Liverpool Biennial

The Unexpected Guest

Art, writing and thinking on hospitality

Edited by Sally Tallant and Paul Domela

ART/BOOKS

First published in the United Kingdom in 2012 by Art Books Publishing Ltd
in association with Liverpool Biennial of Contemporary Art

Art Books Publishing Ltd
77 Oriel Road
London E9 5SG
Tel: +44 (0)20 8533 5835
info@artbookspublishing.co.uk
www.artbookspublishing.co.uk

British Library Cataloguing-in-Publication Data
A catalogue record for this book is available from the British Library

ISBN 978-1-908970-03-9

Edited by Paul Domela and Sally Tallant
Assistant editor Vanessa Boni
Texts by Jacques Rancière and Achille Mbembe translated
by Gregory Elliott
Designed by Sara De Bondt studio
Printed and bound in Belgium by Die Keure

Cover design: Jakob Kolding and Sara De Bondt studio
Inside cover: Dane Mitchell, *Ghost Paper*, 2012

Distributed outside North America by
Thames & Hudson
181a High Holborn
London WC1V 7QX
United Kingdom
Tel: +44 (0)20 7845 5000
Fax: +44 (0)20 7845 5055
sales@thameshudson.co.uk

Available in North America through
ARTBOOK | D.A.P.
155 Sixth Avenue, 2nd Floor, New York, N.Y. 10013
www.artbook.com

Contents

Art

Writing

Thinking

Sally Tallant
Welcome

Stranger, parasite, ghost, lover, mother, host, friend, tenant, dependant, carer, prisoner, child, pirate, alien, vampire, spectre, virus, slave, parent, guardian, ward, consumer, oppressor, thief, victim, tourist, traveller, guest, hostage, pariah, migrant, foreigner, citizen, visitor ... welcome.

Art 'hosts' the values and ideas that are at the heart of how we articulate contemporary urgencies and possibilities, how we express our fears and our hopes. Artists are often invited (and sometimes uninvited) guests, working in places that are not their own. As such, they bring a different perspective to specific situations and locations, as well as simply to the everyday – and that is especially so with an exhibition like a biennial. The personal and gentle unfolding of content that emerges from their work can disrupt the status quo and enable us to ask questions about where we are, who we are, and how we are accountable to one another.

In order to think about how artists, writers, architects and curators construct sites where art is possible, it is important to understand the value of the relationship between host and guest. Cities are defined, and changed, by the people who occupy them. Those occupations can be momentary or last months, years, decades or generations. As we move through the world at great speed and find little time for intimacy, hospitality becomes a crucial issue. To whom do we extend it? For how long? And on what terms?

The guest is often used as a literary device to represent the unexpected, and sometimes the unthinkable. In this publication there are many guests: artists, writers, poets, critics, theorists, activists and others, each welcomed to the distinct space of the book. Setting out to create a platform to present art, writing and thinking prompted by different aspects of hospitality, we adopted an editorial strategy of opening up and actively welcoming guests, hosts and ghosts to use the format of the book as a site in which to make visible the processes of thinking and making. We have complicated this approach yet further by inviting our invited contributors to bring guests into their spaces, should they so wish. The resulting publication is a rich gathering of diverse visual and written material that prompts thinking and leaves questions with the reader.

Published on the occasion of the 7th Liverpool Biennial, the book is not intended as a catalogue or documentation of the exhibition, nor is it simply a reader on the subject; instead, it is a complex anthology of newly commissioned writing, artists' projects and texts that together excavate the terrain and explore the possibilities of occupation and leakage that can take place in the context of a book. Unlike the exhibition, the publication exists as a site that is neither time specific nor geographically determined; and we have curated it to capitalize on that fact, so that it can resonate beyond the temporal and actual constraints of the biennial itself. The rules of engagement are simple and reminiscent of literary games. Piracy and occupation are central strategies that test and extend the notion of hospitality. The texts and the art works exist as prompts and possibilities that urge us to reconsider the present.

The book has been divided into three sections: art, writing and thinking. Artists have been invited to make a contribution that reflects upon a particular aspect of hospitality, or to invite a guest to occupy their space. Many have made new work and used their pages to present it. Some have brought along others as fellow contributors or collaborators: Sylvie Blocher, for instance, has invited a new text from philosopher Jacques Rancière, while Suzanne Lacy appears in conversation with curator Stephanie Smith. Others have handed over their pages entirely: Andrea Bowers, for example, has given her space in the book and in the exhibition to City of Sanctuary, a grass-roots movement to build a culture of hospitality towards people seeking refuge in Britain, in order to give visibility to their campaign; and Jiří Kovanda has invited six other artists, each of whom has made new work. The result is a collection that exists only in these pages and hence becomes an exhibition in book form.

American poet Kenneth Goldsmith was invited to curate an anthology of writing on the subject. In turn, he invited twenty-nine poets to write new texts that explore two key areas of relevance to contemporary hospitality: technology and geography. I am grateful to him for his engaging introduction to the section and for his inspired selection of writers.

New essays have been commissioned to elaborate specific notions of hospitality. Pelin Tan reflects on spatial politics and the ethics of the host–guest relationship in the urban context; Rosi Braidotti argues for a more hospitable place for critical practice, and new possibilities through strategic, affirmative politics; Costas Douzinas explores past, present and future ideas of Europe as they relate to hospitality; Achille Mbembe evokes the spectre of slavery and the radical hospitality of the anti-museum; and Stuart Hall, the subject of John Akomfrah's new film *The Unfinished Conversation* (2012), discusses the subject of hospitality and black history with David Scott.

This Liverpool Biennial, perhaps more than any other previous edition, with its multiplicity of guests and layers of hospitality, focuses attention on the difficulty of being hosted, of being a guest and of potentially becoming unwelcome. Lorenzo Fusi, the curator of 'The Unexpected Guest' exhibition, articulates these complexities in his thoughtful contribution to the book. In Luis Buñuel's film *The Exterminating Angel* (1962), a party of dinner guests arrives at their host's home twice over. They ascend the stairs and walk through a wide doorway, only to find themselves entering again. Having so thoroughly arrived, they are then incapable of leaving. They are mysteriously compelled to spend days and weeks squatting in the house. They become imprisoned in a room, hostages of their host. They become restless and their worst tendencies are revealed. Hours lengthen into days, and their dilemma takes on a ritualistic quality. Similarities are often drawn between the film and Jean-Paul Sartre's existential play *No Exit* (1944), where recently deceased guests are trapped together in Hell in perpetuity. While there are clear artistic and philosophical distinctions between the two men, it is apparent that Buñuel shared Sartre's celebrated sentiment that 'Hell is other people.' Both the play and the film are allegorical and refer to the complex politics of class and bourgeois society. In this sense, they extend our understanding about the role of hospitality in constructing society. We hope that this book, too, prompts similar thinking, writing and art as a way of developing a deeper knowledge of hospitality in the twenty-first century.

I am grateful to the team that have made this Liverpool Biennial publication possible: to my co-editor Paul Domela, whose careful and considered editing has ensured that the book is challenging and ambitious; Vanessa Boni, who has guided and assisted the process; Lorenzo Fusi, who has brought together an extraordinary group of artists and written an insightful text; Rosie Cooper and Lucy Johnston, who have both worked tirelessly on the delivery of exhibition and the publication; Laurie Peake, whose commitment has made the durational commissions by Fritz Haeg and Field Operations and Jeanne van Heeswijk possible; and Sam Baldwin of the Sara De Bondt studio who has designed the publication with care and vision. I am also grateful to Andrew Brown, our publisher, who has guided the process and been invaluable throughout. We are proud that this publication is part of the Art / Books imprint. I am especially grateful to the artists and writers and all the unexpected guests for their thought-provoking contributions.

I give special thanks to Lewis Biggs, the previous director of the Liverpool Biennial, who intially proposed the theme of hospitality and started us all on this journey. I would like to thank each one of the many individuals in our partner organizations, without whom the Biennial would not be possible. And I thank all of our supporters. Our principal funders, Arts Council England and Liverpool City Council, have continued to support us in challenging circumstances, and we are grateful to them for sharing our vision. We also appreciate the support of our project funders, particularly the Esmée Fairbairn Foundation for their instrumental support of our work in Anfield, and Bloomberg for their support of our public programme, as well as the many international embassies and agencies who support our artists' participation.

Finally, I am delighted to welcome our group of founding Patrons, as well as Liverpool John Moores University, Partner of City States, and Liverpool ONE, Liverpool Hope University, Boodles, Virgin Trains, The Monro Group, Hotel Indigo and The Macallan, who join John Lewis and BAM Construction as Partners and Sponsors of Liverpool Biennial 2012.

Paul Domela
Delineation of a subject

This publication appears at a juncture when hospitality appears in several forms:
as the most valued welcome of strangers; as an attitude and a code of conduct;
and as a metaphor that regulates the stability of notions such as the body, territory,
politics or the circulation of data. It has also been captured, polished and turned
into an industry and a mode of occupation. In its modern European guise, it
dates to the nineteenth century and the age of Romanticism, with Byron's *The
Prison of Chillon*, the Grand Tour, mountaineering, the birth of *hôtellerie* and, the
emergence of the international exhibitions and *biennale*. While leisure increased
for some, others experienced famine, emigration or colonization. *The Traveller's
Guide through Scotland and its Islands* was published around 1800, in the middle
of the period of the Highland Clearances, which saw mass expulsion from the
Scottish Highlands – the book described to visitors a view of nature stripped of its
inhabitants. *An Gorta Mór*, the Irish potato famine, doubled Liverpool's population
in the late 1840s at a time when no permission, passport or application was needed
to emigrate from British or Irish ports. Sarah Mytton Maury, an English author from
Liverpool who emigrated to the United States in 1846, wrote two years later:

> The season of Emigration is fast approaching, and there is no justifiable
> ground of hope that the stern necessity, which causes the people of this
> country to become exiles has been arrested; on the contrary, it has been
> augmented. It is a matter calling forth our gratitude that such a relief exists,
> and the mother country is imperatively called upon to facilitate, in every
> possible way, the passage of those whom she can no longer support, to a soil
> less rigid, and to a lot less inflexible.[1]

If ever proof were needed of the precedent to and validity of economic migration,
here it is – economic migration not only permitted, but sanctioned and facilitated.
The right to leave is not the same as the right to settle, however: in Maury's day
the corollary to emigration were, of course, the colonies.

   The choreography of hospitality and leisure has now become so perfected
that smiling attendants on Chinese high-speed trains bare the ideal six to eight
teeth.[2] While such hospitality is increasingly filtered from our everyday lives into a
complex of service economy and immaterial labour, hospitality has itself become
a 'travelling concept', visiting and hosting, as it were, other disciplines, including
anthropology, philosophy, economics, theology and political science. But rather
than examining the distinction between host and guest in each of these fields and
accentuating their divided nature, we see hospitality as an event. Unfurling in
two-faced fashion, like Janus, the patron god of doors, presiding over change, over
the transition between one idea and another, over the birth of life, and over the
beginning of time. It is a liminal hospitality that is by definition time-bound, arising
in the undivided meeting between host and guest. In other words, as Raymond
Williams taught us, let us not place a circle around our subject but draw out
relations until the whole is described. We have therefore brought together in this

publication more than one hundred responses to hospitality with the aim of inviting not a singular definition but a conversation on how the idea of hospitality may continue to speak about, to and for unexpected guests.

I

Other species are moving northwards. A 2011 study in *Science* found that animals are migrating to cooler zones. But not only animals. The internet of things has brought Google to Hamina, Facebook to Luleå, and Verne Global to Keflavik. Mining companies from Australia and China have arrived in Greenland, and while the Antarctic Treaty retains the aspiration of a 'Common Heritage of Humankind', the Arctic Council subsumes the rights of indigenous peoples to exploration of oil and gas and shipping. In *Hermes V: The North-West Passage,* Michel Serres uses the image of an unnavigable sea route between the Atlantic and Pacific oceans to evoke the difficult passage between the humanities and the natural sciences. Hermes, the communicator and messenger, charts the ice to break open channels between conceptual and disciplinary fixities. Both precise and full of imagination, translation becomes for him a process of invention. Within thirty years of Serres's publication, climate change has opened up the northern sea routes, both north-west and north-east, changing the North–South geopolitical dichotomy and giving rise to new forms of agency in the knowledge of 'natureculture', the term introduced by Donna Haraway to indicate the human/non-human entanglement. From this perspective, nature is no longer an instrument for humankind to adjust to its image, nor an all-enveloping host with an interminable capacity for self-correction. The emphasis is on codependency, interaction and what we may call mutual specification – which is to say, Darwin's idea of adaptation working in both directions, organism and environment specifying one another.

II

These interactions between humankind and nature have accumulated to such an extent that they have acquired geological force. Named by the ecologist Eugene F. Stoermer as *Anthropocene,* this geologic period is said to have started with the invention of the steam engine by James Watt in 1775 and is roughly synchronous with modernity, the Enlightenment and the Industrial Revolution.[3] Not only does this periodization of climate change collapse the epistemological divide between human and natural history, it also suggests a link between the ideals of the Enlightenment and the burning of fossil fuels. If we agree that the pursuit of freedom is foremost among these ideals, then in the words of Dipesh Chakrabarty, 'In no discussion of freedom in the period since the Enlightenment was there ever any awareness of the geological agency that human beings were acquiring at the same time as and through processes closely linked to their acquisition of freedom.'[4] Indeed – and yet it seems that the evidence is hiding in the light.

III

Any convention, discipline or closely held belief has its border conditions. While regulating cordial relations within specific social, historical and cultural domains, such conventions – tolerance, for example – are unable to question the assumptions of power that allow those beliefs to be sustained. Could we say that our sense of freedom has created a boundary of meaning and expectation that limits our interaction with a wider environment to which we are nevertheless structurally coupled? Accommodation becomes compliance or adjustment, the space within which to give to difference, a concession to the unexpected guest. If we distinguish procedural from substantive difference, it is with substantive difference that fault lines appear and expose (cultural) hegemonies. For example, Marcel Mauss famously described the *potlatch* of the North Pacific tribes as gift exchange, a radical alternative to commodity culture. The gift retains the spirit of the giver, and this inalienability creates the social bond. By contrast, the commodity passes in its entirety from seller to buyer during the transaction. Even though Mauss based his view on accounts written at a time when capitalism had already taken root in indigenous societies and had imbued the *potlatch* ceremony with a sense of striving and competition,[5] the practice was nonetheless considered such an obstacle to conversion to Christianity that Canada outlawed it until 1951.

IV

Conversion implied not only proselytizing but also submission to the ideas of citizenship, property, law and domestic order. 'Natural man' is, by definition, outside the bounds of the state and is therefore, in the sense of John Locke, open to expropriation, particularly if the land in question is ruled under the principle of common right. The parallel between Charles I's enclosure in 1637 of wasteland between Hampton Court and Richmond for a hunting park and the pressure on the Masai homelands to make way for tourism and game reserves is striking.[6] What occurs to hospitality in such instances of severe asymmetry? Could it be extended to a dissensual hospitality, one that embodies disagreement rather than consensus? Now that we have discovered more of the world, the question becomes one of relation. What forms of agency can be enacted? The struggle of endangered tribes such as the Suruí people of Brazil poses such questions in the context of human rights and development. As their ancestral forest is under threat from illegal logging and mining, they have sought the help of Google Earth Outreach and embarked on what is called ethnographic mapping using Google Earth, Google Maps, Blogger and YouTube to report and make visible the loss of forestation, but also their efforts at preservation. A replanting scheme is linked to global cap-and-trade programmes, providing resources to the tribe. Are these the assemblages of technology and resistance that produce the new 'atmospheres of democracy'? How to recognize the active participation of human and non-human forces in such a weblike unfolding of events? If Janus rules over the duality of host and guest, Indra's net presents a metaphor for the interconnectedness of all encounters, with each knot an instance that reflects every other. 'When we look at ourselves in the Net of Indra, we are not only the selves who inhabit our own bodies, but also a series of reflections and possibilities – all the minds we could savour, all the bodies we could transit through, all the imaginations that could enrich ours.'[7]

1   Sarah Mytton Maury, *An Englishwoman in America*, Liverpool: George Smith, Watts & Co, 1848, Part II, p. 3.
2   'China tests its high-speed rail link from Beijing to Shanghai', *Guardian*, 27 June 2011.
3   Paul Crutzen, 'Geology of Mankind', *Nature*, 3 January 2002, p. 23.
4   Dipesh Chakrabarty, *The Climate of History: Four Theses*, www.eurozine.com, 30 October 2009, accessed 4 August 2012.
5   See Lewis Hyde, *The Gift*, Edinburgh: Canongate Books, 2007, pp. 29–31.
6   Andrew Renton, 'Tourism is a curse for us', *Observer*, 6 September 2009.
7   Ilja Trojnanow, based on the manuscript *Confluence* by Ranjit Hoskoté and Ilija Trojanow. From a lecture to mark the fifth anniversary of the Passa Porta International House of Literature, Brussels, 25 September 2009.

Lorenzo Fusi
'Disappearing human beings, not problems'

Hospitality has a limited lifespan

According to an old Italian saying, after three days a guest starts to smell of rotten fish. Italians are generally considered to be rather hospitable people, certainly more than most, but this proverb reminds us that even among the friendliest of folk, hospitality has its bounds. Time is clearly one of the yardsticks by which it is measured, perhaps the central one. The presence of a new guest may be welcomed at first precisely because it disrupts the monotony of daily life. Routines and schemes are destabilized, creating a state of excitement and novelty for the host as well as the guest. This temporary 'state of emergency' must be brought to a close relatively quickly, however, to avoid undermining the equilibrium upon which the household is founded. It is down to the guest to recognize when it is time to leave and release the host from his/her duties. Prolonging a stay shifts a mutual agreement built on generosity and gratitude into an altogether different social and psychological realm. An extended visit sets new parameters that highlight the asymmetric relation between the host and guest. After a while (three days, according to the Italian maxim), there can be only feelings of imposition, unease and annoyance. The contract enters a critical phase when the guest is unable or unwilling to leave at all.

As for the household, so for the nation state. Faced with the arrival of refugees or asylum-seekers, a hosting agency usually opens its doors to receive the newcomers, whether it be for humanitarian, diplomatic or political reasons. In the longer term, however, initial good intentions are problematized by the need either to integrate these alien bodies within the system or to push them out once again, delegating to someone else the responsibility of dealing with their future. And therein lies the conundrum for civil society, especially in the West: how can we articulate, politically, and demonstrate the notion of hospitality to those seeking shelter if hospitality is supposed to be temporary. Can we find alternative models of the host–guest relationship that respond better to current global politics?

The implications and dangers of extending political hospitality indefinitely are evident if one looks at the refugee camps that have been set up in Europe in recent years. This 'zoning' strategy of confining the Other in some kind of suspended reality outside of normal society – one that is based on an inequality of rights within and beyond the limits of the camp – exemplifies the potential aggressiveness of the host once its initial welcome has come to an end. The literal and symbolic removal of these subjects (including those born and raised within the camp's confines) compounds their sense of displacement, alienation and disempowerment. By embedding in their psyche a permanent dependence on the host authority, these immigration policies consolidate the state's power over the lives of the refugees. It is here that one is reminded of the etymological link between the words 'host' and 'hostage'.[1] These refugees are held hostage by a political and social system that aims to freeze them in a state of permanent exception (paraphrasing Giorgio Agamben).[2]

The non-places of such camps demonstrate both the inability and unwillingness of nation states to solve the problem of asylum-seekers beyond formal resolutions (for instance, redesignating them as 'accommodation centres'). Jacques Derrida argued that, unlike invitation, hospitality requires 'absolute surprise': 'I must be unprepared, or prepared to be unprepared, for the unexpected arrival of any other.... The other, like the Messiah, must arrive whenever he or she wants.'[3] We can only conclude, from the evidence of the way it treats refugees, that Europe is not yet prepared to be unprepared for its unexpected guests.

Speaking the inhospitable

We live in a highly inhospitable time and place. In fact, there is a certain irony in investigating ideas of hospitality in this new era of the so-called Fortress Europe and in light of the increasing restrictions on immigration adopted by many countries in the West. Financial crises, the shift of economic power to non-Western regions, and the potential flood of migrants originating from the Arab uprisings in north Africa and the Middle East – all of these have created an unprecedented fear and general xenophobic psychosis in the people of the 'old continent', to the extent that even long-established practices and international treaties such as the Schengen Agreement are now being questioned. It appears that the only way Europe believes it can re-establish its authority is to exercise power around its borders: an ultimate and somewhat desperate act of self-affirmation and determination. And yet at the same time, Europeans face the dilemma of needing the migrant for their economic survival. Shifting our attention momentarily to the United States, we see a similar scenario of contradictions and confusion. There, as here, economists reason that the economy requires 'guest workers', and argue that the gains from lowering barriers to immigration would be substantial.[4]

Despite this, we seem unable to make up our minds when it comes to hospitality at a macro level. Do we want and need these people or not? Shall we leave our doors open or securely lock them? And if we decide to receive this influx, are we politically and psychologically able to behave as their neighbours (and equals) here in 'our' land, rather than act as their hosts? Or do we want instead to perpetuate a model according to which those who arrive are placed in a subordinate position of dependence that simply validates our 'right' and authority to be the host and to look at them from a dominant and favourable standpoint?[5]

The events of 9/11 symbolically marked and officialized a new permanent state of fear that replaced the Cold War axis of antagonism between two ideologically opposed superpowers with a different set of oppositions that pitches the 'good' *us* against the 'bad' *them*, wherever 'they' might be – even, and especially, within our very midst. The resulting emotional and political distress in the United States heightened a situation that long predated the attacks on the Twin Towers, which has been described as a 'prison nation': a paradoxically hyper-hospitable jail system where the governmental laws of hospitality (that is, hospitality as tool of control) are extended to the largest community of inmates in the world.[6]

But to feel fear within one's own borders does not necessarily require a terrorist attack or war. There are some countries that have been equally traumatized by the recent financial crisis, such as Iceland. A similar fear is felt at present by many in the United Kingdom as a result of the government's policies on public spending and the economy, which appear unconnected to the lives of large sections of the population, but driven instead by a backward-looking ideology. Most other Western states are likewise witnessing the systematic dismantlement of welfare schemes, cuts at all levels in state-aided sectors, job losses and unemployment in both the public and the private arenas. In what it is becoming a prolonged state of crisis, national governments are unable to meet the costs of the systems they created and are turning to one another or to supranational bodies for help.

Curiously, a new nostalgia for the 'old times' is emerging from this 'deranged' political scenario: an almost irrational need to clearly pin down and classify the categories of Good and Bad according to an ideological schema. This might be one reason why Marxism is experiencing a revival across many countries and, conversely, why neo-con (and far-right) parties are gaining support from the electorate. Another result of this nostalgic political backlash is the reinvigoration of racism among civil societies – but racism of a different kind. It has been argued (following Adorno)[7] that liberalism is presently giving voice to a new meaning of the term: a racism that has been 'democratized' and made less direct but more diffuse, one that is sometimes called 'Euro-racism', 'xeno-racism' or 'everyday racism'.[8] Étienne Balibar's analysis is illuminating in this respect. He maintains that we are currently experiencing a race-less racism, which has shifted its attention from the notion of race as expressed before and during the era of the bourgeois nation state. Instead, this new version is intimately connected to nationalism, in that race has been replaced by the category of immigration: 'It is a racism whose dominant theme is not biological heredity but the insurmountability of cultural differences, a racism that, at first, does not postulate the superiority of certain groups or peoples in relation to others but "only" the harmfulness of abolishing frontiers, incompatibility of lifestyles and traditions: in short what P. A. Tanguieff has rightly called a *differentialist racism*.'[9] In other words, we have entered an era of 'racism after race relations' where 'the Other of immigrant origin occupies within Europe a social position which exposes the limits of bourgeois democracy, as well as the effect of racist exclusion'.[10]

This nostalgia and its associated political revisionism have reactivated the Cold War psychological device of claiming the presence of an incumbent or pending threat. But what is it, exactly, that we are so scared of? Communism, as such, can no longer be targeted as a 'demon' to be fought in defence of capitalism. Capitalism won, convincingly, so it seemed. And yet in its latest manifestation (international liberalism), capitalism is nonetheless in a state of impasse with no further possibilities of growth, at least not in the West. We are at an endpoint, stuck, as it were, between fast forward and rewind. As Chantal Mouffe suggests,[11] the current lack of antagonism between opposing political forces has shaped a self-centred and somewhat depoliticized arena, where the debate and confrontation between adversaries formerly competing on purely political grounds have shifted to a form of witch-hunt of the 'enemy'. This so-called enemy generally happens to be the stranger, the immigrant, the other-than-me who is instinctively disliked and opposed not on political grounds, but on the basis of religion, ethnicity, gender or sexual orientation. Inevitably, this process places the immigrant (the unwanted 'guest') in a highly uncomfortable position. But most importantly, it provides the perfect agency for projecting, exorcizing and giving voice to our otherwise unverbalized fears.

A new model of hospitality?

Hospitality is linguistically and semantically an ambiguous term. Just to look at the Latin roots of the word – *hospes*, standing for both host and guest, and *hostis*, signifying both foreigner and stranger, but also enemy (as in hostility) – reveals the multiple, sometimes contradictory meanings at its heart. The word also shares the same etymological root as both hospital and hospice. Asylum (long before it was attached to '-seeker') was the term for a shelter for 'lunatics'; while psychiatric hospitals were conceived and designed in the same fashion as prisons (the panopticon) and informed the notion of state control. This train of associations and intersections creates a connective thread, binding together a variety of institutions, agencies and disciplines under the same hospitable roof.

I wonder, therefore, if we might try (at both an individual and a collective level) to reinterpret hospitality anew, to look again at the dichotomy that opposes guest and host, by taking inspiration from other 'systems'. Biology, physics and medical studies, for instance, have informed new hybrid disciplines and approaches (such as evolutionary psychology and anarchic evolutionary theories) that might help in this task. Or we might draw on the notions of biopolitics and biopower as informed by Foucault and articulated by Agamben and others.[12] Particularly interesting here is the analysis of the role played by 'bare life' and the 'exception' in the construction of sovereignty and the juridico-political order, as articulated by Agamben in *Homo Sacer*.[13] When it comes to systematizing the notion of hospitality in political terms, we might say that the immigrant, the guest and the refugee represent his 'sovereignty exception' or 'bare life' component. By being positioned outside the rule (the house, the state, etc.), the guest is not excluded by or from that rule as such, but rather defines it. And since the guest indicates where that rule suspends its authority or power, any political, psychological or metaphorical 'household' exists only because the guest remains outside its internal logic.

Shifting to biological grounds, the human body gives us many insights into the interactions between a hosting entity and external agents. Our skin is considered the demarcation line that separates inside from out, defining us from the other-than-us. But it is also a highly porous border where a multitude of continuous negotiations take place, making the distinction between 'internal' and 'external' somewhat nebulous. Bacteria, fungi and viruses represent three remarkable categories of immigrants. Once they have entered our system, they quickly learn how to survive and cohabit in the new environment. Often their presence is asymptomatic and manifests itself only if an internal disequilibrium occurs. To classify these intruders as 'enemies' and eradicate them is not easy – each has developed techniques of resistance. But as long as our immune system is efficient, these pathogens are apparently kept under control. And yet these 'immigrants' are working endlessly against or in response to our defences, especially when their own existence is at stake.[14] What might we learn from this in political terms?

The threshold is a device we constructed to justify tolerance

The *limen*, or threshold, separating the private and public spheres is conventionally understood as the dimension where our first transaction with, and hence acceptance or refusal of, the Other takes place. This is the site

where the differentiation between 'political self' and 'political otherness' is
thus formed (a negotiation that Foucault challenged by introducing the notion of
'transsubjectivation', suggesting that this 'false alterity' is in fact resolved within
the spectrum of one single identical self).[15] This threshold is generally thought
of as a linear measure: a line that demarks and informs our understanding of
an outside and inside. Its alleged linearity has been questioned in philosophical
terms, however, most notably by Derrida, Emmanuel Levinas, Jean-Luc Nancy
and Luce Irigaray. They identified a new locus, as expressed by the term 'vulva's
schema'. This metaphorical and anatomical structure suggests that the threshold is
not a line but a 'space' contained between the inner and outer labia. Upon entering
someone's sphere, we are placed in an antechamber: a site of suspension of
judgment where pleasure and violence (coitus and resistance) are not yet ratified.
(Some might argue that political discourse in relation to hospitality is instead
constructed on the notion of anality, where there is no penumbra between the
territorial 'in' and 'out'.)

What are the psychological dynamics that induce us to embrace and
'welcome' the alien/stranger into our intimate space in this way, and what
are the implications of doing so? Why do we allow some to penetrate and not
others? Where is the division between public and private? Is there a difference
in being hospitable in the public sphere (in the political arena) and in the private
realm? According to whose rules are the boundaries drawn, pushed, distorted
and ultimately redesigned? And at whose cost? What are the socio-political and
emotional implications facing those who are hosted? Given that any hospitable
environment is regulated by conditions imposed by the host, are the guests
subjected to a form of psychophysical disempowerment? Is there a way to elude
the host's authority, liberating the guest from a sense of dependence? Or is the
host equally disempowered by having to suspend his/her authority? And can the
realm of politics even afford to undermine the very power structure that binds
together 'giver' and receiver' and renegotiate its legitimacy?

These are just some of the questions 'The Unexpected Guest' as an exhibition
aims to tackle. I myself do not trust the rhetoric of hospitality very much. I
see the interrelations that it establishes as a means of fostering gratitude, thus
consolidating a form of power that acts in a similar way to dominance and control.
It breeds anxiety in the guest, since he/she is continually testing the host's
tolerance and its limits. Hospitality is a subtle 'violence' because it manifests itself
as a charitable act, an offer and a demonstration of goodwill. In Foucault's terms,
hospitality is 'dangerous': 'Not everything is bad, but everything is dangerous,
which is not exactly the same as bad. If everything is dangerous, then we always
have something to do.' His position leads not to apathy but to hyper – and
pessimistic – activism. That is so even with apparently neutral (if not benign) terms
such as hospitality or tolerance, an attitude that asserts one's right to tolerate and
someone else's need to be tolerated. As a consequence of the lack of innocence
in the term, I wish to see 'the end of tolerance'[16] and the reintroduction of mutual
acceptance and understanding – as key philosophical and socio-political discursive
arguments – to emancipate the debate and to bring it to a new level.

In today's world, both legal and illegal citizens are spied on and monitored
constantly, but they are also willing to share a vast amount of information about
themselves. We have developed an ambivalent relation to intimacy that suggests that

the notion of the threshold has come to a critical point: it can no longer be centred on dichotomies such as intrusion and exclusion, permeability and resistance, desire and castration. Hospitality needs to conform to these changes. It may well be too late; it may already be an obsolete notion altogether. Marcel Duchamp could have predicted its end in 1953 with a work entitled *A Guest + A Host = A Ghost*.

Personally, I hope this exhibition will mark the end of the 'hospitality era' as we know it. It is time to define a new relational structure – perhaps one based on 'cohabitation', where everyone has the same right to be in a space at the same time – a structure where inalienable human rights are not questioned or granted as a gift by someone who has more authority or privileges than others. The right 'to be' cannot be mistaken for an act of generosity.

1   Emmanuel Levinas identifies the subject as guest/host and the subject as hostage in *Otherwise Than Being, or, Beyond Essence*, trans. Alphonso Lingis, Boston, Mass.: Kluwer Academic Publisher, 1991, further analysed by Derrida (e.g., 'Hospitality, justice, responsibility', in *Questioning Ethics: Contemporary Debates in Philosophy*, eds. Richard Kearney and Mark Dooley, London: Routledge, 1999).
2   Giorgio Agamben, *Stato di eccezione: Homo sacer, II, I*, Turin: Bollati Borighieri, 2003, p. 113.
3   Quoted in François Raffaoul's 'The subject of the welcome: on Jacques Derrida's *Adieu à Emmanuel Lévinas*', p. 11 (article downloadable by browsing the following link: http://lsu.academia.edu/Fran%C3%A7oisRaffoul/Papers/358556/The_Subject_of_the_Welcome_Derrida_on_Hospitality)
4   See for example Martin Ruhs and Bridget Anderson (eds.), *Who Needs Migrant Workers? Labour Shortages, Immigration, and Public Policy*, Oxford: Oxford University Press, 2010; Saskia Sassen, *Guests and Aliens*, New York: The New Press, 1999; Michael A. Clemens, 'Economics and immigration: trillion-dollar bills on the sidewalk?', *Journal of Economic Perspectives*, vol. 25, no. 3, Summer 2011, pp. 83–106; and Philippe Legrain, *Immigrants: Your Country Needs Them*, London: Abacus, 2010.
5   Another example of the ambivalence of the West in regard to immigration is provided by the Utah House Bill 116, which proposes that illegal immigrants who are already working for an employer (and are responsible for their debts and obligations) can apply for a 'guest worker permit', thus legalizing their position. It is easily imaginable that those illegal workers who fight for their rights or do not perform to the expectation or satisfaction of the employer will be refused a permit, mistakenly confusing efficiency with human rights.
6   See Sasha Abramsky, *Hard Time Blues: How Politic Built a Prison Nation*, New York: St Martin's Press, 2002.
7   Theodor Adorno, 'What does coming to terms with the past mean?', *Bitburg in Moral and Political Perspective*, Bloomington, Indiana: Indiana University Press, 1986, p. 115.
8   This recrudescence of xenophobia and racism in Europe are the subject of Gerard Delanty, Ruth Wodak and Paul Jones (eds.), *Identity, Belonging and Migration*, Liverpool: Liverpool University Press, 2008.
9   Étienne Balibar, 'Is there a "neo-racism"?', in *Race, Nation, Class: Ambiguous Identities*, London and New York: Verso, 1991, p. 21, and the therein cited P. A. Tanguieff, 'L'Identité française au miroir du racisme différentialiste', in *Espace 89, L'Identité française*, Paris: Editions Tierce, 1985.
10 Robert Miles, *Racism After 'Race Relations'*, London and New York: Routledge, 1993, p. 216.
11 Chantal Mouffe, *The Return to the Political*, London and New York: Verso, 1993.
12 Biopower and biopolitics as informed by Michel Foucault in *The Will to Knowledge* (*Histoire de la sexualité, 1: La Volonté de savoir*, 1976) refer to the practice of modern states and their regulation of their subjects through 'an explosion of numerous and diverse techniques for achieving the subjugations of bodies and the control of populations' (Michel Foucault, 'On the genealogy of ethics', in *Michel Foucault: Beyond Structuralism and Hermeneutics*, eds. Hubert L Dreyfus and Paul Rabinow (Chicago: University of Chicago Press, 1983), pp. 231–2).
13 Giorgio Agamben (*Homo Sacer: Sovereign Power and Bare Life*) claims that biopower and sovereignty are fundamentally integrated, to the extent that 'it can even be said that the production of a biopolitical body is the original activity of sovereign power'. See also Catherine Mills' reading of Agamben: 'Agamben's messianic politics: biopolitics, abandonment, and happy life', *Contretemps*, no. 5, 2004, pp. 42–62 and 'Playing with law: Agamben and Derrida on post-juridical justice', *South Atlantic Quarterly*, special issue on Agamben, ed. Alison Ross, 107:1, 2008.
14 Viruses never abandon our system. Their presence might not provoke illness, but they still exist within us and never leave. The transmission of viruses from one body to another happens even when the infecting body shows no apparent symptoms. Bacteria do us good and bad; they can be removed, but once you treat the bad ones with antibiotics the good ones also go; wrong or insufficient treatments result in stronger and genetically modified bacteria that cannot be treated (antibiotic-resistant).
15 Michel Foucault, *The Hermeneutics of the Subject*, New York: Picador, 2004.
16 Citing Arum Kundnami, *The End of Tolerance: Racism in 21st Century Britain*, London and Ann Arbor, Michigan: Pluto Press, 2007.

The title of this essay paraphrases American author and activist Angela Davis, whose analysis of the 'Prison Industrial Complex' explores the 'masked racism' within US prisons. According to Davis, they 'do not disappear problems, they disappear human beings'. She argues that, 'The seeming effortlessness of magic [of imprisonment] always conceals an enormous amount of behind-the-scenes work'. 'Masked racism: reflections on the Prison Industrial Complex', 1998, accessed at http://colorlines.com/archives/1998/09/masked_racism_reflections_on_the_prison_industrial_complex.html.

Art

Doug Aitken

The Source
Sook-Kyung Lee

When Doug Aitken published a collection of conversations with leading artists, film-makers and architects under the title *Broken Screen* in 2006,[2] his focus was on notions of non-linearity and fragmentation and the ways in which fractured perception and ruptured images have begun to dominate modern life. Multiple voices and the conscious absence of absolutes were prevalent, and the conversations between Aitken and the other artists proposed several possibilities and various perspectives rather than a unified direction or agreement. Common grounds appeared, however, which were their passion for creating art and their unique vision and ability to respond to and shape the changing world around them.

Sky Arts Ignition: Doug Aitken – The Source, the artist's project for the Liverpool Biennial, is a platform for a conversation as much as for conversations. Taking *Broken Screen* as the starting point, he has developed a series of filmed interviews with a number of creators, not only artists and film-makers but also architects, musicians and actors who share experimental spirits and innovative approaches in their chosen fields. Crossing across different art forms and disciplines, the artist and other participants talk about creativity and other seemingly abstract notions around making art. Articulate and engaged, both Aitken and his conversant delve into the very essence of the creative process in each conversation, turning and returning to another conversation, literally and conceptually.

Aitken's conversations demonstrate the radical betweenness that is inherent in this form of language. Presented as a sort of multidimensional medium – a social event, a philosophical exchange and a poetic dialogue – a conversation reflects on culture while resisting a given form or a unified set of rules or knowledge. In the philosophies of Socrates and Plato, in particular, conversation was regarded as a method of seeking the truth rather than as a tool of communication. Through the writings of Plato, Socrates teaches how to 'conduct' a conversation, being at once a speaker, an actor of speech and the one who embodies what he speaks about. Both the 'signifier' and the 'signified' are present in the figure of Socrates, and such a convergence enables the dialectics of conversation for Plato's philosophy.

While dialogue is an encounter of two – two points of view, opposing sides, identities and worlds – conversation emphasizes the possibility of participation.

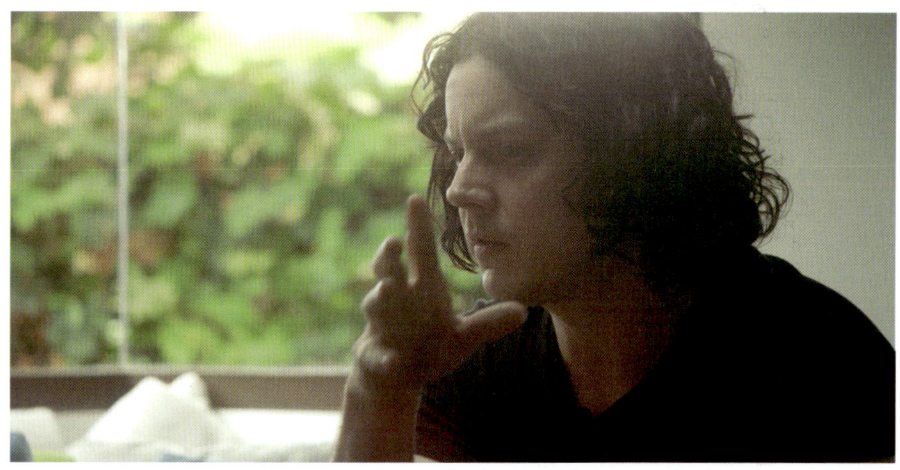

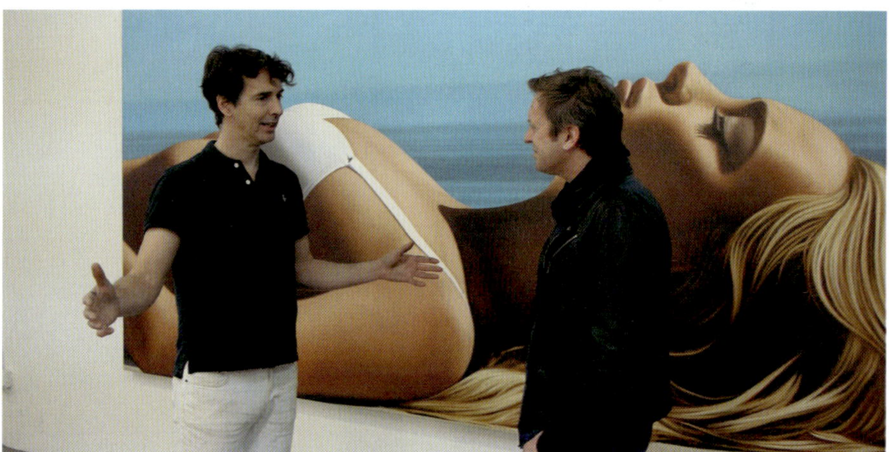

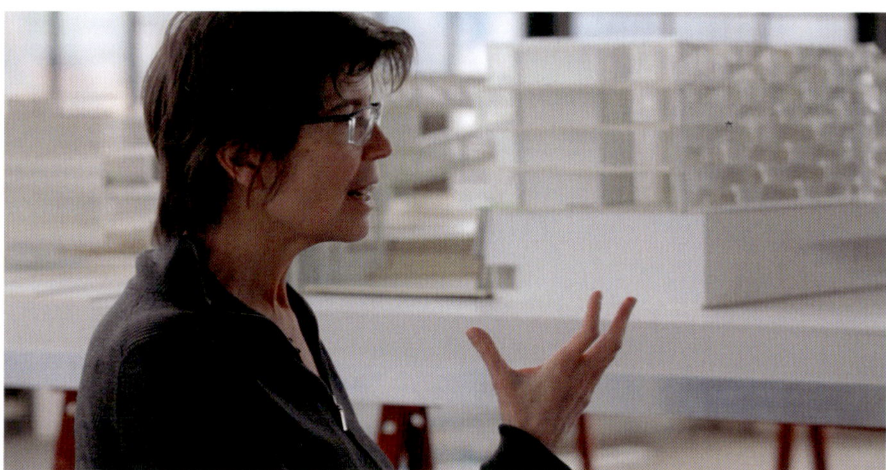

From the top: Jack White, Richard Phillips and Liz Diller
Overleaf: Paolo Soleri

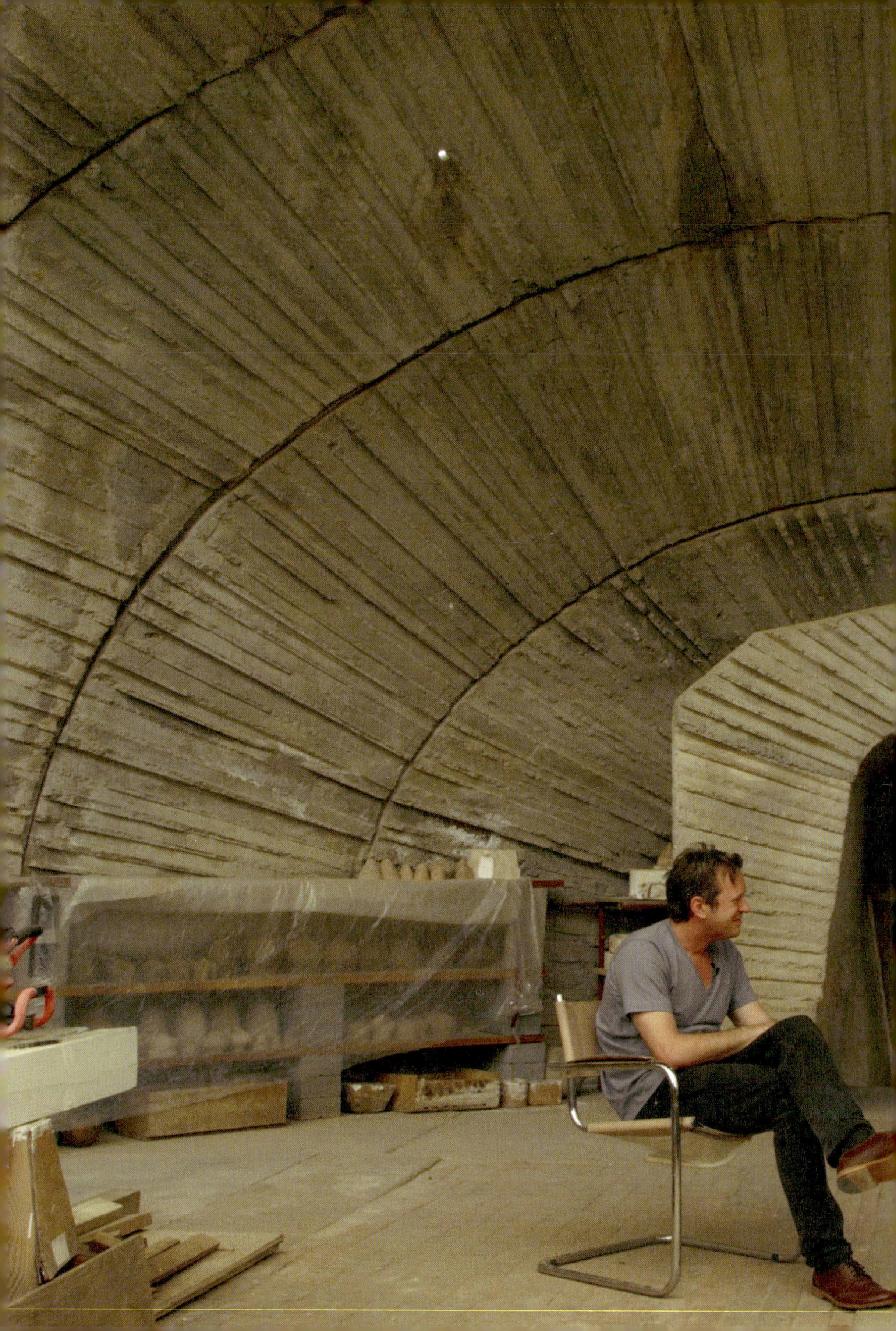

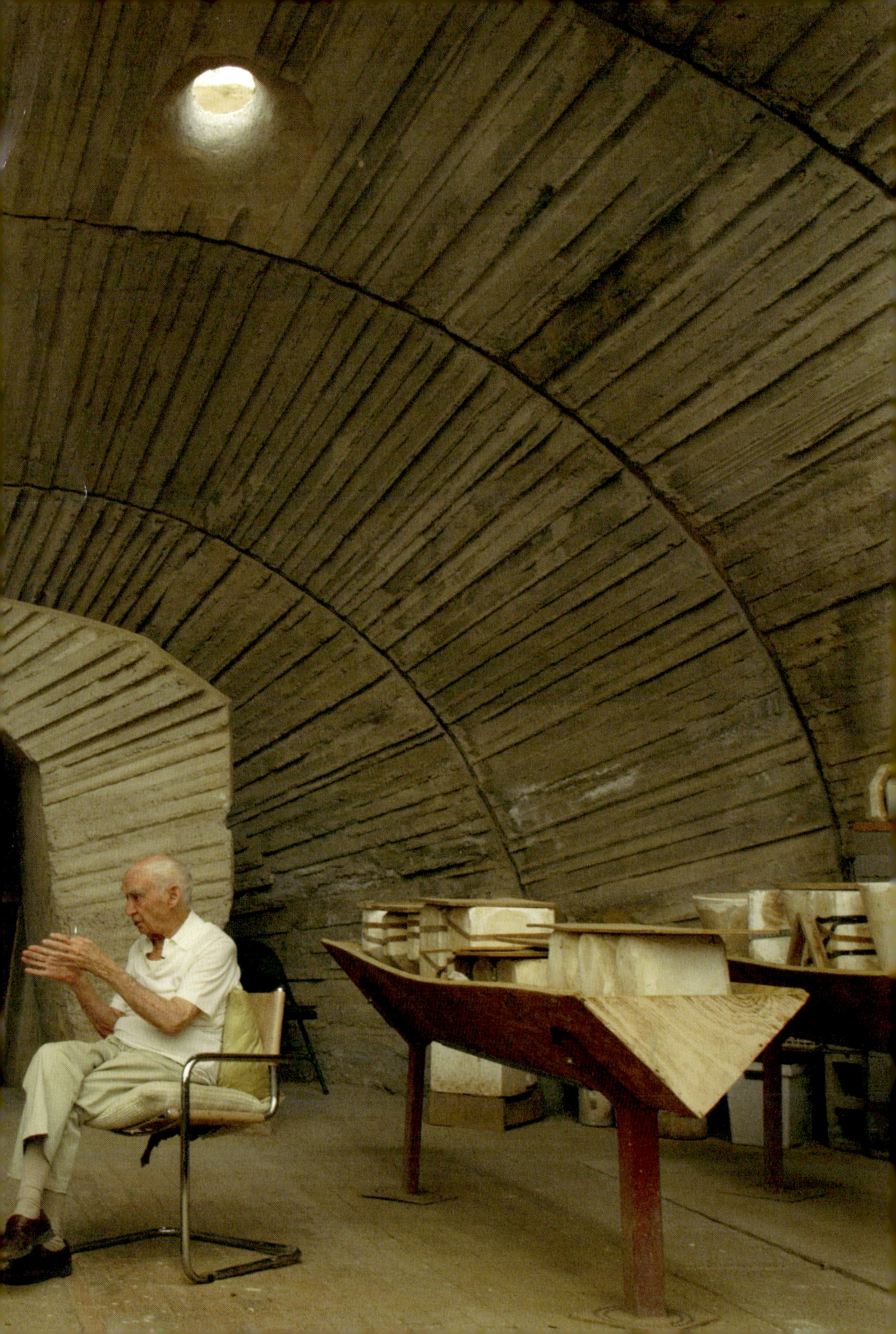

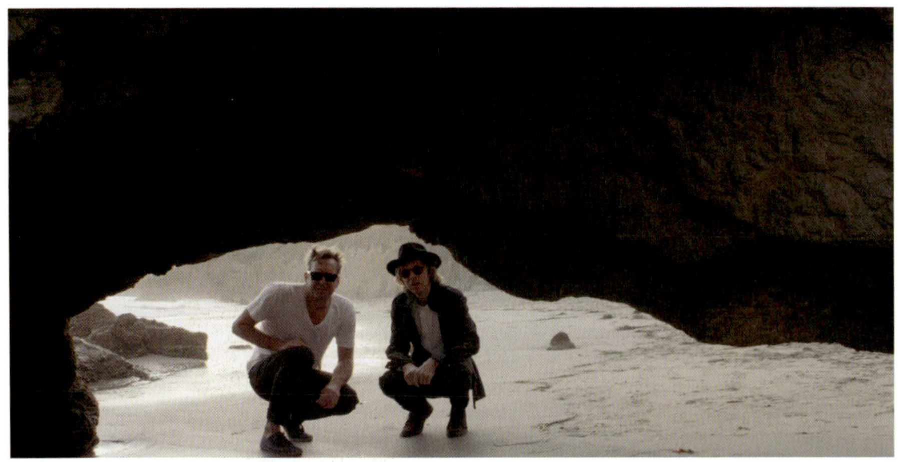

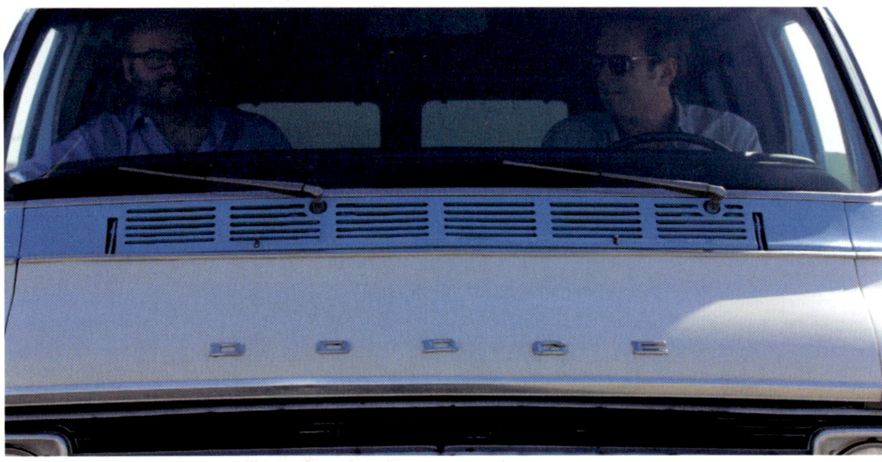

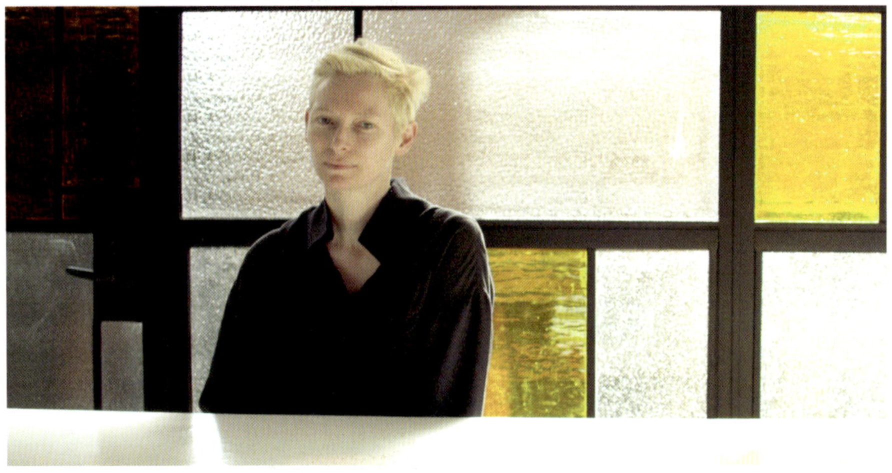

From the top: Beck, Thomas Demand and Tilda Swinton
Opposite: David Adjaye

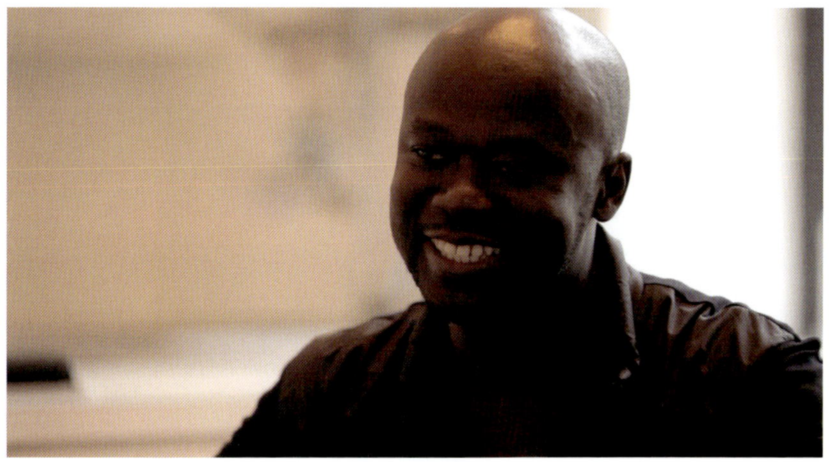

When we enter Aitken's installation, we are entering not only into a space but also into a conversation itself. A silent conversant is no less significant in the structure of conversations, and the way the artist presents his installation ensures the inclusion of the viewer. As Aitken says: 'I want the work to be a destination. It's about the new form of access, using moving image as a tool to open up a discussion, to share, to create something that is completely democratized.' Filmed conversations are displayed in a pavilion specifically designed by the artist in collaboration with the architect David Adjaye. Their collaboration itself is a form of dialogue, embodied in the architecture that hosts conversations and protects the moments of encounter and participation.

Aitken says that 'the starting point of creativity is words, experience and dialogues'. *The Source* explores the creative drive behind the works that are shaping our cultural future. Moreover, it is about empowerment, 'the empowerment of the viewer, not necessarily of the creator'. To listen to the conversations between Aitken and other creators is not merely to receive their messages but to be an active participant in their purposefully open dialogues. Unlike a finished work of art that might be housed in a museum, this work exists as a place of and for conversations, which engenders further conversations, and creates a fast-moving road trip through the modern landscape of creativity.

The most fruitful and natural exercise of our mind, in my opinion, is conversation. I find the practice of it more pleasant than that of any other action of our life.
Michel de Montaigne, 'The Art of Conversation'[3]

1   All quotes by Aitken are from conversations with the artist, held between
    October 2011 and May 2012
2   Doug Aitken, *Broken Screen – Expanding the Image Breaking the Narrative:
    26 Conversations with Doug Aitken*, edited by Noel Daniel, New York: D.A.P., 2006
3   Michel de Montaigne, *The Complete Essays*, translated by M. A. Screech,
    New York: Penguin, 1991, pp. 1044–69

GA
CTOR
...

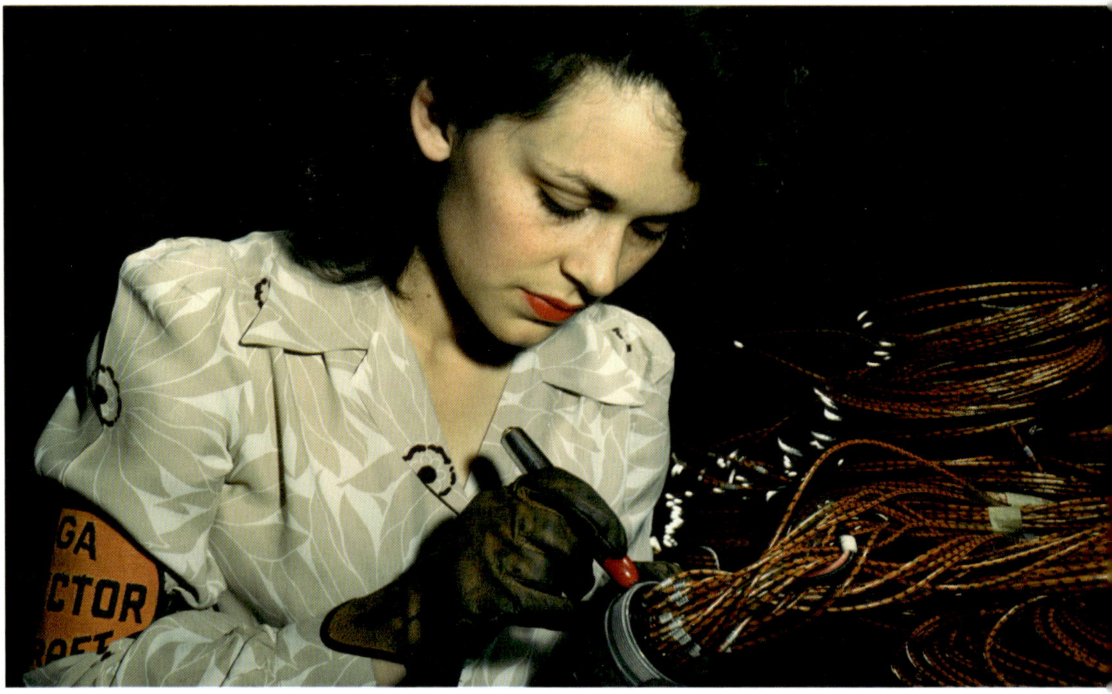

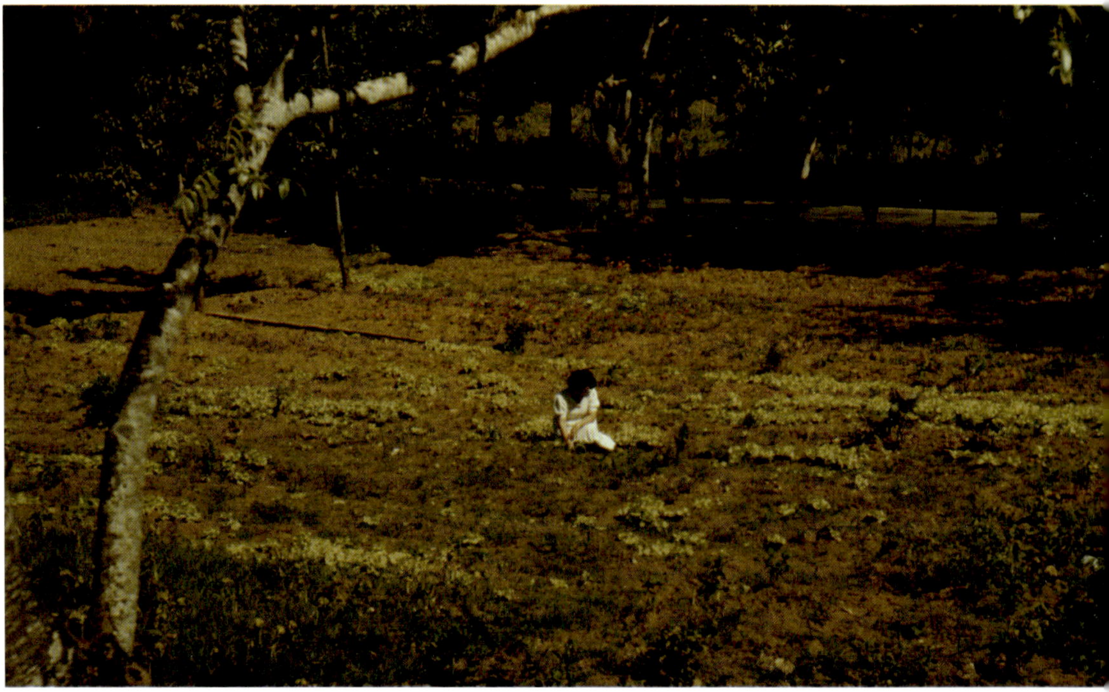

These and following pages:
Astrocartographies from Inhospitable Climes,
2012, with special thanks to Trevor Mathison

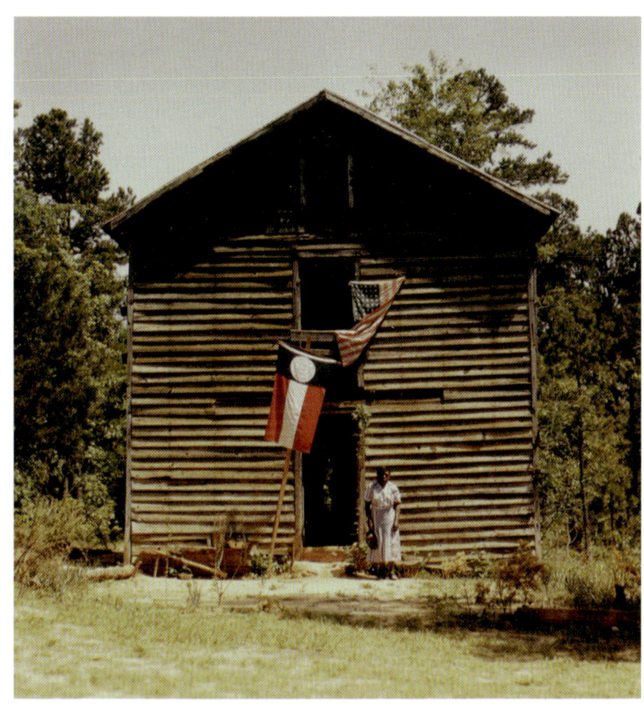

Told Mama
I told mama yesterday
I can't see her no more.
No one must know who I am.
Or what I am.

Dirt
Pay's real good. But she never
got used to the stares.
And maybe the dirt, I think.

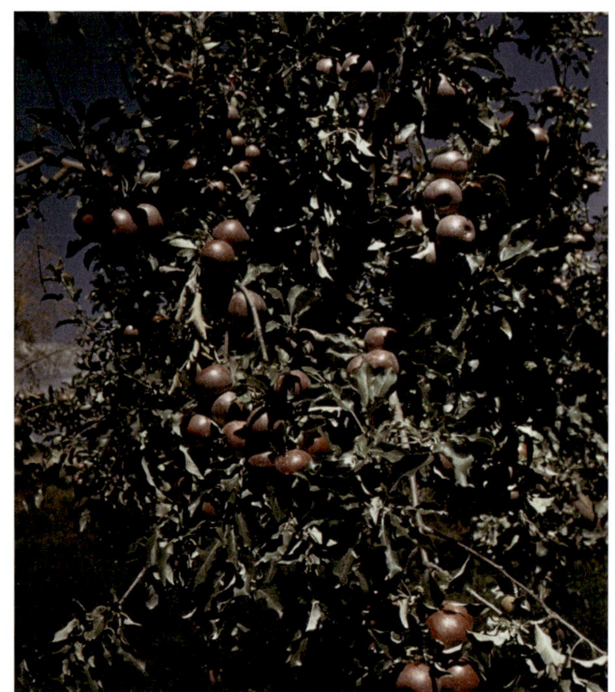

Never Left the Woods
Once mama told her she couldn't
marry him, that was it.
She never left the woods.
Still there right now.

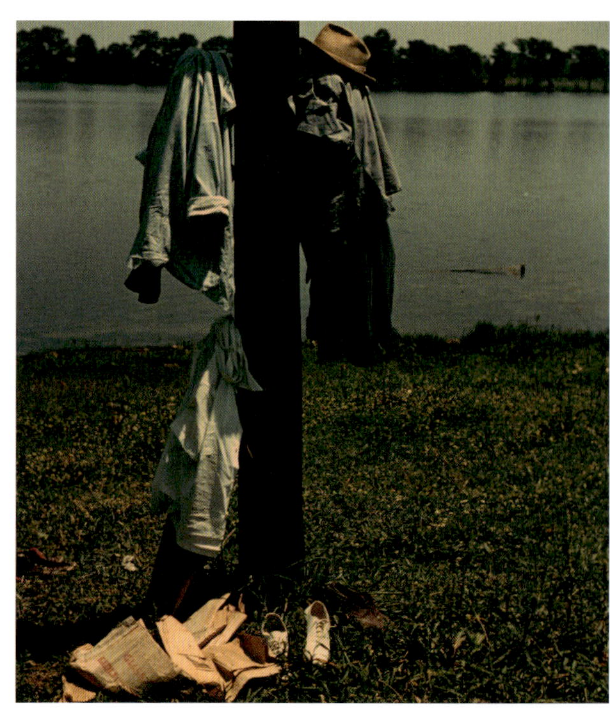

Catfish
Sunday afternoon catfish sandwich.
That's all I miss.
Going to the Promised Land;
that's what I told them.

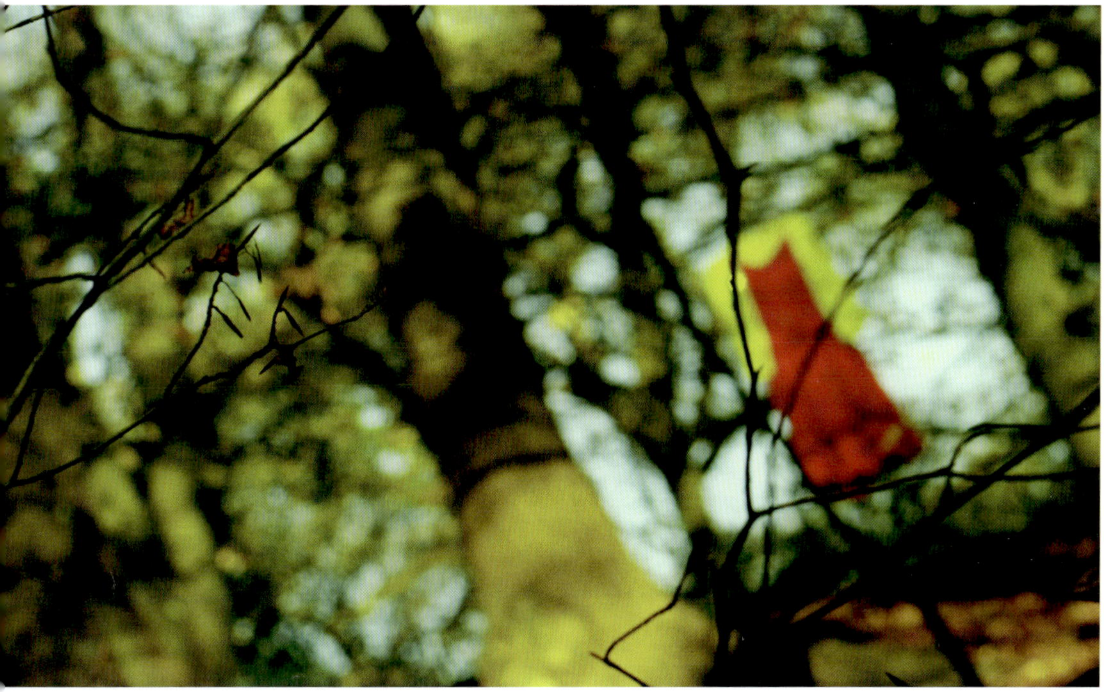

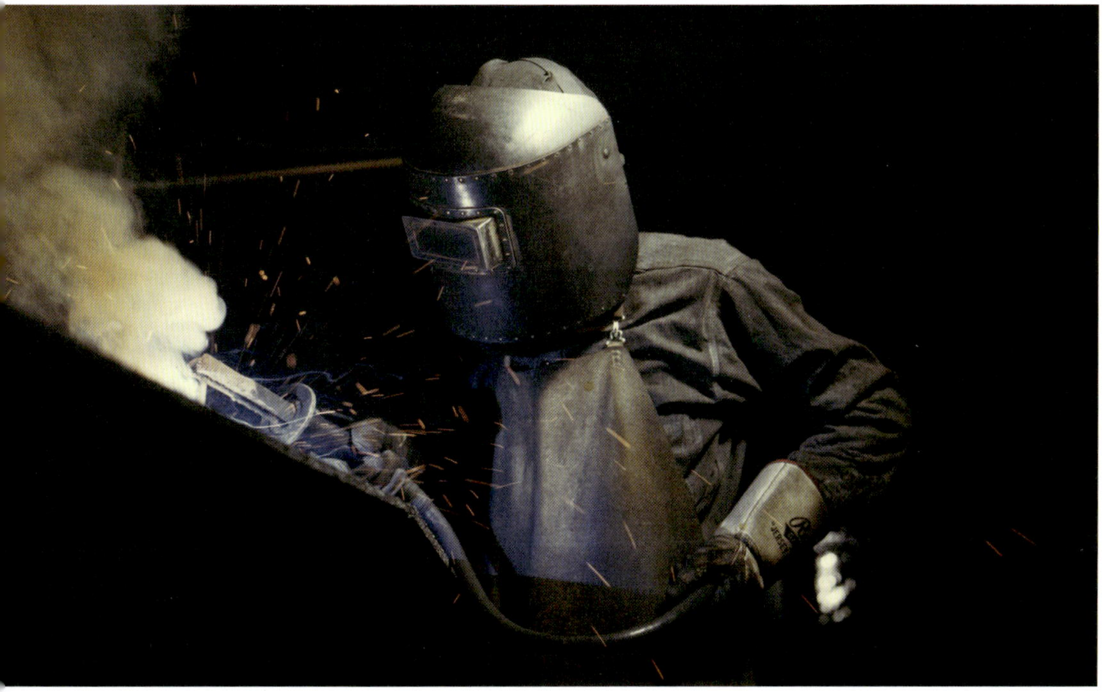

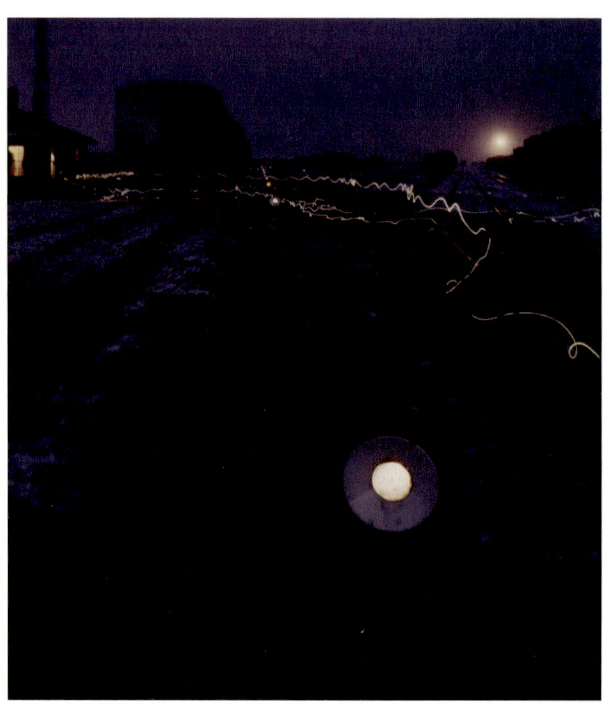

Purple
I waited all night. That's
when I knew I'd lost him.
Don't know what to think
right now.

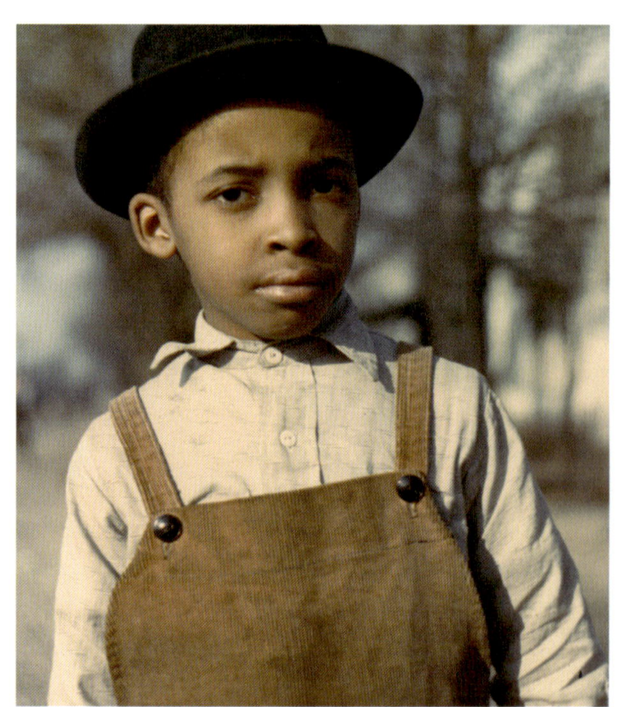

Not Your Sister
She's not your sister no more.
And you'll never see her again.
That's all mama said.

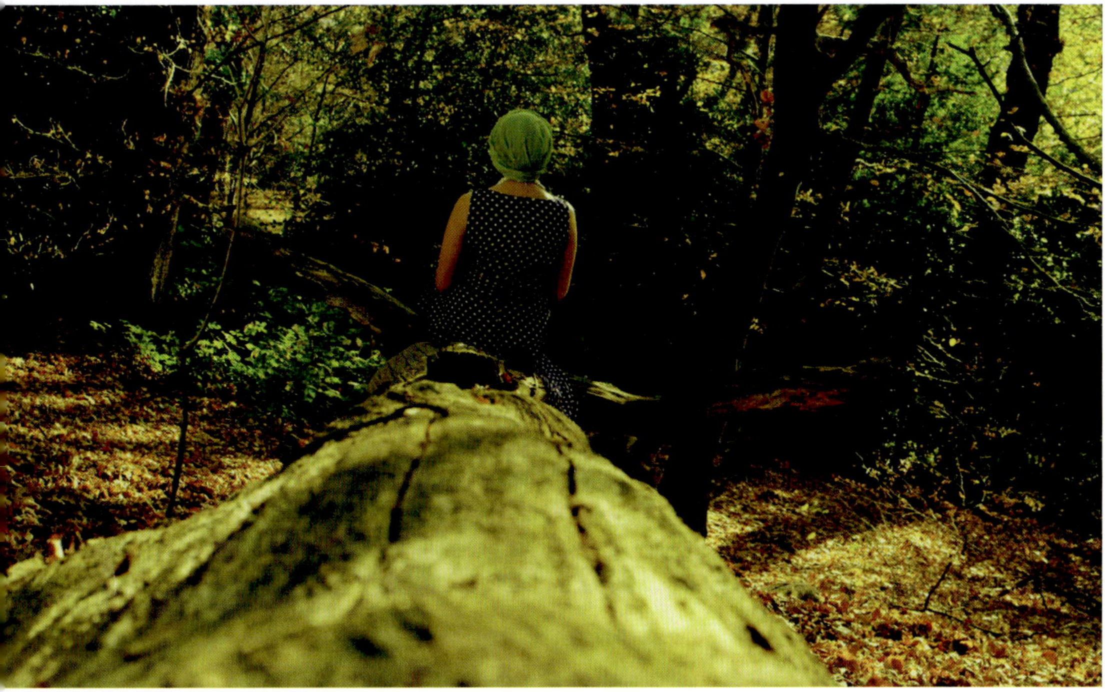

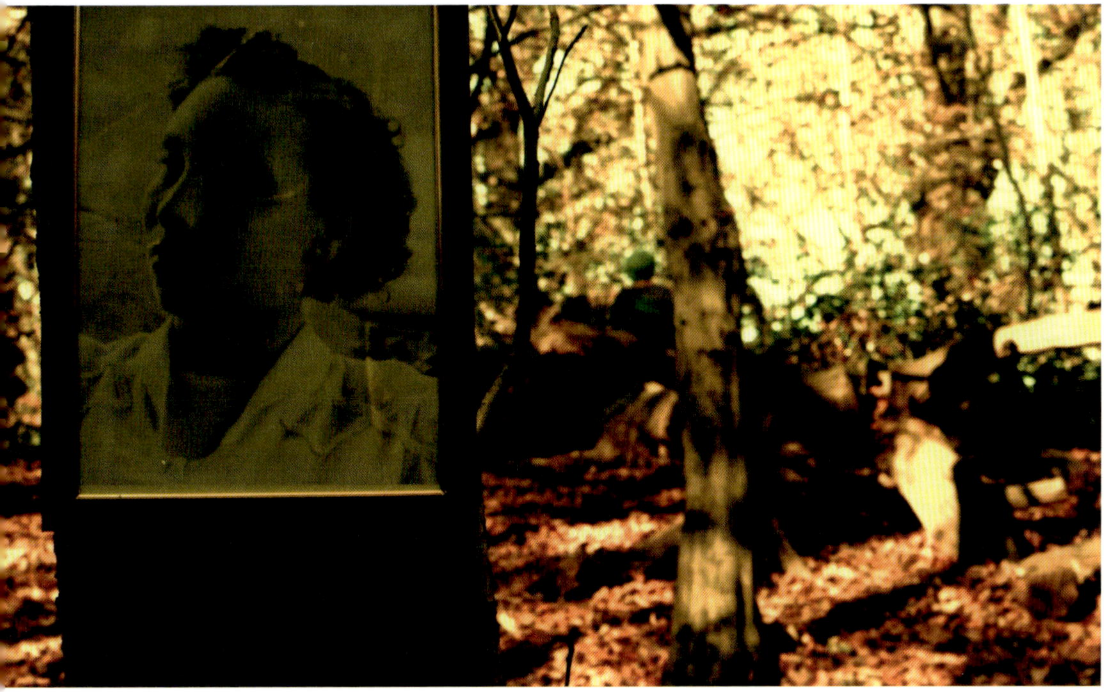

Janine Antoni

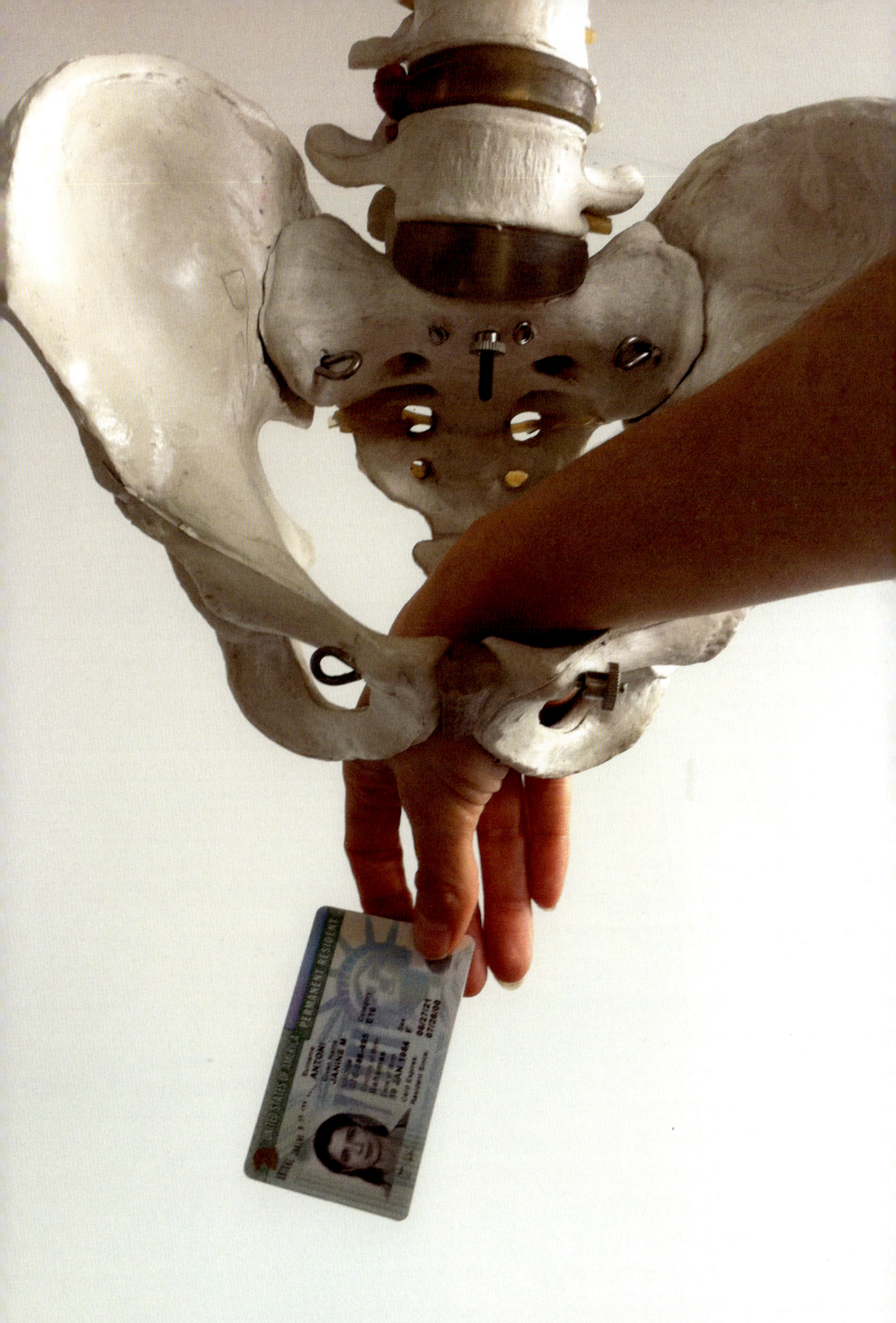

Sylvie Blocher
invites Jacques Rancière

Tariq Teguia's beautiful film *Inland* tells the story of the meeting between Malek, the surveyor and ex-militant who no longer believes in anything much, and a young, nameless woman from Mali (the girl), whom he initially wants to help make it to Morocco and then accompanies to the border of her country. In southern Algeria, while Malek is asking a friend to lend him a vehicle to continue the journey, the girl is questioned by an old woman of the house: 'Who are you? What country are you from? Say something so we can hear your language. Why don't you want to speak?' She does not reply, but smiles bashfully. Perhaps she does not want to speak; perhaps she simply does not understand the language in which she is being spoken to. The old woman concludes: 'Welcome, even if you don't want to speak.'

Obviously, this scene brings to mind an earlier episode in the film where the police harass one of the girl's unfortunate companions on his hospital bed. And it might easily supply its symbolic antithesis: the tradition of serving friends and welcoming strangers as opposed to the violence of the collective order that blocks the path of migrants. In short, hospitality would be the age-old virtue of openness to the other, the last resort in a world where the dual law of the State and Capital rules without appeal over the free circulation of capital and the barriers erected against the circulation of human beings. We are familiar with the current popularity of the word and the way it assumes the value of an incantation urging us to welcome the other, the different; to make way for her and recognize her customs and values. But those passing through do not ask people to recognize their culture, but to help them pass through or simply to make them a friendly gesture. And those who stay hardly wish to be singled out as different beings to be understood and respected. For them it is enough to be regarded as fellow creatures. In sum, hospitality thus conceived is unconducive to a collective settlement of the relationship between peoples and groups. From this, some philosophers have even concluded that things should be inverted. With Levinas, Lyotard and Derrida, they have construed the guest not as the one who must be benevolently welcomed, but as the irreducible other of which the I is the hostage, and who deprives the community of citizens of its tranquillity.

But maybe there is too much pathos on both sides. At stake in the encounter between the women of Béchar and the young black girl is not recognition of the other. The welcome is precisely addressed to someone who furnishes no indication of her identity and hence no opportunity to practise toleration of that identity. It is addressed to someone who does not speak, without us knowing why she does not speak or even whether she has understood the question. Rather than identifying it with the uncompromising virtues of respect and toleration of the other, I would therefore be tempted to associate it with certain scenes that are seemingly of less import: mute encounters between non-communicating worlds – for example, the memory of an old woman on a path in Korcula, silently offering the stranger a fig, as the only word of welcome she could speak to him – or comic dialogues of the deaf. *The Bulgarian Conductor*, one of Dezső Kostolányi's most wonderful short stories, recounts a long nocturnal conversation between a passenger and a conductor who interminably unwinds the yarn of his life in words accompanied by various relics – a photograph

of a dog or two buttons from a greatcoat – to which the passenger can only respond with the sole two words of Bulgarian he knows: a 'Yes', which allows the other to go on, or a 'No' that is the wrong answer to the narrator's sudden tears and that ruptures communication, until the final reconciliation of a 'Yes' on leaving the train.

In the first instance, hospitality might be this: not recognition of a community by a different community, but a sign made to someone with whom nothing else can be shared – the sign of a community of those who have nothing in common except the very possibility of making that sign to the person one meets in passing. For in any event, the young black girl will start out for the border again; the tourist will return home; the passenger will not see the conductor again. That is why the word so often sounds hollow when one seeks to make it a rule of coexistence grounded in recognition of the other. Accordingly, it is fitting to restore to it something of its levity, even its comical side: not the heart-rending sharing of an ailing human condition, but the initiative, sometimes inopportune, that seeks to convey a decision to treat someone as a fellow being even though we do not know precisely how she is our fellow, since we do not know who she is, what she is feeling or what she is expressing – a question of trust, therefore, rather than of understanding. An idea of humanity which is that neither of the friends of difference, nor of the priests of the absolutely Other.

This idea finds it difficult to get a hearing in politics – a sphere where levity is held in low esteem and where signs are requested to be clear. Others must probably come to its aid. This is what artists are perhaps doing today in their own fashion. The film-maker who has the women of Béchar speak is well aware of this: the film is not there to preach the virtues of hospitality, but to practise a form of aesthetic hospitality. Such hospitality is not the eclecticism that welcomes everything because the major explanations of the world and the major artistic models of service to the oppressed have failed. Instead, it is an attempt to explore anew the ways in which community is woven, to hold together places, bodies, gestures, words in new ways, when the meaning of the assemblage is no longer constituted in advance, when one no longer really knows what signs mean or what they will produce, without resigning oneself to the doleful wisdom of non-meaning. So it involves trying out the many ways in which beings can beckon to one another, exploring the ways that they can invent communities the formula for which does not as yet exist. This is a task that must be taken seriously, but also lightly.

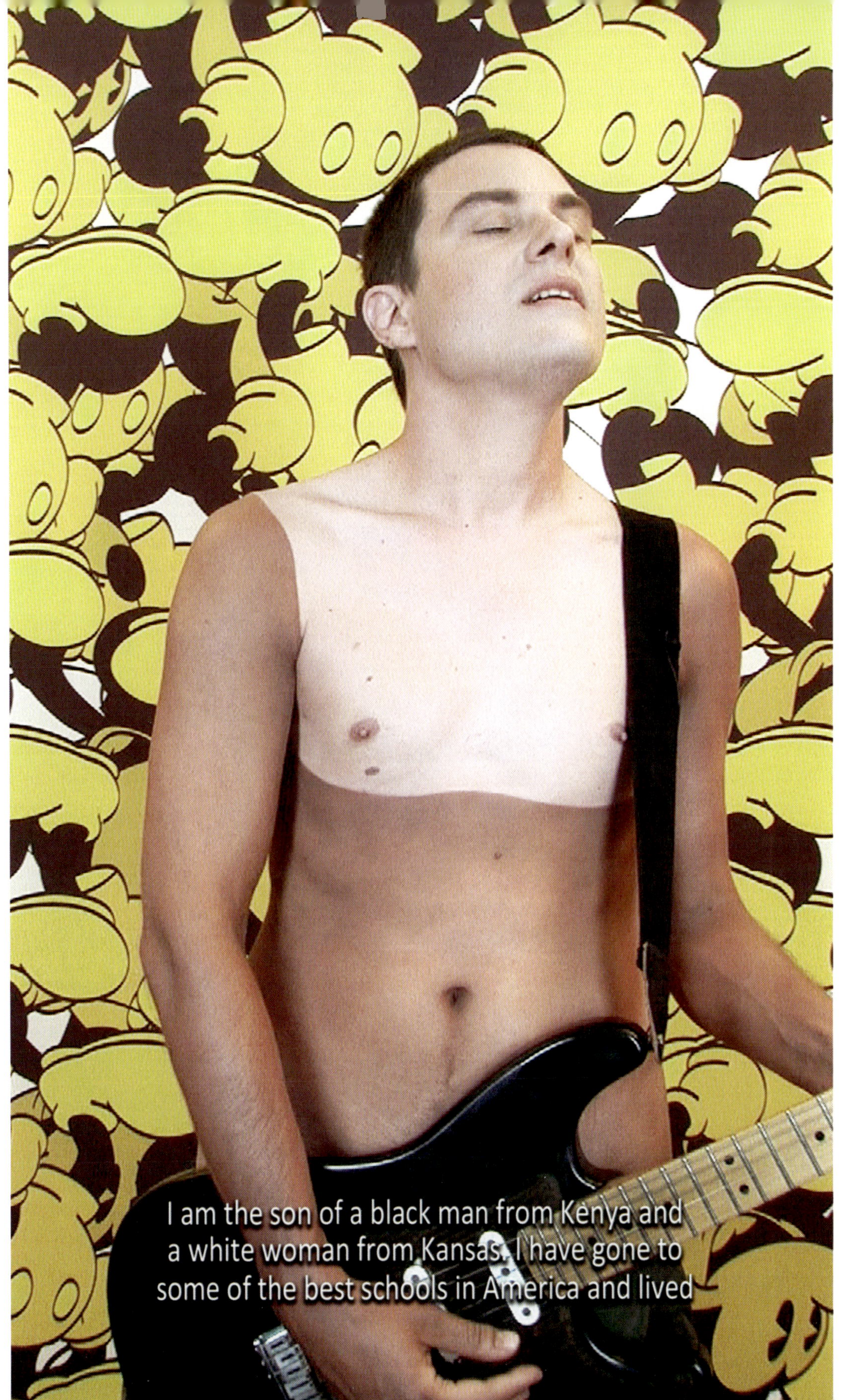
I am the son of a black man from Kenya and
a white woman from Kansas. I have gone to
some of the best schools in America and lived

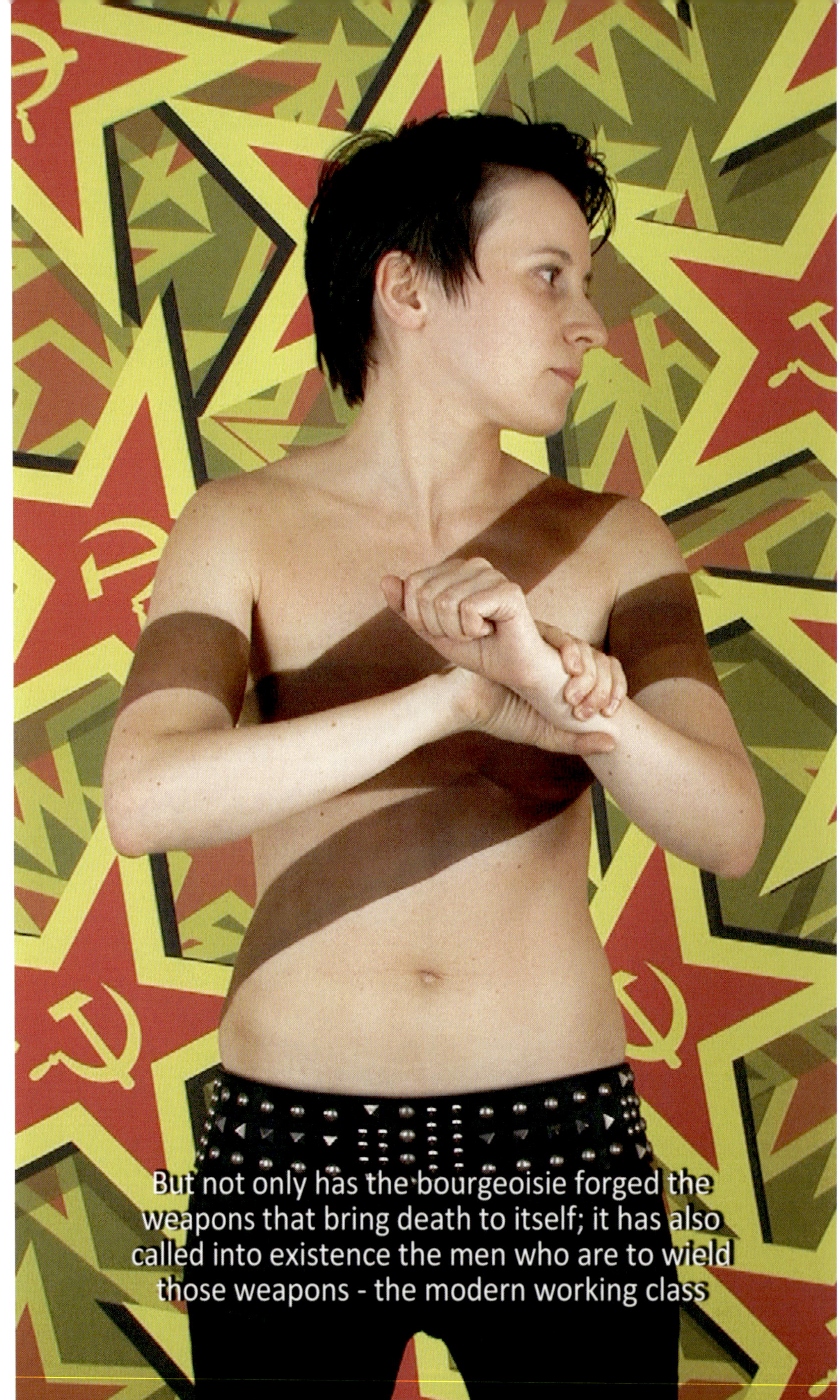But not only has the bourgeoisie forged the
weapons that bring death to itself; it has also
called into existence the men who are to wield
those weapons - the modern working class

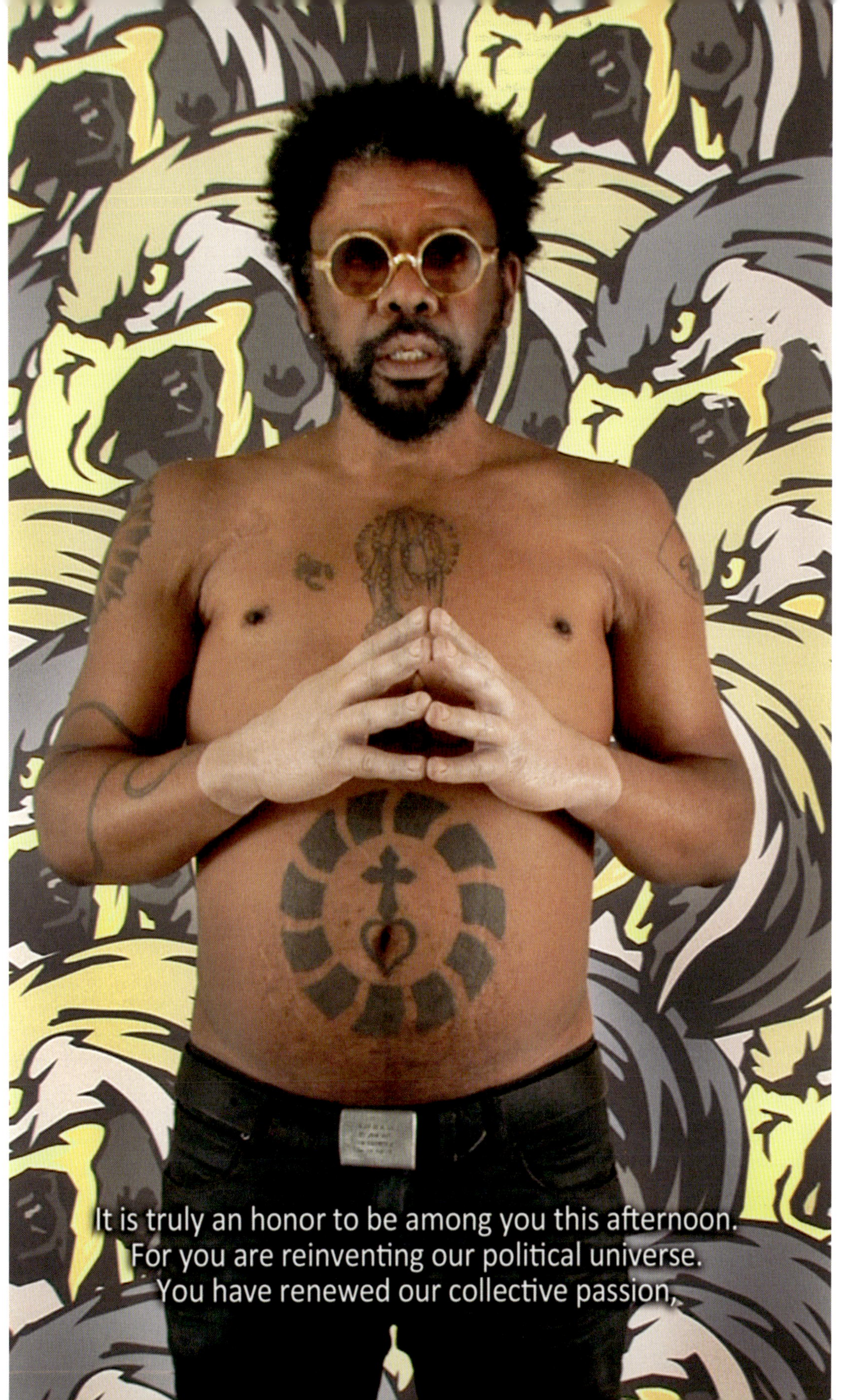

It is truly an honor to be among you this afternoon.
For you are reinventing our political universe.
You have renewed our collective passion,

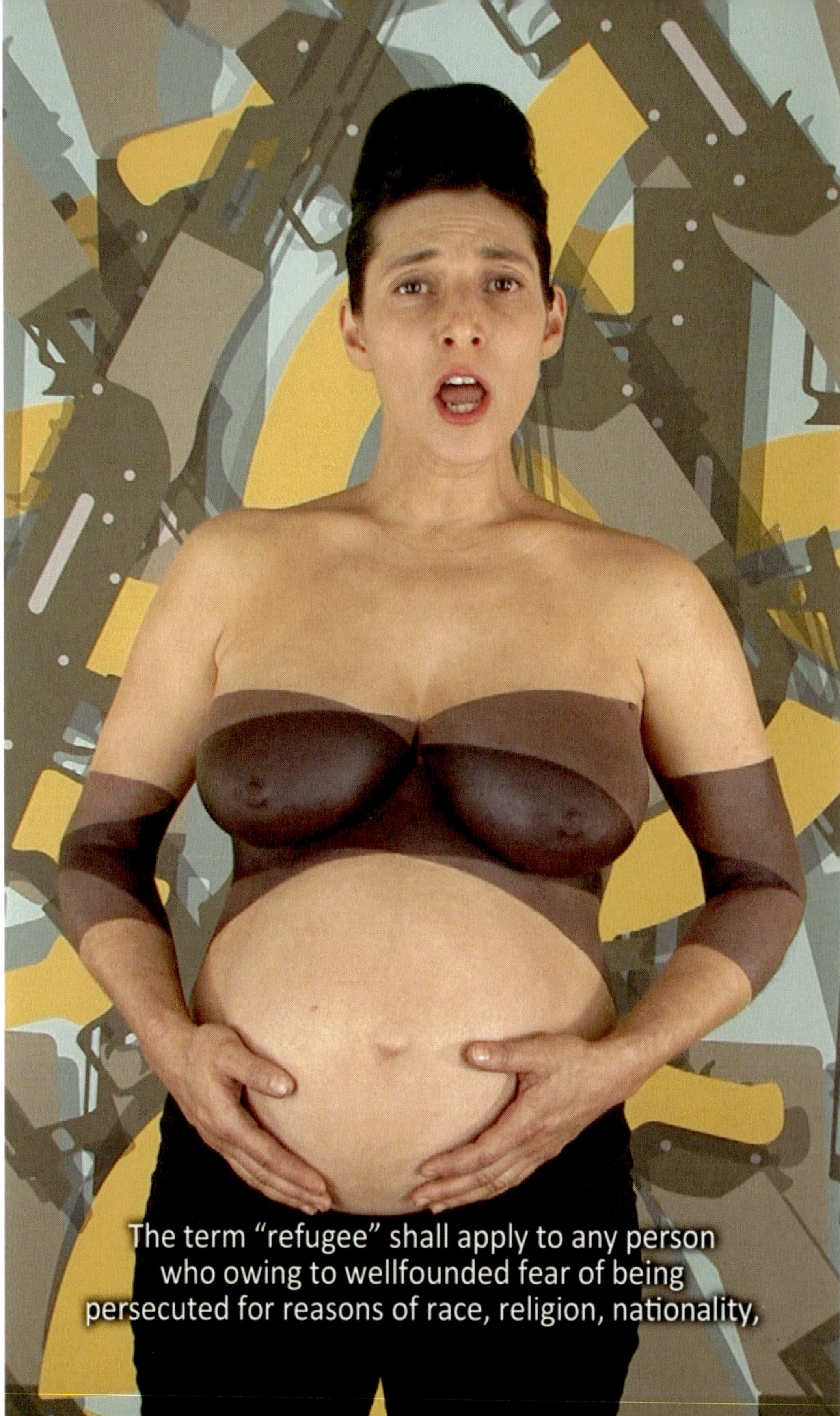
The term "refugee" shall apply to any person
who owing to wellfounded fear of being
persecuted for reasons of race, religion, nationality,

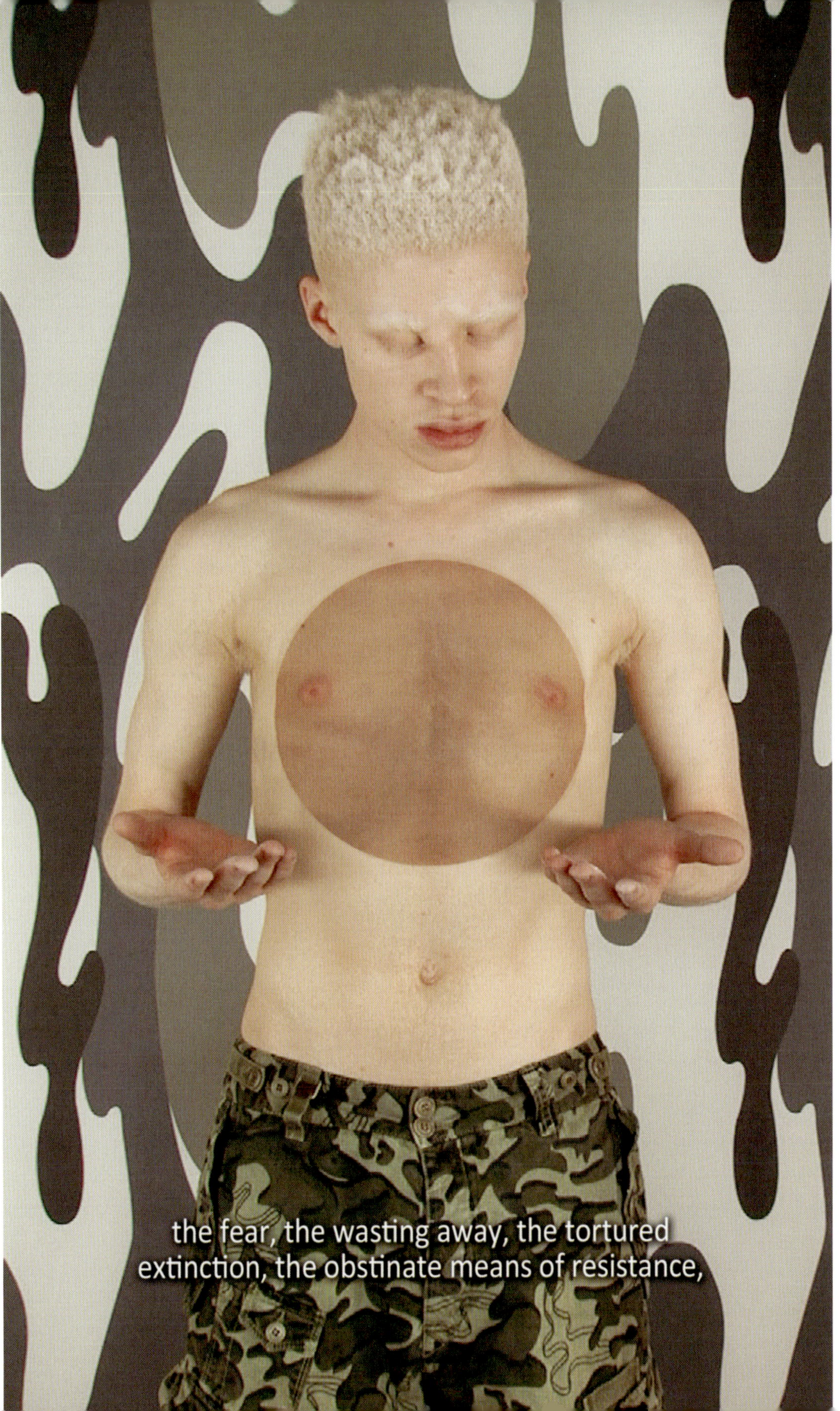
the fear, the wasting away, the tortured
extinction, the obstinate means of resistance,

Andrea Bowers

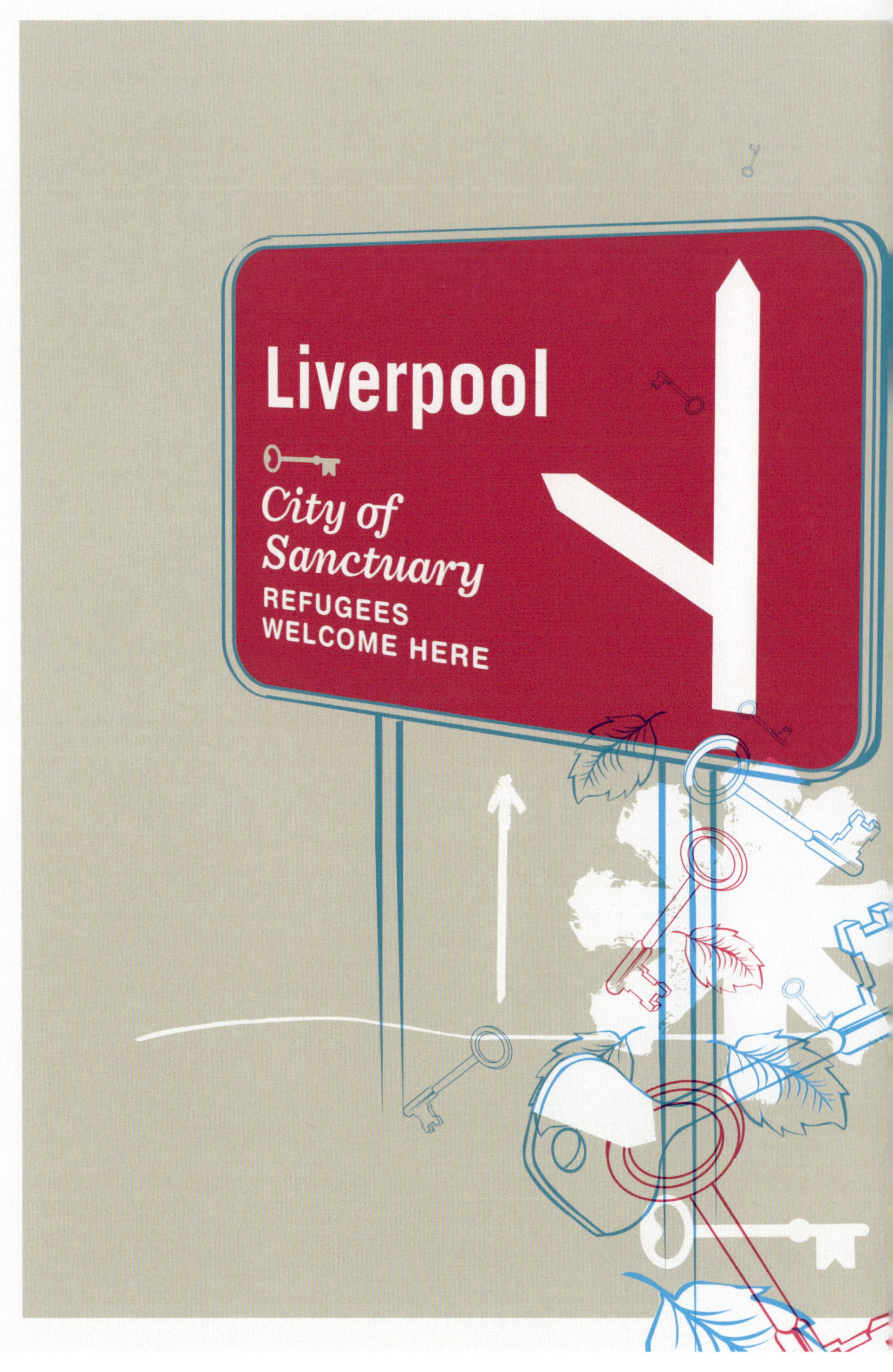

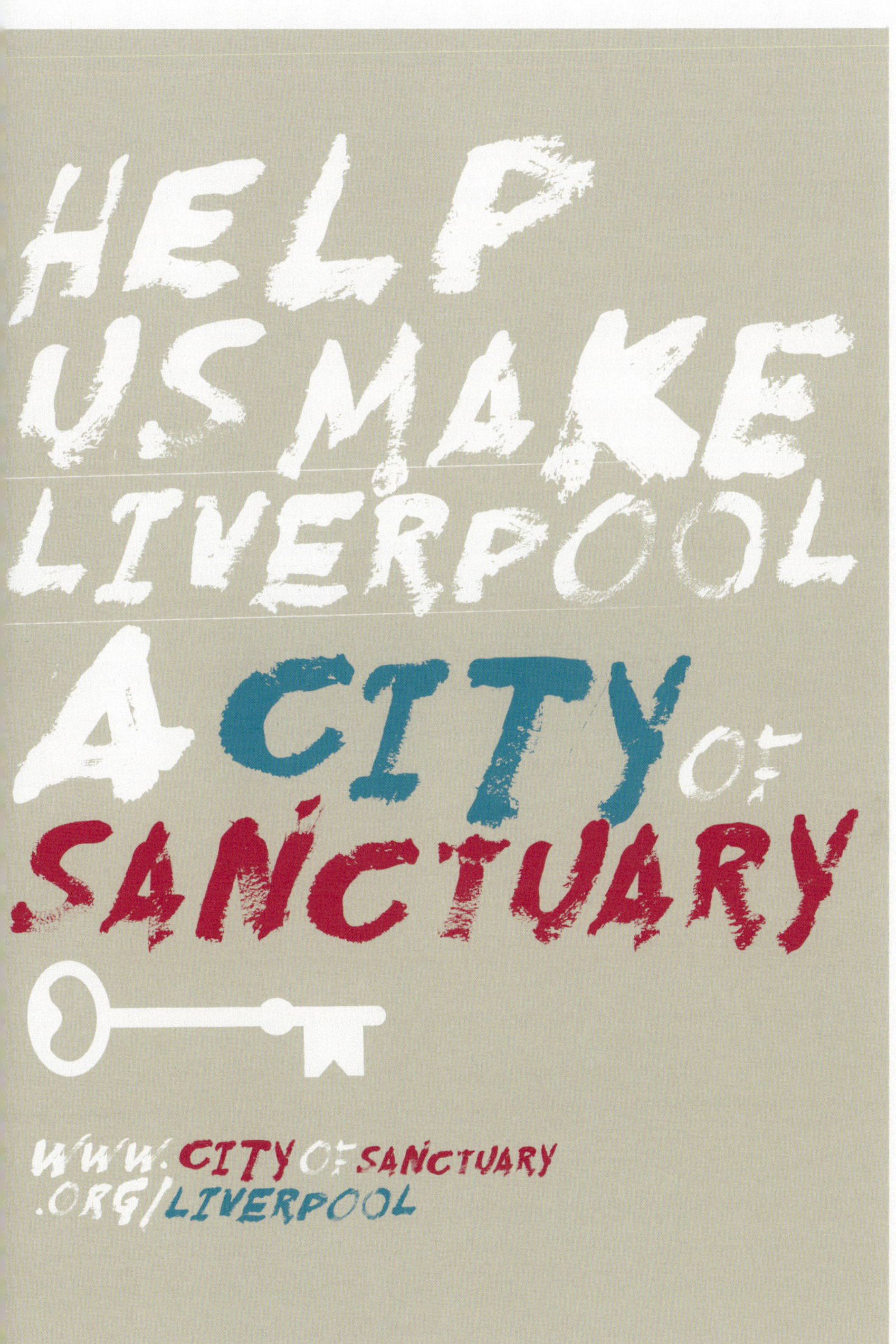

HELP US MAKE LIVERPOOL A CITY OF SANCTUARY
WWW.CITYOFSANCTUARY.ORG/LIVERPOOL

A national movement of local people,
community and public-sector groups
working to make their cities a place
of welcome and safety for people
seeking sanctuary from war,

Liverpool has a rich cultural heritage
and for generations has offered a
home to people fleeing persecution
from around the world. People seeking sanctuary have lost their homes

We are striving to spread a culture
of hospitality and support throughout Liverpool. We want to celebrate

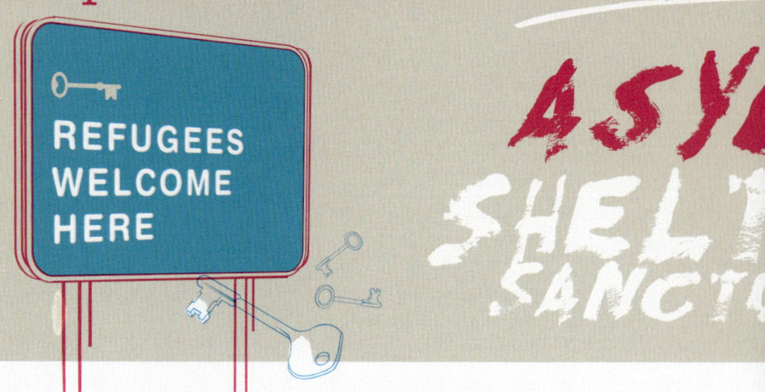

conflict and persecution. Liverpool City of Sanctuary is a movement currently led by an informal partnership of community, voluntary and public-sector organizations.

and families, yet bring diverse skills, arts, culture, food and social commitment that have contributed to the development and culture of the city.

the contribution of those who have come here for safety. We hope to reduce isolation, fear and exclusion.

From media myths to simple facts: a little bit of information about refugees

Under the 1951 Geneva Convention, a refugee is a person with 'a well-founded fear of being persecuted for reasons of race, religion, nationality, membership of a particular social group or political opinion' (Article 1A[2]). In the UK, an asylum seeker is someone who has applied for refuge and is waiting for a decision.

AN ASYLUM SEEKER IS NOT AN ILLEGAL IMMIGRANT

According to the Geneva Convention, 'States shall not impose penalties, on account of their illegal entry or presence, on refugees' (Article 31). Asylum seekers and refugees make themselves known to the authorities and are in a legal process of asylum.

AN ASYLUM SEEKER IS NOT AN ECONOMIC MIGRANT

Asylum seekers are not allowed to work, although among the people we meet, there are health professionals, engineers, teachers and others, most of whom expected that they would have to work to get by! Those who are supported are entitled to only £5 a day (less than 70% of mainstream benefits).

Asylum seekers must report regularly to police stations or immigration centres, and are subject to detention at any point during their claim (including pregnant women and children). Those whose claims are rejected face a choice of going back to where they originally fled or else destitution and homelessness in the UK.

Where do people come from?

Afghanistan, Iraq, Iran, Sudan, Sri Lanka, Zimbabwe, Somalia, China, Pakistan, Nigeria, Eritrea, Syria

HOW MANY

The UK is home to less than 2% of the world's refugees. Home Office statistics from March 2012 show that there are 20,993 supported asylum seekers across the UK at the moment. In Liverpool, there are about 1,000, barely enough to fill 1/40 of Goodison Park.

Who's living in the North West?

92.1% White
4.4% Asian or Asian British
3.4% Other ethnic groups
0.1% Supported asylum seekers

Information sources: UN High Commissioner for Refugees; Home Office; The Geneva Convention; Refugee Council / Oxfam; Refugee Action; Student Action for Refugees

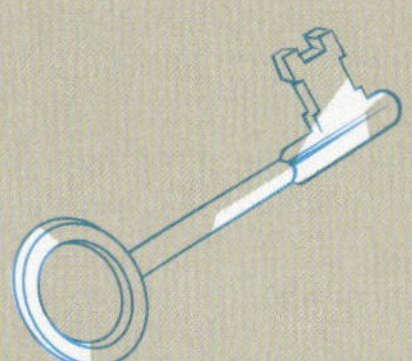

Pledge YOUR Support.

The first step in your support for City of Sanctuary Liverpool is to pledge your support and send it to the City of Sanctuary group. We would like to be able to include your name and/or organization as part of a pledge and contact list.

Pledge your support at www.cityofsanctuary.org/liverpool and then see the practical ways you can show your support.

STEP TWO

Other Ways YOU and YOUR Community can Welcome People Seeking Sanctuary ...

Positively support your colleagues, friends or staff to understand the real reasons why people seek sanctuary and the problems refugees face. This is in contrast to the inaccurate and negative media that exists about them. Donate preloved clothes, furniture, pots and pans and other useful items (via Asylum Link, STAR and Healthy Inclusion's Women's Group). Offer your skills and volunteer with one of the local asylum or refugee support charities (any of those listed on the right).

Become a mentor and help folk move back into their professional roles.

Join a conversational English class (STAR).

Smile more often: it uses fewer muscles and helps you and others feel happy and welcome.

Fundraise for or donate to an asylum or refugee charity.

Publicize City of Sanctuary, Refugee Week and other refugee events within your community.

What YOUR Local Organizations and Community Groups are doing ...

Merseyside Refugee Support Network (MRSN) runs communication and information exchange for all groups and partners working with and for refugees and all asylum seekers. It also provides English and interpreting classes, employment and training support, as well as benefits and housing advocacy.
0151 707 0566
seana@merseysidenetworkforchange.org
www.merseysidenetworkforchange.org

Asylum Link (ALM) provides a safe space for asylum seekers and refugees to meet and discover their new community. A wide range of services are available, from advice and English classes to bike repair.
0151 709 1713   www.asylumlink.org.uk

Refugee Action provides advice and support to asylum seekers and refugees in the UK.
0151 214 3020   www.refugee-action.org.uk

SOLA ARTS uses the arts to support mental health and well-being, predominantly with refugees and black and ethnic-minority communities. Creative and social projects to support personal and community development.
0151 726 8440
www.solaarts.blogspot.com / www.solaarts.org

Sahir House Support is an information and training centre offering a wide range of services to individuals and families living with or affected by HIV.
0151 237 3989   www.sahir.uk.com

Family Refugee Support offers project support and therapy through horticulture for refugee and asylum seeking families who are struggling with mental health issues as a result of traumatic experiences.
0151 728 9340
www.familyrefugeesupportproject.org.uk

STAR (Student Action for Refugees) A national network of student groups campaigning for, volunteering and raising awareness for refugees in the UK. Projects in Liverpool include a weekly conversation class and women's group, and a monthly Circle of Silence in Liverpool city centre.
liverpoolstargroup@gmail.com
www.star-network.org

Any questions?

www.cityofsanctuary.org/liverpool
info@liverpool.cityofsanctuary.org

Libia Castro and Ólafur Ólafsson

Asking the question 'who has the right to right?' seeks to explode something regarding the rhetoric of rights, to make explicit the tensions and hypocrisies in the way in which rights obscure real, material exclusion. Let us then begin to rewrite the declarations in a way that addresses the metaquestion of the right to right and begins not with a philosophy of right but with a philosophy of wrong, of the wronged …

Article 1
All human beings are born. Freedom and equality in dignity and rights is heavily dependent on where you are born, who your parents are and which government is bombing other people in your name.

Article 2
No one is entitled to all the rights and freedoms set forth in this Declaration. Distinctions of any kind, such as race, colour, sex, language, religion, political or other opinion, national or social origin, property, birth or other status will be used to divide you whenever your economic and political rulers deem it useful. Furthermore, every distinction shall be made on the basis of the political, jurisdictional or international status of the country or territory to which a person belongs, whether it be independent, trust, non-self-governing or under any other limitation of sovereignty.

Article 3
Everyone has the right to life, liberty and security of person. The police will let you know when and where these rights are operative.

Process-fragment from the work
ThE riGHt tO RighT
by Libia Castro and Ólafur Ólafsson
in collaboration with Nina Power

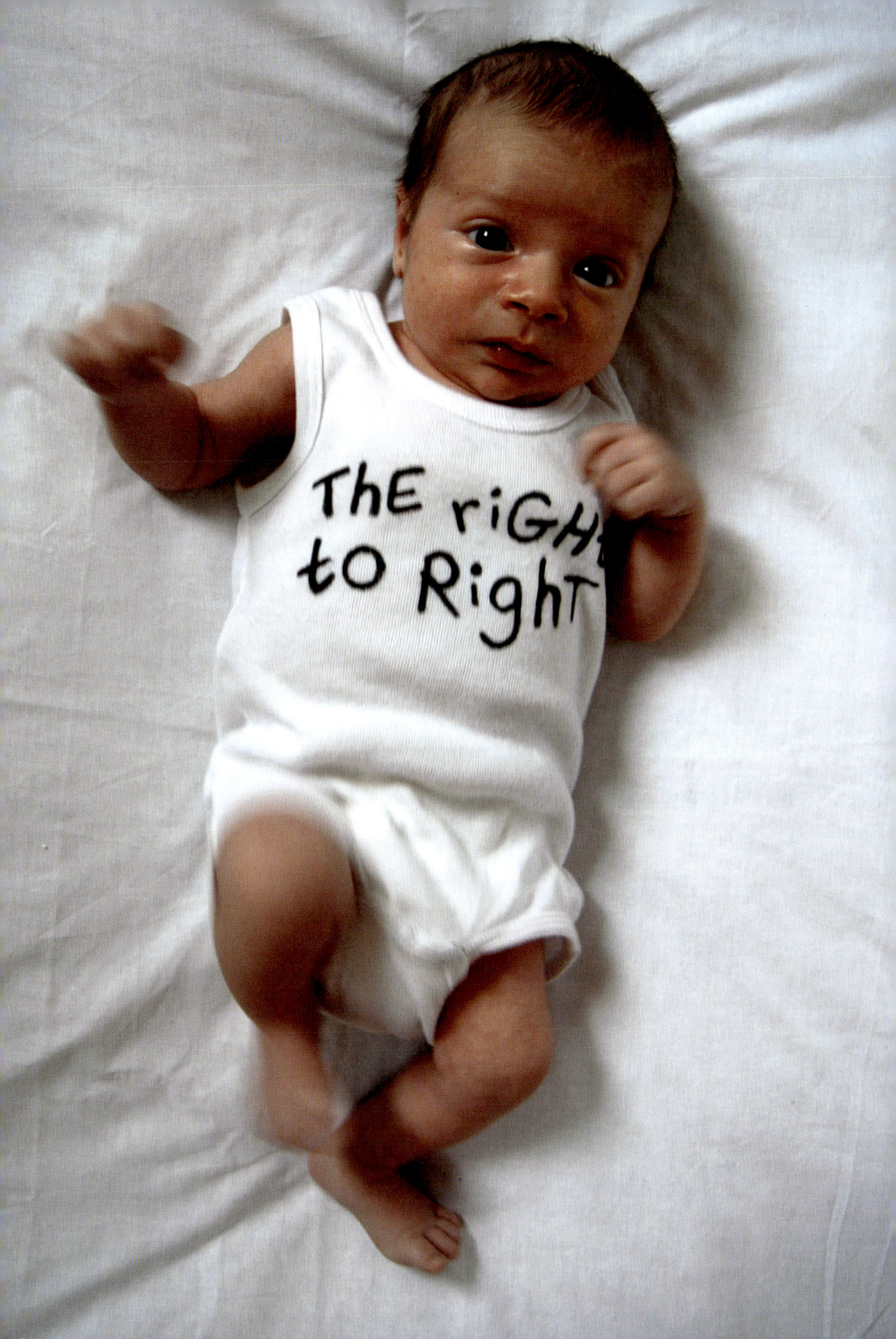

ThE riGHt
tO RighT

Good evening, I'm Patrick Mefang

I was born in New-Bell (Cameroon). I grew up in New-Bell. I had a childhood like all the other children there. I am the firstborn of a family of five children, three girls and two boys. I attended elementary school and got all the required diplomas. I finished high school and got my Baccalauréat F3.

Right. My troubles start from the moment of my mother's death in 2001 … February 2001. So, after her death I was desperate. I had to find a job in the brasseries.

Right. I worked for one year … afterwards they didn't hire me. Right. It was necessary for me to keep going; I had to provide for my little brothers, so I had to do other things. As I couldn't find anything to do, I decided, with a group of friends, to set out on an adventure. So, one morning, I decided to leave. I had a bit of money saved, on me, and as usual, I had to touch my grandmother for cash.

So, with that, I left. On D-day, I was the only one to leave because all of my friends backed out at the last minute.

I didn't take … because there's two ways out, two ways out of Cameroon to Nigeria. The first one is by Mamfe. You pass through Mamfe and you arrive in the water via Ikok. I didn't take that one because I'm afraid of water. Instead, I went by Yaounde. Ngaoundere, the great North!

Right. Near Maroua, Maroua is a border city, there is a city next to the border called Maroua-Mora, Mora-Banki. I spent the night in Banki. Anyway it took me three days to get out of Cameroon, because it's not easy. Because I have to sleep in the train in Ngaoundere. And then again in the train from Ngaoundere to Maroua, which also takes all day. I have to sleep another night in Banki, at the Cameroon–Nigerian border, in order to cross into Nigeria very early in the morning.

Right. So, how does it work when you don't have papers? There are those who are called the traffickers. When you get there, you find the traffickers. They ask you these questions: 'What are you here for? Where are you going?' You explain. They tell you, 'Right, ok, you are going to go like this, like this, like that. You are going to produce this sum that sum … because you don't have the papers.'

Right. Anyway, it worked out like that! To start with I slept. The next morning my trafficker took me to take the cars. They are those old 504s that are used on the borders over there. Right. So I took the 504. I drove until Nigeria, from Banki to Maidougouri. I paid the customs along the way, the Nigerian police. I paid 500 nairas which is equal to, about… which is equal to about 4000 francs CFA.

In Maidougouri I took the bus for Kano. Six hours of driving. It takes for ever. You are tired.

Right. In Kano … I stopped in Kano. I spent the night there, at the train station. There's a place there where everyone sleeps. It's a big station. Everyone sleeps there; all the travellers, even the Nigerians. You pay 50 nairas, that equals 250 francs CFA … just for sleeping, with mosquitoes all around and everything. The next morning I took … the car for … I think, the car for Agades. I took the car for … yes, yes for Zenden, Kano-Zenden. It takes for ever. It's really a long trip, and then the only annoying thing on the way was the border police. Otherwise the journey through the country doesn't bother you. But it's the border police that bother you. So, when you don't have the papers, you have to pay the customs in order to go through.

That's what I did, because I had saved. I left with almost 350,000 francs CFA.

Right. As a newcomer I thought that was a lot and yet it's nothing. I had no idea what was in store for me.

Right. So, in Zenden, I spent almost a week in Zenden because there's a ghetto of Cameroonians, Africans. That's where everyone gets together. If you go there, you're looking for your brother; you ask, they'll tell you, 'Yes, he's been here, well, that was … about a month ago, he went through to that country.'

So, there I made a break. I spent almost a week there. I found myself with a lot of other Cameroonians, even some who had left the US to come and learn the work. Because that's the crossroads where you come to learn the work; it's not the work you think of as 'work'. The work. The work, that's … how to screw the whites? How to steal their money without attacking them? You know what I mean, that's where you learn how to be a 'feyman'. It is there that you learn how to be 'the fey'. They show you the B. ABA. They show you how to forge money and all that, and all that.

Right. I was there for about a week. When you have the feeling that you're ready, when you know that you have learned the work a bit and you can move on … yes, yes, you move on. And, let me tell you that to learn that kind of work over there is a lot less expensive, but if someone wants to teach you that here, you will pay for the rest of your life. Even before I left I had a friend who was a feyman. He did the Dubai route. He had refused to teach me because it costs a lot of money to learn that kind of work. But over there, you can learn it for free.

Right. After I'd had a little bit of training, I went on to Agades. Agades is already a border city. It's on the border, and that border separates three countries: Nigeria, Algeria and Libya. To get to Libya you have to cross there. Even if you are someone special? No matter how you try to do it? At the moment it's very difficult to cross over there.

So, I preferred to go via Algeria by crossing through the desert. Now there, that's another thing, man! The desert, crossing the desert takes a long time, if you're not lucky you won't make it, it's just a matter of luck. You pray to God to protect you … until you arrive. Right. This time I was lucky. It took me a week and two days' travelling.

All you have with you is water and these biscuits. You leave from there with a huge quantity of water. Almost 20 litres of water, which doesn't even last you, it's not even enough. And the biscuits, those are some special biscuits. You buy them; they sell them at that market in Zenden. These are special biscuits, made specially just for that. You eat one biscuit, you can last all day. So, that's what you carry with you.

And then there's different ways of keeping the money. If you don't have cash on you, maybe you have it in Cameroon; they'll constantly send it to you by Western Union. But then, that's only when you have the papers and when you have your passport with you. If you don't have your passport, you can't get money from 'West', so you have to keep the money on you. That means you have to thread it into your belt loops. You fold the money and put it behind your belt loops, that's where you hide the money. Yes, you hide the money in the belt loops. So apart from the belt loops, you can put the money in your shoes. You take off your shoe and you put it in the heel. You put the money in there. Apart from the heel, you can also put money into a 'Colgate', the toothpaste tubes. You open the end of the tube, you open the end of the tube, you put the money inside, wrapped up well in plastic, and then you know it's your tube. If they come to search you … if they come to search you, you know all they are going to find is toothpaste, I tell you! So, it's kind of like that. This means that when you don't put your money in those places, they'll 'bobele' you; they'll 'choa' you. This means, you get searched; they strip you.

So, I was lucky, I got all the way to Tamanrasset. Tamanrasset, that's where you'll find … there's patrons. There's a Cameroonian there, a Cameroonian who has lived there since … the age of Ahidjo. He has lived there since the age of Ahidjo. He is like a representative. He is like a councillor, but he is not a councillor, it's not official. He is like a representative. We can him, we call him … we call him … anyway, I forgot the name. I forgot what we called him, I tell you! But … he's a representative anyway, who has lived there since the time of Ahidjo and everyone who gets there, you say that you are Cameroonian, you say that you are Cameroonian, he welcomes you. He's also a Bamileke, he's already married with kids and everything. Right. So, he welcomed me, he welcomed me. I spent almost a month there with him, because, when you get there, you have to stop, you have no money, you have to stop. He finds you work, you work and most of the money's for him. So, for, say, 100 euros, you get 35 and the rest is for him. Yeah, you know you have to try and save up a bit of money like that before going on.

Anyway, I spent some time in Tamanrasset. I took the route to Oran. Oran is a lot like Douala. Algiers is the economic capital. Oran is also one of the big cities in Algeria; it's the third capital. So, I stopped in Oran.

I left with a friend. I met a Cameroonian in Banki; we did the trip together. He's a Bamenda; he came from the North West. So, we met over there. And we stayed together as we were two Camer'. We went on together until we got to Algeria. Wow, he had his way of life. You see, I lived, I lived … I knew what I was looking for, what I had set out to do there. He, well, he had some cash, he was always having money sent to him, because the Bamenda, they really are too supportive – the family and all. Whenever he cried, someone always sent him money. He used it for the girls; he was always looking for girls. He lived … he thought he was in Cameroon; he lived like we do here, when we have some cash. Yeah, so that's what he did when he was there. Right. I couldn't handle being with him because, well, his lifestyle did not allow for saving; he got me used to living like him. Right. Unfortunately for him, he got sick, sick for a long time. He caught a sexually transmitted disease. So, right … it paralysed him. He stayed sick, for a long time, a long time until he … until he died. Peace to his soul. When he died, they tried to repatriate his body to Cameroon, because all the Cameroonians back there knew each other. There are places where everyone meets up at night, where you go when you've got nothing to do, you hang out there. We do all sorts of things…. And if anyone can help you out, he helps you out, and so on.

So, anyways that was how we lived! And little by little, we got by. We were already a group. And we stuck together. There's a reunion of Cameroonians there. And we stuck together. We lived like we do here, and we saved so we could go on.

Right. What made me feel bad is that I never sent money to my family. Of course I didn't have much. But anyways, it was symbolic, even to send 100 euros even one time!

Right. I made the effort. When my friend died, I went on by myself. We tried to repatriate him back to Cameroon, we paid our respects and then I went on my way. I couldn't stay there any longer because I was alone. I went on to Morocco. In Morocco … Morocco is too … it's a country … there's too much racism. They think they are whites. The Moroccans think that they are in Europe. So life isn't easy there, it's not easy to live in Morocco. It's hard for a Cameroonian to find work there. For Africans it's not easy over there.

So, I managed. I was lucky because as I am a nice guy, I was lucky to stumble upon a nice girl. So, she helped me out … she helped me out. And if it were only with food, every time she gave me food and then a place to sleep. So, I was with her, she was a friend for me, she was everything for me, a mother. Right. So, that's just how we lived. All just waiting for the day … the big day of crossing, because everyone crosses on their particular day. You train yourself because there is a barrier, a barrier of six metres. And that's the border; it's in Tangier, Tangier is the border. So you train yourself to sprint and to climb because the barrier is real high, six metres and sometimes electrified, at night they electrify it; on the other side there are dogs. So, even if you make it over the barrier, you need to run, with the policemen over there. Policemen with those things they put on you – to electrocute you. You know, these things they put on you to like, shock you! Don't know what it's called.

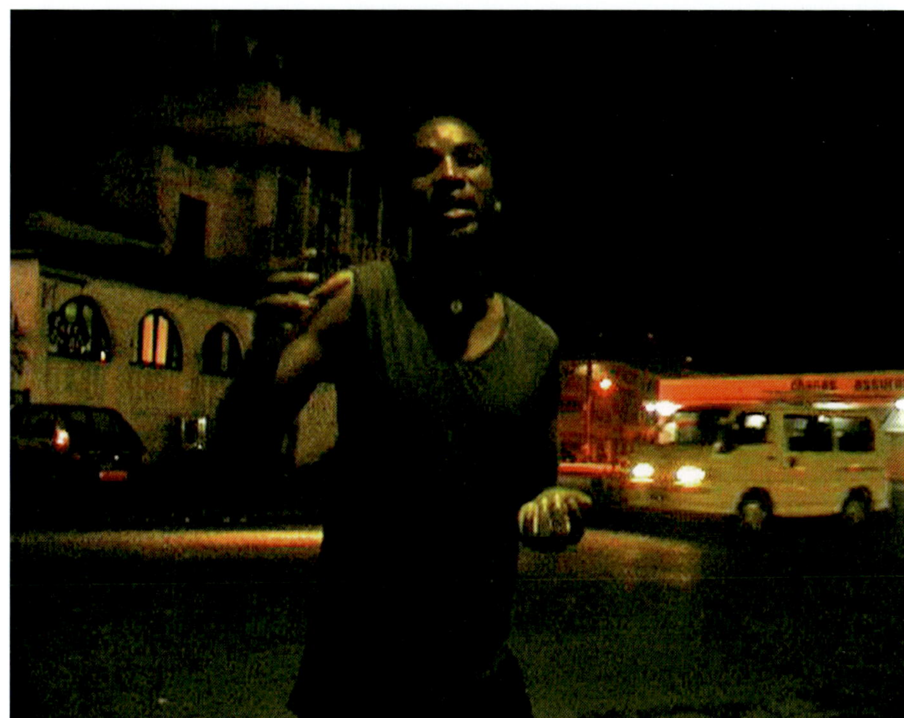

Right. So, in a sense, the training in Tangier is for that. There's also a camp of refugees there. We all stayed there. You live … you live … in French we call that … so … there's no house to live in, so we live, we call it … I can't remember the expression, or maybe it's 'under the stars', we often say. Yes, ok, under the stars, we live like that. You sleep; you sleep on the bare ground. You have nothing but sheets to cover yourself from the cold and the mosquitoes.

So, in the morning, if someone has a bit of money, he helps you out. If the government is aware, they give you bags of rice and cans and stuff like that. That's how you live. Right, all the while waiting for your day to cross over. When you cross over, you are on the other side, if you are caught they make you go back again right there. They make you jump across the same barrier again. Tough luck. You fall, you get cut up … you break your bones. Tough luck. It's none of their business. It's your problem.

Right. That's how you spend your time there.

Actually, life isn't so different from here. It's the same life. Except that over there, there's a distinction: there's blacks and whites. The whites, the Arabs, they take themselves for whites, think they're whites; they quarantine us.

Right. The Spanish government, the European Union, they hang together; they had an agreement, had their deal because they already had a lot of immigrants. I don't like water. Otherwise I would have crossed by water.

I don't like water, and it costs 1,000 euros to cross by water, and it's not even sure you'll make it.

You are in a little pirogue that can hold 200 people. You're there with almost 5,000 … in the middle of the sea … a little pirogue with a motor. And then the trafficker, when he crosses with you, he leaves you on the open sea. He leaves you like, umm … I'm here and then, umm … Spain is … like, till the 'Flower Market' cross-roads. He leaves you like at that distance. He takes a lifeboat. He goes back. He leaves you there; up to you to make it. You leave, you get caught, or you do whatever you want.

Right, that's how it is! And even if you succeed in crossing … because amidst … inside there, we are so packed that people die! So packed that there's no oxygen, you can't even breathe. You die! You die … First … first it's the cold

that kills you. You are on the open sea. You also die from famine. You also die, … it's that you can die of suffocation because we're so packed. A boat that can normally take 200, they put in 5,000. It's terrible! And on the other side, when you cross over, the border police, the water police stop you, the Spanish.

Right. Those are the things. I didn't try that. But those are the things that, when you are in Tangier, they tell about to prepare you. They prepare you for what you are going to say when you get to the other side. When the police catch you, from what we've been told, when the police catch you, now there, you have no papers on you to identify you. When they catch you, they ask you questions, you don't reply. You pretend to be deaf. If you really need to speak, you speak the way you do back home. For example, if you ask me, 'What is your name?' I answer in my local dialect. I am Bamileke; you can't tell. I can even insult you in my dialect because you can't tell. So, it's a bit like that. I don't have any papers so they can't identify me. I don't speak the same language as you do. And then, when you're in a situation like that, they put you in a camp of refugees.

But then, that's already on the Spanish territory, in the camp of refugees.

There's also another tactic: you arrive, you say there is war in your country; you are trying to escape, you are trying to escape the war. Now this is a special case. They call your country and ask if there's really a war going on there? Is that city really at war? Between which people? How many people have left Cameroon to emigrate? And all. And so on … they enquire on all that. So, if it is really the case for those who are at war, like at the time, the Sudanese, the Sudanese, you know? It's Sudan, Rwanda, Sudan, and Chad even; those were the countries at war.

Right. When the refugees were from Chad, the people from Darfur, between Sudan and Chad, when you come across them there, everyone knows that they were real refugees, that there's a war and all. They are taken aside. They treat them differently. This means they were given special treatment, more food to eat, more things than the others who had crossed over illegally just to get in.

Right. And at that point…. These things I tell you, they told us in Tangier.

I didn't get there. At that point, as we had been prepared for when we would be in situations such as these, we would be able to get out easily.

Right. At that point, when you play mute, you don't answer a single question, you don't have a single paper on you, they put you in the camp of refugees, you live, you live, you live there, you live there until the day that you don't have any family, you have nobody, you are tired. Even now some people are still living over there. If you manage to escape from the camp, you leave. If you don't succeed, because it is a big camp, guarded and surveyed.... And they feed you; they take care of you, because over there, there are a lot of injured people. Always injured people … injured people over there, and … it's even because they are injured that they put them there. Because if you arrive in good shape … they look for a good reason to send you home.

Right. I made it till the fence.

We also lost another Cameroonian over there. But for him, it wasn't because he wanted to cross, it's not because he wanted to jump over the barrier, but because he wanted to cross the road. It's a guy from New-Bell. His name was Joe, a little guy, but he was pretty old. A little guy, but pretty old. Now he is a special case: it's for a girl that he sets out on his adventure. Because he was in love with a girl, she was so beautiful, he doesn't want to lose her and he didn't have enough money, too, to keep her, so he decided to leave.

Right. We were together over there, in Algeria and in Morocco. He even has a family. He had an older sister who had a good position. But for him, it's not the barrier that kills him; it's crossing the road. Because over there it's not our little roads, it's these huge major roads. Morocco, that's a little like the white man. They think that they have made it. But life over there is good, too. The infrastructures are good, the roads, big. Right. Crossing the road, he has that accident and he dies. Because there … that's heavy traffic roads. The cars there go by 180 to 200 per hour. Right. We had to repatriate his body to Cameroon.

We … our repatriation came from the fact that we didn't have any papers and moreover the Spanish government and the European Union have subsidized this project of repatriation. And then, normally, according to the regulations the person being sent back should be given 200,000 francs CFA. Now, we had no papers, so they sent us back again to the desert, without any money, without papers. There they could give us 250,000 francs to go back to where we came from, because they didn't know where we had come from. According to them, we hadn't told them where we had come from because we didn't have any papers to identify ourselves. I told them that I had come from the Ivory Coast. Because I know that at that time, the Ivory Coast was better than Cameroon. I said that I came from the Ivory Coast. Where's the

proof? There's no proof. So, all these people, all of us … Others said that they came from South Africa, because if they send you back to South Africa you have also made it! There, you've also made it. So, as we didn't have any papers, they dumped us all in the desert, and this time in the desert, they gave us each 250,000 francs CFA.

With that, well, I went back by the same route. I went through Niger. I took the same route, as I knew the way.... I went back. I run out of money at the border, in Banki. Ok, there I'm already in Cameroon. I called home in Douala. They sent me a … what's it called? What's the company? A Union Transfer, Union Transfer or something, whatever Union that is. Yes, that's what they did for me. And I went all the way back home to Douala, but I have been away nine months, I have been away nine months. I came back just how I had left, so, with nothing. I came back; it was even worse than when I left! Right. Still, a man shall not give up hope, because I know that spirit that I have. And the spirit of New-Bell. I am a New-Bellois. We have our spirit. I didn't give up hope. I went on. Right. With my same girlfriend, my same friends and everything and everything and everything. And I thank them today because without them, I would have been lost. They supported me. They said, 'It was nothing, you didn't make it, but it is not worth dying over.' Because, when I came back I always had my lonely corner. I was always alone there; I thought to myself, I analysed.

Right. In this period my friends really supported me. I have a friend in the United States who told me not to do it again, that it was stupid. And so on, and so on.

Right. But I didn't understand that. Instead, I prepared for the real thing this time, that is, with my papers to begin with. So I was prepared, the second trip I had a passport on me. I had my passport that I had made.

Right. I left again last year in November. I left again last year in November. I left … as I was already used to it, I took the same route. But now, this time, in Kano there was a curfew. I didn't know that there was a curfew. I went out for a walk, why, we're in Africa. I went out for a walk and a beer before going to bed because sleep didn't come easily. I was restless and anxious to go. So, in Kano, the curfew, they picked me up, the Nigerian police picked me up. Because there was a curfew they said that there was unrest in Nigeria; there were presidential elections coming up, the general elections coming up and everything. So, there was a curfew because there was disorder. Right. I made a break in Kano. The night of the curfew they stripped me. They took my passport and the money that I had on me. Because I had kept the money in different places, as I already told you, in my belt loops, or in the toothpaste, or in my shoe. So, they bobeled the money that I had in my pockets. They took the money that I had in my pockets and my papers. With all that, I was trapped. I don't

have any papers.... I only have a little money left, and as I know that without papers you can't go on to Europe, I rather went back to Cameroon.

I only spent a month there. Why one month? Because I stopped over in another city in Nigeria where I met some really great Nigerians. They were in the phone business. They sold telephones, telephone accessories, chargers, batteries, telephones as well. I stayed with them over there. Right. As I had been stripped, I explained my situation to them. They took me in for a while.

What made things go wrong, what even made me go back to Cameroon was that I didn't speak their English so well. I tried with pidgin and they didn't understand that. They don't understand French. I couldn't speak that kind of English that they spoke over there. Otherwise I would have stayed in Nigeria, because Nigeria is ahead of Cameroon like the elephant outgrows the chick. Nigeria surpasses Cameroon in everything, for everything. In money, in everything, they are ahead of us! So, I was doing well over there in Nigeria. They took good care of me. I spent my time with them. For about a month. Right. One day I said, 'Well, I have to go back to Cameroon.' They gave me some money. They counted the exact amount to get to Douala, and I arrived in Douala with that money on me. I had just about those 150 to take the moped to get home, and that's what happened. Right. That is … I think, in short, that's what happened.

Patrick's Story, 2008
from the project *Avant-garde Citizens*, Douala, Cameroon
A video work by Libia Castro and Ólafur Ólafsson
French transcription: Marilyn Douala Bell
English translation: Marianne Kirch and Peter Kann
First published in *Fucking Good Art*, no. 25, March 2010

Enrico David

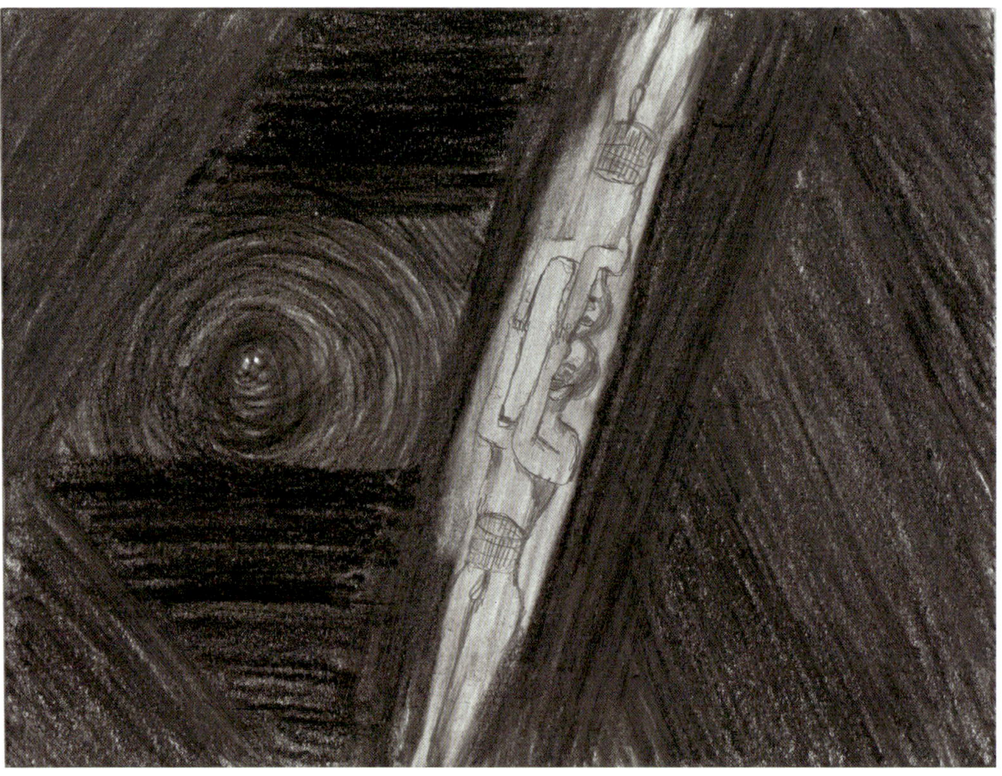

Phobic Sketch I, 2012
Graphite on paper, 28×35.5 cm
Courtesy Michael Werner Gallery, New York

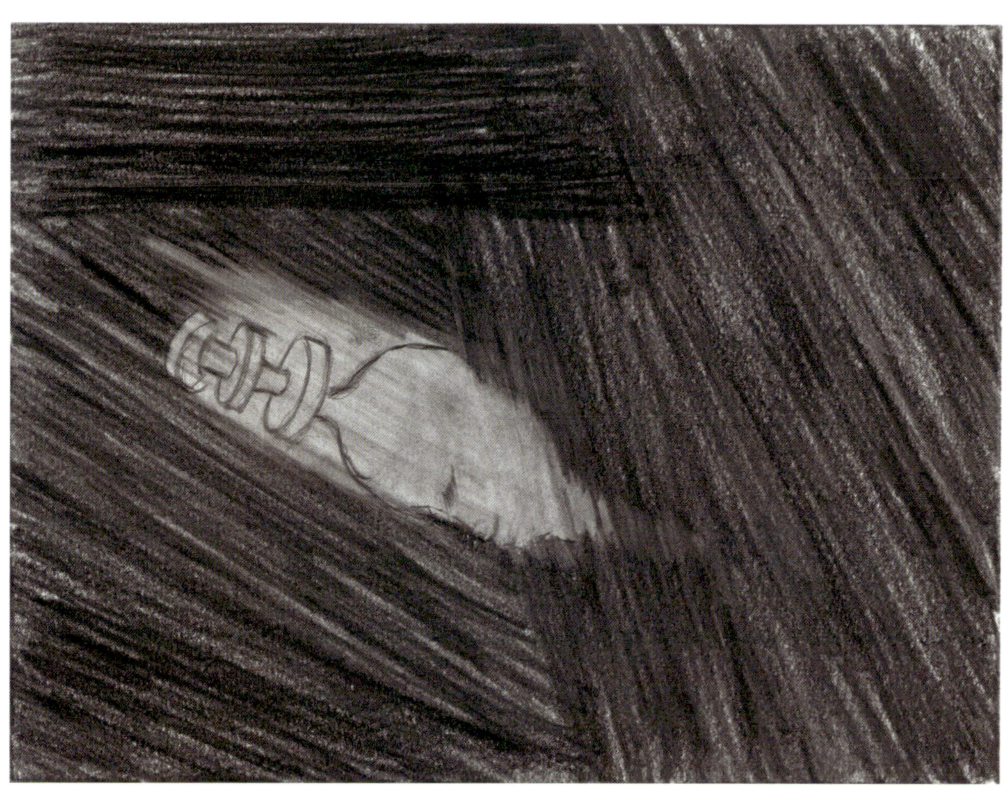

Phobic Sketch II, 2012
Graphite on paper, 28×35.5 cm
Courtesy Michael Werner Gallery, New York

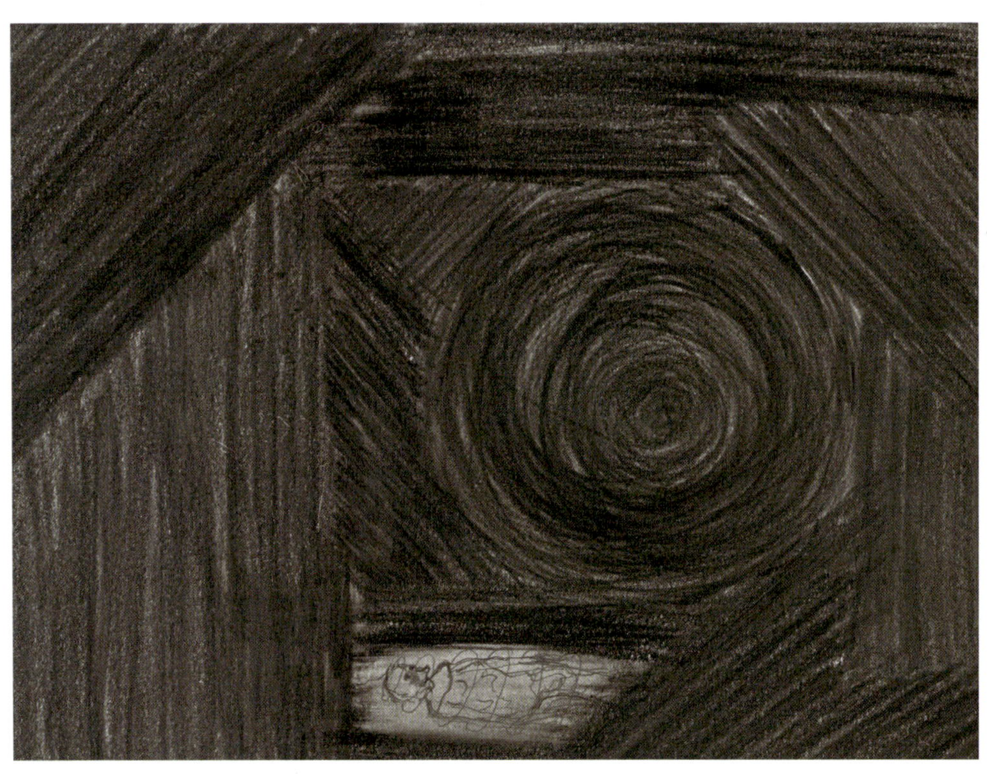

Phobic Sketch III, 2012
Graphite on paper, 28×35.5 cm
Courtesy Michael Werner Gallery, New York

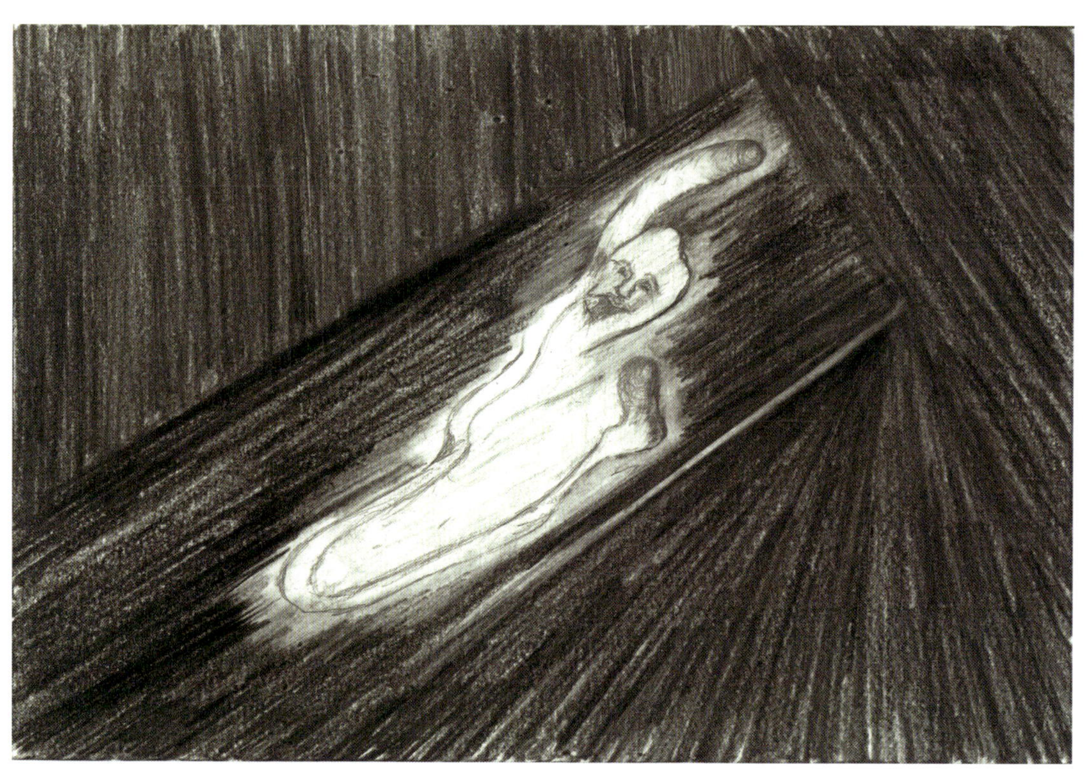

Phobic Sketch VI, 2012
Graphite on paper, 29.5×42 cm
Courtesy Michael Werner Gallery, New York

Elmgreen and Dragset

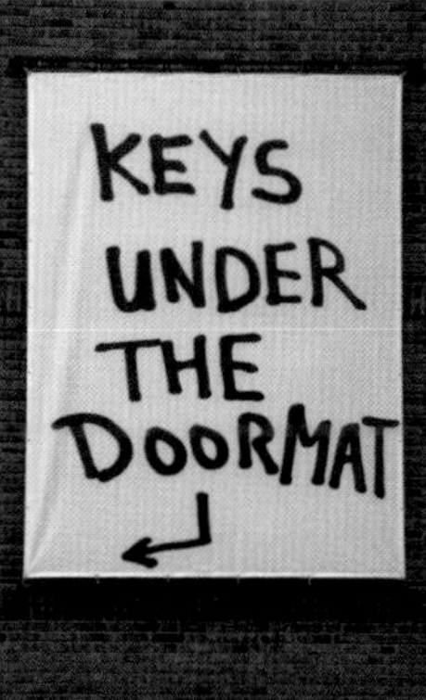

KEYS
UNDER
THE
DOORMAT

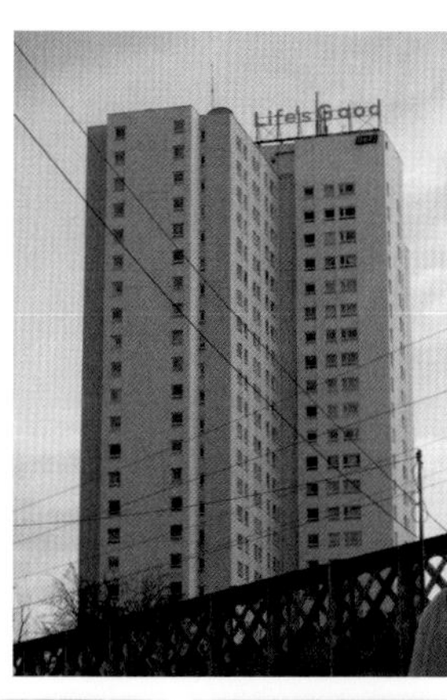

Life's Good

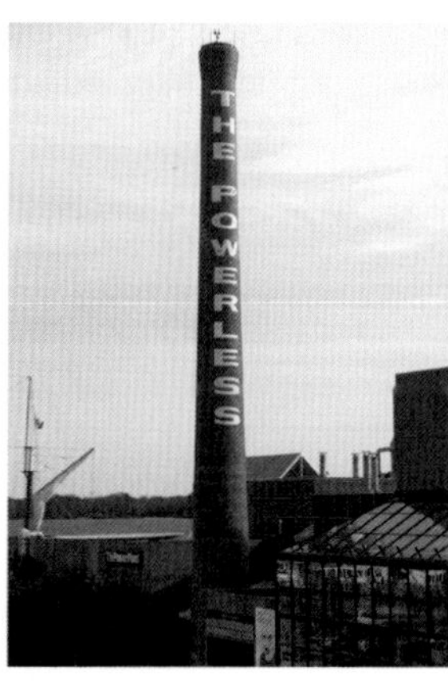

THE POWERLESS

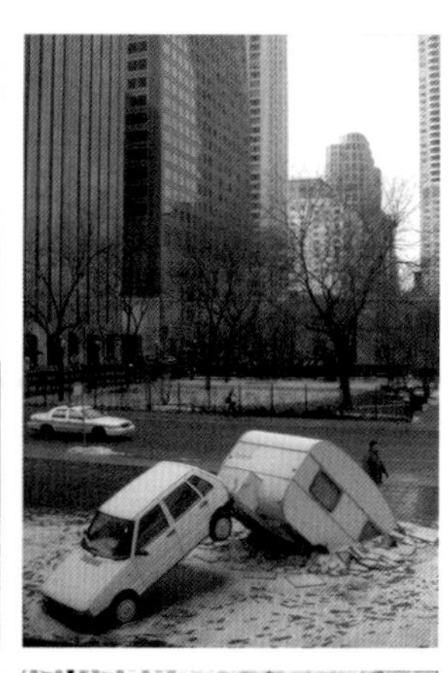

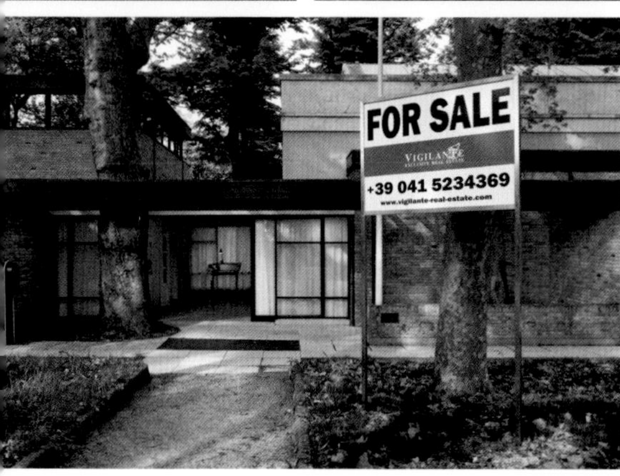

FOR SALE
VIGILANTE
ESTATE REAL ESTATE
+39 041 5234369
www.vigilante-real-estate.com

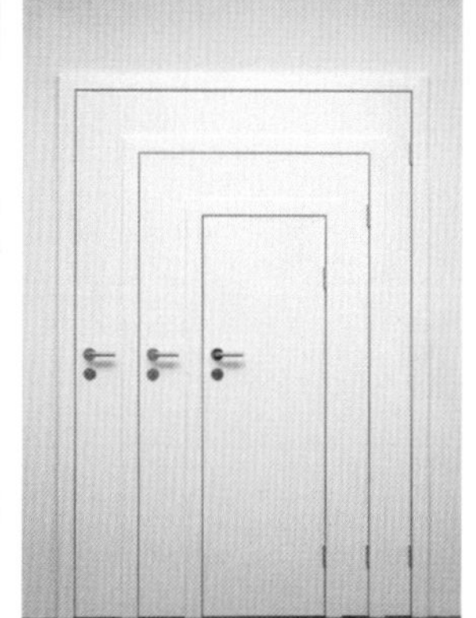

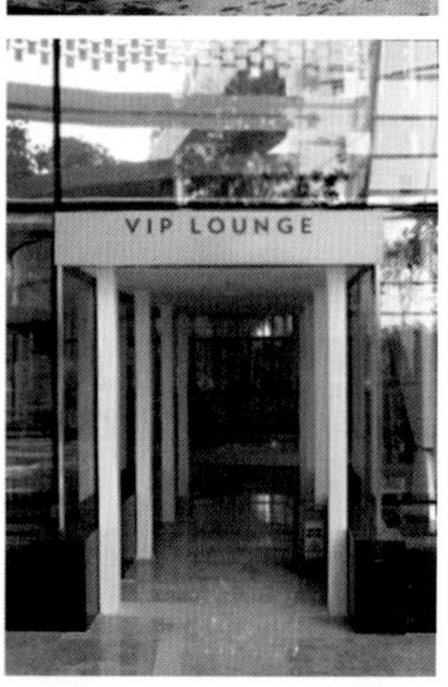

VIP LOUNGE

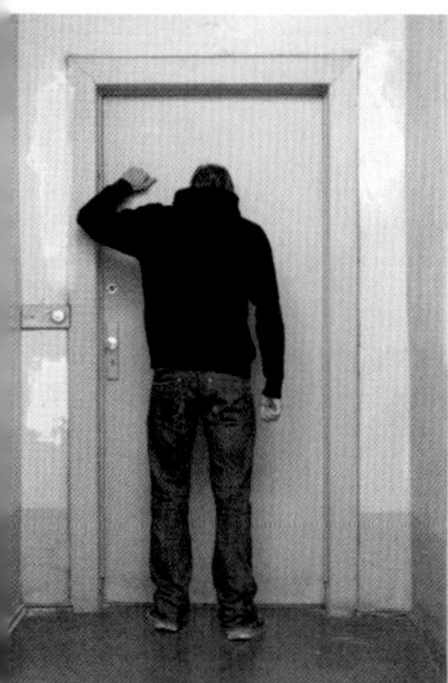

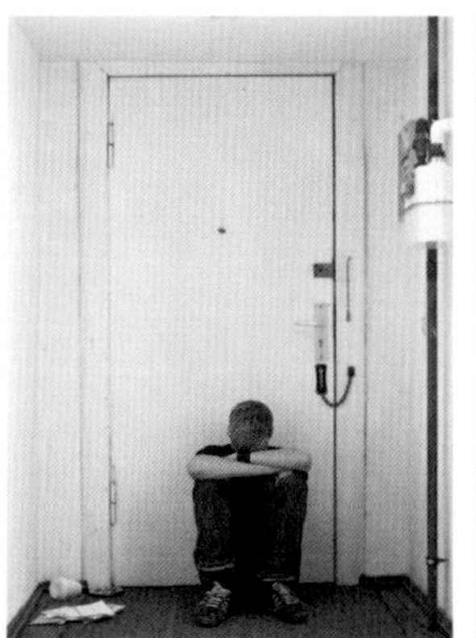

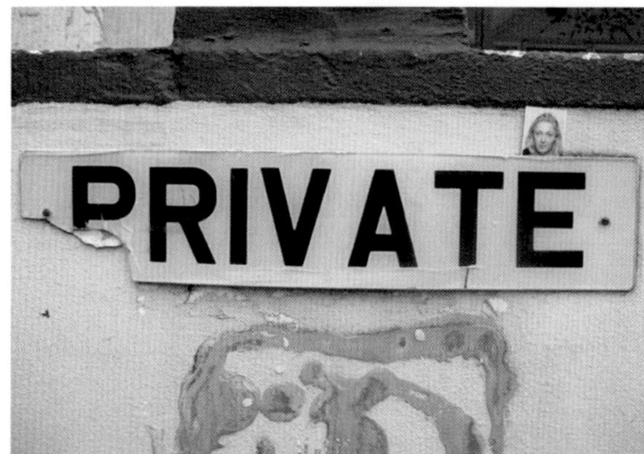

PRIVATE

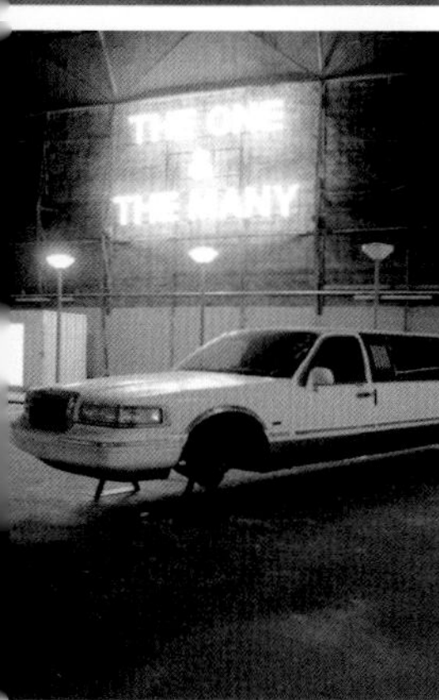

THE ONE
&
THE MANY

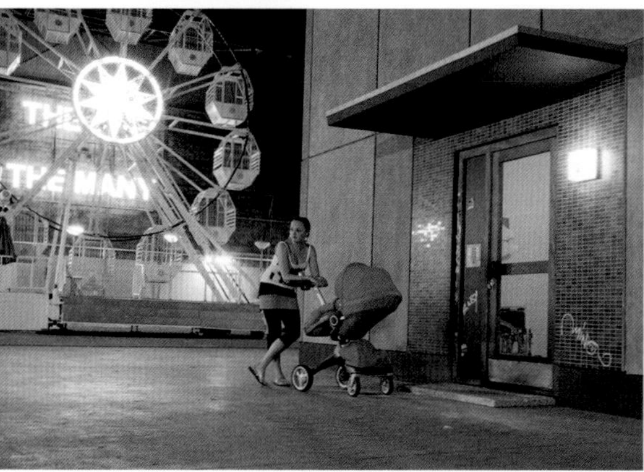

THE
&
THE MANY

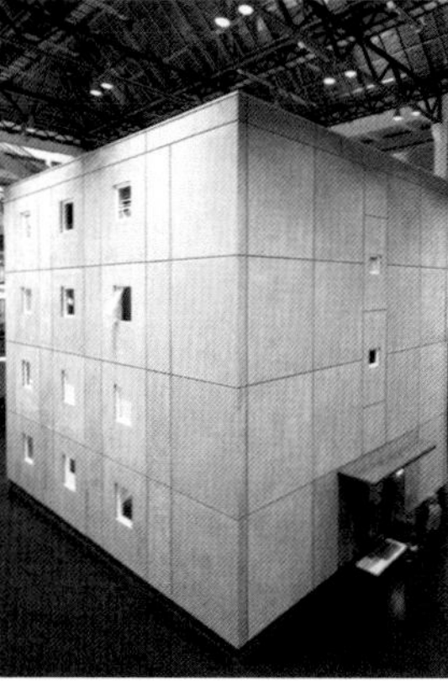

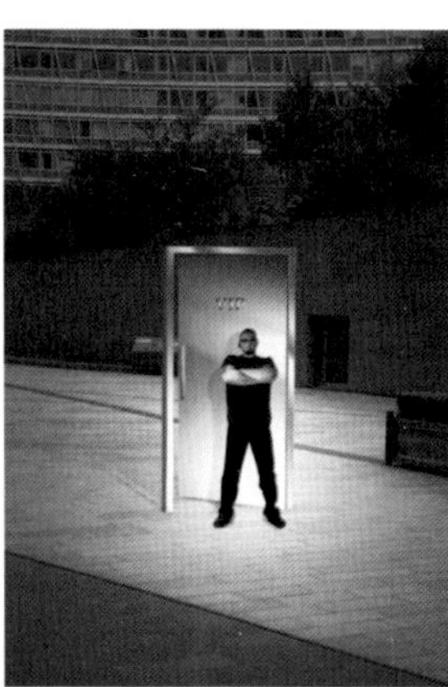
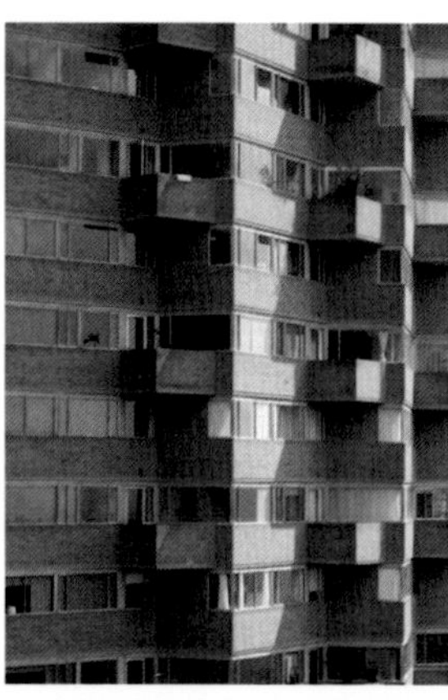
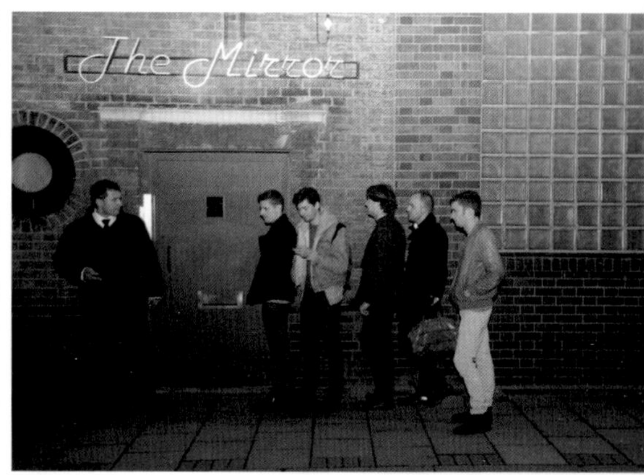
The Mirror
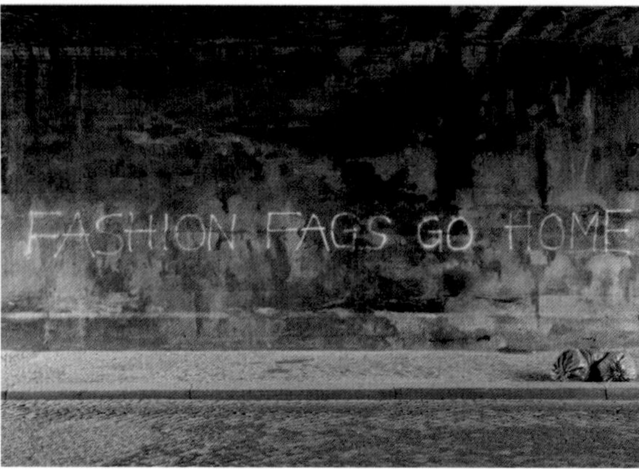
FASHION FAGS GO HOME
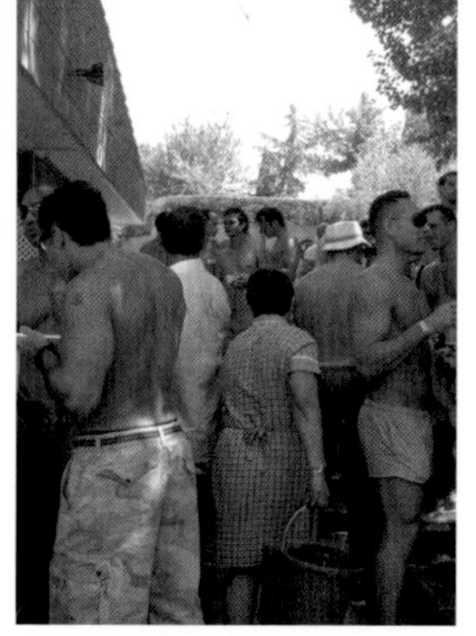
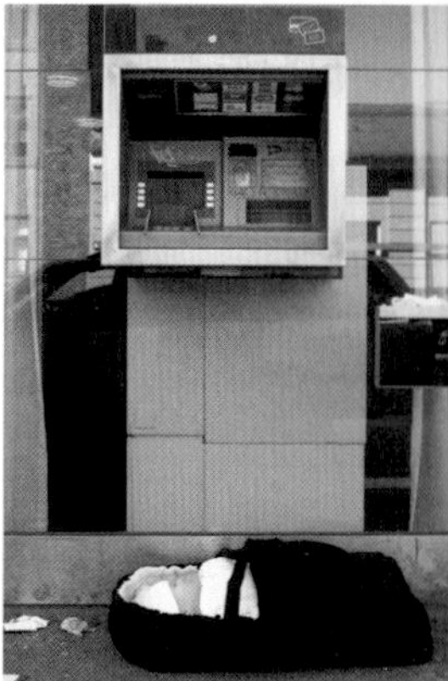
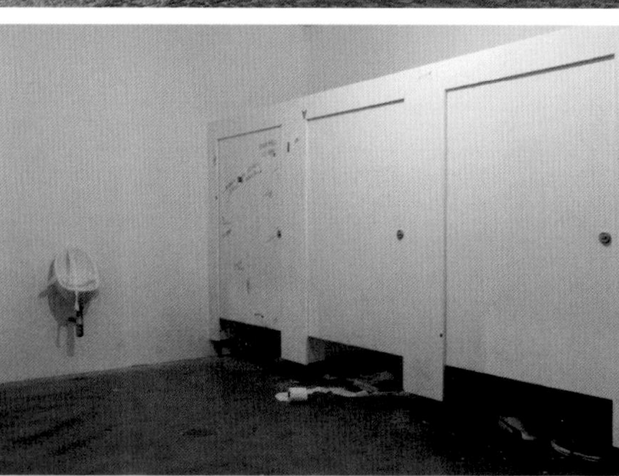
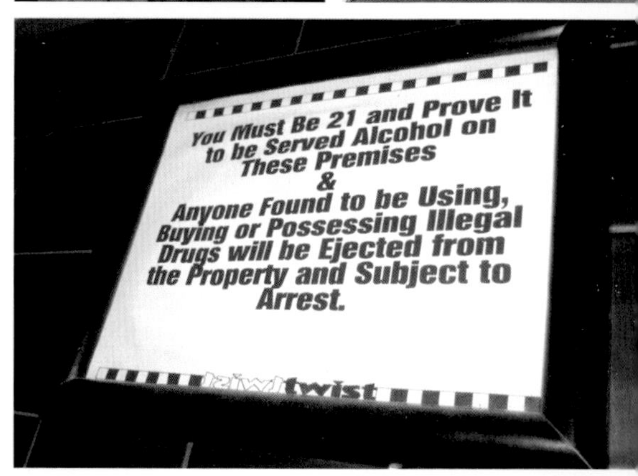
You Must Be 21 and Prove It
to be Served Alcohol on
These Premises
&
Anyone Found to be Using,
Buying or Possessing Illegal
Drugs will be Ejected from
the Property and Subject to
Arrest.
kiwi twist
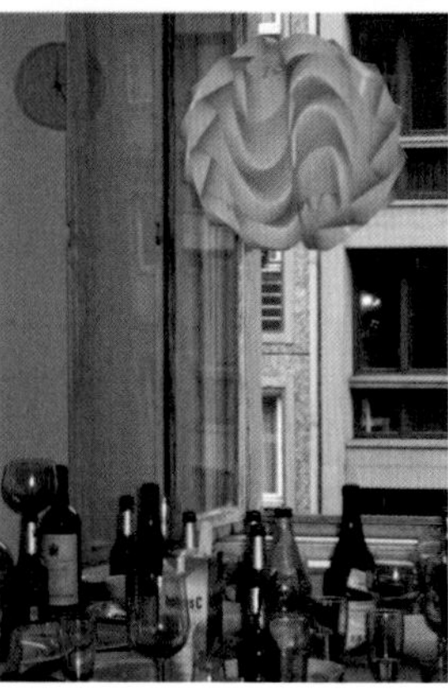
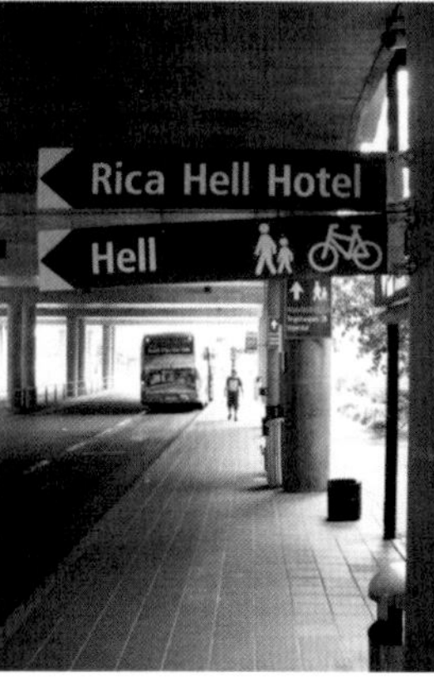
Rica Hell Hotel
Hell
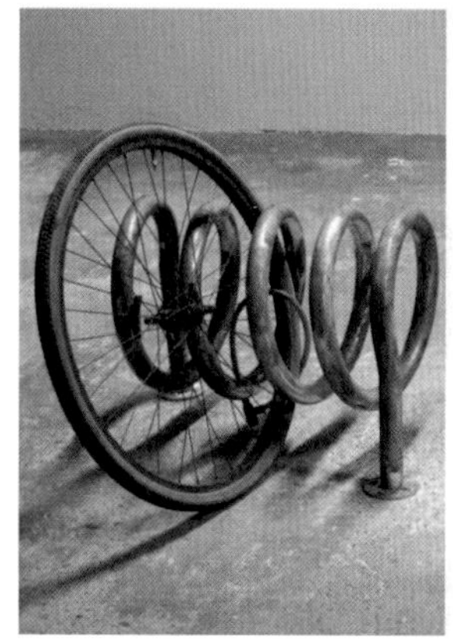
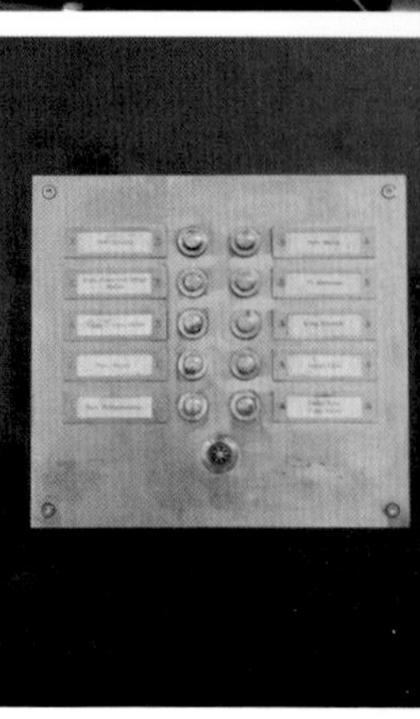

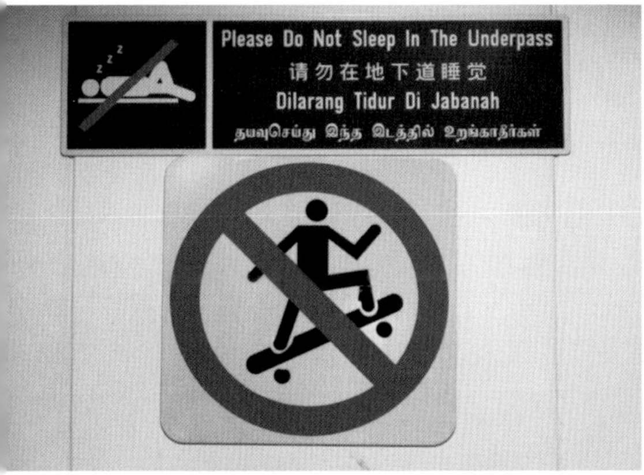

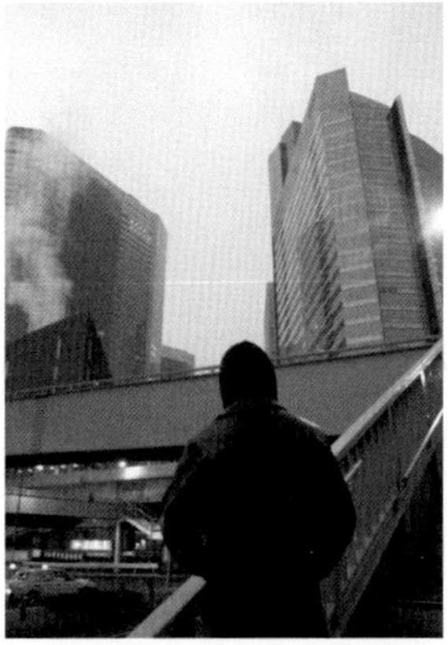

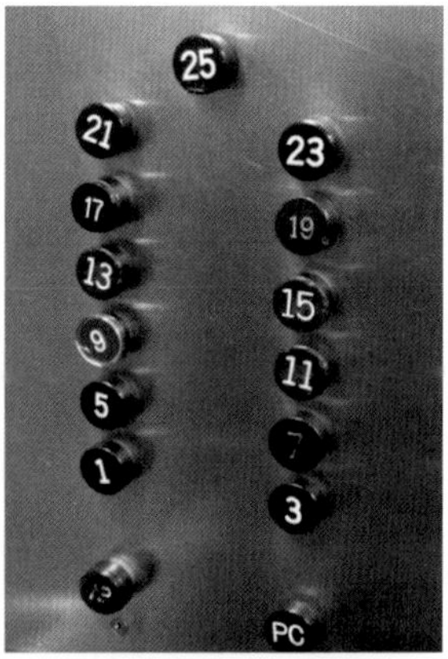

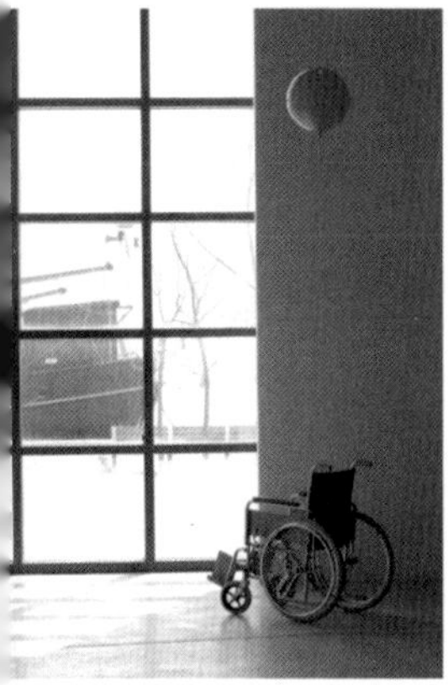

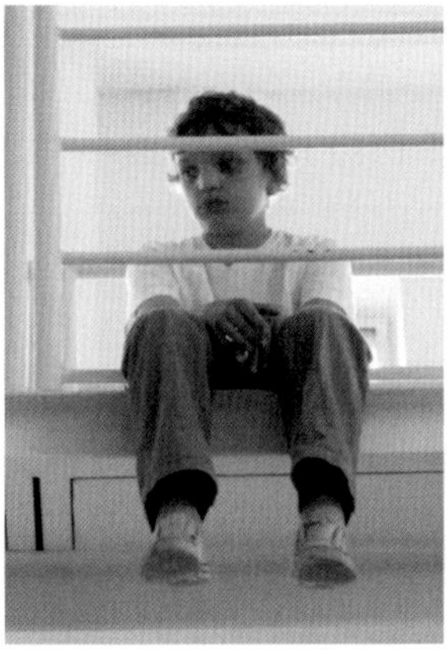

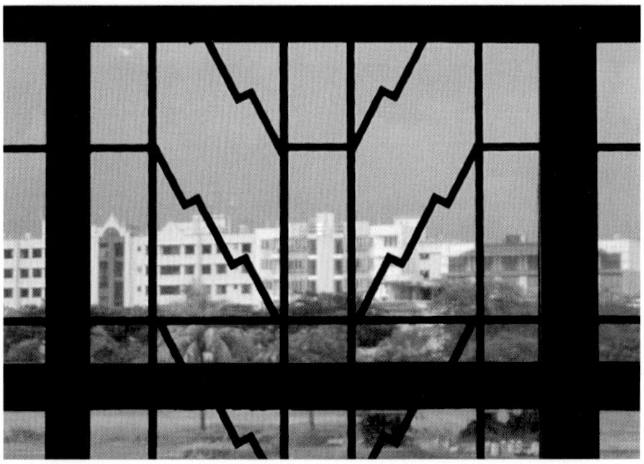

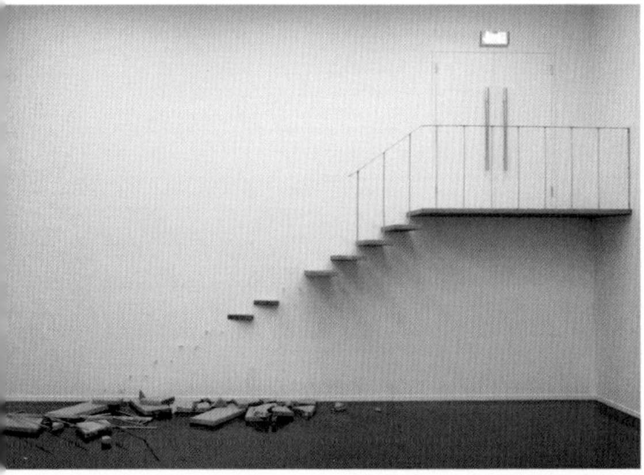

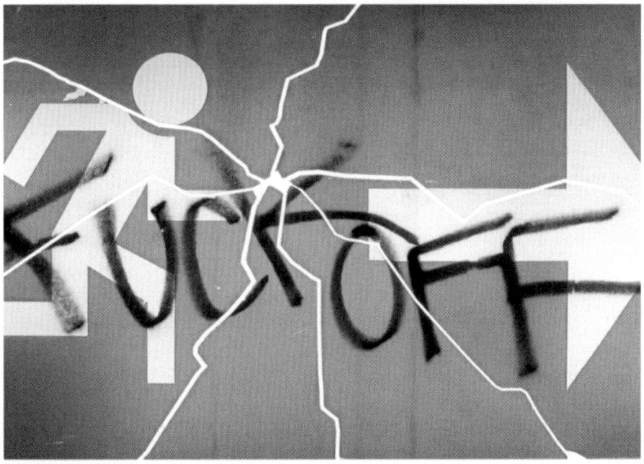

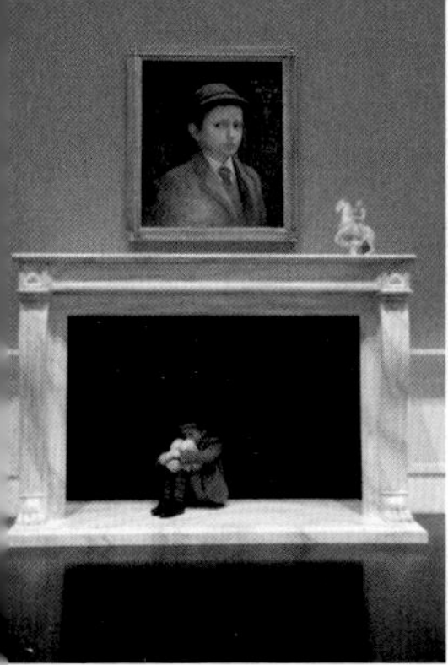
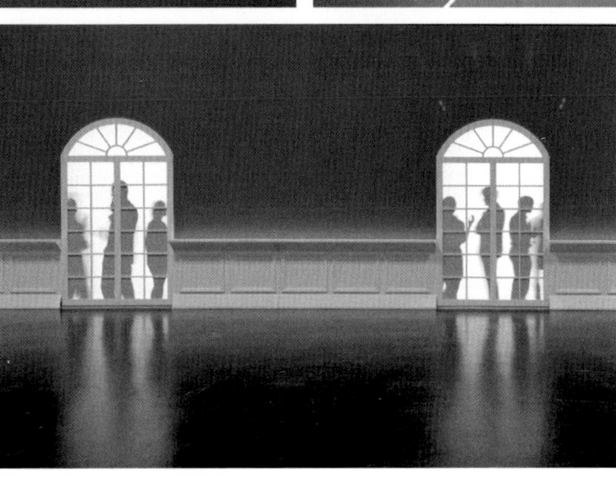
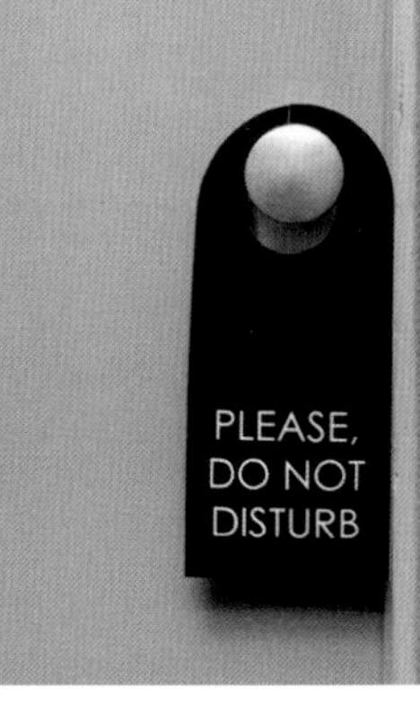

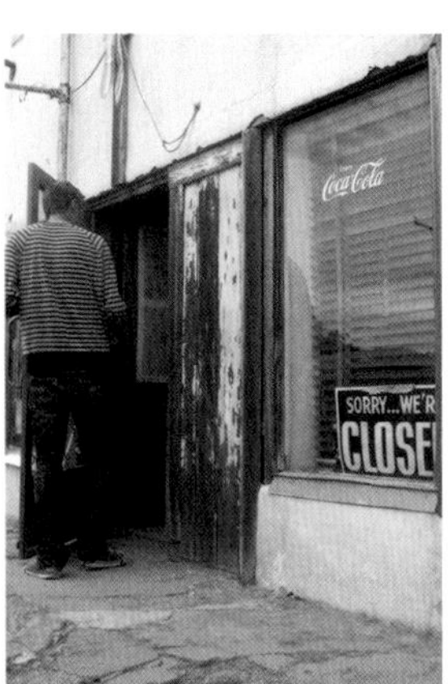
Coca-Cola
SORRY...WE'R
CLOSE
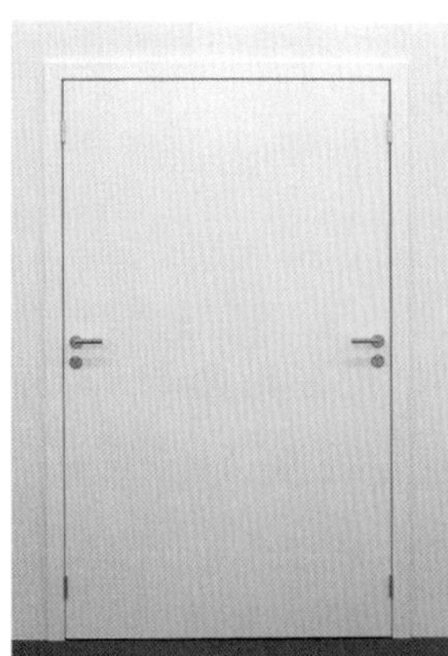
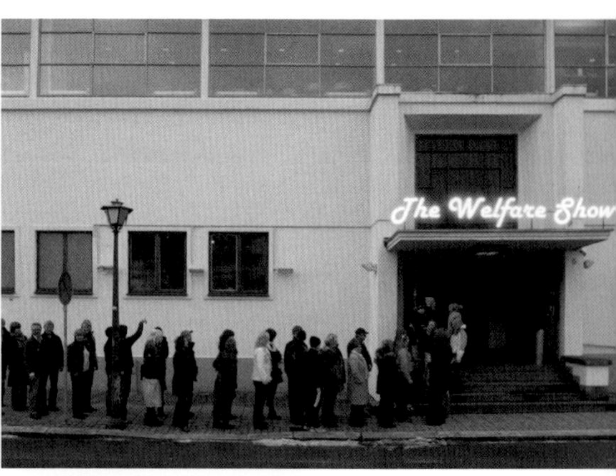
The Welfare Show
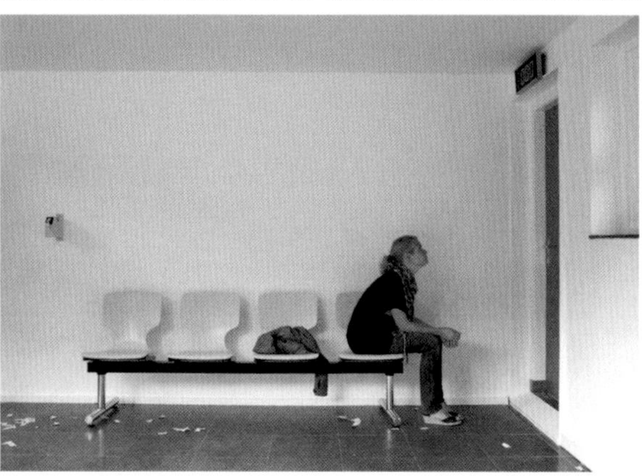
Coca-Cola
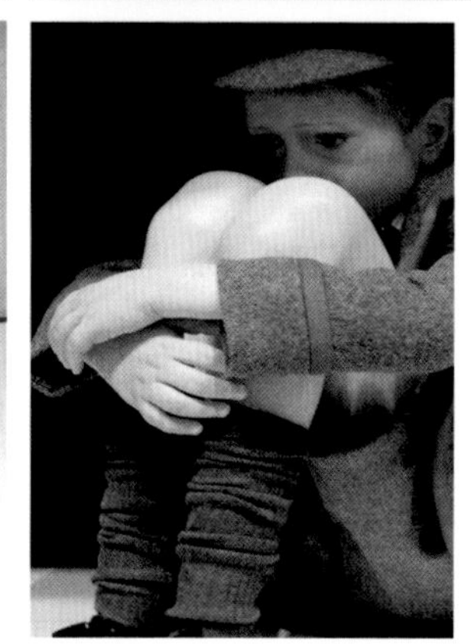
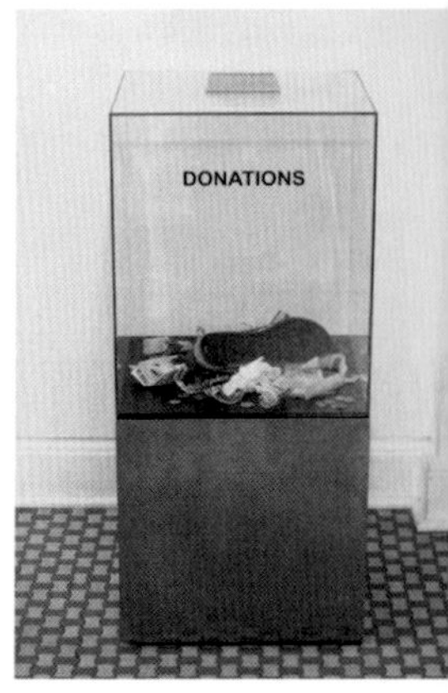
DONATIONS
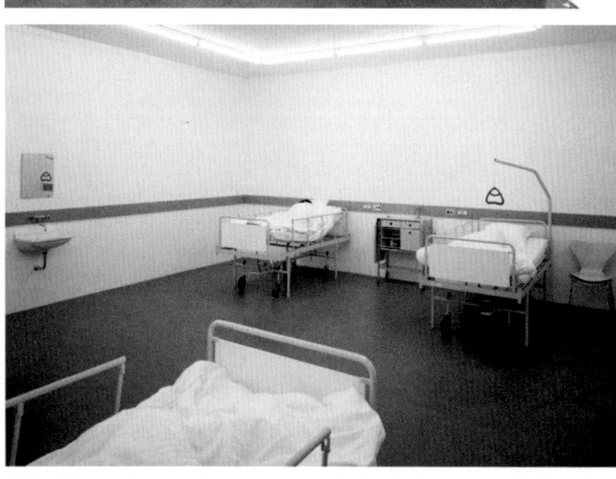
Coca-Cola
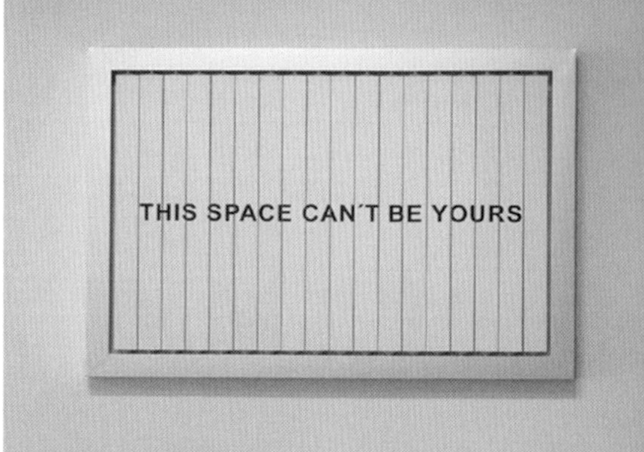
THIS SPACE CAN´T BE YOURS
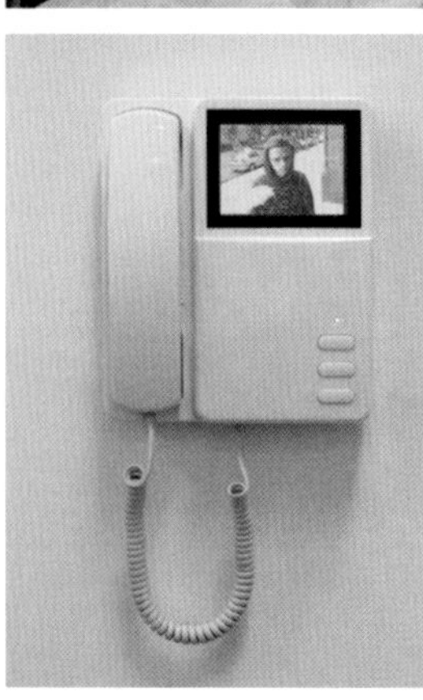
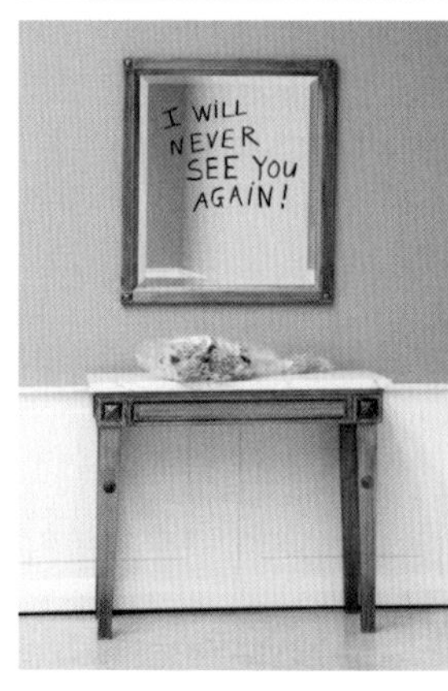
I WILL
NEVER
SEE YOU
AGAIN!
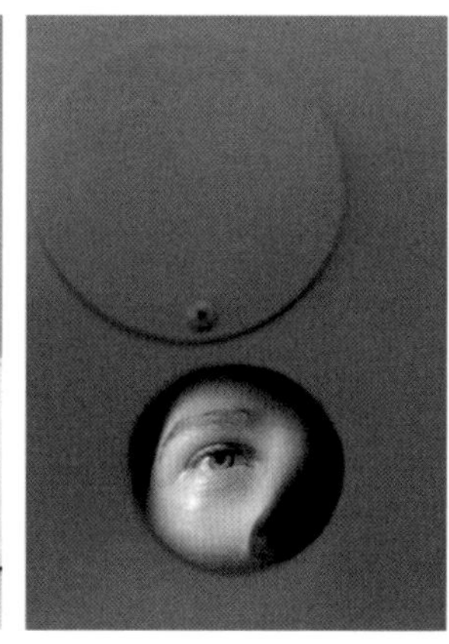
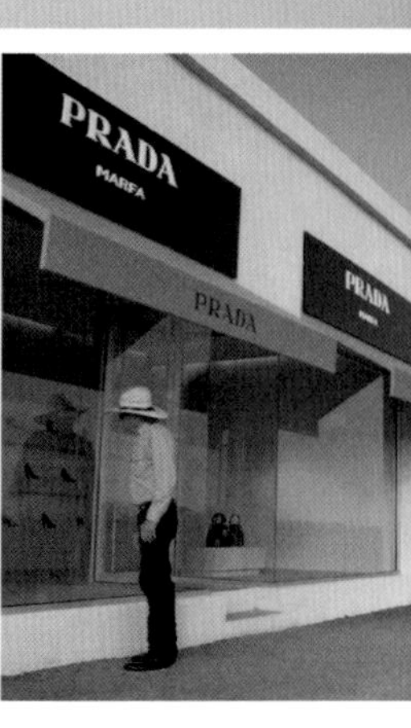
PRADA
MARFA
PRADA
PRADA

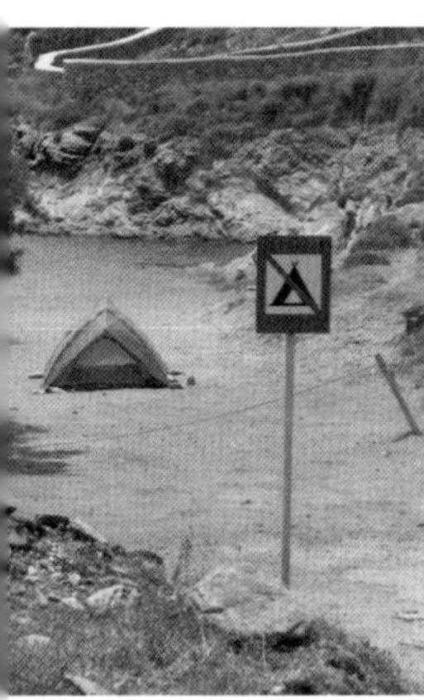
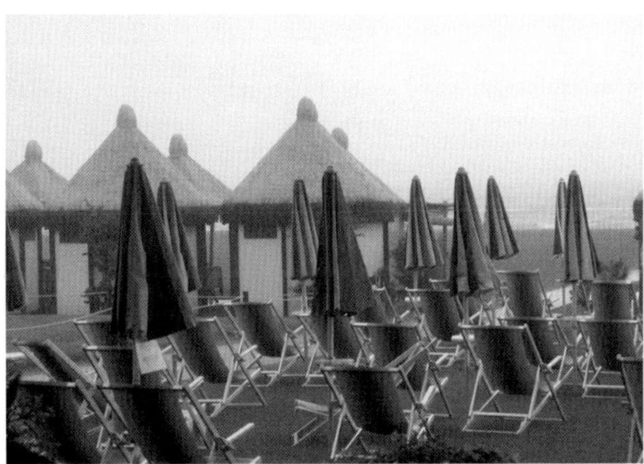
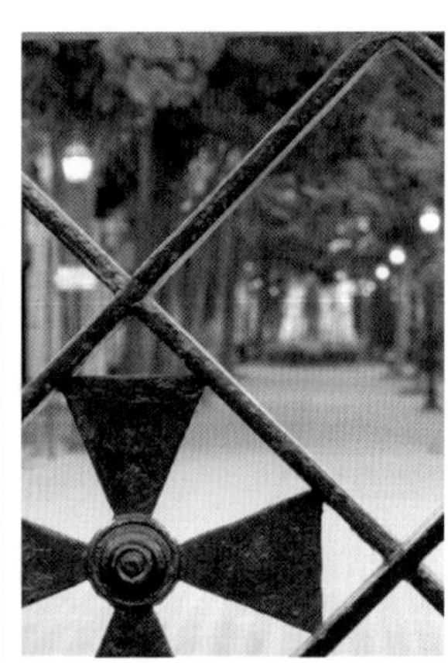
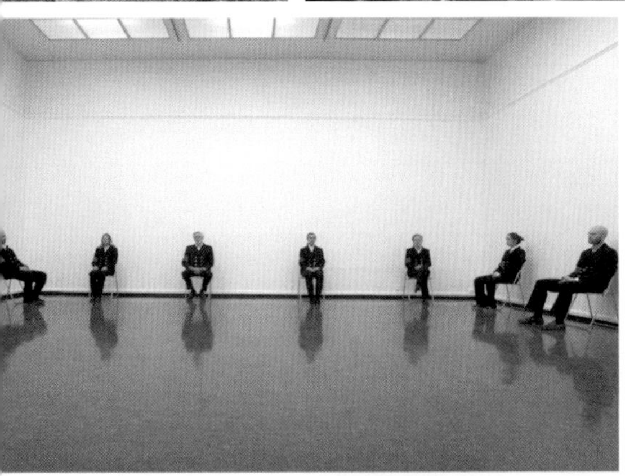
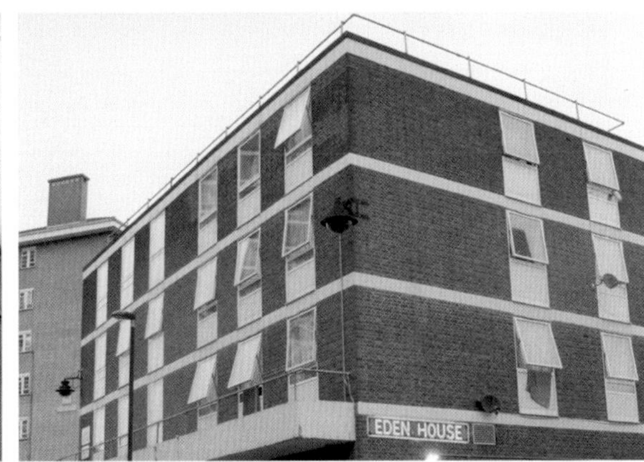
EDEN HOUSE
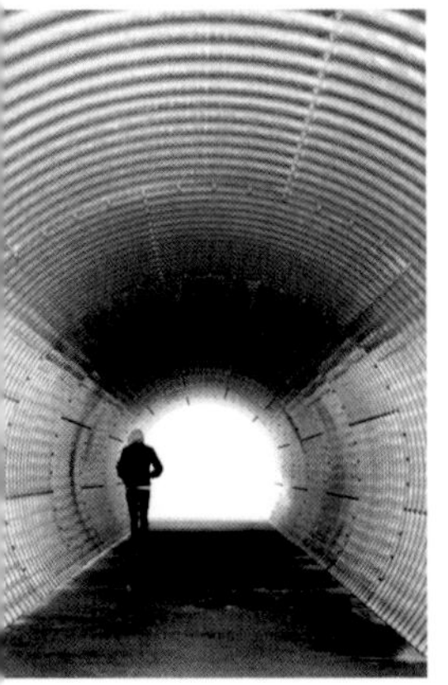
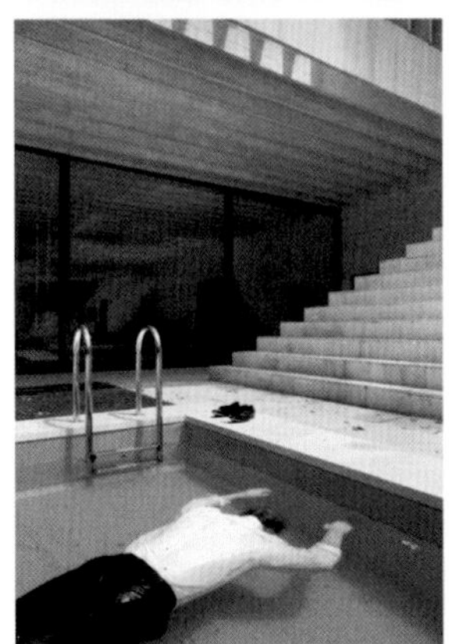
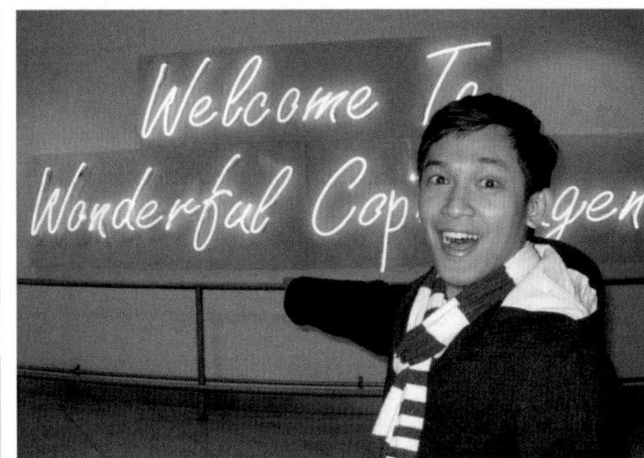
Welcome To
Wonderful Copenhagen
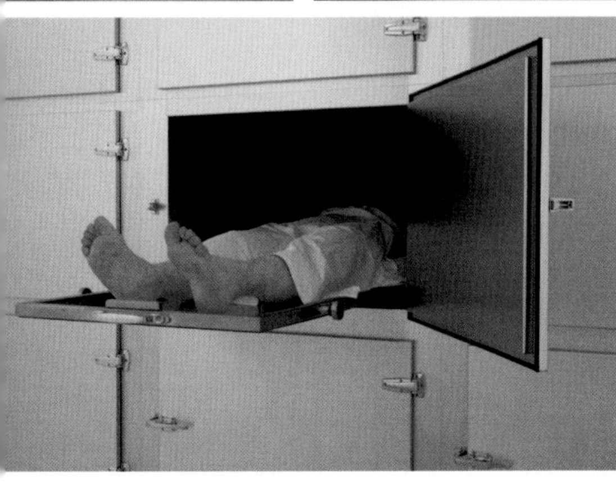
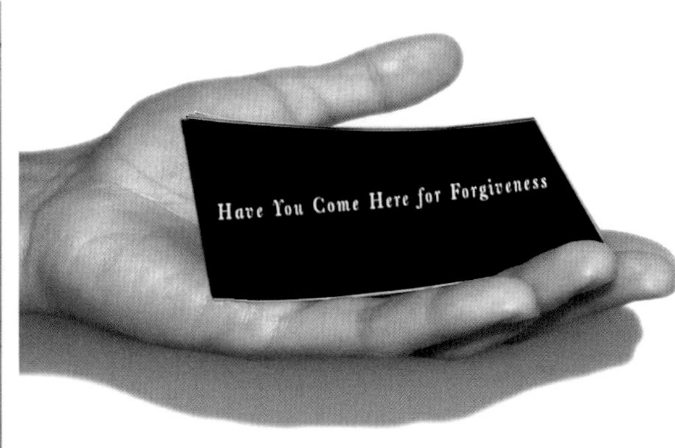
Have You Come Here for Forgiveness

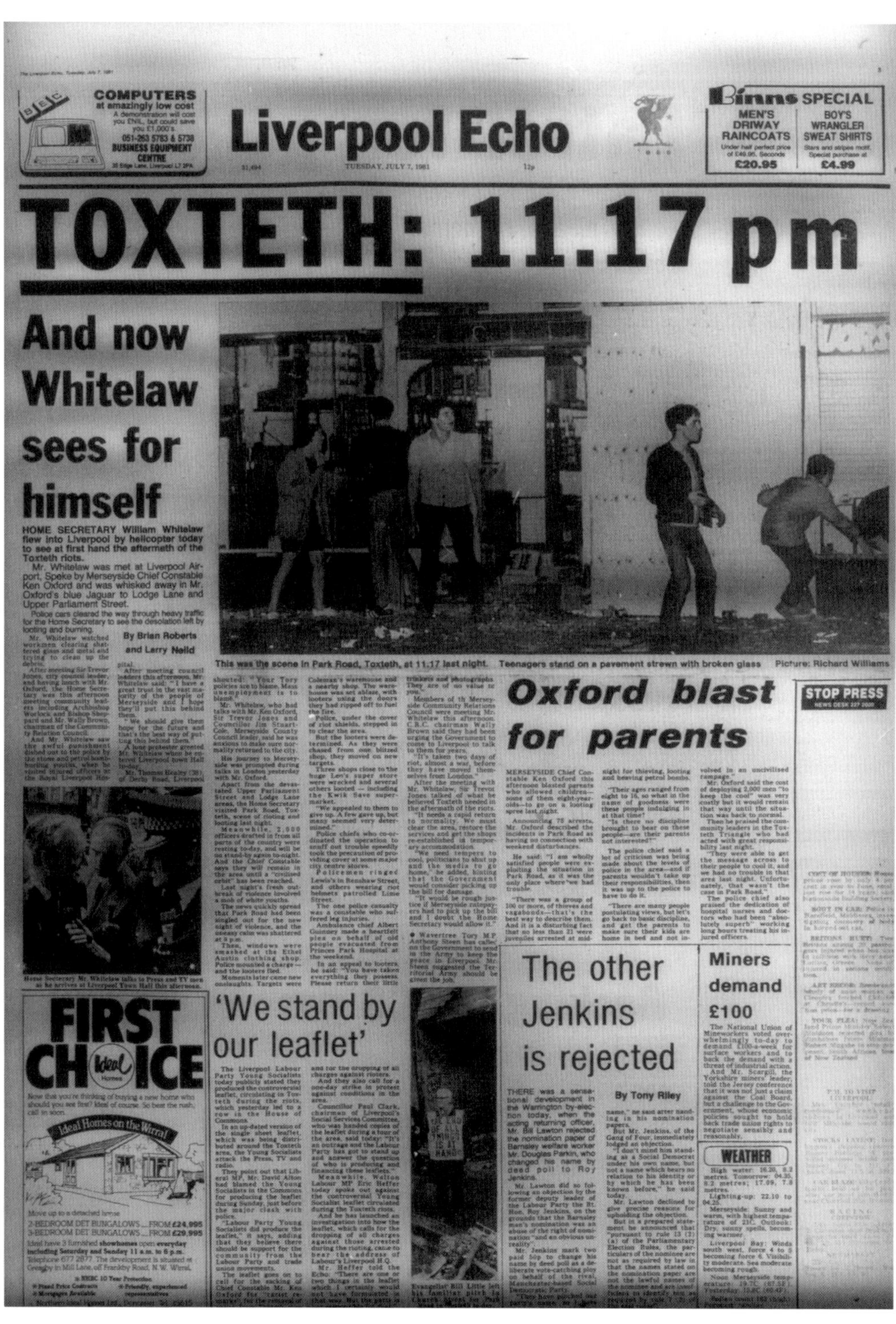

The Liverpool Echo, Tuesday, July 7, 1981

Liverpool Echo

TUESDAY, JULY 7, 1981   12p

TOXTETH: 11.17 pm

And now Whitelaw sees for himself

HOME SECRETARY William Whitelaw flew into Liverpool by helicopter today to see at first hand the aftermath of the Toxteth riots.

Mr. Whitelaw was met at Liverpool Airport, Speke by Merseyside Chief Constable Ken Oxford and was whisked away in Mr. Oxford's blue Jaguar to Lodge Lane and Upper Parliament Street.

Police cars cleared the way through heavy traffic for the Home Secretary to see the desolation left by looting and burning.

By Brian Roberts and Larry Neild

Mr. Whitelaw watched workmen clearing shattered glass and metal and trying to clean up the debris.

After meeting Sir Trevor Jones, city council leader, and having lunch with Mr. Oxford, the Home Secretary was this afternoon meeting community leaders including Archbishop Worlock and Bishop Sheppard and Mr. Wally Brown, chairman of the Community Relation Council.

And Mr. Whitelaw saw the awful punishment dished out to the police by the stores and petrol bomb-hurling youths, when he visited injured officers at the Royal Liverpool Hospital.

After meeting council leaders this afternoon, Mr. Whitelaw said: "I have a great trust in the vast majority of the people of Merseyside and I hope they'll put this behind them.

"We should give them hope for the future and that's the best way of putting this behind them."

A lone protester greeted Mr. Whitelaw when he entered Liverpool town Hall today.

Mr. Thomas Healey (38) of Derby Road, Liverpool

This was the scene in Park Road, Toxteth, at 11.17 last night.   Teenagers stand on a pavement strewn with broken glass   Picture: Richard Williams

'We stand by our leaflet'

First Choice Ideal Homes

Oxford blast for parents

MERSEYSIDE Chief Constable Ken Oxford this afternoon blasted parents who allowed children—some of them eight-year-olds—to go on a looting spree last night.

Announcing 70 arrests, Mr. Oxford described the incidents in Park Road as having no connection with weekend disturbances.

The other Jenkins is rejected

By Tony Riley

THERE was a sensational development in the Warrington by-election today, when the acting returning officer, Mr. Bill Lawton rejected the nomination paper of Barnsley welfare worker Mr. Douglas Parkin, who changed his name by deed poll to Roy Jenkins.

Miners demand £100

The National Union of Mineworkers voted overwhelmingly to-day to demand £100-a-week for surface workers and to back the demand with a threat of industrial action.

STOP PRESS

WEATHER

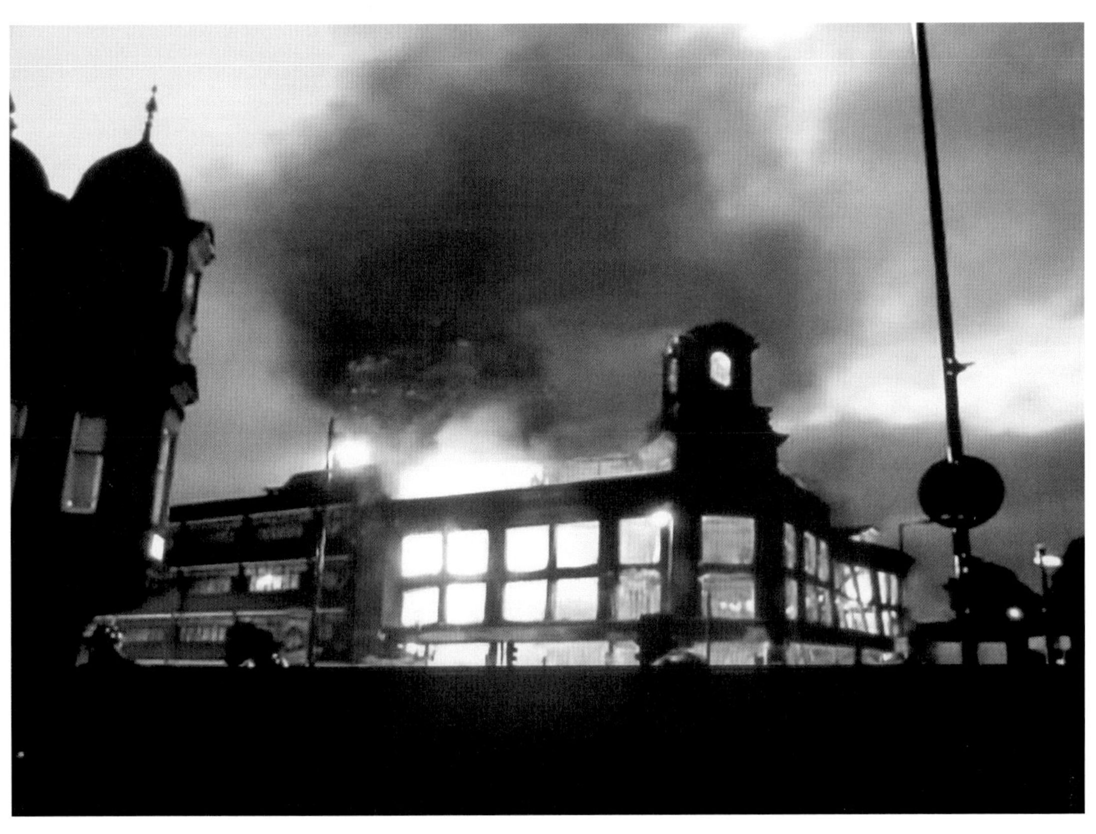

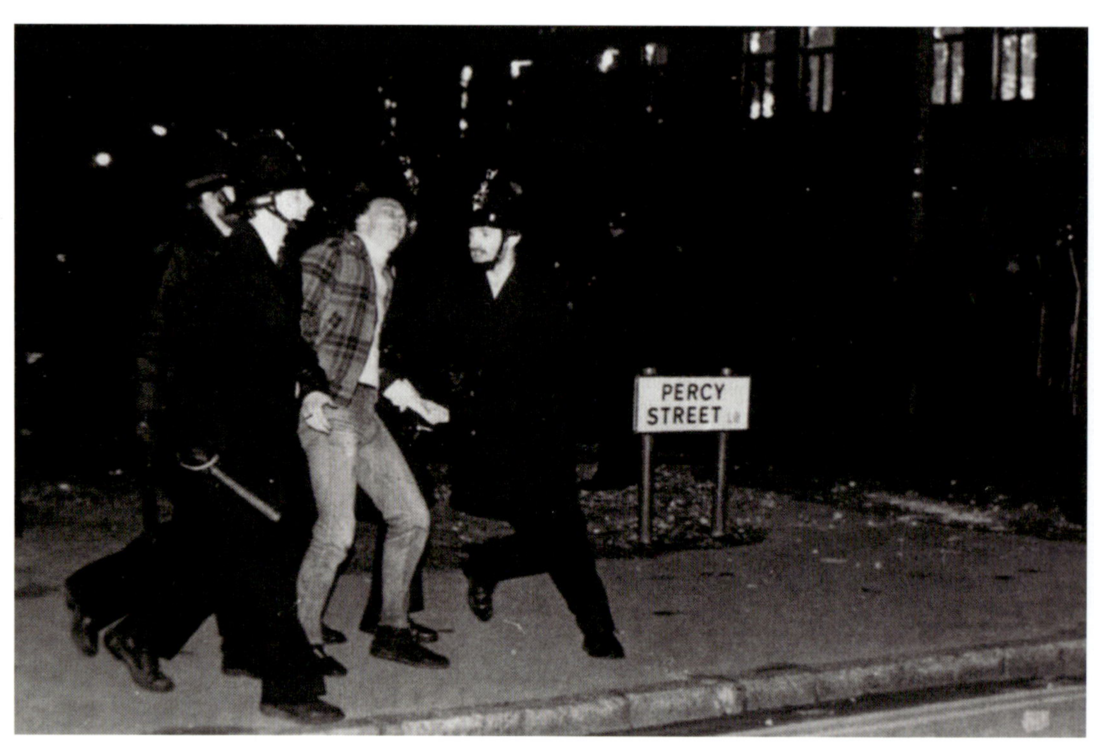

Outside!
On the complexities of hospitality and hostility
www.newsfromoutside.co.uk
Opposite: photograph by Francesco Mattarese

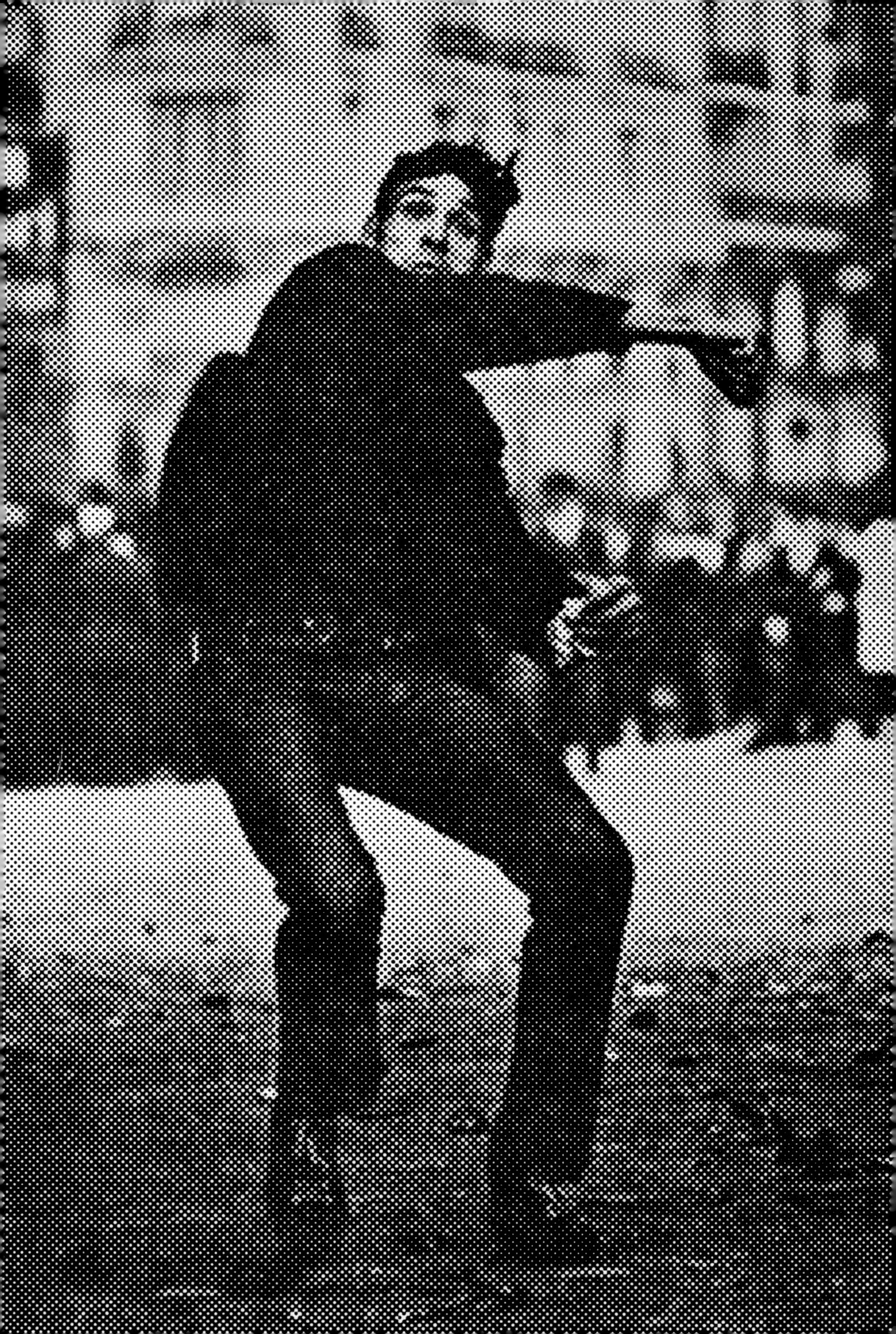

Dan Graham

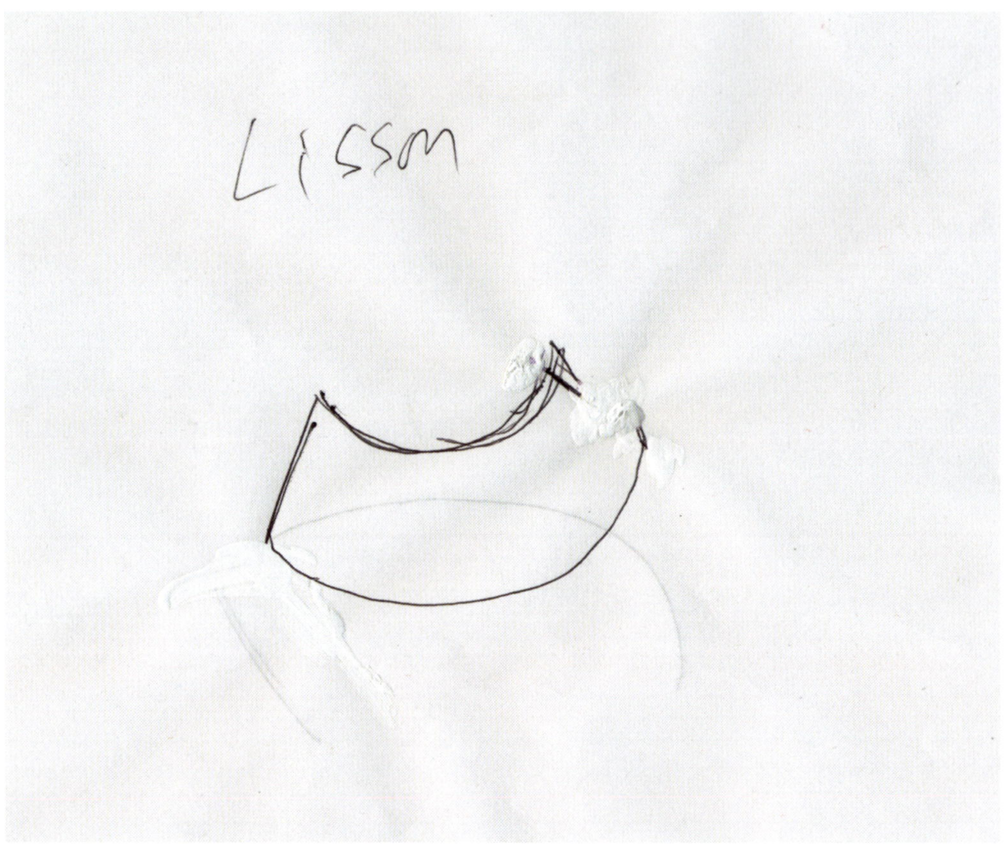

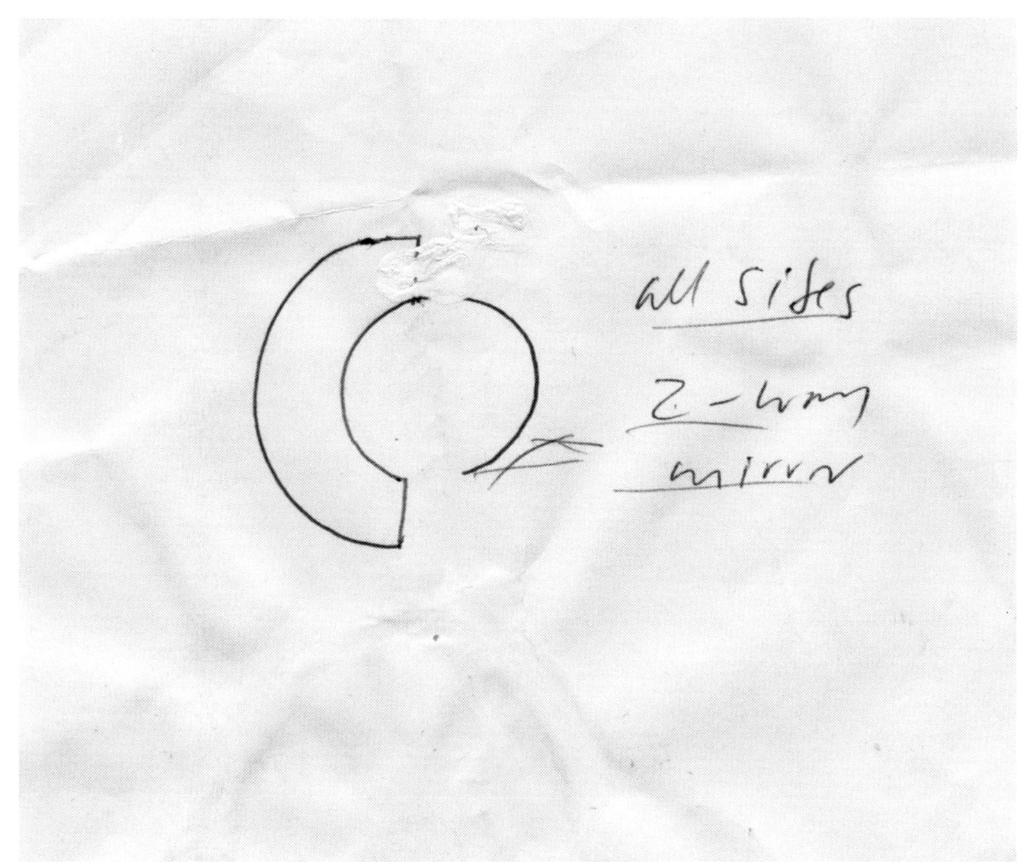
all sides
2 - way
mirror

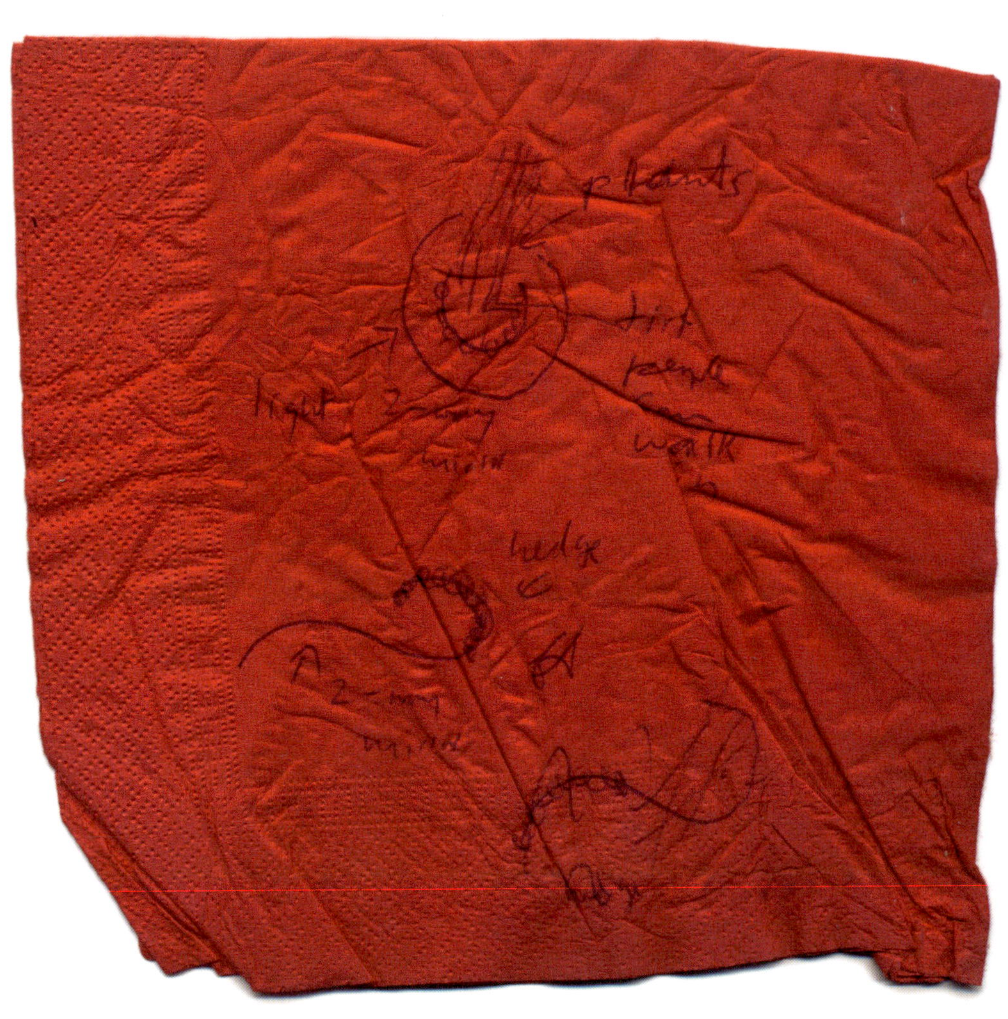

Untitled drawings, pen on paper

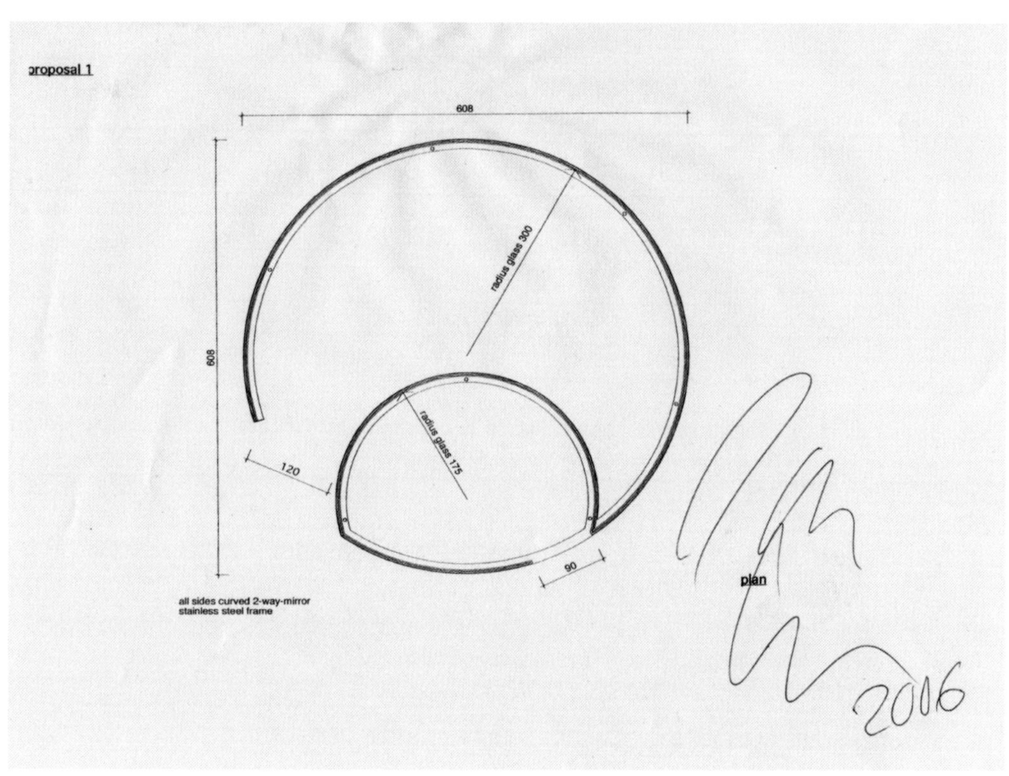

608
608
radius glass 300
radius glass 175
120
90
plan
all sides curved 2-way-mirror
stainless steel frame
2016

Mona Hatoum

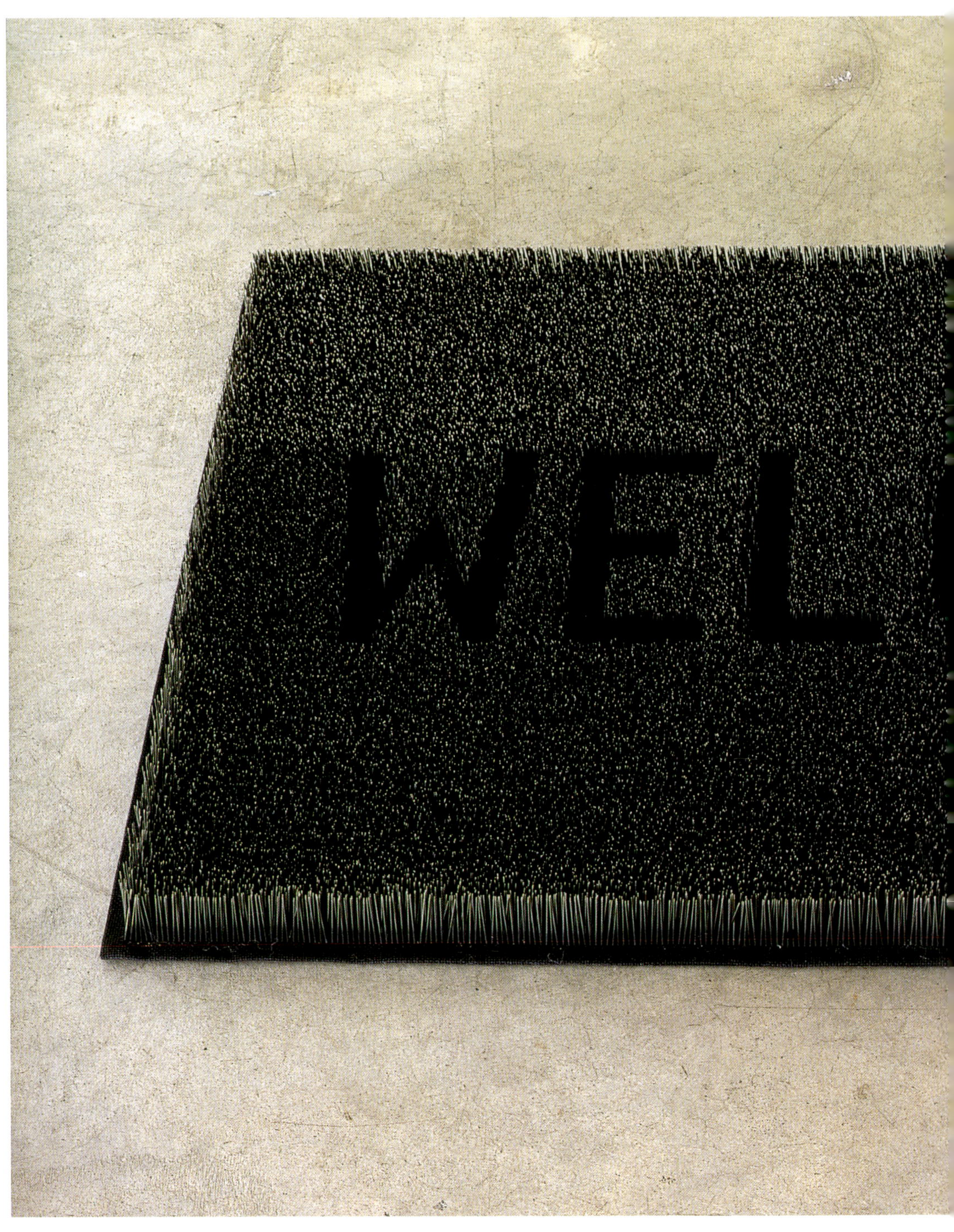

Doormat II, 2000–1
Stainless steel and nickel-plated brass pins,
canvas and glue, 3×72.5×42 cm
Photo: Oren Slor. Courtesy Alexander and Bonin, New York

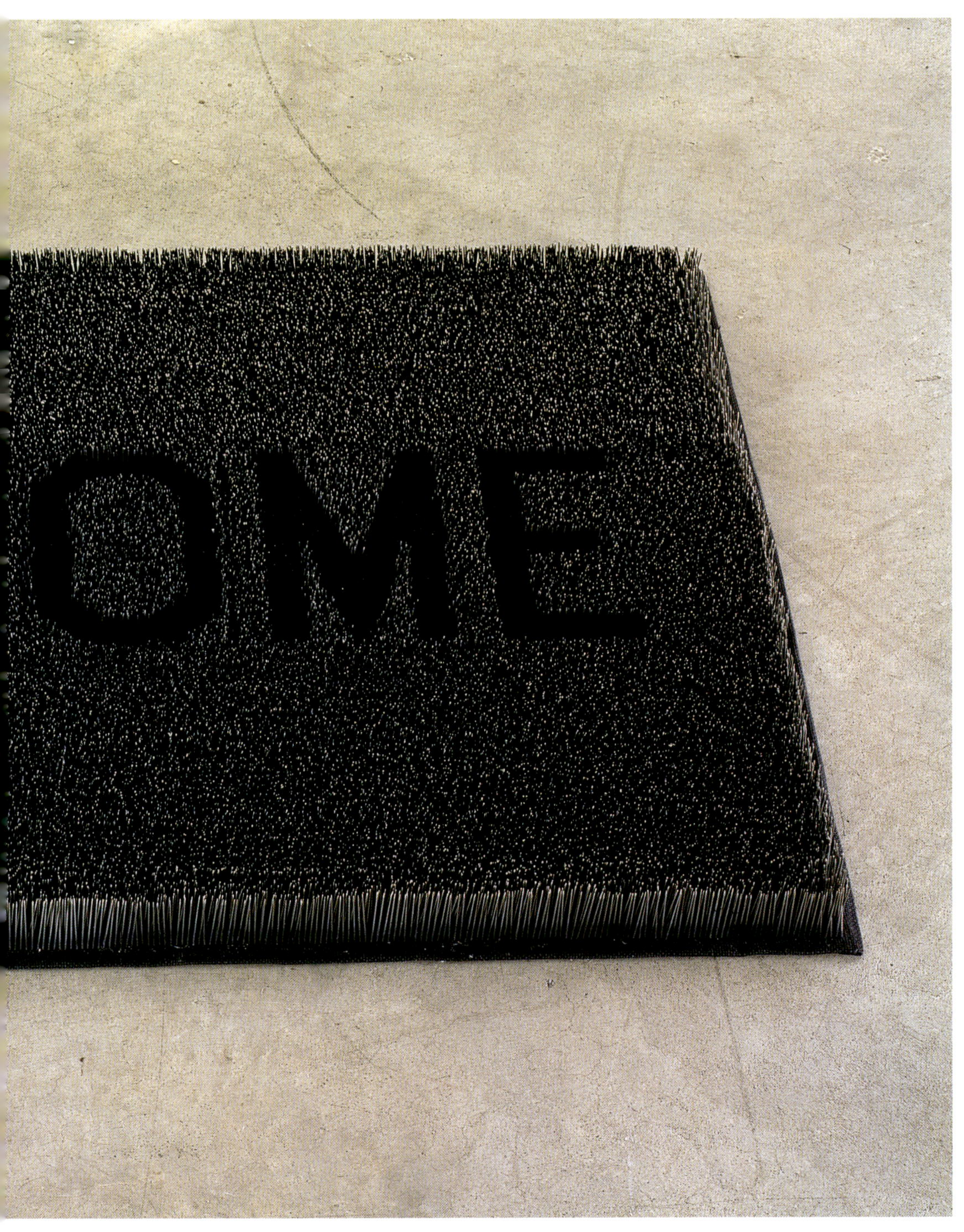

OME

Fritz Haeg

Welcome

In 2000 I landed in a geodesic dome on a hill in Los Angeles. This peculiar, partially subterranean home was designed by William King for a young pediatrician named Joy Gaertner. She died of cancer just months after it was completed in 1984. The realtor who sold me the house gave me a newspaper clipping showing her holding an abandoned three-hour-old baby boy she nursed back to health at the General Hospital Children's Ward. I think of her often and wonder what she had in mind for this place, what sort of life she expected to lead in this unusual home.

Three levels of open spaces are connected by a circular stair. You enter from the street into 'the cave', a poured-concrete curvy space carved into the hill and illuminated by skylights. Going up a few steps, you land on a stagelike upper level. From there, a few more rotations up the stairs lead you into the small gathering space of the kitchen, an angular woody perch with a long table facing the mountains. One last spiral up the stairs deposits you into the middle of a 24-foot-diameter geodesic dome, a bright-blue hemisphere. A triangular window faces the garden to the south, and the city below is framed by a large hexagonal window from which you could imagine a Bond villain plotting world domination.

The house faces north, overlooking the 2 Freeway as it snakes through Glassell Park towards Eagle Rock, then meets the 134 Freeway, which can be seen hugging the base of the foothills heading towards Pasadena, with the long jagged backdrop of the San Gabriel Mountains dominating the horizon. To the west are Atwater Village, Los Feliz, Silverlake and Hollywood. To the south are Mount Washington, Cypress Park, Chinatown and downtown. To the east are Highland Park, Garvanza, South Pasadena and the infinite flat expanse of the Inland Empire extending out to San Bernardino over sixty miles away.

When I moved in, the land around the house was overgrown with weedy shrubs and virtually inaccessible. I spent my first year mostly outside, strategically clearing the vegetation, creating terraces out of the slope, by hand, with a shovel, digging up the native decomposed granite rock and covering the roof and garden with it, planting native wildflowers, fruit trees and vegetables and making a big fish pond. The gardens, like the house, are a precarious balance of careful design and casual chaos. I began my occupation of the house with an architect's preciousness for surfaces and desire for permanent order. As I loosened my grip, the house and I mellowed, becoming open to more wildness in the yard and unfinished, lived-in roughness inside.

My house shares Sundown Drive with seven other homes. It is a narrow dead-end street that each new house has extended further into the hillside meadow where it terminates. There are no sidewalks, and barely enough room for two cars to pass. Sharing a street this small could be an intimate social situation, but it isn't. On the rare occasions that I see my neighbours, we are moving in opposite directions separated by the two car shells between us. It is a 'diverse' street, featuring a variety of ethnicities and familial arrangements. I suppose we have little in common, apart from geography, sharing this quiet cul-de-sac of Los Angeles. Each home turns inward, creating its own world away from the city and street.

I had three friends in Los Angeles when I arrived from New York City in 1999: Melissa Thorne and Katie Grinnan, artists with whom I had gone to school, and Andrea Zittel, whom I had met when we both lived in New York. Melissa was a recent MFA grad, and through her I met the CalArts crowd, including Mark Allen (Machine Project), Malik Gaines and Alex Segade (My Barbarian), Marc and Robby Herbst (*Journal of Aesthetics & Protest*), Kimberly Varella (Department of Graphic Sciences), and many others. I was quickly indoctrinated into their world of self-organized culture – living-room wrestling parties, curated closet exhibitions, etc. It was my first taste of what might be uniquely possible at home in Los Angeles.

In New York I saw friends everywhere – on the street, in the stores, on my bike – even when I didn't want to. Social plans could be loose adventures that involved being swept away by whatever events emerged or people were encountered. It became apparent that in LA human contact needed to be choreographed. This was especially clear at home on Sundown Drive, which delivered me into the new world of twenty-first-century isolation: work at home, communicate by computer, travel by car.... I knew that if I didn't create a structure for seeing people in a stimulating, meaningful way, I might lose touch completely. This eccentric house also seemed to be built for crowds and gatherings.

In early spring 2001, I sent out an email, an open call to everyone I knew at the time, describing the home and announcing the beginning of Sundown Salons on periodic Sundays as 'a gathering place for the free exchange of ideas and art through events, happenings, gatherings, meetings, pageantry, performances, shows, stunts, and spectacles' and welcoming any proposals or ideas. The inaugural Sundown Salon was on 4 April 2001. More than one hundred people gathered in the cave just before sunset to see my friend Melissa's band, Book of Giant Pets, perform their gentle 'romanticore' songs, illuminated by twenty programmed, spinning hemisphere disco barnacles attached to the walls by Mark Allen.

Over time the salons grew increasingly elaborate. Some were intimate gatherings, while others drew hundreds. With each event, the Salon network grew exponentially. The idea of community started with geographic proximity on the east side of town, and gradually expanded to encompass friends of friends with a similar spirit of homemade culture from New York (LTTR), Mexico (Bordermates) and London (Janfamily). Each Salon was catalysed by a friend with an idea, an inspiration: knitting, boys, dance, deliveries, gardening, haircuts, children, magic, trannies, animals, fashion, political ennui, and it grew from there. Who else was thinking about this? The 'project' of the Salon began with the preparation for the event, meetings over potluck dinners, and climaxed as a gathering of people for a moment of focused thought, activity, experimenting and sharing.

The gatherings took place in a private home, but anyone who found out about them could show up. In fact, I often did not know more than half of the people who came, or how they had sniffed us out. Because it was in a house, there was an immediate intimacy and familiarity among friends and strangers. The house is made up of many welcoming places to gather – complex, diverse and assertive spaces that played a central role in how people interacted with one another and the work that was presented. And even if a performance was boring or an event bombed, the unique, intimate spaces of the house made everything seem

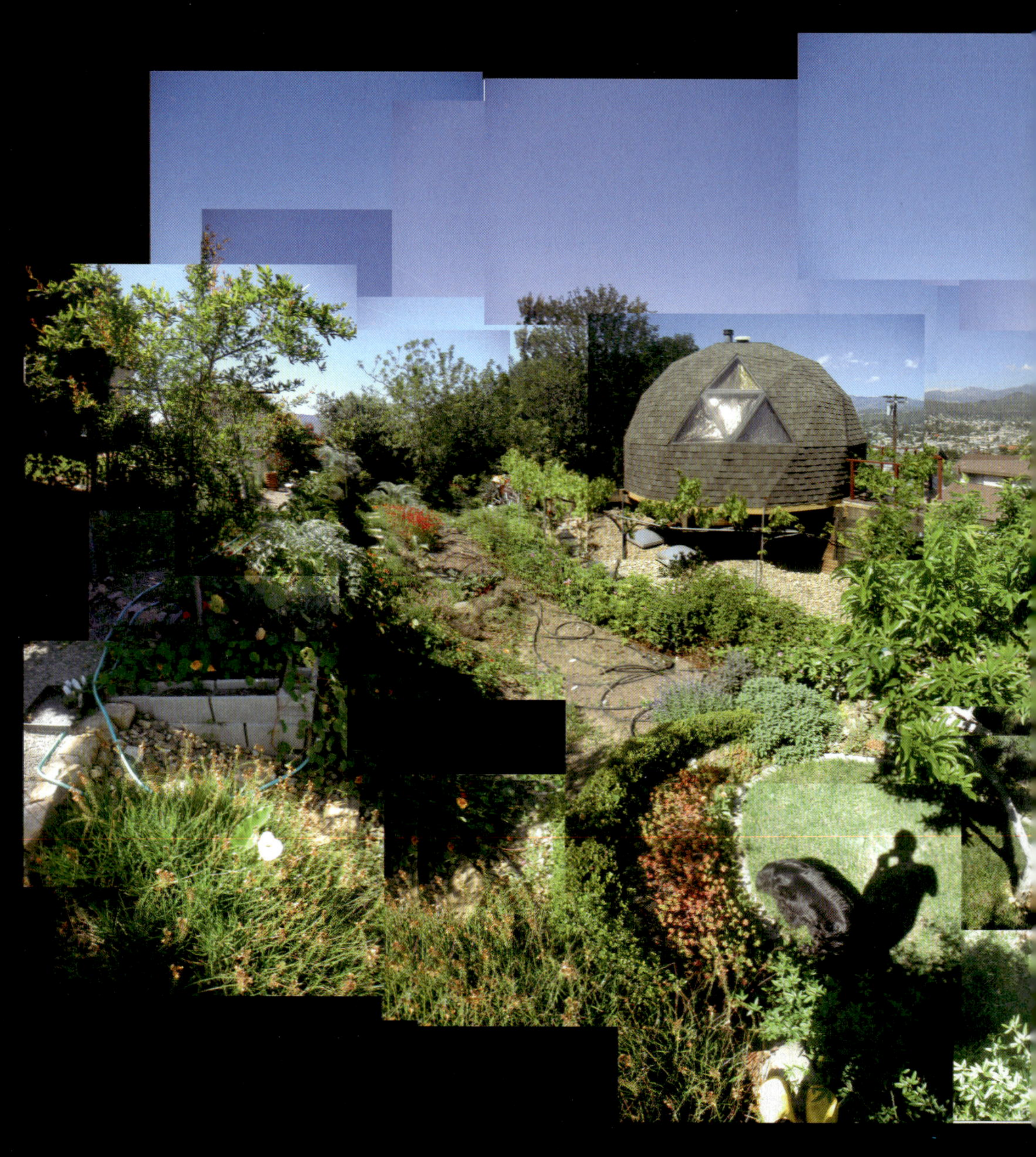

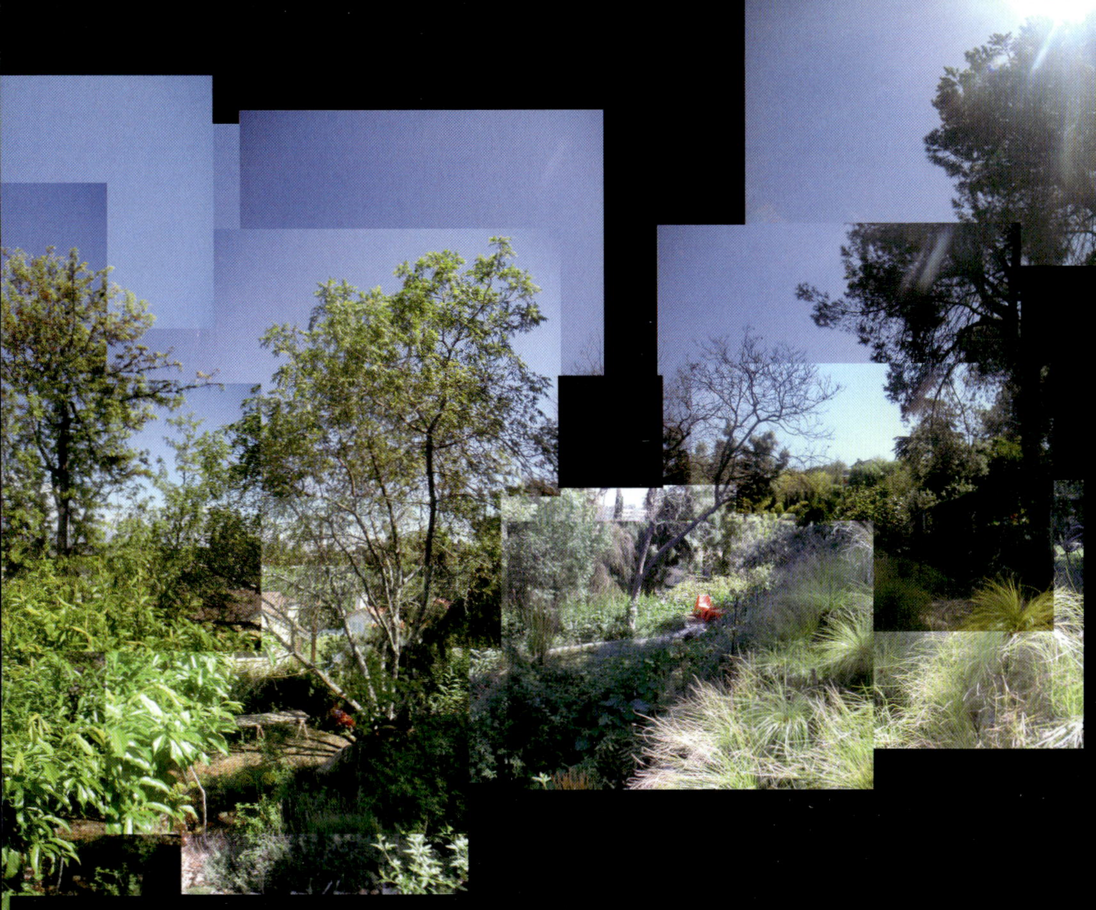

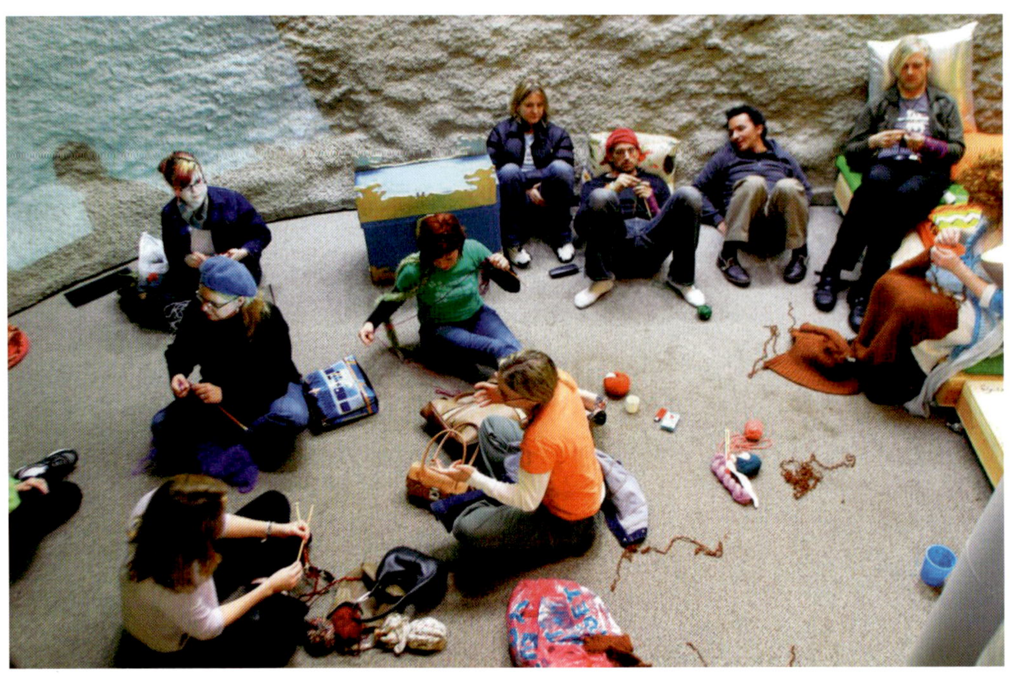

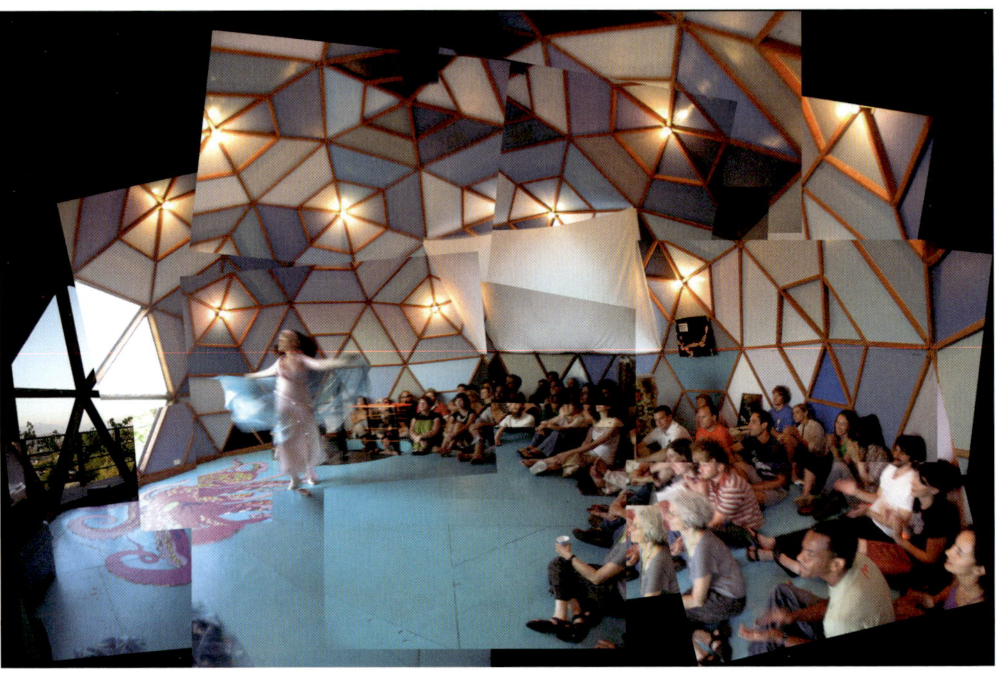

Top: Sundown Salon #9: 'KnitKnit', 22 February 2004. Photo: Jeaneen Lund
Bottom: Sundown Salon #29: 'Dancing Convention', 9 July 2006. Photo: Fritz Haeg
Previous pages: Sundown Garden, Sundown Salon #2, 5 June 2001. Photo: Fritz Haeg

worthwhile as we shared a moment together, huddled on the floor of the cave or facing each other in a circle in the dome.

Art schools, museums, studios and galleries are still plagued by an assumption of solitude. Work is often made alone in one white box to be then experienced alone in another white box. Of course there should always be a central place in our society for both work and experiences of this sort, but perhaps we need some balance, with equally serious attention to the more collective, engaged and social possibilities. Often it is assumed that to have an experience with art one must leave daily life and enter into the enlightened institution or place of commerce. A line has been drawn between banal daily existence and the transcendent realm of Art. The church that provides a sacred, spiritual place for communion with a higher power has the same message: religiosity happens here, and a similar level of communion is precluded from occurring elsewhere. Part of the message of the Salon and other forms of homemade culture is that meaningful Art can happen anywhere, even at the very core of your daily life, at home with friends.

In a capitalist society, our private property – and our home in particular – is one of the few places we exert immediate control. The way we administer our small private realm can be a public declaration of what we believe in and what direction we would like to see things go. We want to connect; it is our most basic human need. Every step forwards in our increasingly homogenized, processed and 'connected' culture further isolates us physically and numbs us mentally. In a world of engineered foods where every apple in the market looks the same, we also long for the unique, the eccentric, the handmade, the local, the unexpected, the not-quite-ready, the unformed thought. More than anything, these moments together at home on Sundown Drive gave us a taste of potential alternatives and unexplored possibilities.

Reconsidering the role of the home in our society has become a central theme in my work since beginning the Sundown Salons. How do we make more effective use of the rooms, landscapes, neighbourhoods and cities that we have inherited? How can we make them more welcoming to the complex interdependent lives of the plants, animals and people that share them?

From the rather insular gatherings at my home among friends, these ideas expanded in 2005 when I started working with families in cities across the country to replace their front lawns with edible landscapes. This ongoing series of Edible Estate Regional Prototype Gardens extends the idea of the Salons by repurposing part of the private home for public function. By deploying the old-fashioned kitchen garden as a contemporary form of gentle anarchy and poetic provocation, a previously unwelcoming, wasteful and polluting space is transformed into a productive and social space to be enjoyed equally by the owners and their neighbours.

The social and cultural agenda of these gardens is similar to the series of gatherings at my home, in which the antiquated form of the salon is reconsidered for a new generation. What does it have to offer us in an age of Blackberries and Starbucks? I like the idea that anyone with a living room can try this for themselves. You don't have to live in a dome, but hopefully what happened here may serve as inspiration for other homes to open, and who knows what that could lead to.

Visit sundownsalon.org for more stories and photos.

2Up2Down / Homebaked

Subject: Too Sexy?
From: Carl Ainsworth <carlitosway@yahoo.com> Wednesday 11 July 2012 3:44pm
To: Michael <michaelbroadhurst@btinternet.com>
⎘ **2 attachment(s)** – poem_dad.jpg (374.84KB), meandmichael.jpg (2.1MB)

All right Michael
We got the results of the last 'consultation' today. This is it: clearance of
Gilman St to the even side of Pulford St which means clearance of 156 properties
(76 occupied; 80 voids) with 60 retained in the odd side of Pulford St to even side
of Burnand Street. It also means the retention of the old Phase 7 area with only
68 properties being demolished with in this area of which (32 occupied; 36 voids)
314 being retained in all.

    Confused? Well, no news there. It's finally us now, as if once wasn't bad
enough, but having to go through all of this again? It's bad enough what's going
on in this area, and now, they're changing the goalposts at the last minute, again.
The worrying thing is that my Dad hasn't said a word all day. He's been upstairs;
rummaging through boxes of his old writing. I can hear him cough. It's all that
bloody mould. We'll have to wait and see what happens now.

    Great to see you in The Park on Sunday for Bob's 65th. Larry, behind the bar
ended up giving us a stay behind after you'd left. Donkey ran out of money as
usual and bummed a bevvy off me. This woman, some relative of Bob's, was
standing next to me at the bar, asked why he was called Donkey, and I said it's
because he's never got a carrot. She didn't get it. It was her first drink. Thought I'd
forward you this pic of us, just as pure proof of exactly who has the charisma, the
good looks, and a sexy, sexy, beard. Yes, you live in a new house, and you now
have a new garden, but they're not gonna get you a girl!
Carl

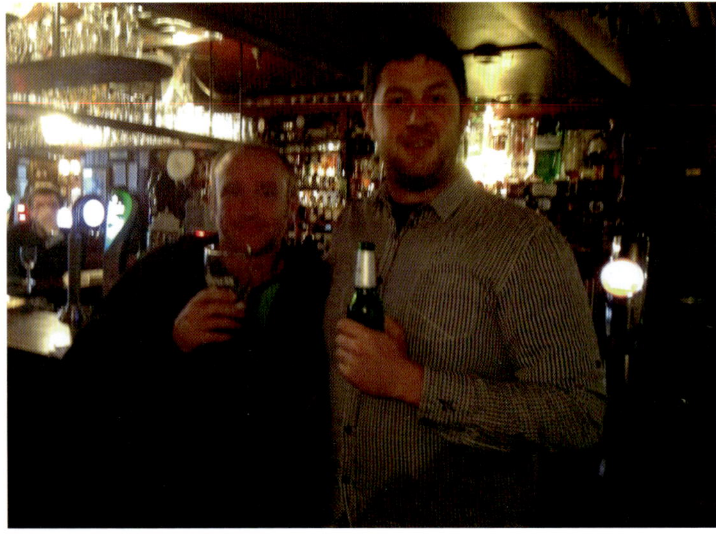

Reincarnation of a Home

If I could choose
I'd come back as a caravan
Then nobody could slap
a C.P.O on me.
And the ~~fire~~ only fire to come
within six feet of me would be
a campfire.

I could join the circus
draw up a crowd.
The oldest Victorian caravan in town.
They would change to look at me.
Do me up like a dog's dinner.

I'd make friends with a lion
Let him curl up against my wheels.
Sit under my belly.
Fill up the holes.
I could circle around it for years.

Subject: remember Gary Melford?
From: Carl Ainsworth <carlitosway@yahoo.com> Friday 13 July 2012 8:43am
To: Michael <michaelbroadhurst@btinternet.com>
📎 **1 attachment(s)** – mitchells-bakery.jpg (6.3MB)

All right Michael
Guess who I ran into yesterday? Gary Melford. Remember him? Had a moustache since he was twelve and always came to school with biscuits in his pockets? He's over from Jersey for the weekend. He couldn't believe the changes he saw. Last time he was over was ages ago. He was going on about Mitchell's bakery closing down. He was looking forward to a steak and gravy pie and a funny face. Have you heard about the bakery, Michael? A bunch of middle-class knobheads have hijacked it. Knock on that door now, you'll need more than one pound ten pence for a pie. It'll be champagne and caviar on the menu now. But what would I know? Suppose something happening is better than nothing happening, right?

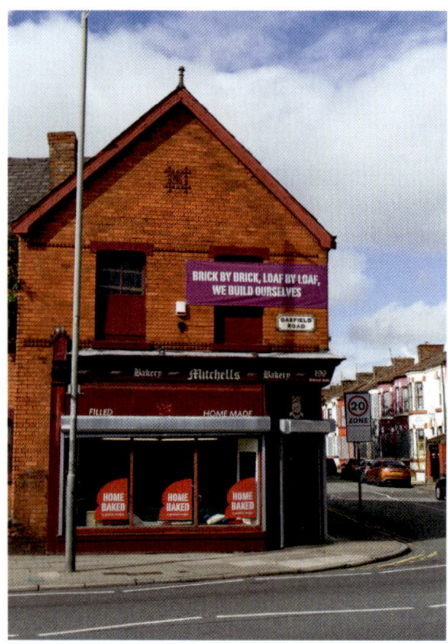

Subject: dirty big hole
From: Carl Ainsworth <carlitosway@yahoo.com> Sunday 15 July 2012 12:43am
To: Michael <michaelbroadhurst@btinternet.com>

All right Michael
Just came home from the pub. On the way I paid your old place a visit. There was a pair of blue suede shoes on the step. Nah, messing. But outside, in the road, right in front of the house, there's a dirty big hole in the ground. It wasn't there the last time I visited. You can see pipes and cables and it looks like a giant wound with black arteries that nobody's taking any notice of. If you fell down there you might never get back out; looks like it needs a giant plaster on it. You have to see it. It was quiet sitting on the step. I could hear myself breathing. A street full of houses side-by-side and I could hear myself breathing. Listen to me, I sound like one of my Dad's poems.
Carl

Subject: none

From: Carl Ainsworth <carlitosway@yahoo.com> Wednesday 18 July 2012 11:47pm

To: Michael <michaelbroadhurst@btinternet.com>

⌀ **1 attachment(s)** – dearsirs.jpg (1.2MB)

How are you? Wasn't too great Sunday, sorry for coughing all over you. And no, I haven't got swine flu, been to the doctors, so you can stop marinating the chops in Lemsip. I found the dear sirs letter in some stuff Dad told me to bin.

I've had a go at doing one myself, minus the politeness.

Dear Sir or Madam

How would you like it if somebody came along and told you your home had reached its sell-by date and you had to move out? That's exactly what happened to me and my family. These homes are solid, and they're ours. They've stood for over one hundred years and they'll easily stand for another hundred. Idiotic, meaningless terms have been attached to our homes and our streets. Terms like 'low-demand areas' and 'deprived areas'. I have never felt deprived in my life. My parents saved up to buy our home. We have lived here for forty-six years. Then somebody behind some desk somewhere decides to knock the whole lot down. These are perfectly good homes. It doesn't make sense until you dig a little deeper. There are reasons why councils become spineless and ignore our existence. First of all, they don't want us to know things. The last thing they want is educated, well-informed residents, that would be devastating, that would mess up their plans. They make sure we're not informed. They want control, they want your home, and you know what, they will get it. It's the last supper; it's Judas Iscariot all over again. Sitting at a banquet we're not invited to. They don't give one, nobody gives one; they're all in it for the pieces of silver. Cross my palm and I'll draw a little map, I'll even colour-code it, I learned that in nursery. We'll scatter them. Well, let me offer you, Mr Pathfinder, a pittance for your home. What kind of racket have you got going on here? Making my parents take mortgages out at their age? It reminds me of when I was a kid, sitting on our step. Squishing ants dead between my fingers, watching how more crawled out from under the concrete, all searching, I thought for the lost little fella; who ended up a smudged dark mess between my fingers. Forgive me, won't you, if I seem a little off. I have lost my family home now, and we are all out of pocket. Excuse me while I limp off, and try to find a new path to follow.

Carl Ainsworth

Your ref APP/5091/A/80/02944
dated 7.5.80

Dear Sirs! thank you for the opportunity of supporting the Liverpool City Council decision to refuse consent to demolish 46 houses in Kemlyn Rd etc

The houses are a worthy memorial to a builder who made houses good to look at & to live in — I know because for the past 70 years I have done just that

To destroy these houses to make way for extra ground facilities on Saturdays mainly once a fortnight would be an act of organised vandalism

The above address is my present home & has been for the past 43 years — The destruction of this house matters to me but the deprivation of 46 families who need homes matters a great deal more.

Yours faithfully

Dep of the Environment
Room 11/11 Tollgate House
Houlton Street
Bristol

MR. G L HILL
65 WALTON BRECK ROAD
LIVERPOOL 4

BS2 9DJ

Subject: our step
From: Carl <carlitosway@yahoo.com> Friday 20 July 2012 6:07pm
To: Michael <michaelbroadhurst@btinternet.com>
🖉 **1 attachment(s)** – bricks for london.jpg (3.9MB)

Michael

Do you remember that Saturday when Charlie Massey's dog shit all over our
front step? Dad went ballistic; marched down to number forty-two. And after he
hammered the hell out of Charlie's door, he flung it open wide, so excited to have
a visitor. He invited Dad in for a beer and to watch the match. Dad didn't have the
heart to kick off on him after that.

Me and you cleaned all the shit up. Remember?

Someone from the Council came to make us a final offer for the house today.
But instead of telling them to stick their money where the sun don't shine, like
he used to, Dad said nothing and walked back upstairs to his room.

Carl

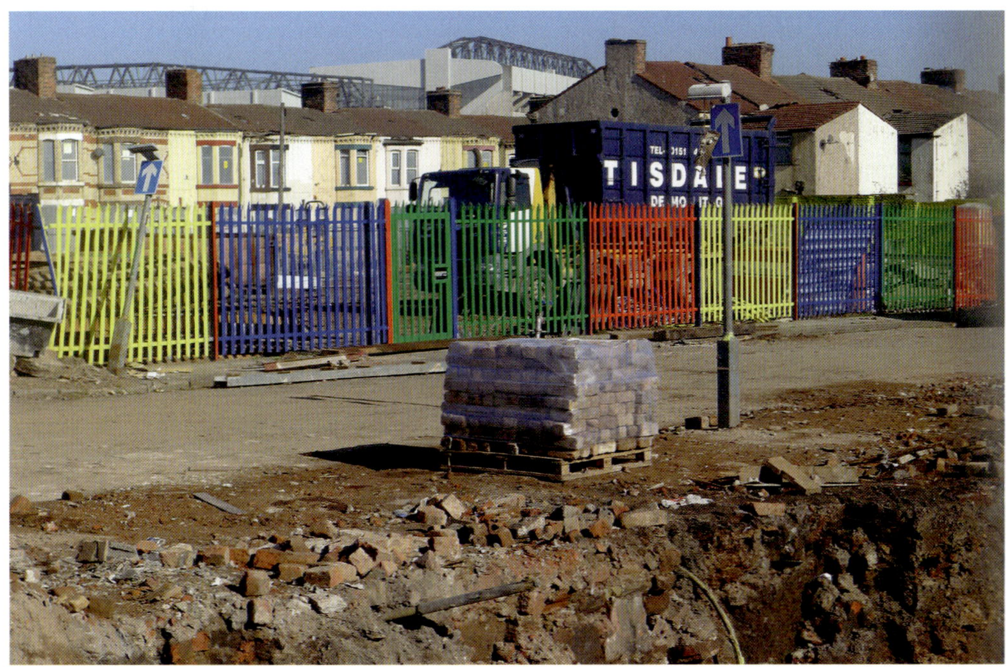

Housing is the battlefield of our time and the house is its monument.
'Brick by brick, loaf by loaf we build ourselves'

2Up2Down/Homebaked, 2012, is a project by Jeanne van Heeswijk and the residents of Anfield

Oded Hirsch

A few weeks after I moved away from the countryside, I felt an urge to fill up my newly rented quarters with soil. The apartment was located on the fourth floor of a typical prewar walk-up building on the outskirts of the city. The plan was simple: to get as much soil as I could, carry it up to the apartment and cover the floor. Then, I would place a camera in one of the corners of the room in order to capture the muddy interior along with the grey street appearing through the only window.

I went downstairs, equipped with a bucket and a small shovel, determined to dig up some earth and transport it up the stairs. I managed to collect a handful of compost from a fenced lot and scraped a few chips from below the trees along the pavement. After hours of scavenging, I ended up with only a shallow layer of earth in the bottom of my bucket.

I rented a car and headed north. One city block after another, the asphalt stretched through hills and valleys, through neighbourhood after neighbourhood. In a distant suburb, I encountered a pile of dirt. It was a guarded construction site. I could not get in. On the margins of another town, I saw an open field for the first time, but it was blocked by an electric fence with very clear signs: 'NO TRESPASSING'. A few hours' drive west, on another hilly site, I was followed closely by a suspicious pick-up truck that did not welcome my presence on this private land. Only at the end of a very long day, did I finally find unclaimed territory in the depths of thick woods, where I could load precious soil into my burlap sacks.

Back in the city, I parked the car with the treasure in the trunk and waited for the early hours, so I could haul the heavy load upstairs without having to explain myself. It was two or three, maybe even four o'clock in the morning, when I made the final trip with the fifty-pound freight on my shoulder. The superintendent opened his door, first a crack to quietly survey the situation, and then releasing the chain, to step out.

'What do you think you are doing?' he asked.

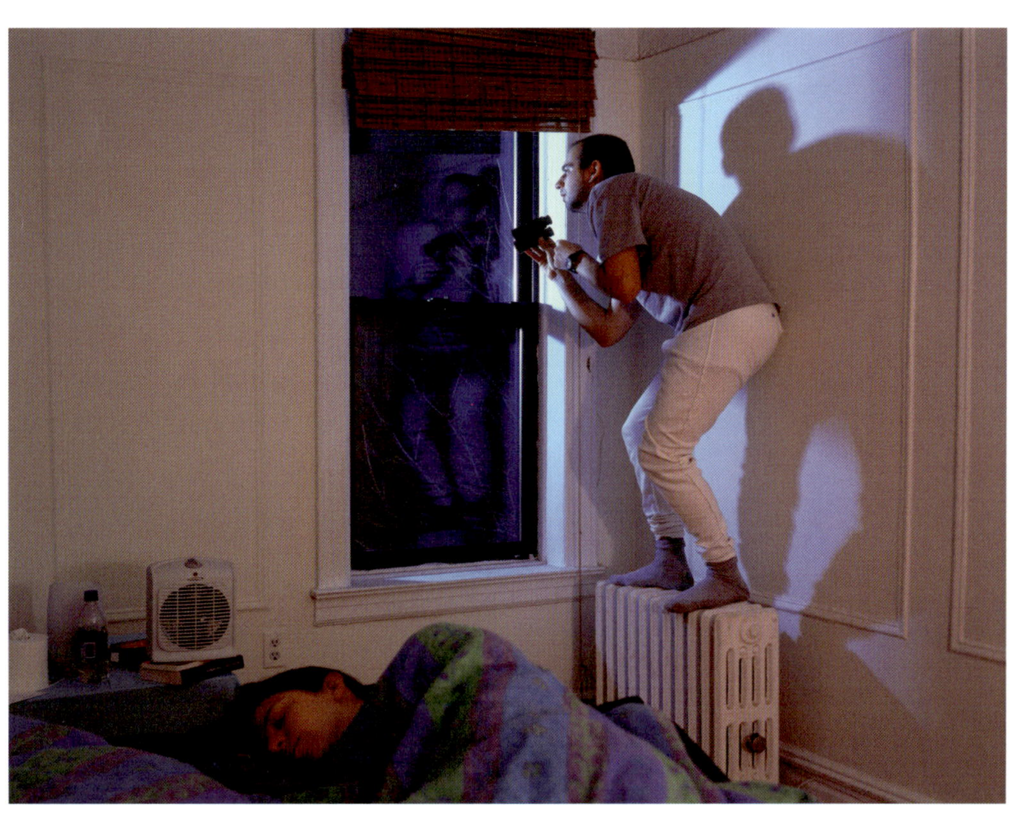

Sleep Tight

Hsieh Ying-chun

**Constructing empowerment
from rural to urban**

Following the massive Taiwan
earthquake of 21 September 1999, Hsieh
took his office to the Sun Moon Lake
disaster area in Nantou County, with its
high population of indigenous Ita Thao
minority, to begin reconstruction efforts
there. Guided by the simple tools and
environmentally friendly materials in
traditional Thao buildings, Hsieh and
his collaborators were able to complete
reconstruction within extremely tight
economic parameters. In the wake of
the devastating 12 May 2008 earthquake
in Sichuan, Hsieh and members of his
Rural Architecture Studio worked to
reconstruct homes for disaster victims
in isolated mountain areas, beginning
with the erection of more than five
hundred model homes.

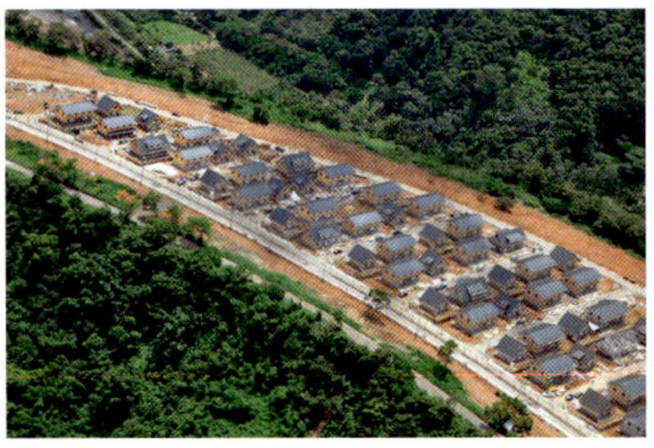

When the August 2009 typhoon
ravaged Taiwan's mountainous and
riparian areas inhabited by indigenous
minorities, Hsieh and his team rebuilt
one thousand homes for members of
thirteen different tribal groups. Among
other projects in 2010, Hsieh also
completed work on settlements for
high-altitude lakeside Tibetan herders.
Observers often connect Hsieh
and his team with post-disaster
reconstruction, or view them as
'humanitarian' architects. But it is
more appropriate to say that they
have picked up the broken thread
of Bauhaus modernism to develop
housing projects of the people, for
the people and by the people, with an
end of eventually guiding architecture
towards sustainable development
where the right to home-building,
and the skills in house-maintenance
are returned to the people. This way
the people, and not mega-corporations,
take ownership of homes and home-
design, the way birds do in the wild.
Under prevailing conditions of rapid
economic development, traditional
lifestyles and values are falling by the
wayside. Villagers are forced to adopt
unfamiliar techniques and materials,
and become thereby impoverished for
life: they have exchanged their savings
for new houses of reinforced concrete,
brick and tiles – materials that are
costly, vulnerable to earthquakes,
unhealthy for the environment, and
unrelated in any way to inhabitants'
familiar cultures. Professional
architects are out of their depth in
this sphere, having never so much as
tested these waters before. Moreover,
the issue of sustainable development
ultimately concerns tests of survival
for humanity as a whole, challenging
both generally understood operational
models in contemporary architecture
as well as contemporary notions of
value, even aesthetics.
With these predicating thoughts,
Hsieh proclaims that architecture is not
a narrow matter of technology; for it
involves considerations of economic,
socio-cultural and environmental

issues. Through the use of local source materials, low-cost building strategies and appropriate technologies, as well as the design of Hsieh's new open structural systems, the team has considerably lowered costs and technological thresholds. Peasant farmers are able to participate in their own modern home-building projects that also adhere to green, energy-saving, low-carbon standards, and vouchsafe the rights of members of this disadvantaged group to live and to work with dignity. At the same time, effective housing design must have flexibility; and sustainable architecture must reflect the diversity of different regions and cultures.

To this end, Hsieh's architectural systems highlight the concept of inter-subjectivity. A designer only provides a platform; from this open platform, the builder and the user can contribute to the project's greater work, whether it be their own images of what the project can become, or a specific standpoint of culture, environment or faith … all participants have the right to develop and to reflect the rich diversity of their particular place and background.

Themes

Sustainable architecture

The core principle of sustainable community architecture is to release people from technology- and commodity-dependency to deploy and integrate the vast available rural labour forces in concert with well-loved traditions in projects of mutual assistance and work exchange, as well as to incorporate elements of environmental protection and diverse local cultures, to establish self-reliant community building systems, cooperatives and other small-scale local microeconomic support systems.

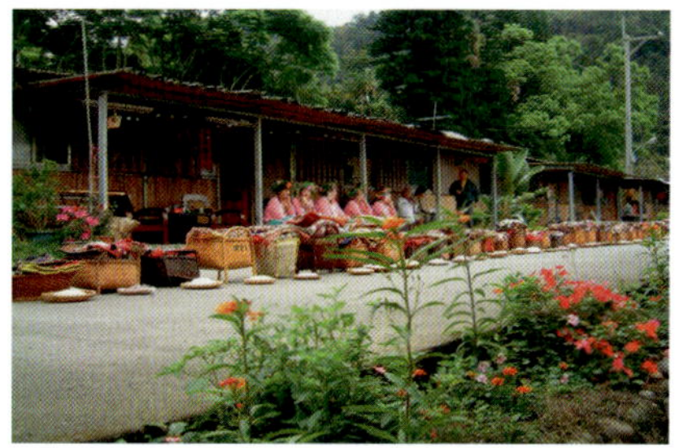

Practical strategies

Environment: green architecture, increased life relevance, greater mass awareness.

Economics: establish self-reliant (non-dependent) building systems; deploy readily available labour power; use locally sourced materials in construction; reduce dependence on mainstream construction markets; reduce reliance on currency; simplify production facilities; reduce capital investment.

Social and cultural: respect every person's right to life and to work; crystallize tribal community consciousness through members' participation, mutual aid and collective labour. Only strong community consciousness can protect, preserve and maintain cultural diversity.

Inter-subjectivity

Completion of ideal architectural projects should not depend solely on the designer. Major contributions in creativity and productivity can and should come from another source: the residents themselves. The designer merely constructs an initial platform on which residents can release their innate talents and imagination.

Opposite: Majia Farm, Pingtung County, Taiwan, reconstruction after the 2009 Typhoon Morakot

Above: Ita Thao community

Overleaf: Yangliu Village, Sichuan, China, reconstruction after the 2008 Sichuan earthquake

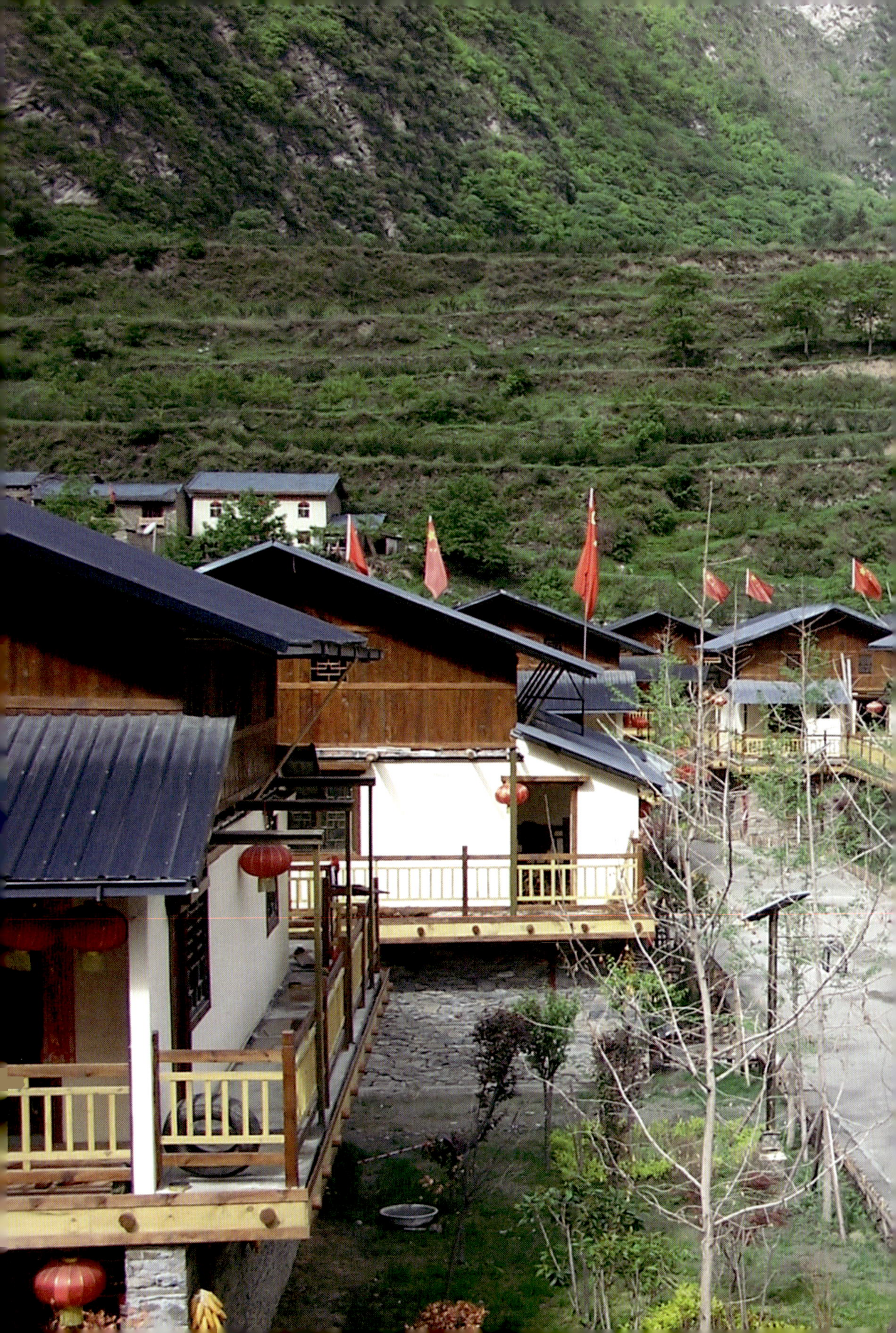

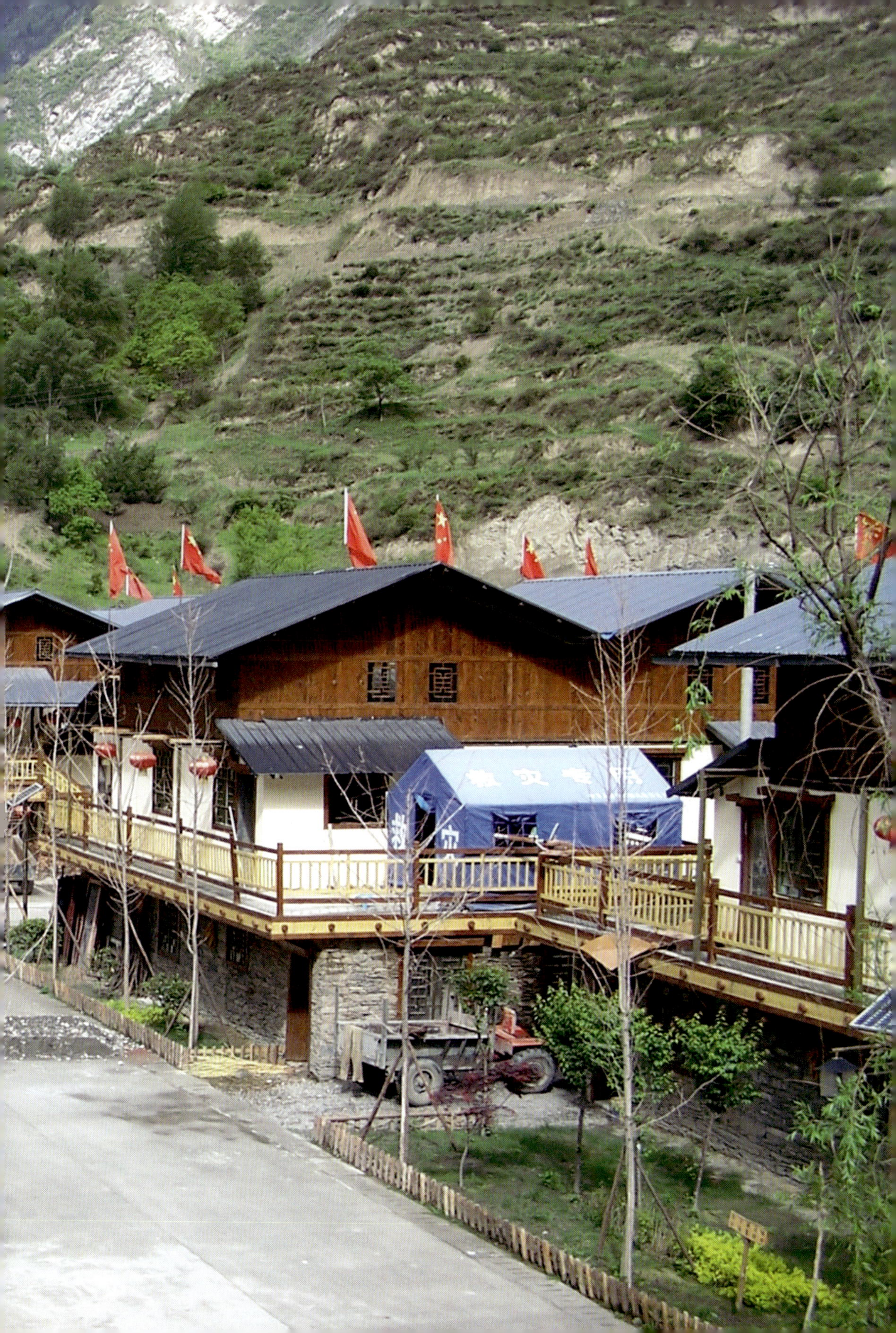

This initial platform must be both *open* and *simple to construct*; besides these characteristics, it must have room for resident participation and for the rich, diverse features that emerge therefore.

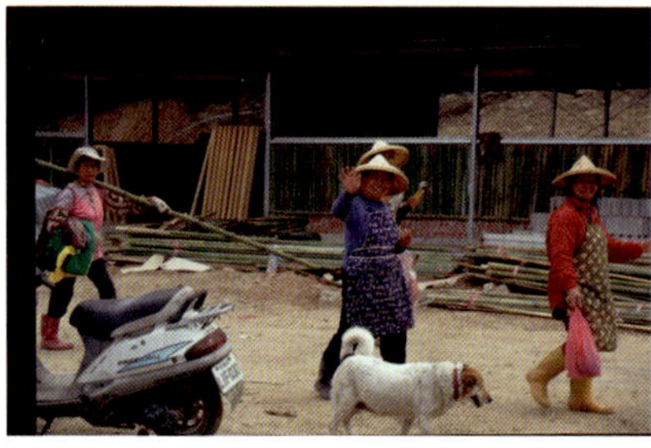

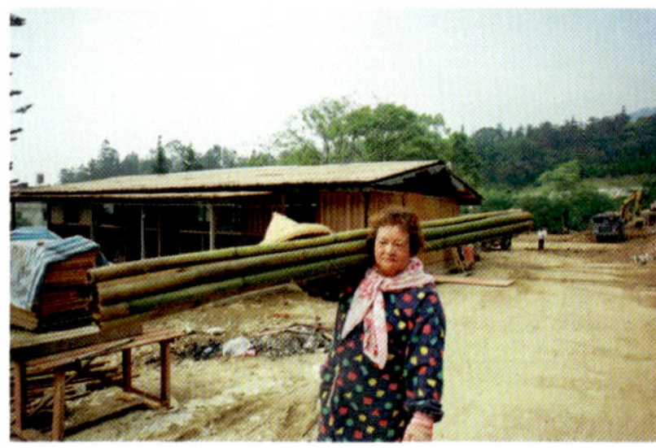

Open architecture
Space, structure and structuring principles are open and flexible: they should adapt to local conditions; incorporate local resources; deploy local traditional materials and craftsmanship; and be flexible enough to shift dynamically in response to changing needs.

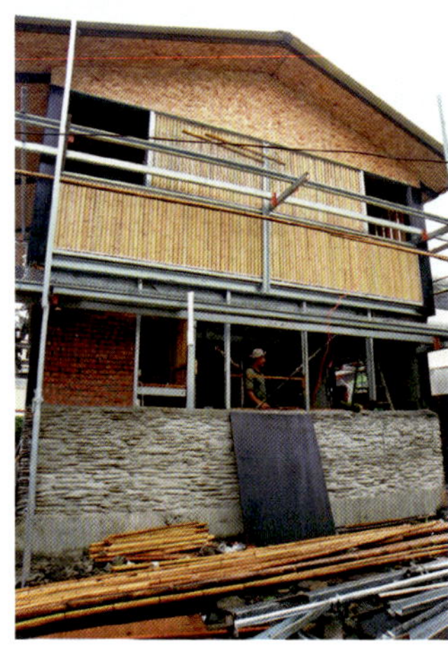

Simple construction principles
Enable members to use simple tools so that even those not trained in architecture can participate in the construction; respect the right of every person to life and to work with dignity; invest excess labour power in material-processing and in construction; reduce dependence on mainstream construction markets; reduce dependence on mainstream 'currency'; simplify production facilities and equipment to decrease the need for capital investment.

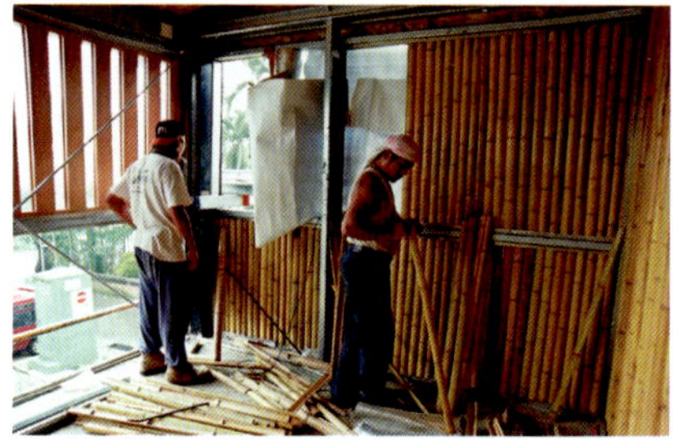

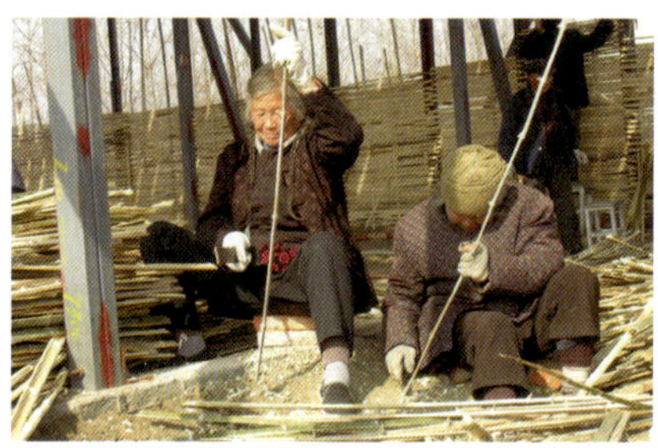

Urban strategy
How do we find the corresponding concept and mechanism within the rapidly changing city? Hsieh proposes a strategy of combining public mega structure and private micro system of self-construction. The mega structure reconciles between the three-dimensional landscape and man-made environment and helps to resolve issues of microclimate control, zoning, structure, municipal engineering, etc. The micro-system of self-construction activates the creativity and enthusiasm from the inhabitants. The strength of

their action is not confined to apartment interior renovation; it can also extend to exterior and surrounding environment, and eventually to the construction of the public space within the community. The power of the citizens can penetrate to the construction of the entire city, bringing back the traditional settlement fabric, richness and nuance in life and space and fostering relationships between people.

Philosophy and aesthetics

The core of the current housing crisis lies in problematic thinking. Over the few centuries that saw the development of 'modern civilization', the future of humanity and Earth has reached an unsustainable bottleneck. 'Sustainability' now challenges our current systems of value, while deconstructing modernity and aesthetics.

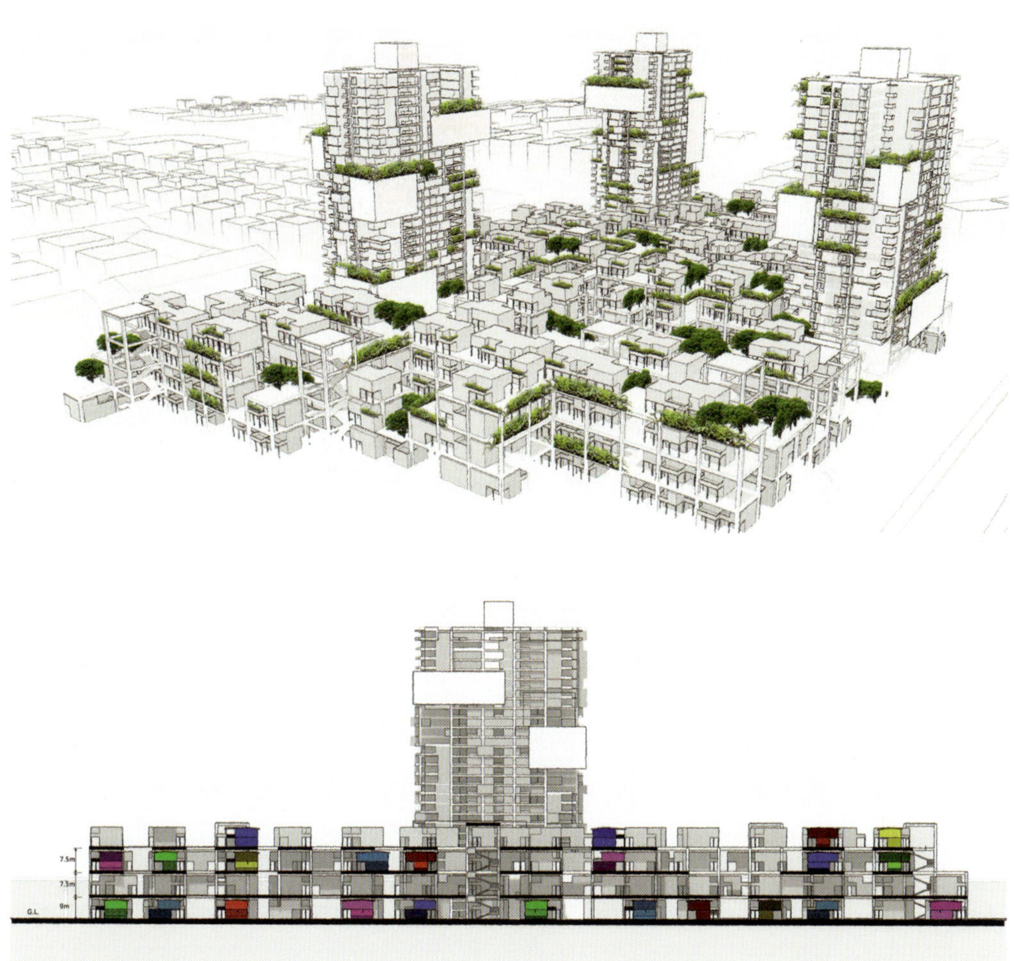

Above: *People's City*, a proposal of collaborative construction vertical city
Opposite: Yangliu Village being rebuilt after the 2008 Sichuan earthquake

Nadia Kaabi-Linke

Z-205862
34185190
33246460
32105147
35131603
34223302
12022580
32569902
12004734
36317587
36721878
35339122
01304990
6531847
35582823
5750977
Missing
33131181
01287456
O-735489
15041860
5600271
O-724000
14045876
36160449
O-689729
Known But to God
35315362
39251163
O-422283
O-436624
20717028
32002089
6246116
35657370
01290357
34315650
35036686
Z-078526
37118084
O-790924
6047393
36448909
13008425
32290320
38314007
33496862
O-884132
6275385
13009901
32277299
38112665
6958966
34120580
16048231
19186814
39836504
O-900559
O-728454
36323753
01012723
37002318
34597054
0-793981
18020197
37449508
Known But to God
35646093
39194428
9305276
17155716

36044141
31048753
31035746
33106577
15046011
6267920
33147315
38063921
20754301
34242505
0358223
01306290
0421477
32316709
34060938
Z86977
39239612
39379366
37368648
32138383
35011615
0659836
15043805
32033171
0686119
01696007
36393862
36442519
38027398
O-423684
35211552
37011083
15048138
31264607
36161572
32577653
12006453
O-729788
2249933
31083253
6471542
33146254
Known But to God
31218820
36159311
O-442769
7086305
O-391859
13120553
O-434366
12011492
12029395
O-141509
16121944
34186134
33068672
37025553
O-659100
37058060
32549972
12045452
19017300
32033671
32161726
12045674
36740310
34288192
O-791071
12045259
12041703
12022411

37042106
38295525
37310983
31134048
33152935
36218514
36038841
0662503
38007560
12003465
36161306
33004372
33179149
33377204
Field Service
0732419
Field Service
35271638
53942
Known But to God
12085885
13015120
31002193
14044267
31001147
11036049
0664252
33101983
Known But to God
35308998
17090050
6330024
Known But to God
20818602
Z3446921
32026653
0579226
Known But to God
39906599
36044170
15057228
35682721
6309928
32804668
7082100
16064397
33074098
15069214
35038240
6026784
38027241
35096207
O-793746
20707679
32568284
37358342
34426800
O-427315
33141257
35682444
35321914
O-884162
O-725135
35201241
35115116
35269066
6173687
Known But to God
32367920
39460356
18079375

34108210
35119517
0346152
Known But to God
35307278
13007431
321614556
Known But to God
35213661
12009747
Known But to God
Known But to God
Known But to God
6880345
31063267
37420453
Known But to God
39300520
35035252
32303935
17001126
7084420
Known But to God
20707241
6006530
69010214
T64551
1838028374
36020153
6297456
31100445
20229671
20329916
11038533
0661781
32452858
35118161
16076719
O-659627
37030832
36277703
O-791182
3415320
8507570
39676241
39251330
8139726
23148
2037528
14031129
16053884
20340856
Z-252650
33137524
34201470
13028214
37472268
O-340041
11114748
36170612
6146990
15057155
Known But to God
32206340
36050388
18085426
32352046
37188786
35164096
32001107
32571866

33151179
2018026
37095757
20804215
32353694
7080258
2025114
32395902
0387374
35289375
13008505
36336379
31048270
32259495
32250971
Known But to God
31164769
0737757
Known But to God
17031193
Known But to God
6968913
33146162
Known But to God
12011533
Known But to God
38036797
Known But to God
0411276
69363225
12016180
Known But to God
Known But to God
7080801
12026441
12022313
0446234
13037661
O-411911
35541018
31223481
O-790493
33570089
37285169
3859575
39150468
37180070
18046608
6947251
O-112859
18201497
38425097
35036682
38510134
14095887
35210519
20829748
11015696
2244295
34597028
32986956
17043268
35355995
32173626
38060747
33548783
14036259
A-603072
O-407297
35300506
O-174808

35259215	14017488	12009754	35462646	Z93243
6975002	0883601	6716806	39247800	16021113
34292019	Known But to God	31142532	35036690	Known But to God
32635244	12060065	Known But to God	32534866	11009182
37025533	7273215	34042429	32221534	16021145
34742257	2564237	139600	33137524	33129730
20701513	0734031	6668790	32065786	19074458
32862294	0790439	Known But to God	Known But to God	13016106
Known But to God	Known But to God	661425	33092708	12038892
38217821	35456345	19032117	32013953	32219067
16030731	35044556	35270732	15055567	33114001
19102960	32774395	37273000	39379916	32209206
32550629	Known But to God	32387860	6277266	39387473
13029175	36500695	Known But to God	32014068	6854717
3501936	19012369	46030043	35150469	15056699
20717409	33066483	01107101	Known But to God	36333339
33114853	040709	39310913	37098057	19177261
37030355	20704727	32068407	35150159	14063217
31052145	37056665	36169996	Known But to God	6122614
31056583	Known But to God	33099447	3323920	33318520
32233200	0801566	0799919	01286134	0737310
13043461	01298427	35288181	Known But to God	32179120
Known But to God	2127901	0813555	0335835	0568179
12018124	0661040	34334291	Known But to God	34041043
Known But to God	0386391	35126618	34437504	33089433
13010369	32282603	19032061	Known But to God	322284681
O-1107548	33188160	32254062	34001364	6403826
8116627	6989054	2660159	13064255	Civilian
33402039	6009094	O-663457	12009758	18050832
33269636	34306534	7082227	36180009	3415482
12183162	34121641	O-789844	35138674	32395856
2507766	3553392	35115901	O-425466	32352299
17034892	33477038	O-659648	20849249	36512216
01292277	O-496112	O-661692	32367983	12017336
O-661425	6592666	2015968	2505529	6947314
14006909	O-791548	6530323	2835871	32461142
38064120	38309552	11998422	39262290	33423068
32066350	O-350826	O-754785	37090193	6956932
32280889	12017102	33363224	37028699	39273316
35170890	O-1533484	2441160	36263260	19147024
32646595	3127126	3684248	35263915	33592064
33452842	6992206	10600234	38057941	O-659443
6702815	O-098080	14046752	32387860	32329208
39385085	35129717	35541070	Known But to God	O-796281
O-660959	16002521	Known But to God	31079407	12004464
Known But to God	38370636	6249007	2724021	7230118
31119903	33214061	O-660444	32249788	33074284
34150277	33137841	31253360	35106914	13028522
19065539	37036944	35109883	16101072	14041220
Civilian	32792671	12026441	11021767	O-730845
32767067	11033349	33110061	34082808	37626504
36227357	36666236	6578144	6122131	10675365
O-726618	36079379	17100727	10600319	32539505
15058811	19058762	O-792672	32181437	34609655
Z-025554	O-743328	37496121	6695724	O-660549
O-413638	O-732211	5560145	32265364	32179819
33068117	O-409873	20285360	19012369	O-728458
35038972	12005983	33065891	31219948	35170197
6143293	6697192	39460359	3562921	38380395
35106794	36242219	35254056	2251804	31310682
12019124	32184761	32284681	O-802982	O-730448
O-732198	Z-377644	36481853	Z-057846	34811027
34723815	6665727	12211677	16127147	32038411
17066944	O-727710	31005166	14120372	32800729
O-664551	35383378	Known But to God	34504709	Z-011109
O-789460	37093937	35698778	Known But to God	12011453
17019902	Z-262695	O-686455	32198893	15054775
38394634	34085015	36222158	37724629	01290380
32800802	Civilian	32056056	Known But to God	34236348
O-394428	O-583215	32268116	Z-013909	32568300
O-499564	11081743	32611060	O-173394	11118446

O-441829	32012044	36412408	32539446	18041376
35545809	O-503275	6149246	O-1290411	36365507
T-120889	35119275	Known But to God	33276699	5517327
O-659660	36349042	O-145649	33132724	O-736124
6323273	31031709	O-661819	O-292598	37374010
7040305	37042051	37559680	O-796988	33331810
6569758	6895034	O-739411	33173441	O-727319
33189146	Z-107416	Known But to God	O-114669	Civilian
13014571	33271942	32200695	37115112	32173341
35599176	34202799	18047754	38194747	19072435
14184597	19019629	17107505	12012155	Civilian
O-792218	Known But to God	39121135	34167540	35356640
34384516	18047358	5601669	8210087	6581905
Known But to God	O-436499	O-398675	35314128	35003111
12012157	6954786	36114922	37119514	36483076
32205435	35000298	34174745	14137399	39163910
34396564	15066105	6372579	39182956	32462991
6240332	O-730383	Civilian	Z-360591	33361164
37496932	19017229	39004902	O-659362	33137440
12021615	17010666	6138186	3005803	32330881
35106829	33591694	Known But to God	32211776	32180912
38148731	36330779	35400452	34595022	Known But to God
32794860	15084173	36387298	O-431950	39169796
38120237	35654866	13044789	13055715	6142982
R-848218	Known But to God	36659122	36293431	17028464
6969628	35206873	6642781	31077486	Civilian
18053536	O1292305	Z-072375	8054823	O-501972
19004120	O1288517	32604812	39840268	6949676
O-857584	O-792222	37027372	35456345	O-250975
Z-093553	35488526	32486946	32000980	39675538
12037816	622679	O-303983	36244938	O-415492
32408755	6684017	32635244	34067817	20804215
8164586	T-223032	13021496	10675378	O-730871
34713733	Known But to God	37320954	70162	32517368
T-060410	6801277	31002162	O-660120	31280802
208700	16097148	6828735	2740147	W-2115164
32059861	15056270	O-444094	W-2109219	O-790523
35010838	17029936	33668088	O-434083	O-1295815
O-795198	3428566	Known But to God	Z-270071	8208533
38249260	O-125581	39039791	17037502	35661579
33187812	11047660	39250907	32337116	R-3224887
Known But to God	O-662883	O-833303	O-676349	15334792
39180747	39906648	37104251	Known But to God	14046779
20703152	O-019572	Z-053619	34201789	Civilian
18166240	6133495	3005020	37505711	37326767
12064147	34191387	32693339	Civilian	35602681
36600938	15014181	32047378	32343102	35647413
O-406634	36019159	7080763	13012903	37169070
33478545	31132857	39036909	O-388652	39911576
34171420	O-792962	13017452	Known But to God	Z-362237
34116696	6535263	6183310	35169772	T-186661
33066483	38137847	33391315	Known But to God	35000720
14069818	36293637	17040314	32868856	O-730391
W2109236	14030216	Z-235123	17015967	34597271
19015552	37101664	32878444	38259378	O-184815
3118244	32140508	15066545	6481906	18051248
T-190439	32864320	35115091	6502113	15055971
14149685	Z-074873	6978393	6507317	8208595
O-728578	38327052	12029464	32368012	35276843
31115921	O-724134	Known But to God	Known But to God	33089307
2018356	31031281	11013678	2025114	2665126
Known But to God	32539852	O-0660243	O-168473	11115307
Known But to God	6975318	Known But to God	32829566	35537363
34388525	O-791283	33333920	18097235	35613424
O-144098	12016758	34308689	O-659690	37181786
20237948	37093807	Known But to God	11002024	39167363
18013973	O-426192	7004874	Known But to God	O-496335
6534732	18014445	R-4568045	13007780	6975196
O-724703	19005129	12087756	32618179	15057166
6910443	O-471887	39084884	35288707	37131969
34004501	6020837	33577056	33412534	15013048
12167714	15057149	33042056	Known But to God	39679264
34596025	38140345	39276569	14000217	35210106
O-501971	O-425636	32142986	13153638	Z-096833

18109753	35101497	33208576	O-562604	36721723
12133696	32784433	16010280	13032844	33108110
O-676452	Known But to God	6085648	O-2043718	33015501
8354178	38171611	36003662	2247138	Known But to God
11116445	O-727438	33079388	2030240	32726038
O-431955	O-732212	12003295	3311388	36157429
20703295	O-434628	Known But to God	6833753	32293106
32328431	32326981	32548865	6814915	T-120021
6699428	O-584367	12073526	5103761	13023449
O-854622	32180700	20310037	2016251	Known But to God
20704487	O-326094	Civilian	6906290	Z-390723
36124345	32465425	3464259	17075793	O-732171
O-317400	A-202190	15077116	O-401378	O-391912
3759524	O-740158	Known But to God	2171543	Civilian
O-325435	36161487	16037552	Known But to God	6972071
6915324	O-791686	W-2118718	38465002	O-520190
16023302	15047013	2015968	35489412	13117014
10600161	36070954	Known But to God	33436359	31226126
15196790	O-663033	Known But to God	2658478	32555158
5564714	37004202	15059984	O-731014	O-732172
O-022234	20701911	A-514811	O-379439	31101569
Known But to God	6582807	34526780	19004906	6940782
39082309	32013953	15058935	Known But to God	13142958
Known But to God	38078620	O-435680	O-465412	12165546
32835971	38312585	6488118	39012399	Known But to God
38450974	35016260	32007109	33496858	32569893
O-530241	33195263	6242145	11048423	Z-268185
31124758	Civilian	O-737757	4113688	36630857
12009610	35577180	7040856	6955895	Known But to God
T-120645	16067033	3758225	14030002	19002493
6181330	36161497	15054422	16006429	Z-235600
37025876	O-381013	18218754	6068670	31125994
32338560	16049614	37245868	O-739244	15044312
O-738361	11009267	34723694	36153883	O-314844
37074657	12007741	3566746	31306873	6630577
33136852	O-396429	34100031	33234693	34506081
12009470	35521541	35683294	37494782	33647923
35745579	Z-053210	O-660981	O-430776	33477229
O-536833	32288793	32486070	Known But to God	Civilian
6124125	32838088	O-280735	35599215	14123311
15045644	33616525	2387933	32767077	12021004
Civilian	15019896	O-731489	33461409	35623839
39685140	33572338	6382953	O-567512	35599306
38340227	37185149	37260515	Known But to God	Known But to God
13037661	12137107	34079249	36630811	6083337
Known But to God	20709112	37499616	35200170	Known But to God
39676400	36500983	39036014	Known But to God	12016180
15057229	32208316	31247371	32668261	32205054
15055392	Known But to God	38266112	35106820	39905493
19180159	16097729	11036049	Civilian	O-426733
2046521	2022089	35599281	12060065	36225381
Known But to God	39906711	2727619	Known But to God	37002606
34612267	91813	37602711	O-173680	32371928
33137255	O-810347	39385471	33494107	O-732203
6658736	31277801	12158911	31132279	Known But to God
19102960	35589254	36701700	Z-113101	20701328
O-413639	35563638	O-580731	32792941	35036698
16057638	34041043	32720135	Known But to God	Civilian
39248949	35004096	2243548	Known But to God	34134000
35676992	6579915	37413962	36568363	O-242872
31136422	35581943	O-726893	33084278	37003332
39828669	32651534	34273008	20806978	16016263
35041632	32882069	11122267	O-819493	6582791
36235461	Known But to God	O-669228	3119642	O-724188
O-427317	34200252	Known But to God	2230460	O-726978
14053728	36815550	37025205	Known But to God	18015467
Civilian	O-801006	17001649	39278362	34309710
37183162	38425348	Civilian	2235995	35263827
16131979	38086339	39379916	6981446	O-791560
16143099	38364139	17076242	O-107079	Known But to God

Markus Kahre

At the local museum office

HEAD OF THE MUSEUM (HM): Nobody comes to my parties any more.
THE FOOL: You must find out new attractions.
HM: But how? I don't know how to do that.
THE FOOL: Then you have to invite a prominent guest to give it glory.
HM: Who could that be?
THE FOOL: I have heard that Guggenheim could come if we promise enough money.

Artists 1 & 2 sitting in a studio

A1: Have you heard Guggenheim is coming?
A2: Yes, they have invited him! What a glorious thing that they will put all that money in the art.
THE CHOIR: Oh, Guggenheim comes to visit us, glory will come upon us.

At the press conference

THE KING: We have decided to give Guggenheim 2 million to investigate how he could be comfortable.
HM: He will give us a party never seen before.

1 year later
A press conference

THE KING: We will build a glorious house for him at the best spot, a real temple.
HM: Guggenheim is everything we dreamt of, it's a totally new thing not seen anywhere. Why lose time on questions?
THE KING: And people from all over the world will rush here to see the wonder.

A1: The party plan looks rather ordinary. Where is the new thing?
A2: Looks more like what has been done everywhere for years all over the world.
A1: And he will stay for twenty years wanting a huge appanage every day.
A2: Not much room for other guests.
A1: It looks more like a parasite.

Extracts from the classical play
Guggenheim in Helsinki

THE CHOIR: Oh, oh, will it cost that much? Will there be food enough for the
    rest of us?
HM (FROM ABOVE): You are just afraid of the new and of foreigners.

AI: What if we would dare to think ourselves. What is the guest we really want?
A2: Let's unite and create a new concept, a new kind of an international party.
THE CHOIR: And the artists come together spreading their message. And they
    get over 150 of the most well-known artists behind them.

ARTIST TO THE KING: Listen, we have a suggestion. Why take Guggenheim,
    we have heard him before. We would like something new, never done before.
    Let's invite the young ones instead. We may not get all that glory at once
    but the future will be ours.
THE CHOIR: That is what we been waiting for.
THE KING: It is very nice of you to think of all this. Now we have to think of the
    house where Guggenheim has to live and start the foundation that would
    provide him with food.
HM: How nice, we want exactly the same as you, only through Guggenheim
    we can achieve what we want.
THE CHOIR: Oh, some in the council listened to the artist, and the council rejected
    Guggenheim with a small margin.
THE KING AND HM (DUET): What a shame, destroying this glorious possibility.
    Nobody will ever want to come to us again.

What we know has happened in Helsinki

2010   The Director of Helsinki Art Museum starts talks with the
                Guggenheim Foundation
17.01.11   The city council decides to order study from the Guggenheim
                Foundation for $2.5 million.
10.01.12   Launch of 'Concept and Development Study' for a Guggenheim Helsinki.
02.12   Artists start to come together exploring other possibilities.
19.04.12   The launch of Checkpoint Helsinki, an alternative to Guggenheim
                developed by artists.
03.05.12   The city council rejects Guggenheim, discussions continue.

On 1 June 2012, Checkpoint Helsinki invited artists, museums and art organizations to an open-space discussion in the Kiasma Theatre to develop the Checkpoint concept.

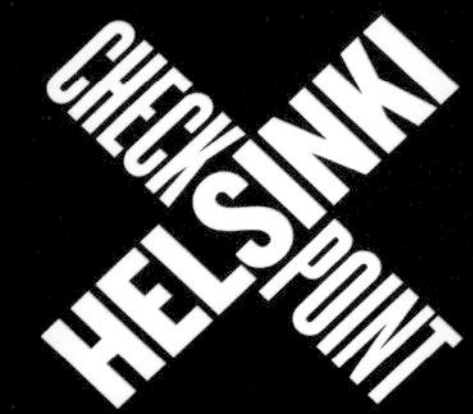

2nd Act

'Behind this is the bigger question of the significance of contemporary art and its impact on people. Publicly funded art museums should be a kind of basic service, like a library. Art is a right for all.'

'Short-term actions by international artists may become superficial; there should be the opportunity for long-term work, and to invite artists again.'

'Artists want on the one hand to preserve the autonomy of the artistic work, but they need support and a collective platform for the testing of ideas and development. Checkpoint Helsinki would be a context provider, providing a community platform for multi-artistic production, for artistic processes of various lengths.'

'Checkpoint Helsinki should give operating aid, facilitate and generate a long-term continuum of visual art, consisting of individual projects. The programme must respond to and actively contribute to contemporary societal, social and cultural issues. An open dialogue outside the field of arts and significant artistic content are essential to ensure the continuity.'

'Checkpoint Helsinki should be developed so that we are attractive relative to the surrounding areas, a "meeting point" of artists from St Petersburg, Stockholm, Tallinn and Finland.'

'Do we need new institutions? Or do we need to develop new ways of operating within the institutions?'

'New: the artists now heavily involved.'

'What would CPH be? An infrastructure that enables the contextualization of productions. Open to different configurations and for different communities and their initiatives. The structural openness, diversity, flexibility would contribute to the dynamics of the field of art.'

'CPH's should be a low-threshold place that is easy to approach by the artists end the citizens. Citizens may approach CPH with project proposals and through CHP make contact with suitable artist.'

'As a mental image, CPH resembles a hybrid of an easily accessible ground-floor space and a construction-site office. A space where ongoing projects are on display and where you can stop by.'

'Working together, without worrying about the theft of an idea.'

'Checkpoint operations should be long term, but at the same time allow short-term individual and collective visits and programmes. It could be based on residencies, focusing on exchange programmes and development of local activities. Long-term residencies enable the understanding of the local context and contribute to a more diverse dialogue, while the short term can give rise to new networks whose activities have long-term effects.'

'Curators, artists and actors are invited to residencies, assignments and projects. Invitations are based on an expert panel consisting of changing names. In addition, there should each year be an open search for the residencies, as well as for new projects and productions. Activity should be based on curators chosen for periods of varying lengths and overlapping periods.'

'We are proposing thinking in scores: an artist produces a score about the spirit of the work according to which the work can be produced again in different contexts. A collection could be made up largely of these scores and their documentation. In CHP, the division between art objects and intellectual works in themselves is not significant, since the collection can also redefine the concept of the art object.'

'Maintain flexibility in operating models, and in relation to the various ways of artistic works. Not everyone necessarily needs to go in depth in the local context.'

'Can CPH happen elsewhere?'

Checkpoint Helsinki would like to invite you to propose a new museum concept.
Please send your suggestion to: utopia@checkpointhelsinki.fi

Anja Kirschner and David Panos

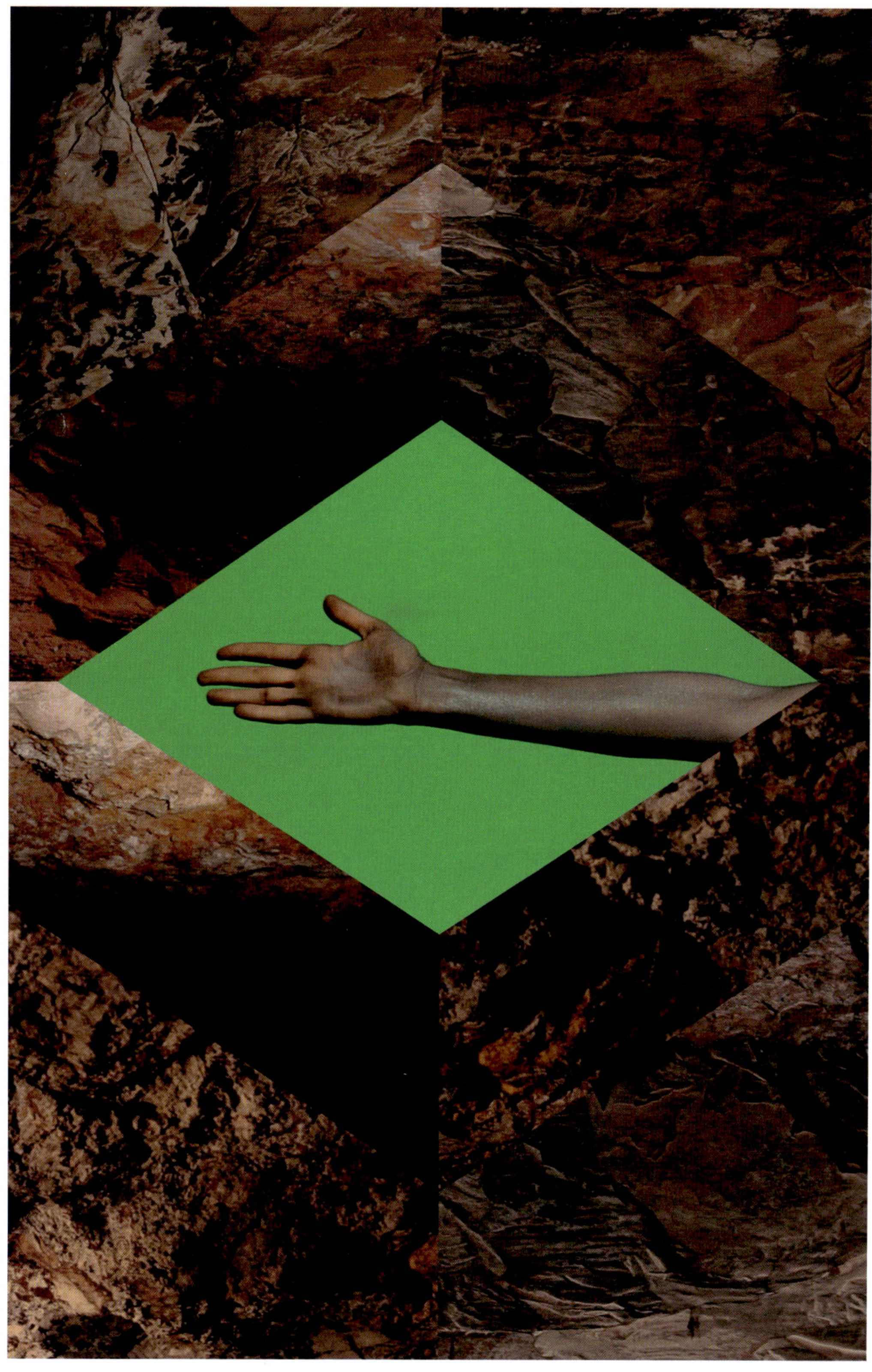

Jakob Kolding

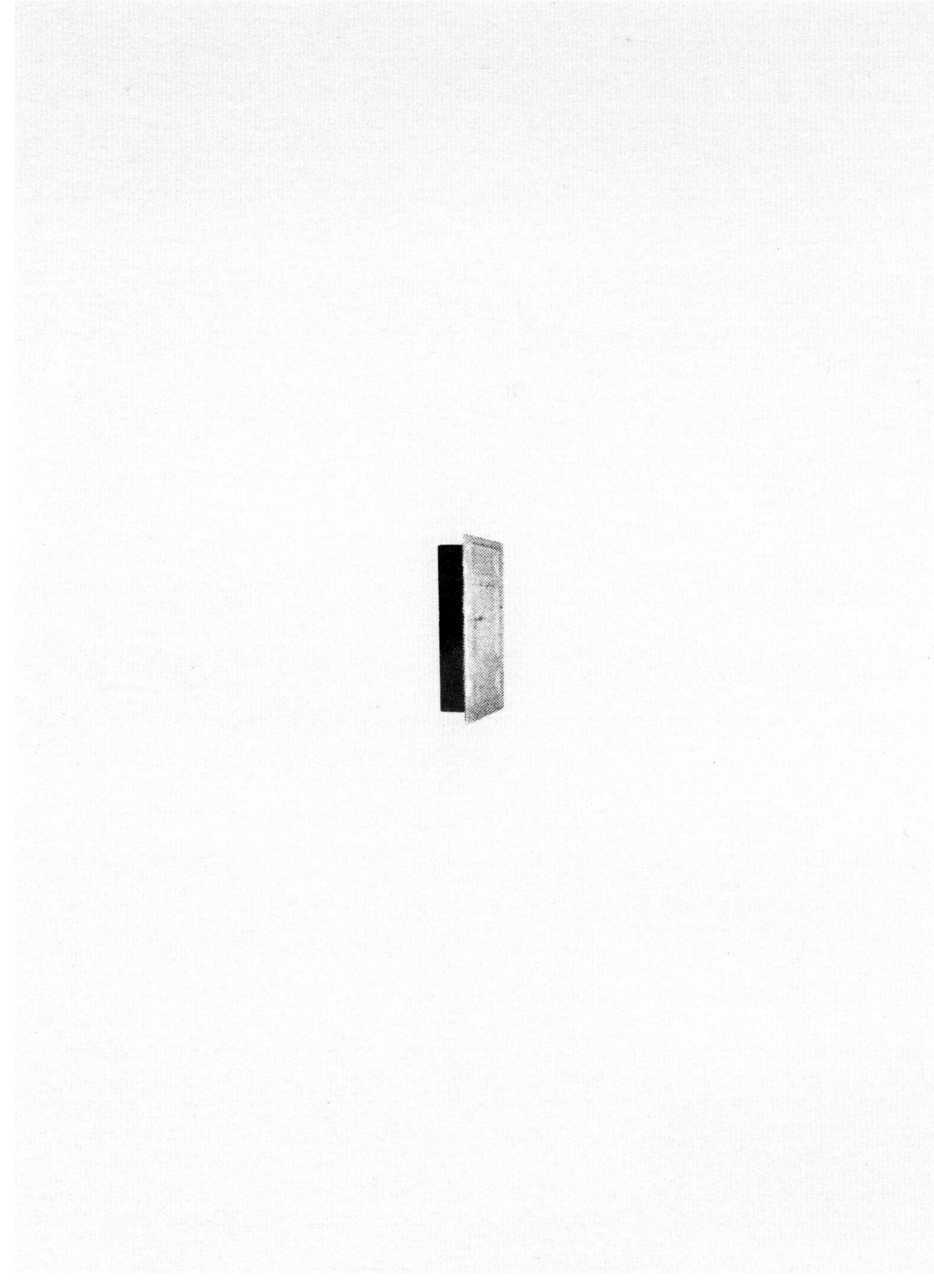

Jiří Kovanda
invites Matyáš Chochola, Stanislava Karbušická, Blanka Kirchner, Barbora Kleinhamplová, Martina Růžičková and Kateřina Zochová

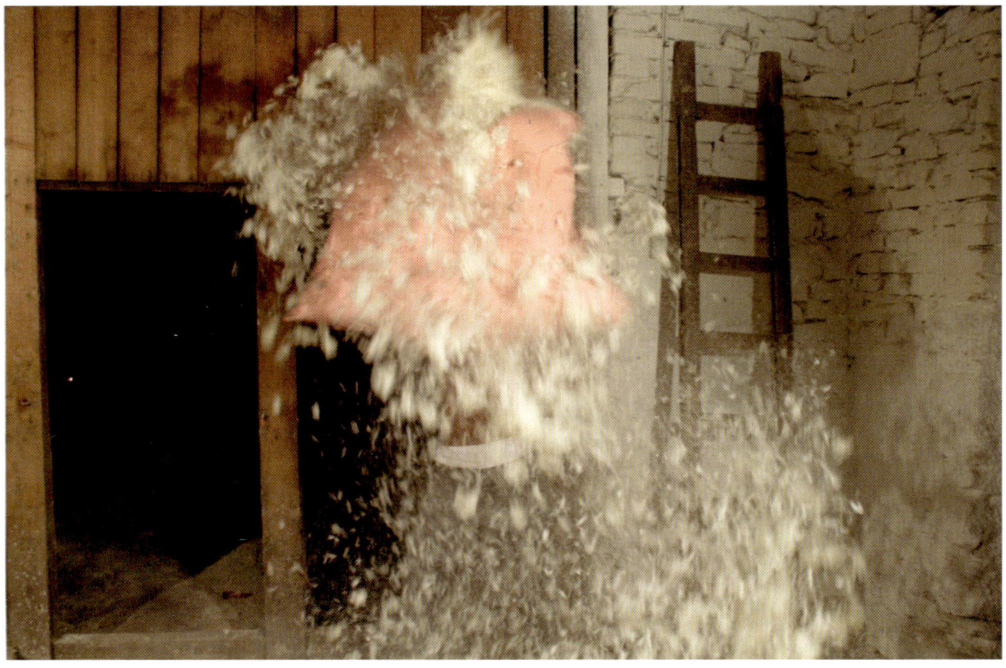

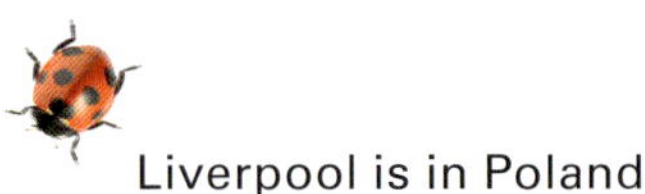

Liverpool is in Poland.

invites Matyáš Chochola, Stanislava Karbušická, Blanka Kirchner, Barbora Kleinhamplová,

Matyáš Chochola

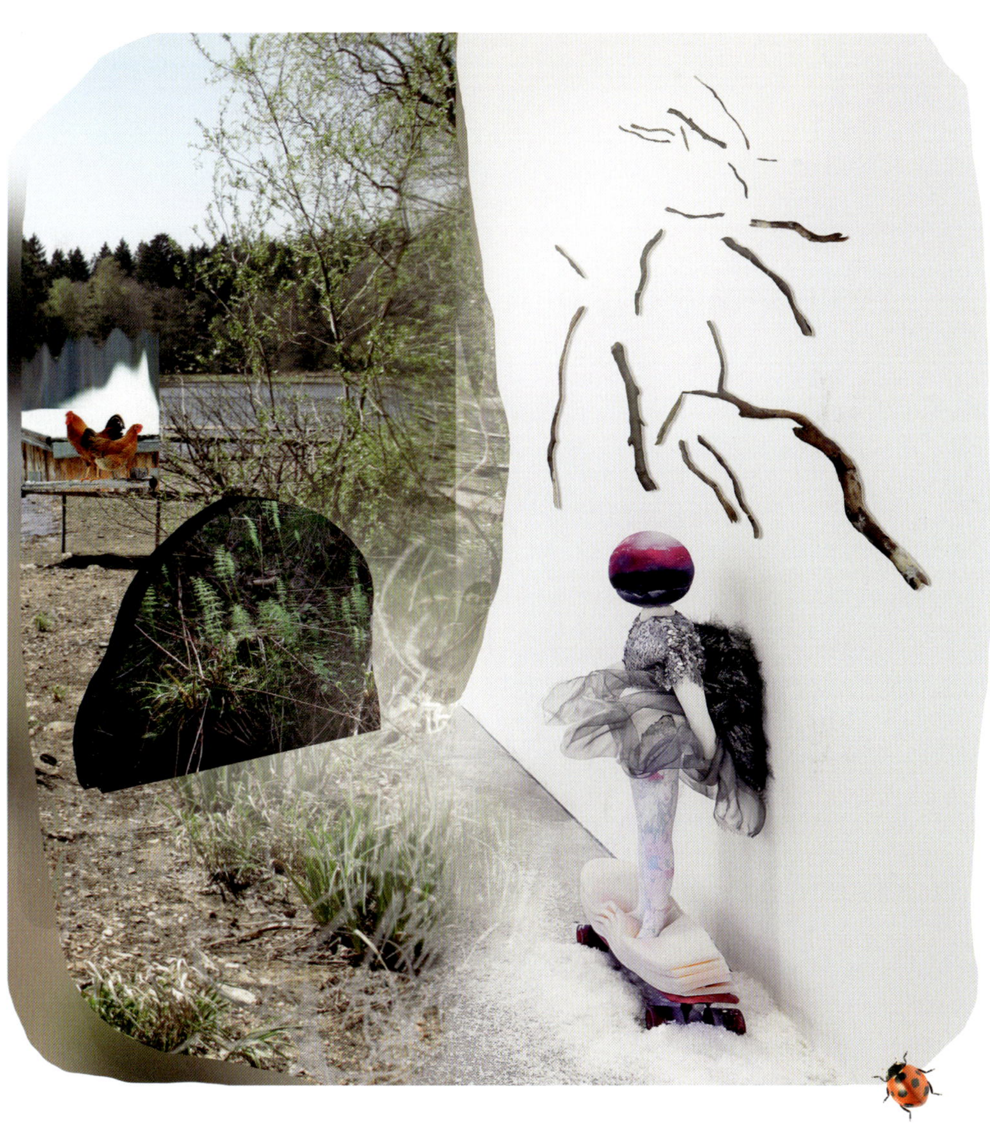

Stanislava Karbušická

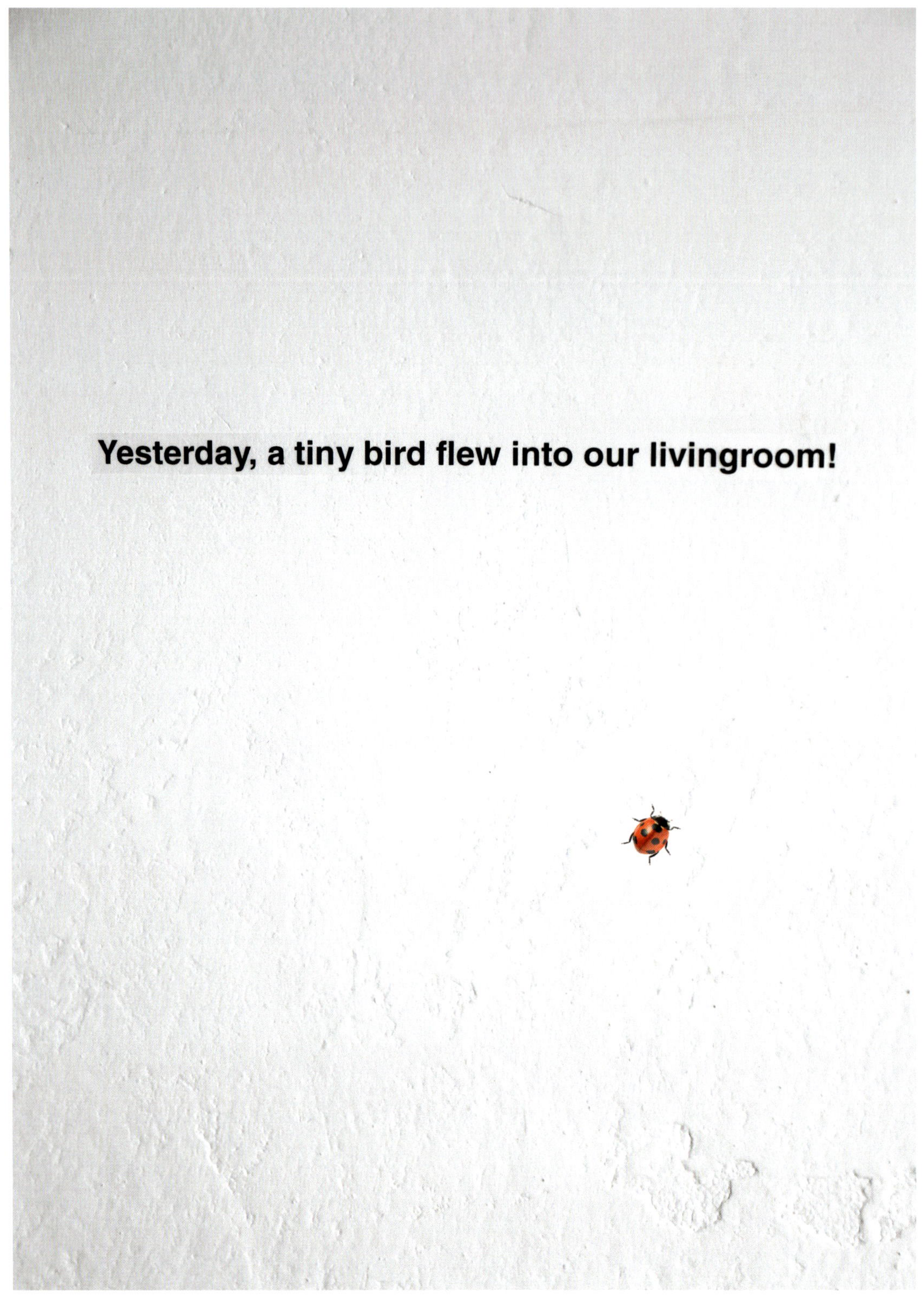

Blanka Kirchner

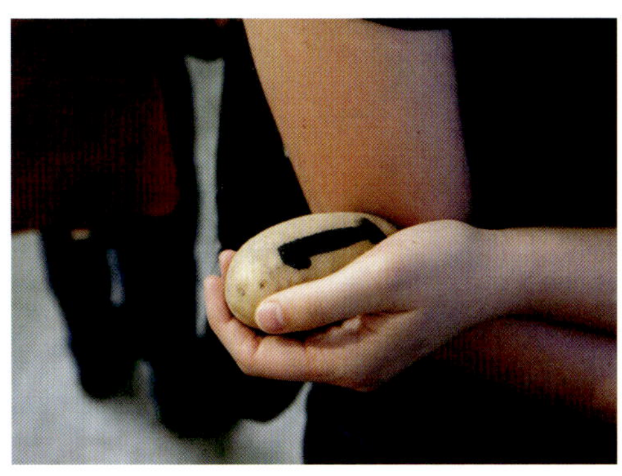
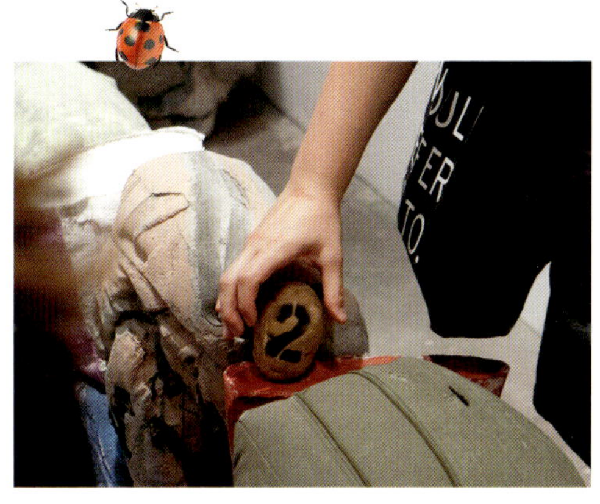

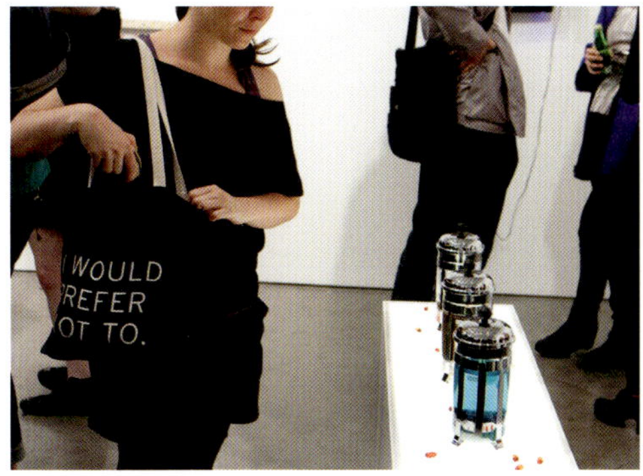

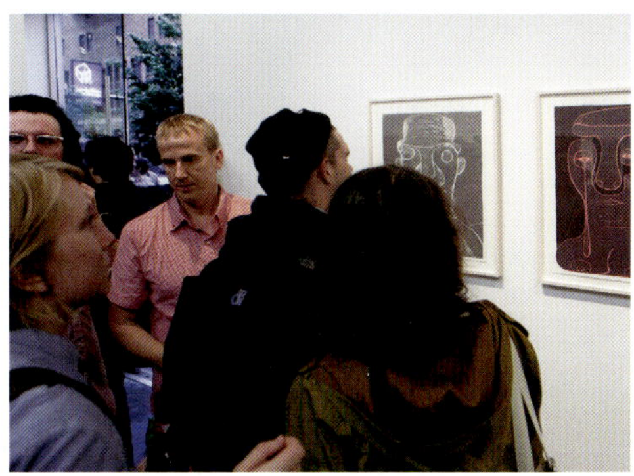

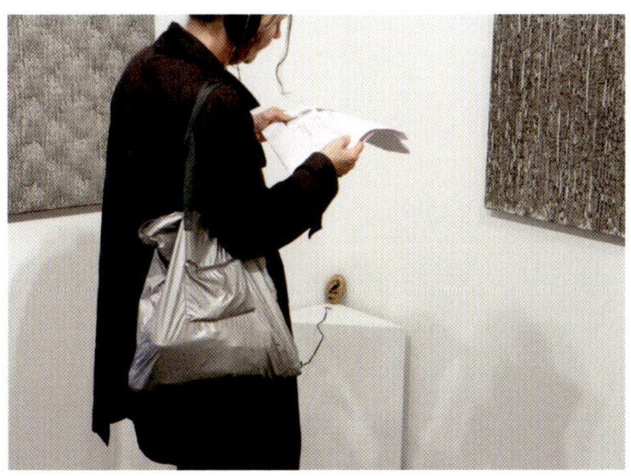
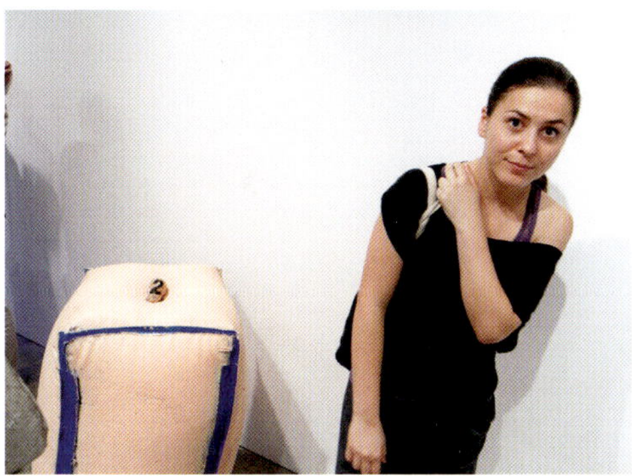

Potato at Chelsea
Performance, 2012

I was interested in the theme of competition in relation to the art market and art production. Following this motive, I decided to work with a kind of senseless abstract classification. I created a pirate invasion attacking galleries in Chelsea, New York. The performance took place during Thursday's night of openings and I integrated my objects (potatoes sprayed with numbers 1 and 2) into the shows, so that they organically penetrated various art pieces.

Barbora Kleinhamplová

At the end of all the stories of sorry remains just one thing/you.
Alone/pure/connections/selfishness.
Chair was not a mercy seat, m.
Protect me from what I want.
Protect me. Protect me. Protect me.
Protect me.
Protect me.
Protect me.
(Excerpt from an unexpected guest story.)

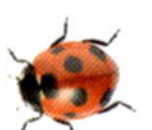

Martina Růžičková

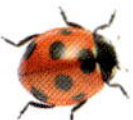

everything is so beautiful,
so magical, so nice
sometimes we are just sleeping or flying
so fucking fast, so fucking fast
sometimes weapons of the dawn are raining from the sky
so fucking fast, so fucking fast

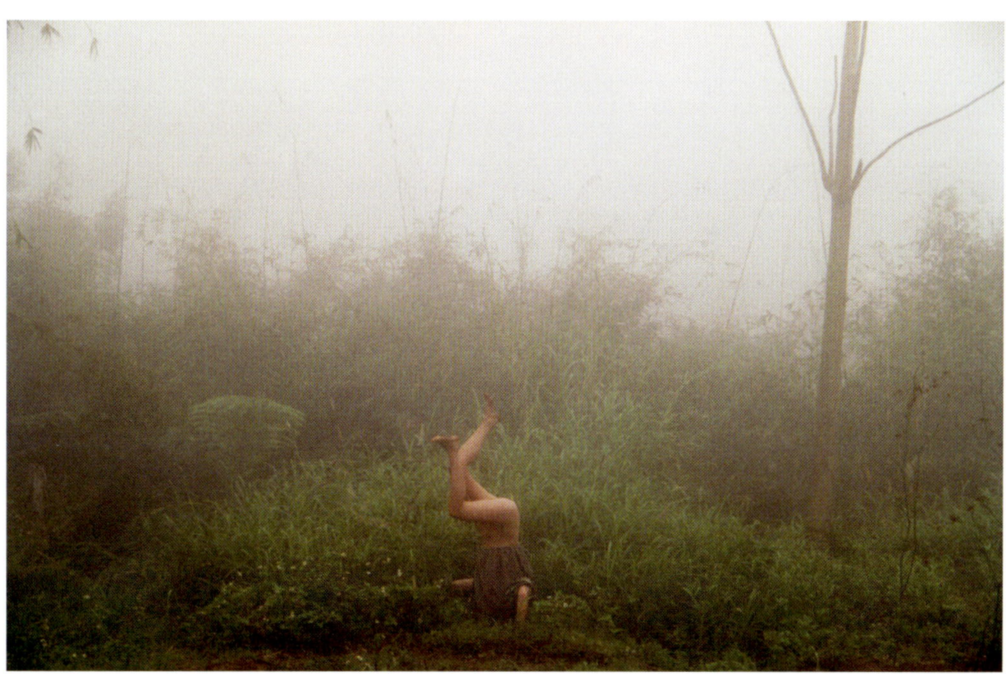

everything is so beautiful,
so magical, so nice
sometimes we are just sleeping or flying

Kateřina Zochová

Suzanne Lacy
in conversation with Stephanie Smith

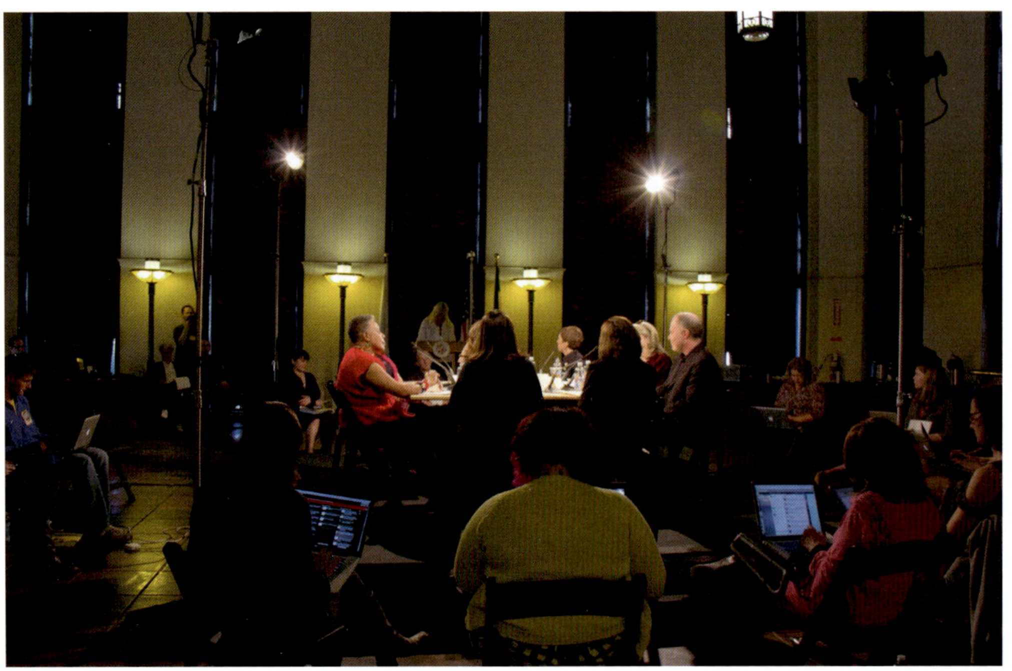

Above:
Storying Rape, 2012, Los Angeles City Hall, one of a series of performances
from *Three Weeks in January*. Photo: Kelly Akashi

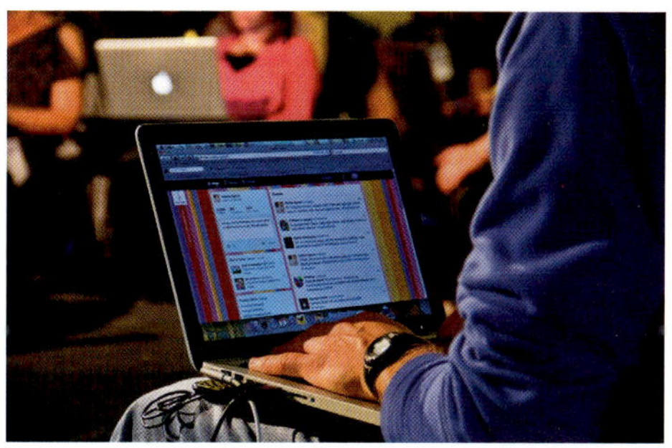

Stephanie Smith: Thank you for inviting me to be part of this conversation about guests and hospitality in relation to your work for the Liverpool Biennial. It's a lovely extension of discussions that we've shared since the early 2000s – most recently working together to revive your 1979 project *The International Dinner Party* by conserving and digitizing materials from your archive and re-presenting the project as a touchstone work for 'Feast: Radical Hospitality in Contemporary Art' at the Smart Museum of Art, University of Chicago, earlier this year.

Since the 1970s, your work has created hospitable situations, in different registers of activity and impact. One strand includes projects like *The International Dinner Party*, in which you've used meals to bring people together and help them feel comfortable engaging in radical discussion, performance and action. More broadly, in projects like *Three Weeks in May* (1977) and the new *University of Local Knowledge* (*ULK*), it's helpful to think of two simultaneous hospitable registers. Most obviously there is your invitation to people who are not usually part of 'art' experiences to engage across race, class and ideology. I think of an aphorism from the great French gastronome Jean Anthelme Brillat-Savarin, who wrote in 1825, 'to invite people to dine with us is to make ourselves responsible for their well being for as long as they are under our roofs'. I see you as host, and your collaborators as invited guests for whom you take responsibility to care.

Suzanne Lacy: I appreciate recent curatorial interest in the concept of hospitality. The nuances under investigation, and the old histories being retrieved, are part of a broader questioning of art's relationship to daily, pragmatic, social and political life. This concept isn't new to visual arts, as 'Feast' demonstrated, but it offers a nuanced enquiry into relationships between makers, participants, collaborators, viewers, covering a host of implicated relationships.

Your quote from Brillat-Savarin reminds me of Arlene Raven's observation as I was making *Three Weeks in May*. She suggested that observer experience was particularly significant in feminist art that dealt with subjects like rape. It was one of the motivators for deconstructing the notion of a universal audience. Audiences were constituted of particular people with different registers of involvement with the work. Statistics indicated that one out of three women in LA would be raped during her lifetime, so for any work of art dealing with violence there would likely be victims of violence in the audience. The ethical artist would take that into account and create work that provided 'safe passage' through it for those whose shame and terror might recur. 'Hospitality' was not simply about 'welcoming' guests, but about concern for the emotional journey of witnessing, a journey built into the process and structure of the work.

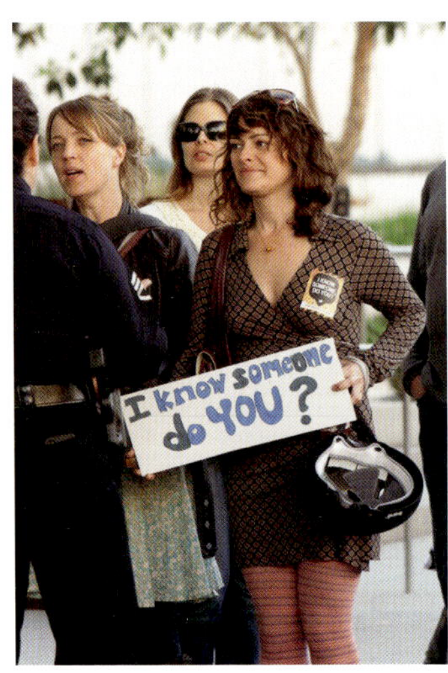

SS: Yes, you clearly have prioritized deep, structural care for both collaborators and core audience members, especially those who might be touched by trauma. That seems a form of hospitality, with you in the role of host. On another register, you flip from host to guest. Your projects, your collaborators and you yourself often behave as uninvited guests. Uninvited and perhaps unwelcome: inserting radical speech into zones like mainstream media and political processes in *Three Weeks in May*, or challenging biases of traditional pedagogical hierarchies in the *University of Local Knowledge*. That's a delicate and potentially very productive position. An uninvited guest might be embraced as bearer of useful news from the outside world, or agent of productive change – but she might also offend her host and be rejected.

SL: 'Hospitality' (or lack of it) in art might also lead us to consider strategies of engagement. At the extremes, you confront some audiences and provide safe passage for others. In the case of *Three Weeks in May*, I was an uninvited and unexpected guest in City Hall, perhaps, but a host for women who had experienced rape. The paradox is that when one works with topics involving oppression, you must simultaneously confront the orthodoxy that oppresses them while creating an empowerment strategy for those oppressed.

With *University of Local Knowledge*, the primary 'audience' is the community of Knowle West in Bristol and their relationship as working-class and disadvantaged people to knowledge hierarchies that operate across many spheres: the University (represented by University of Bristol), the Community (Knowle West Media Centre KWMC), the Arts (Arnolfini Gallery), the City (Bristol) and the Media (BBC). The breadth of this collaboration – one that starts with Penny Evans and Carolyn Hassan (who founded KWMC) and Tom Trevor of the Arnolfini Gallery (who engaged me in the project) – raises a host of questions about hospitality in both senses of your use of the term.

Last summer, for example, we held a series of seminars in public and private sites around the Knowle West estate. These intimate gatherings of residents and academics were videotaped and witnessed by key partners in the project. As they discussed a shared theme from different vantage points, tensions and apprehensions were visible on both sides. While the academics were 'invited guests' of the community residents, the power hierarchies of the British system of higher education and of academic research shifted the typical host–guest dynamic. Professors found themselves under the gaze of observers, challenging hierarchical categories of class-based knowledge. Framing the event as a mutual learning seminar mixed up the rules and everyone felt both welcomed and out of place.

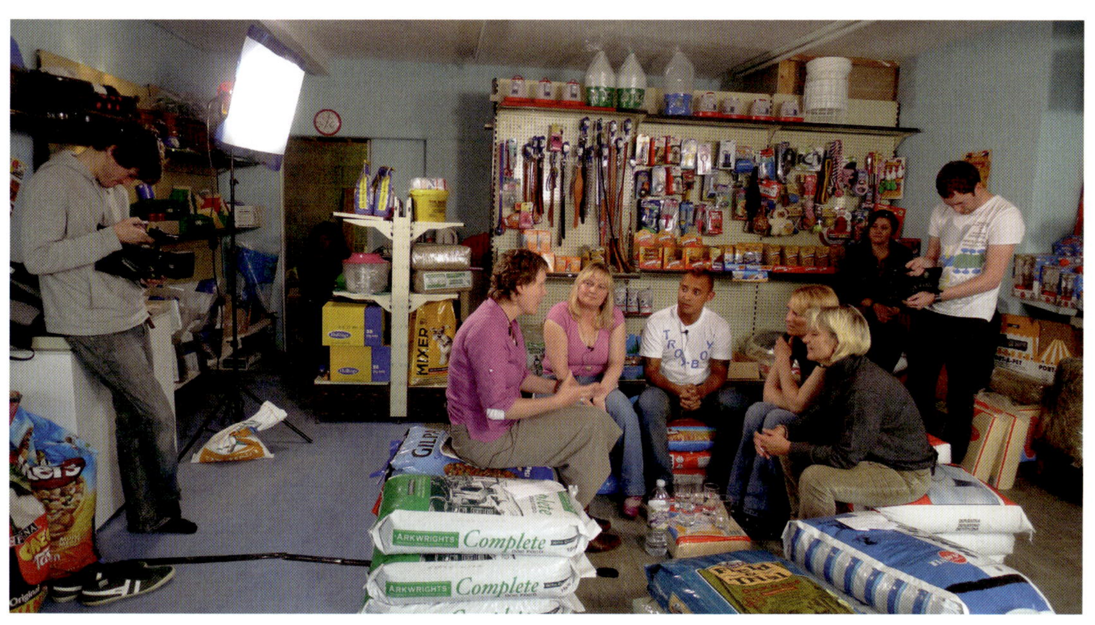

Above:
Fur and Feathers, 2010, Bristol, United Kingdom, one of a
series of performances from *The University of Local Knowledge*.
Photo courtesy of the Knowle West Media Centre

Opposite:
From the social-media campaign in
Three Weeks in January, 2012. Photo: Tara Sterling

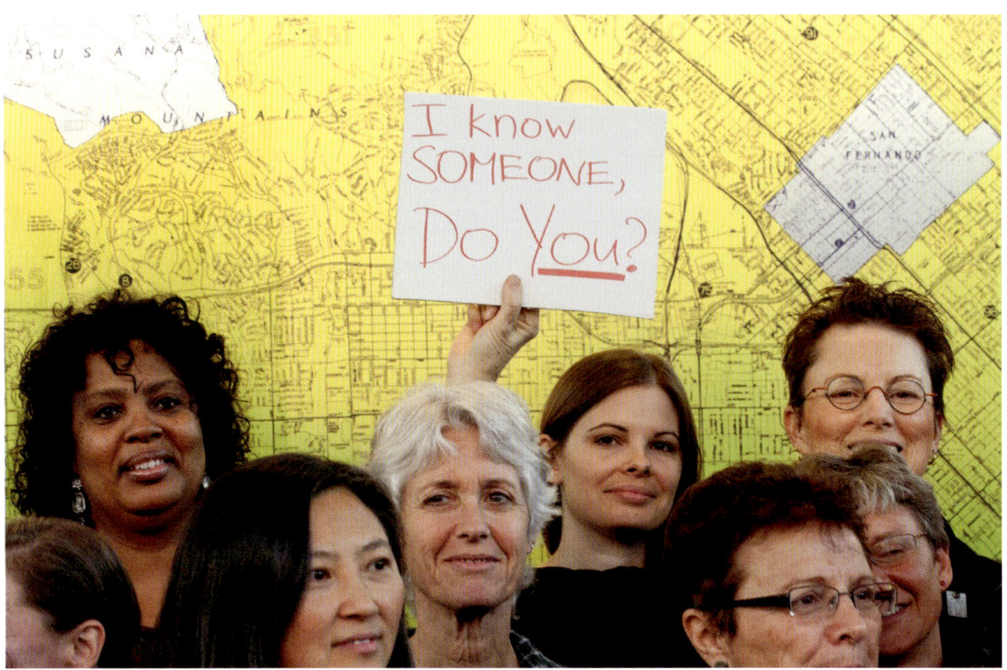

SS: I appreciate your ethically grounded, nuanced discussion of creating 'safe passage' for your collaborators, which complements this idea of being simultaneously welcomed and displaced. You acknowledge the difficulties that might arise in relation to traumatic topics or through participation in potentially discomfiting public/performative settings like the University of Local Knowledge seminars and videos.

How have you decided to give form and material presence to this complex endeavour, for the Biennial? Since you've said that the primary audience is the community surrounding KWMC, are you considering the Liverpool audience? How do you imagine that they will read its social complexity and its challenges? What kinds of guests will they be?

SL: You've hit on one of the central questions in this kind of work: how does it materialize in different venues, considering that the ethical and contextual frameworks can challenge conventions of visual art display? I've seen substantial changes in the way art venues allow and enable artists to negotiate between art and the social. The development of a critical practice alongside the work is also significantly more advanced.

The *University of Local Knowledge* project has been built specifically for KWMC and its community and the larger Bristol region. We have worked to integrate the form of the work into partners' disciplinary interests and agendas and the project is still in transit. The sheer scale and complexity of the work – in process for almost five years now and involving about a thousand short videos from interviews with residents – means that it will ultimately exist in a variety of places, probably in different forms: a website, a piece of research, an ongoing programme, a work of art.

Along the way we've done a series of 'gestures', including the seminars.

For the Biennial we've created another 'gesture' that is also not the whole of the work. We'll use the installation to explore how the community of Knowle West represents itself to other communities; and, as elaborate discussions are still in motion, we might even invite our partners to a performative meeting, or seminar, where we hash out some of the key issues in social practice that the project brings up. But it is one art work along the way to the whole; it won't represent the entirety of the project, nor address all possible audiences.

SS: In the videos and photographs that I've seen so far, while the structure of the project overall feels clean and elegant, this project feels much more informal, visually, then many of your past performative works, which I'm curious about as well.

SL: I think this is a bit of a misperception based on the same artefact – how the complexity and messiness of the work process can be revealed and whether over time the images created trump the process in a work's re-presentation.

I am thinking a lot about the relationship between visuality and conversation. In Los Angeles recently, I rethought *Three Weeks* for the Getty's Pacific Standard Time Performance Festival. As one of more than fifty events, actions and performances that constituted *Three Weeks in January*, I produced a performative conversation at the top of the Los Angeles City Hall in a tower that overlooks the city. Eight people from various professions, including the Chief of Police and the Assistant Mayor, each discussed rape from their own vantage point, but through the lens of literary theory. It worked as a performance on multiple levels. Visuality is important to me, but conceptual 'images' are equally so. I would venture to say that one of the most interesting aspects of presenting my work in art venues is a matter of seeking form.

Runo Lagomarsino

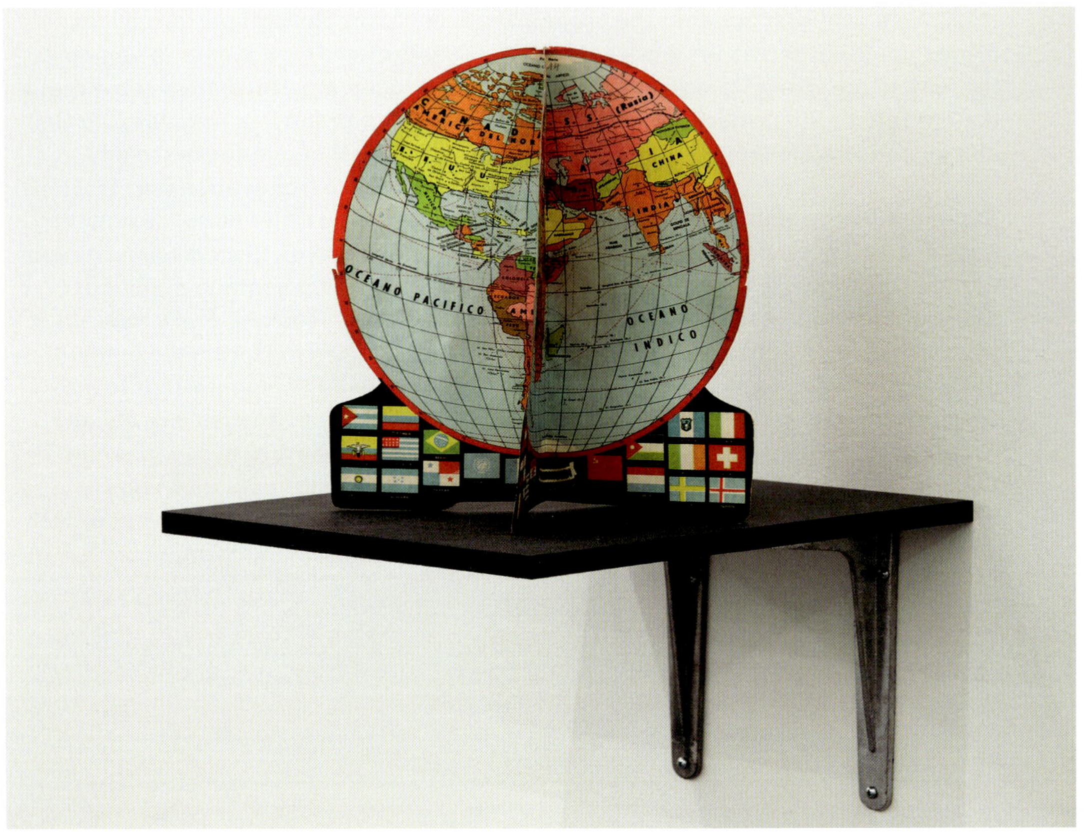

'In the north, politics has always been a dangerous sea.' João Guimarães Rosa

Above: Detail from *Las Casas Is Not a Home*, 2008–10
Photo: Terje Östlind

Opposite: Booth Line Poster, *c.* 1920
Photo: Liverpool Record Office, Liverpool Libraries

Following pages:
Baía do Guajará, 2012

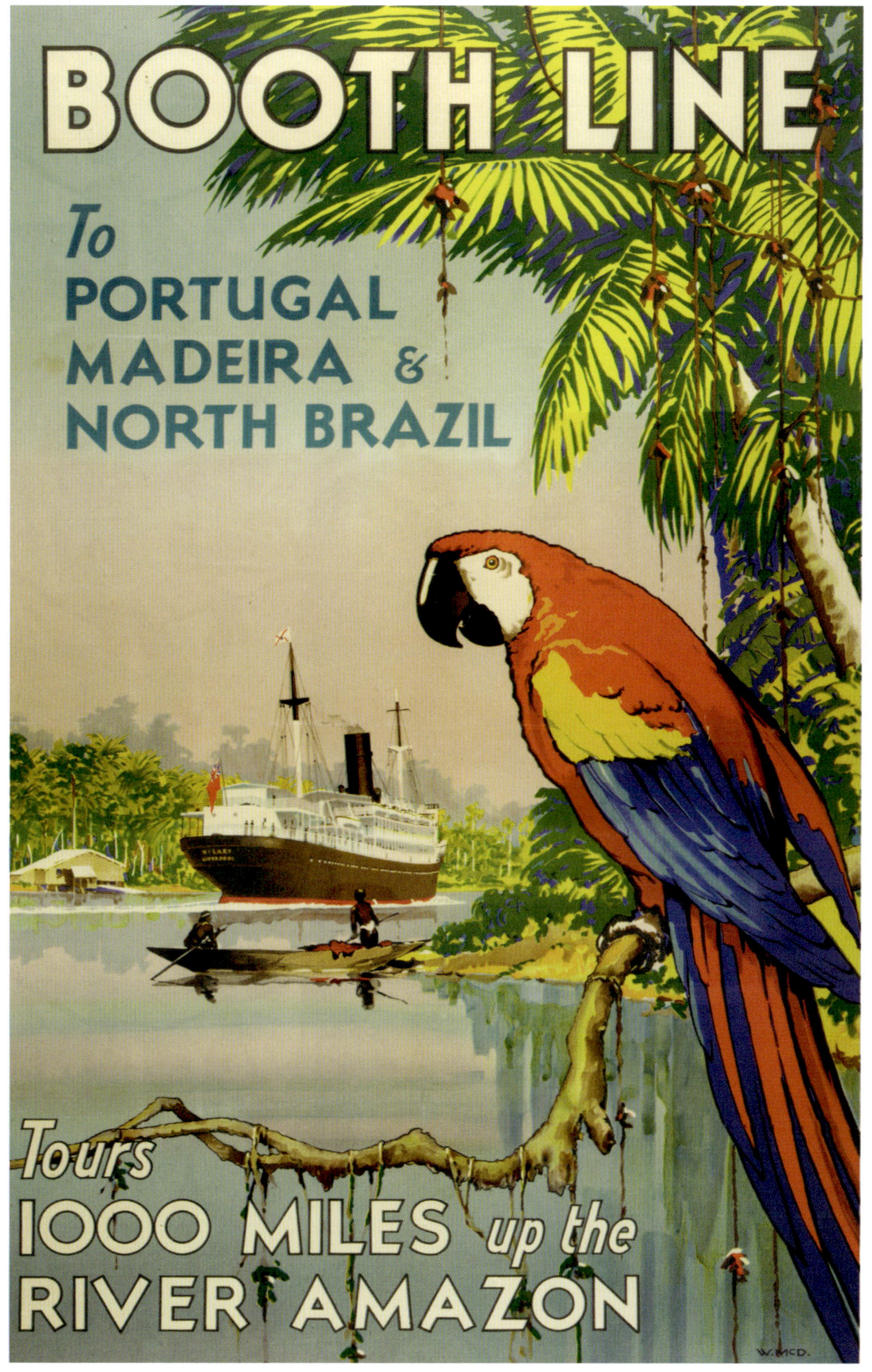

BOOTH LINE
To
PORTUGAL
MADEIRA &
NORTH BRAZIL
Tours
1000 MILES up the
RIVER AMAZON
W. McD.

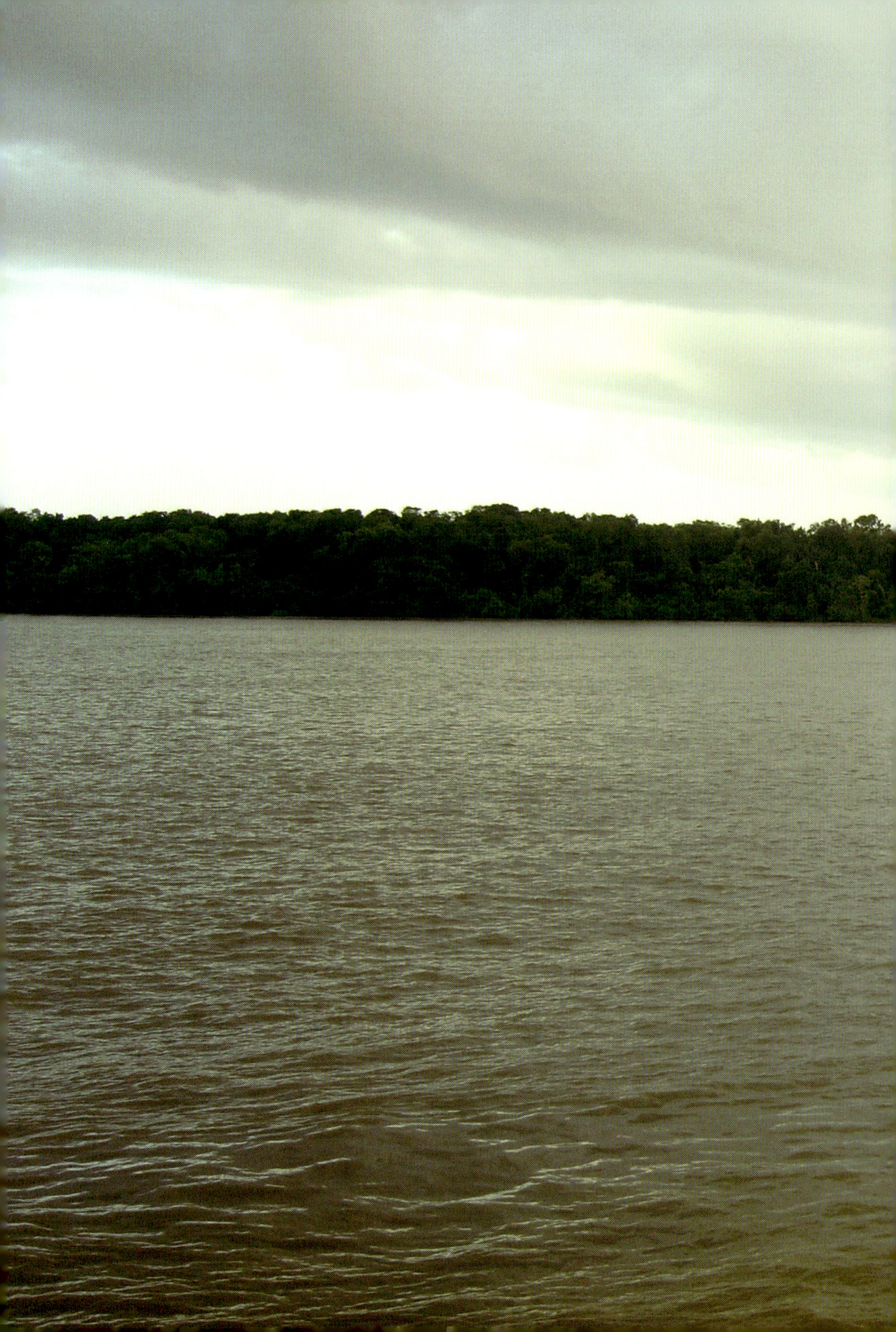

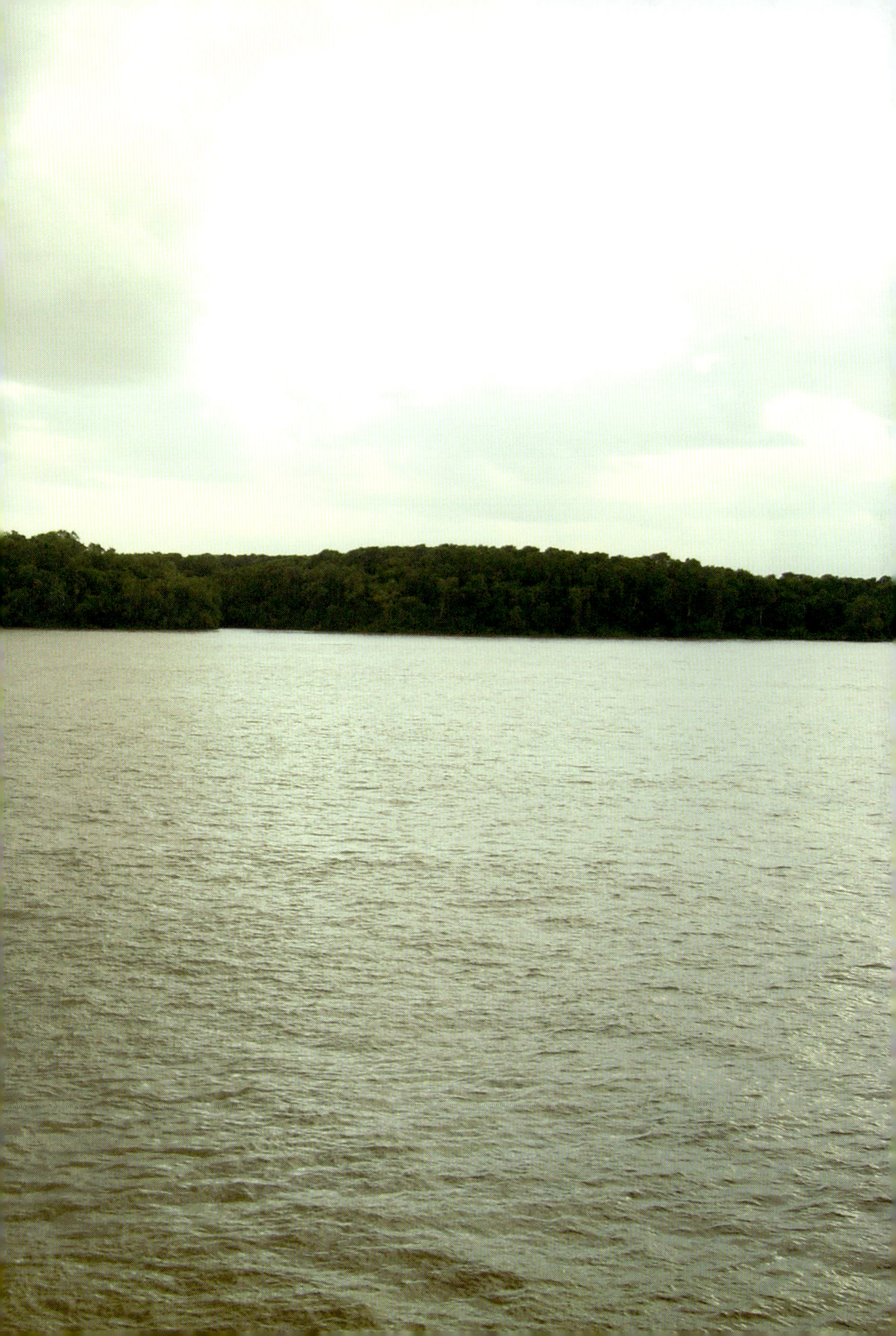

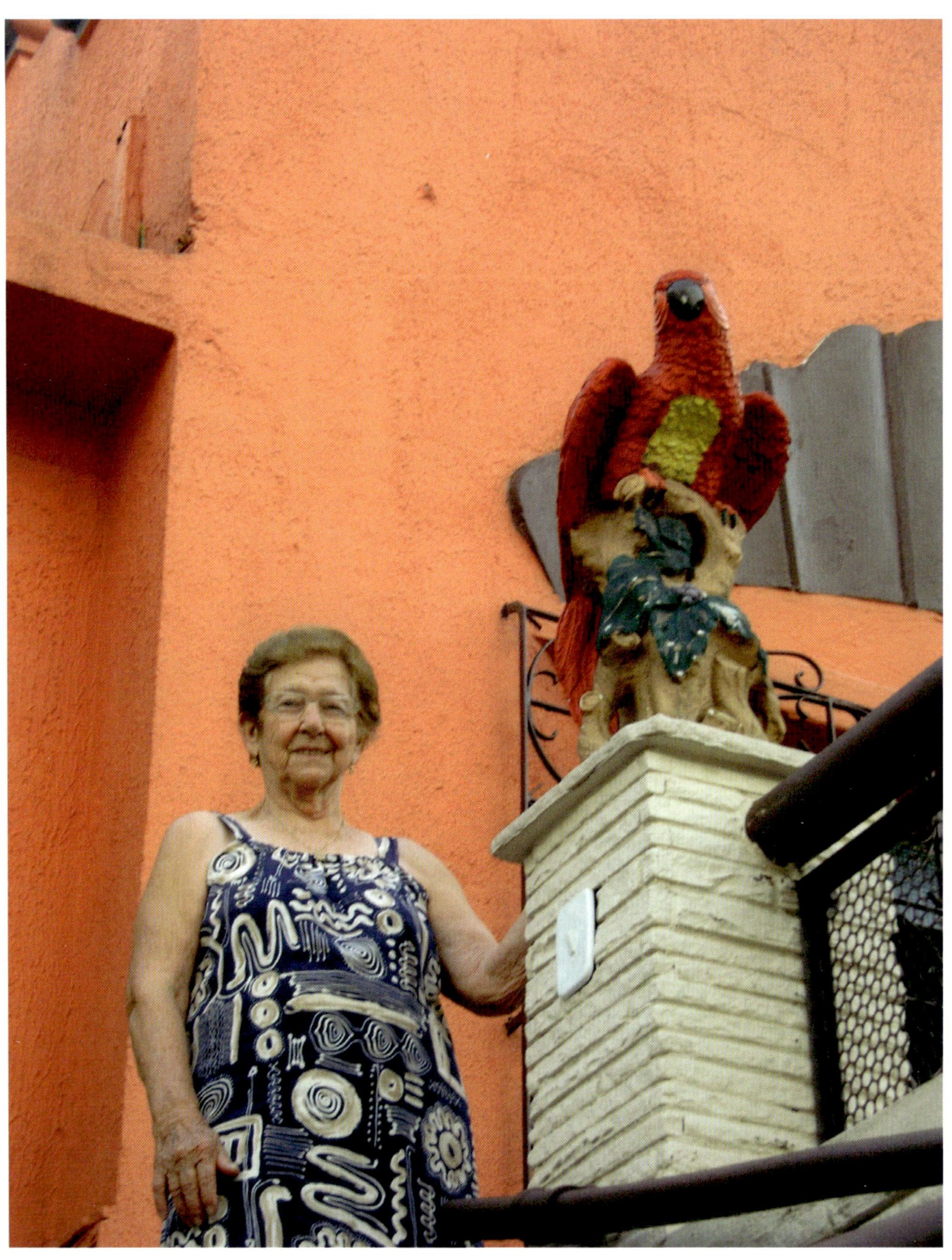

Above: *An Offensive Object in the Least Offensive Way*, Antonia Strazza Prudente
with her macaw, painted by her daughter Neide Prudente. At Rua Desembargador
dos Vale, São Paulo, 2012

Opposite: *Untitled (Leo can't change the world)*, 2011

Leo
não consegue mudar o mundo

either can Romo

Jorge Macchi

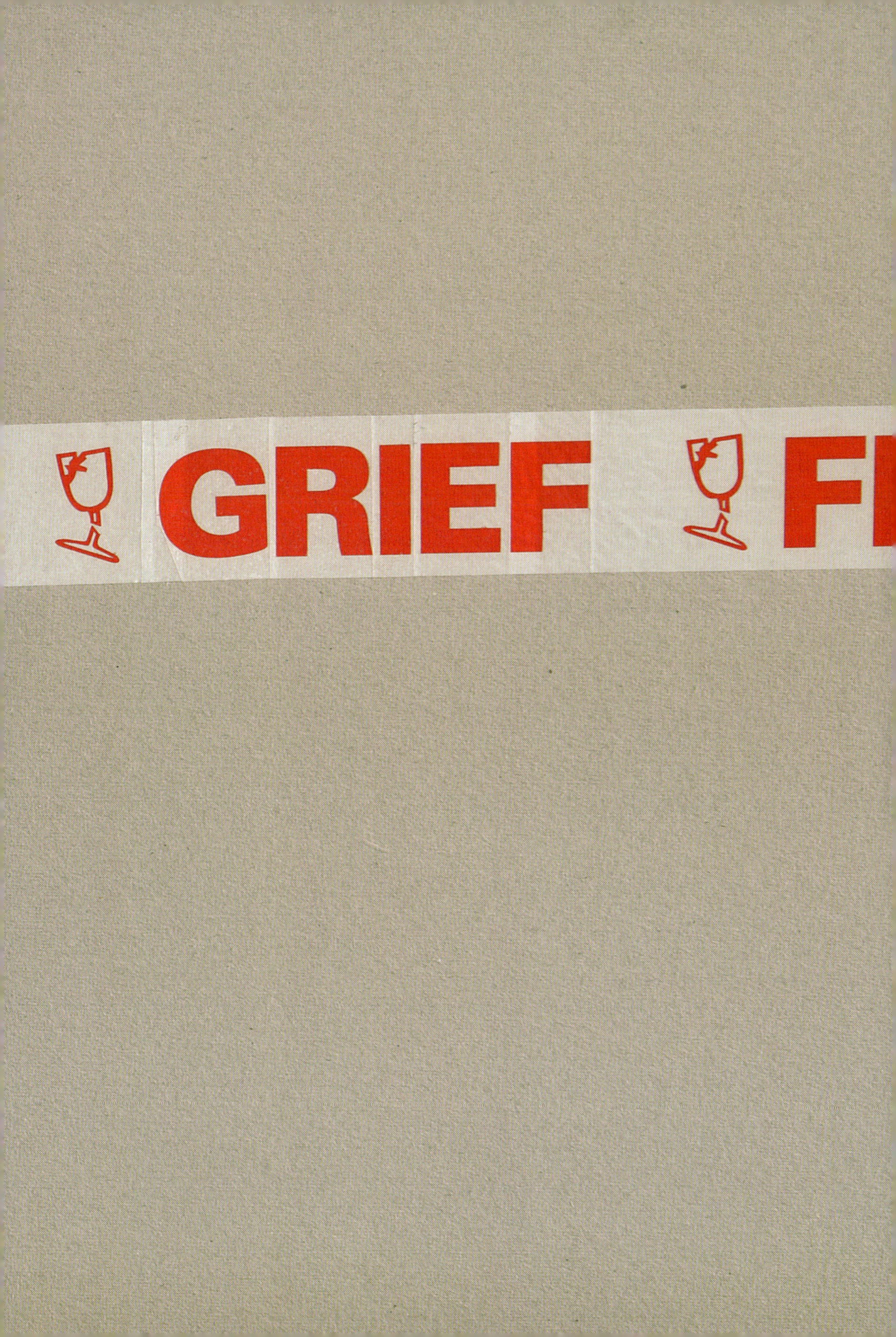

GRIEF
FI

Dane Mitchell

Spirits Lifted
Emily Cormack

Sometimes, in my mind, I see a street from the town where I grew up. Stanley Street. It bears no relevance to me; nothing significant happened there. No momentous childhood happenings or adult crises. It is just there, a ghost street driving across my mind.

In 1999, several people on Bold Street in Liverpool reported a similar slippage in time. Finding themselves surrounded by people dressed in clothing from the 1940s, it was as if they had glimpsed, just for a minute, a world that resides alongside our own. These moments of transparency and overlap between intersecting realities offer evidence (more emotional than legal) of a 'something more'. Despite their being nonsensical, these mutable realities are complete in their fleeting immersion, pointing to the possibility of a non-linear and even spectral version of our 'now'. Taunted by these sensory inferences, we are led to believe that the world is more than our skin and the pain that we feel when we pinch it.

Often it is said that when we die we simply move through to 'another room'. That implies that if we were to tap on our walls we might make out the shapes and feel for the pressures and presences of the dead. If only this were so. If only each world sat neatly adjacent to the other, providing a reflection like inverse twins. These worlds would offer a concrete idea of 'here' and 'there', suggesting that the real and the unreal could be so easily cleaved into distinct and separate spaces. But our desire to diagrammatize existence is futile. How unlike life are the neat circular bubbles of the Venn diagram with their perfect equidistant overlaps? Likewise, ghost stories attempt to organize our awareness into distinct narrative spaces, separating our worlds and creating a safe distance that divides 'our narrative from theirs'. But there is too much shared ground, too many semiotic and spectral escapees to truly delineate with such certainty.

The dead dwell in all kinds of places, spilling from our attempts at containment. Monuments, grave stones and crypts try to stunt the dead's seepage into our everyday, sealing them in with stone parentheses. But there they are, offering themselves up to us in the words of a ballad, in the rain on an autumn afternoon, or in a pocket of air released from a long-closed box. Intangible conjurings of the passed infiltrate the present and we are caught off guard by the completeness with which the dead immerse us in that other world. The world that the grieving person wishes was as simple as a room next door, or a line on a floorplan. But the dead are infamous shape-shifters: they are not anchored by monuments or contained by ghost stories, and they will not dwell in the spaces we build for them. Instead they hover on thresholds, wearing thin the tread that divides.

Overwhelming Presence

~ SITE ~

Liverpool — Walton Junction Station

~ TYPE ~

Haunting Manifestation

~ DATE / TIME ~

1970s onwards

~ FURTHER COMMENTS ~

It is said that ever since the last
steam engine left this site, an evil,
repressive presence has descended upon
the area.

Flag Waver

Liverpool — Area around former
Otterspool rail station

Haunting Manifestation

Unknown

Before closing in 1951, a teenager was
saved by a man from being hit by a train,
although the rescuer was killed in the
process. He is said to wave a red warning
flag in the area.

Time Slip

Liverpool — Bold Street

Other

1999

On various dates, several people {including an off-duty policeman} have reported slipping back in time along this road, finding themselves surrounded by people dressed in clothing of the 1940s, with a cobbled street and old-style shops.

Mirage

Liverpool — Skies above town

Other

27 September 1846

A white city appeared for a short time over Liverpool — it was thought to be a mirage of Edinburgh, though no one could identify any of the buildings.

Cloudy Woman

Liverpool — The Grange Hotel, Aigburth {no longer operating}

Haunting Manifestation

March 2002

While staying at this hotel, one man twice spotted a cloudy shape in the form of a woman, although her features were hard to define. Both times the entity walked past the man and disappeared into a wall.

Sabelo Mlangeni

Hospitality used to be an integral part of the black South African daily life. When you were young, one of the first things you learned was *ubuntu*, which means: 'You are what you are because of the generosity of others.' This philosophy has changed over time as people have become more self-serving. *Ubuntu* is particularly relevant to a photographer because you rely on the generosity of others for your own work.

Men Only is a series that I photographed in 2008–9 at the George Goch hostel on the East Rand of Johannesburg. Built in 1961 to house migrant mineworkers, the hostel is today home to taxi-drivers and security guards, among the many who move to Johannesburg to better their lives. Only men are allowed in such hostels, and in our collective imagination they are places of violence, sexual abuse and illegal trafficking. They are also places where the legacy of apartheid is still clearly evident, in spite of the eighteen years of democracy. I spent several weeks in the hostel, sharing the daily routines of the tenants as I worked. As time went by, and they became comfortable with my presence, my camera became invisible. They shared their food and they even gave me a bed to sleep in; I became one of them. In this context, I was welcomed, I blended in. It was perhaps our shared race, language and gender that made it easy for them to accept me; their generosity stretched beyond what I could have ever imagined.

In contrast, my recent series *My Storie* was photographed in Bertrams. Founded in 1889, it is one of Johannesburg's oldest suburbs. In recent years, it has become a poor community, characterized by dilapidated buildings, illegal immigrants, squatters, drug dealers, thieves and refugees. I became interested in this community and what was left behind after the move of wealthy white people to the northern suburbs after apartheid was abolished. As a black photographer, I was interested in photographing the remaining white residents in their homes, yet most of the subjects didn't allow me inside their homes, and in the five months I spent in Bertrams there seemed to be a barrier that I could not breach. Only one image was taken indoors; all the other photographs were captured from outside. The easiest way to explain the distance between us is race. I don't believe this is the only reason I couldn't get access to their homes, but it remains the only obvious one.

The question of hospitality needs to be contextualized. How do you give a photographer permission to photograph you in unfavourable conditions? Is someone offering you coffee being hospitable? How do you approach *ubuntu* in the face of an increasingly modernized society?

Mark Morrisroe

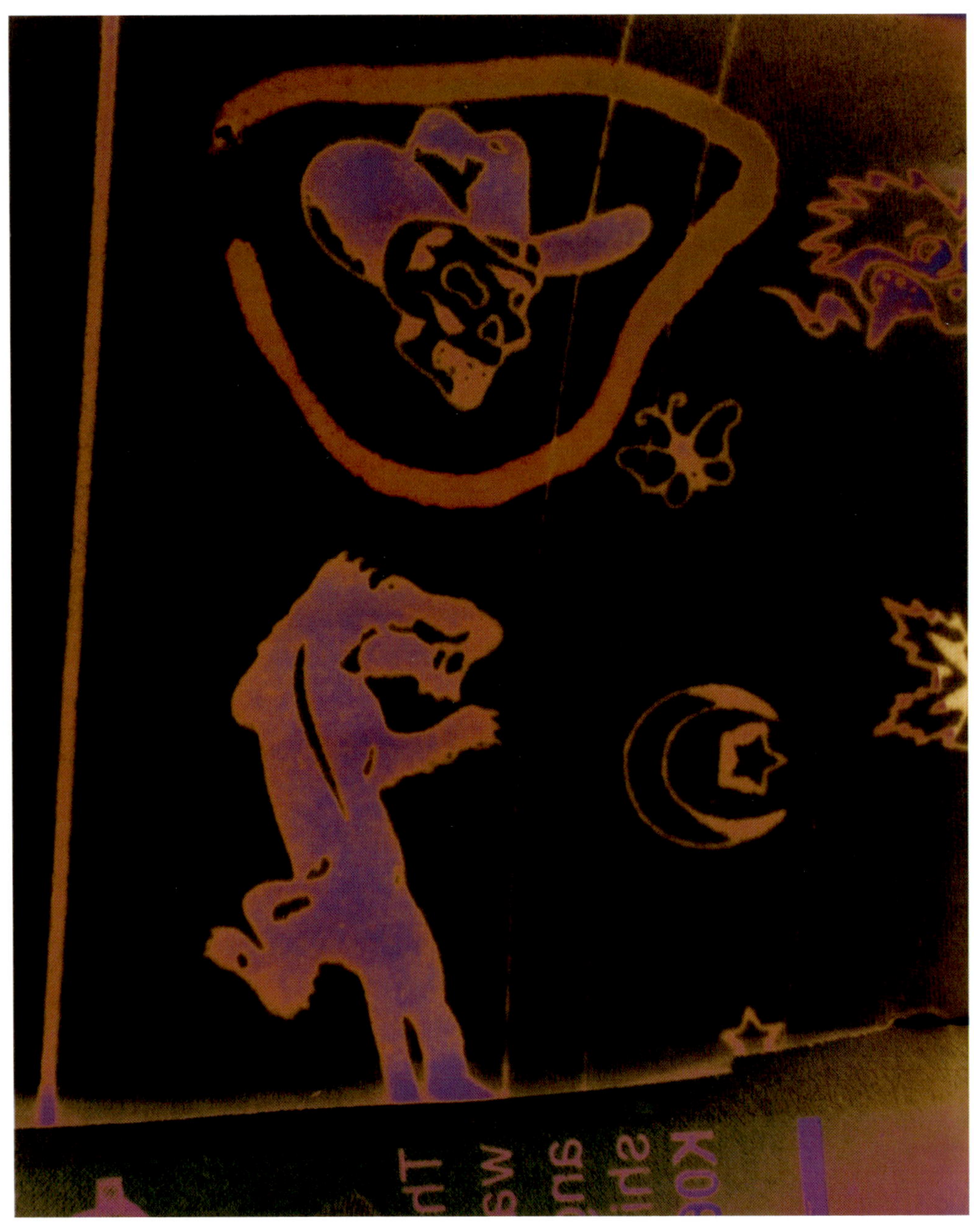

Untitled, 1986
C-print, photogram of printed material, 35.7 × 27.9 cm

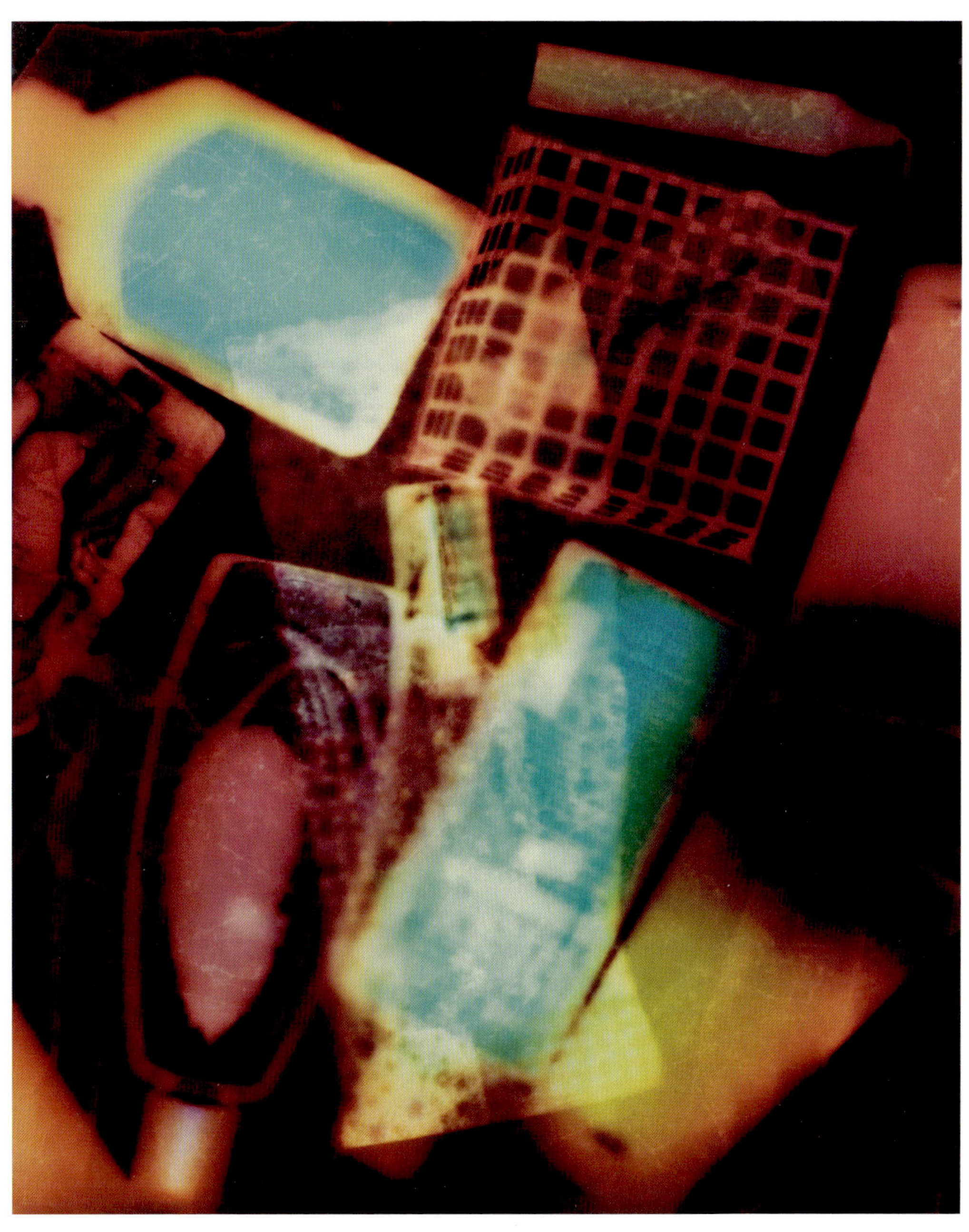

*Untitled, c.*1987
C-print, photogram, 35.6×27.8 cm

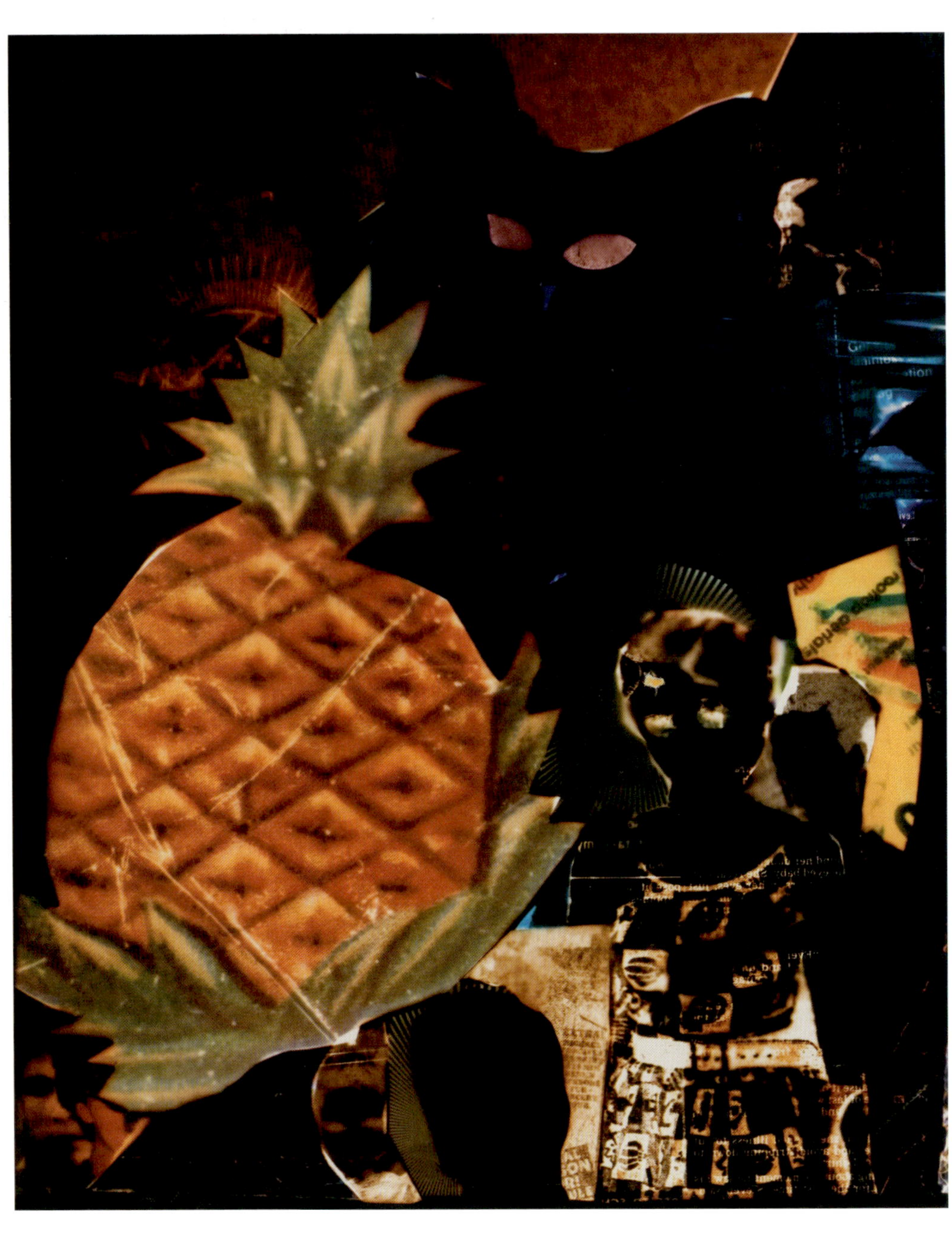

Untitled, c. 1987
C-print, photogram, 35.7 × 28 cm

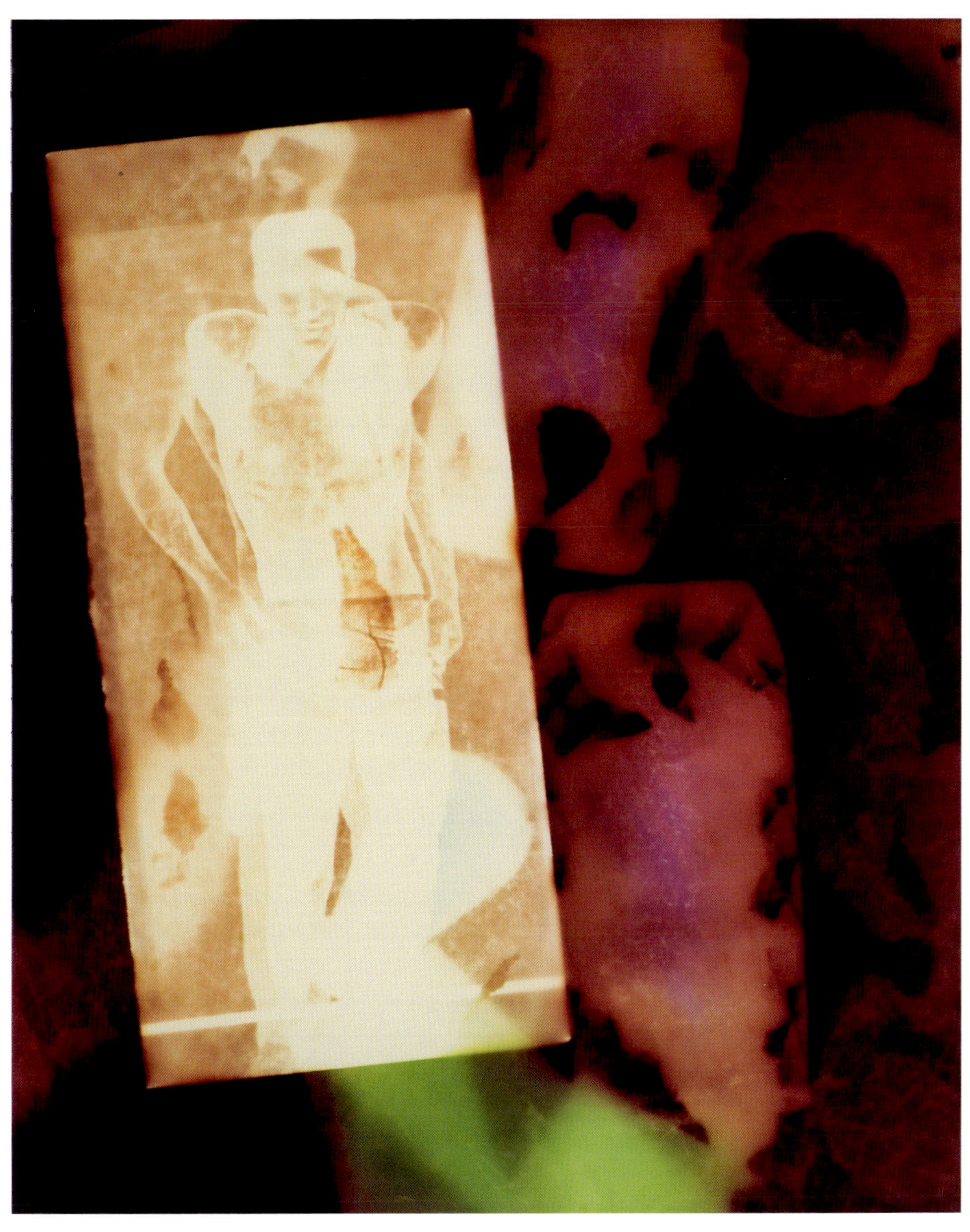

*Untitled, c.*1987
C-print, photogram of printed material, 35.8×28 cm

Patrick Murphy

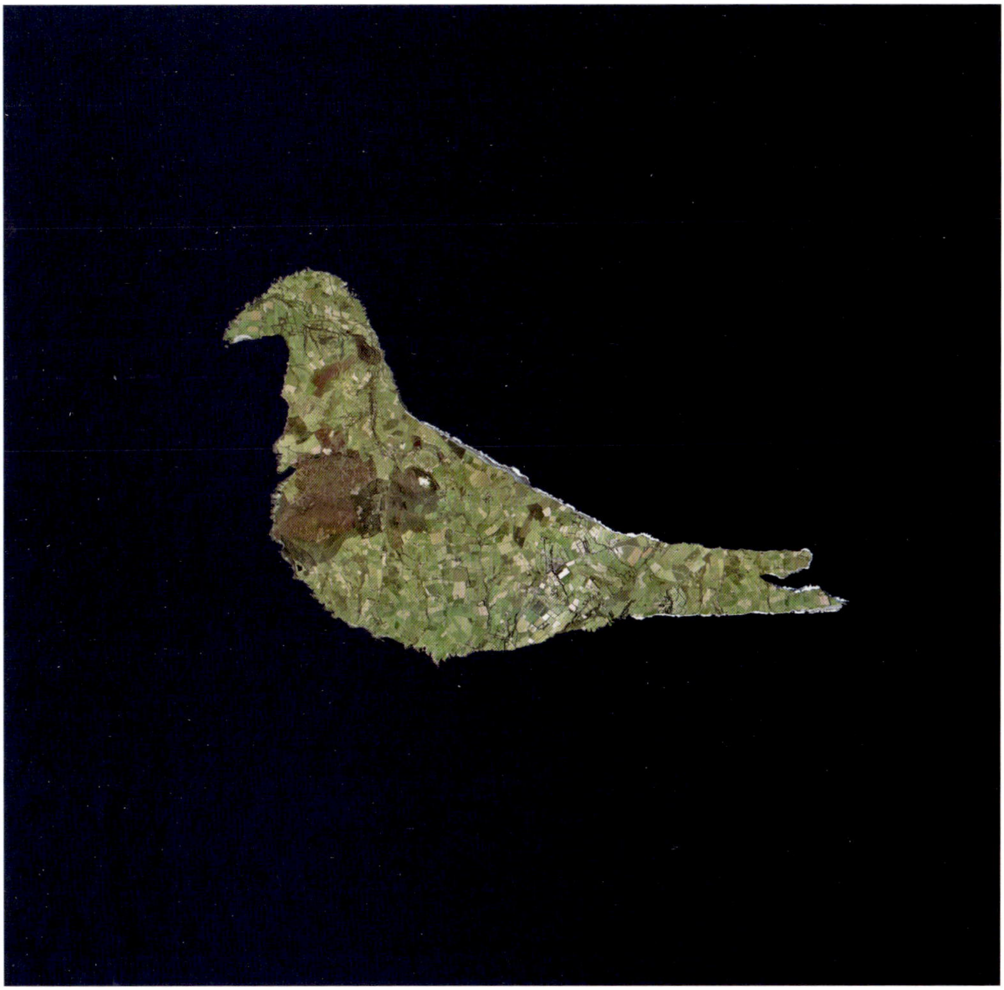

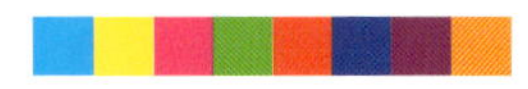

Columbidae Livia, 2012
C-print, digital composition, 80×80 cm

Following pages
Columbidae Livia, Migration, 2012
Digital composition

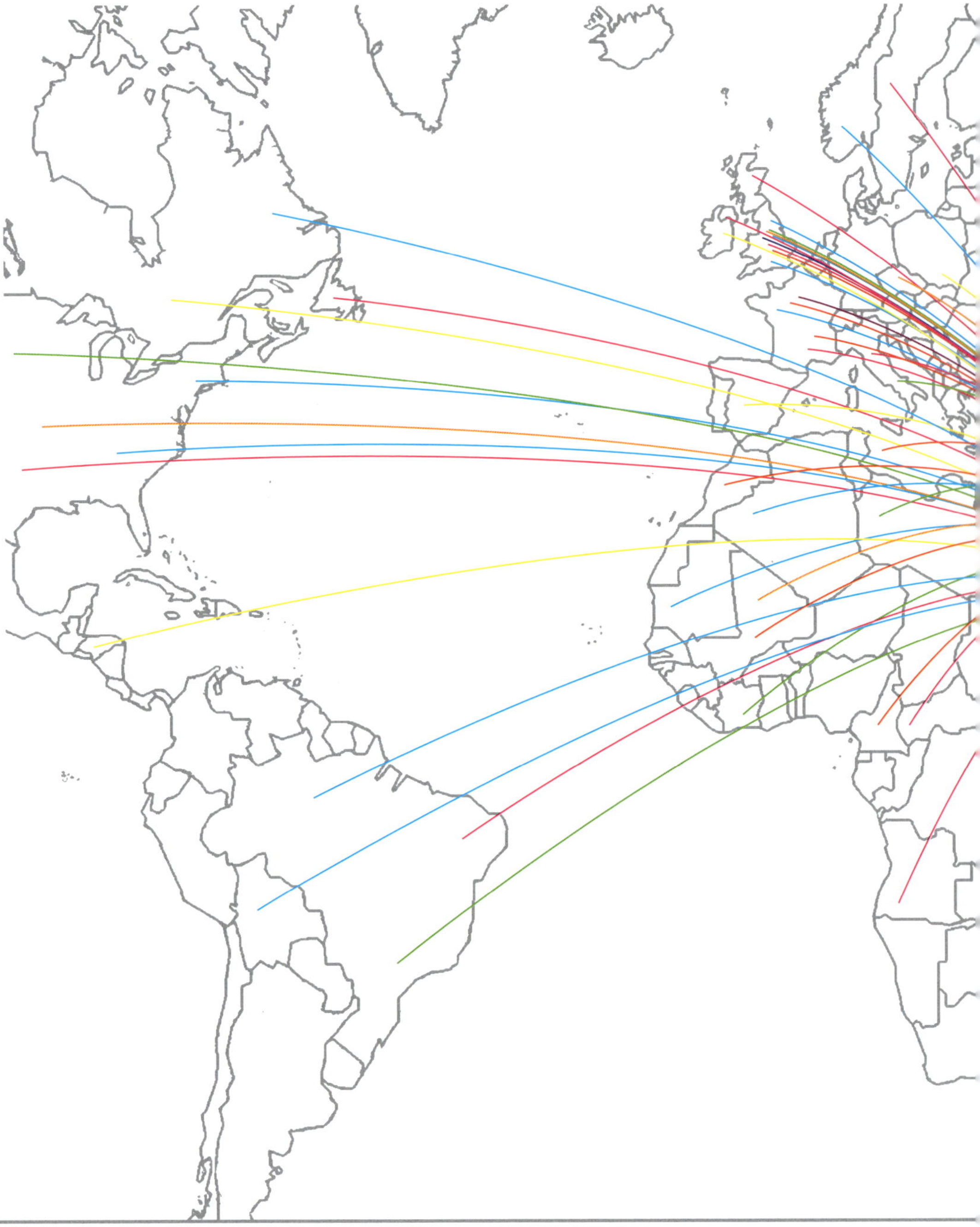

GENUS/SPECIES

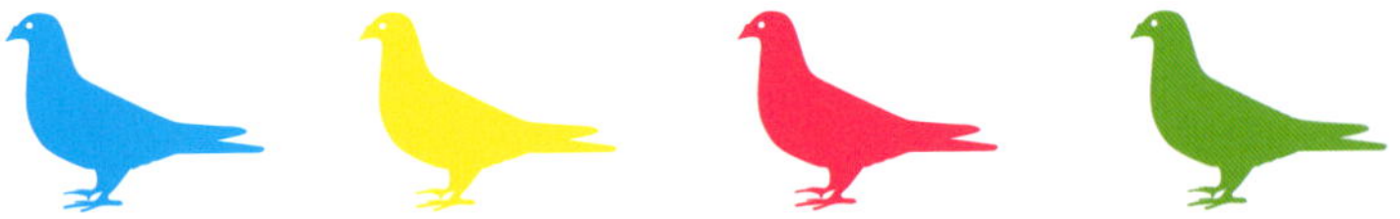

FLAVO
Columbidae

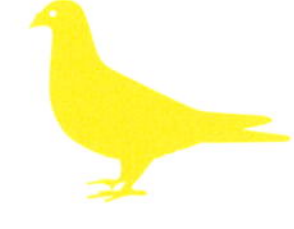
CAESITAS
Columbidae

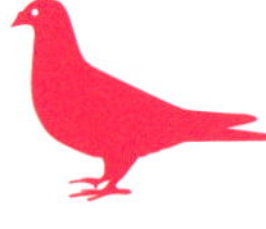
RUBESCO
Columbidae

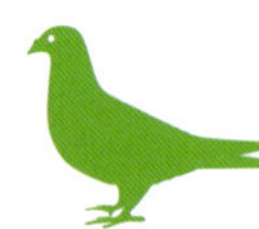
VIRIDI
Columbidae

COLUMBIDAE LIVIA MIGRATION ROUTES

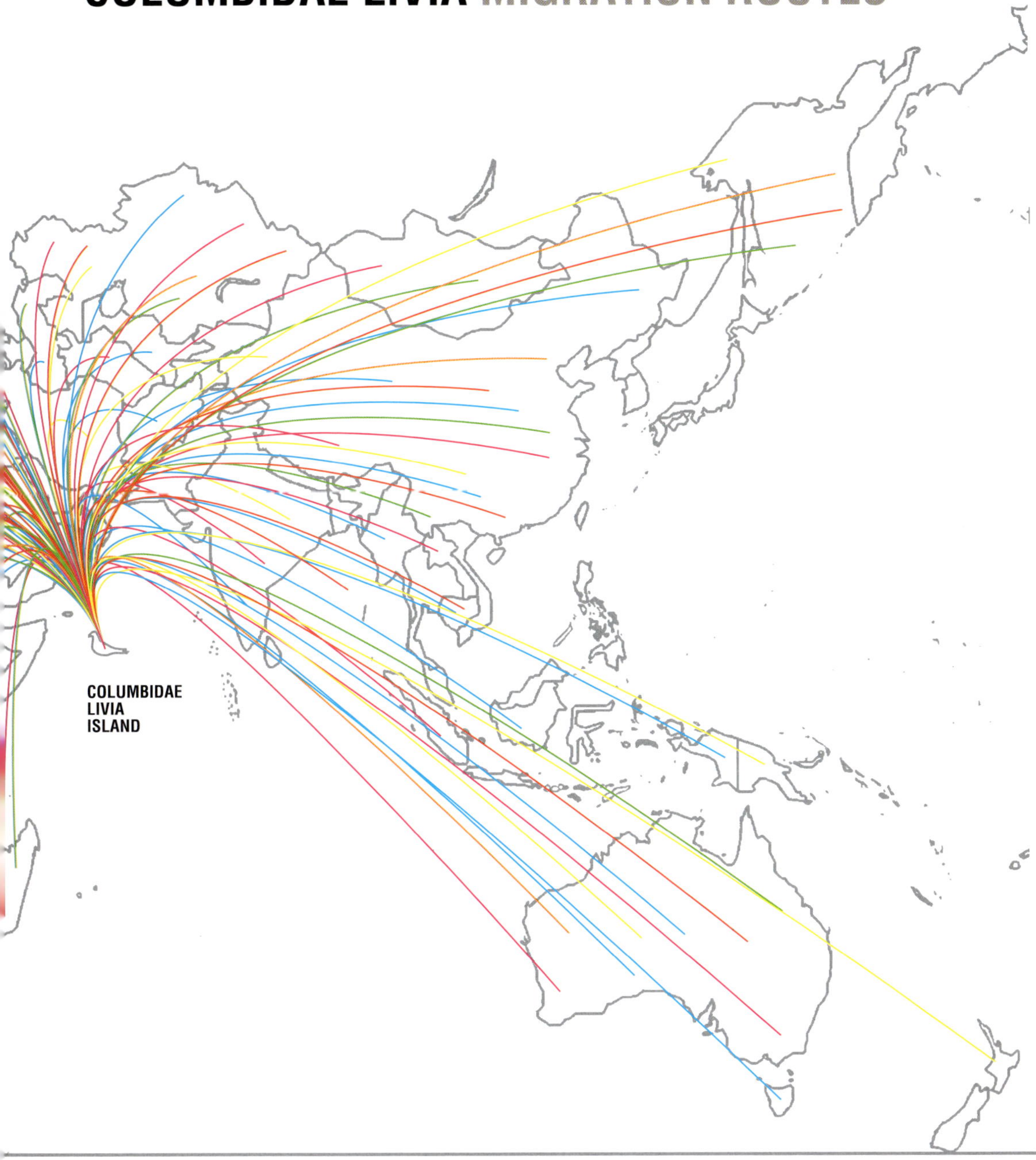

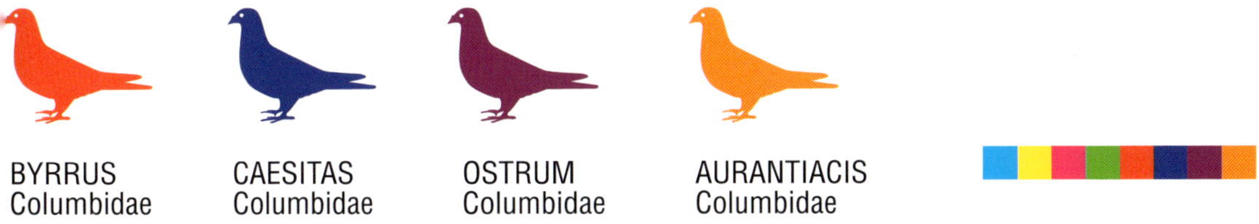

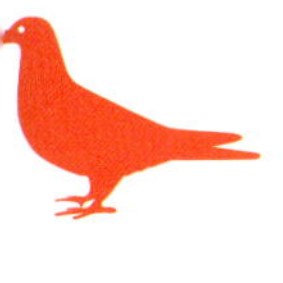

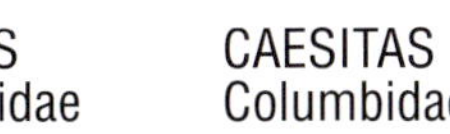

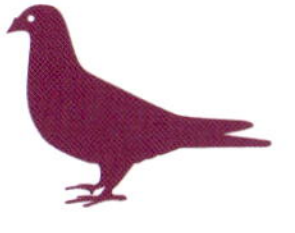

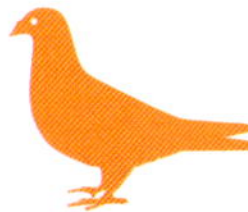

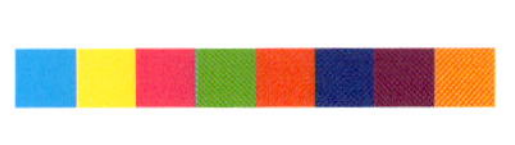

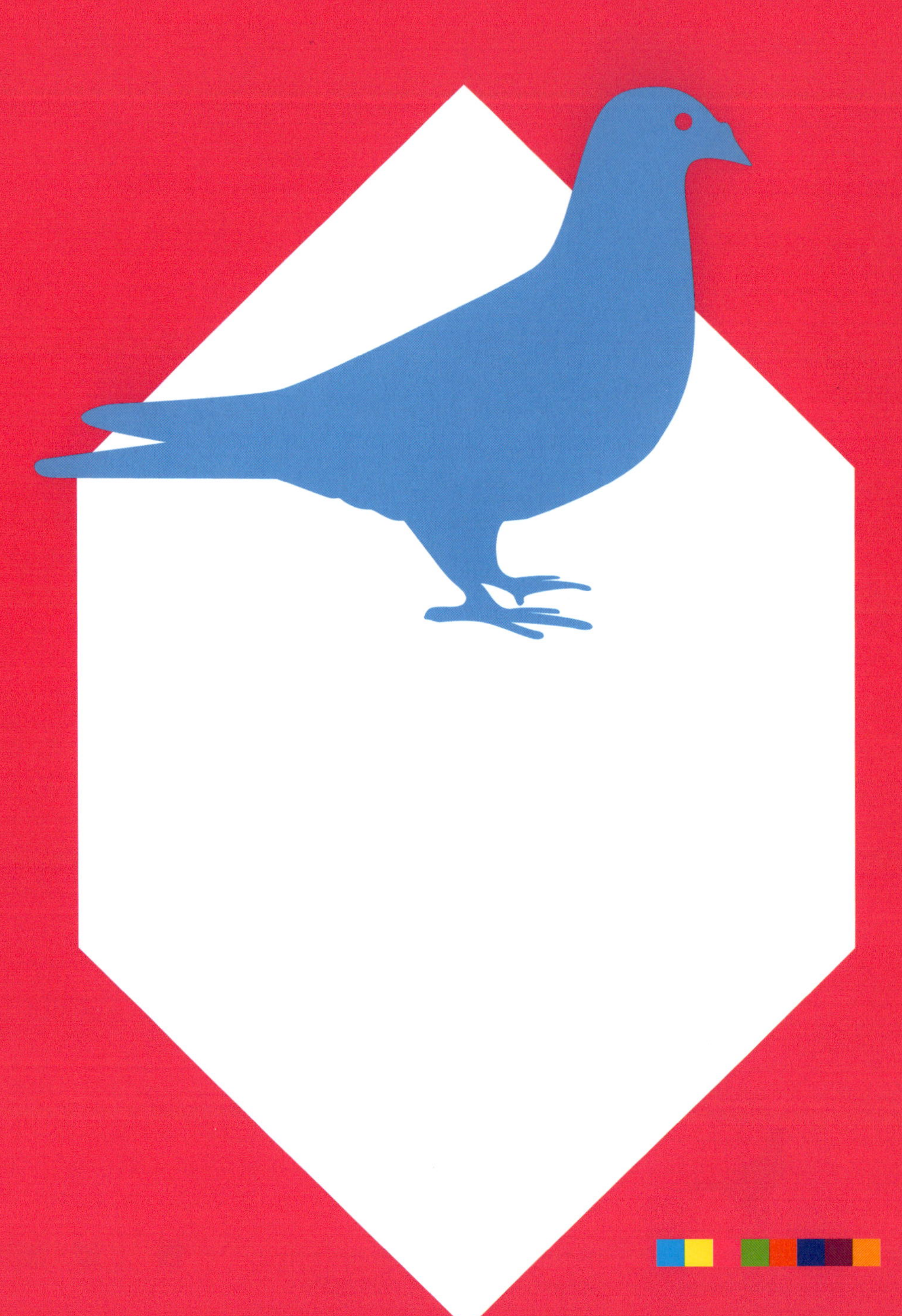

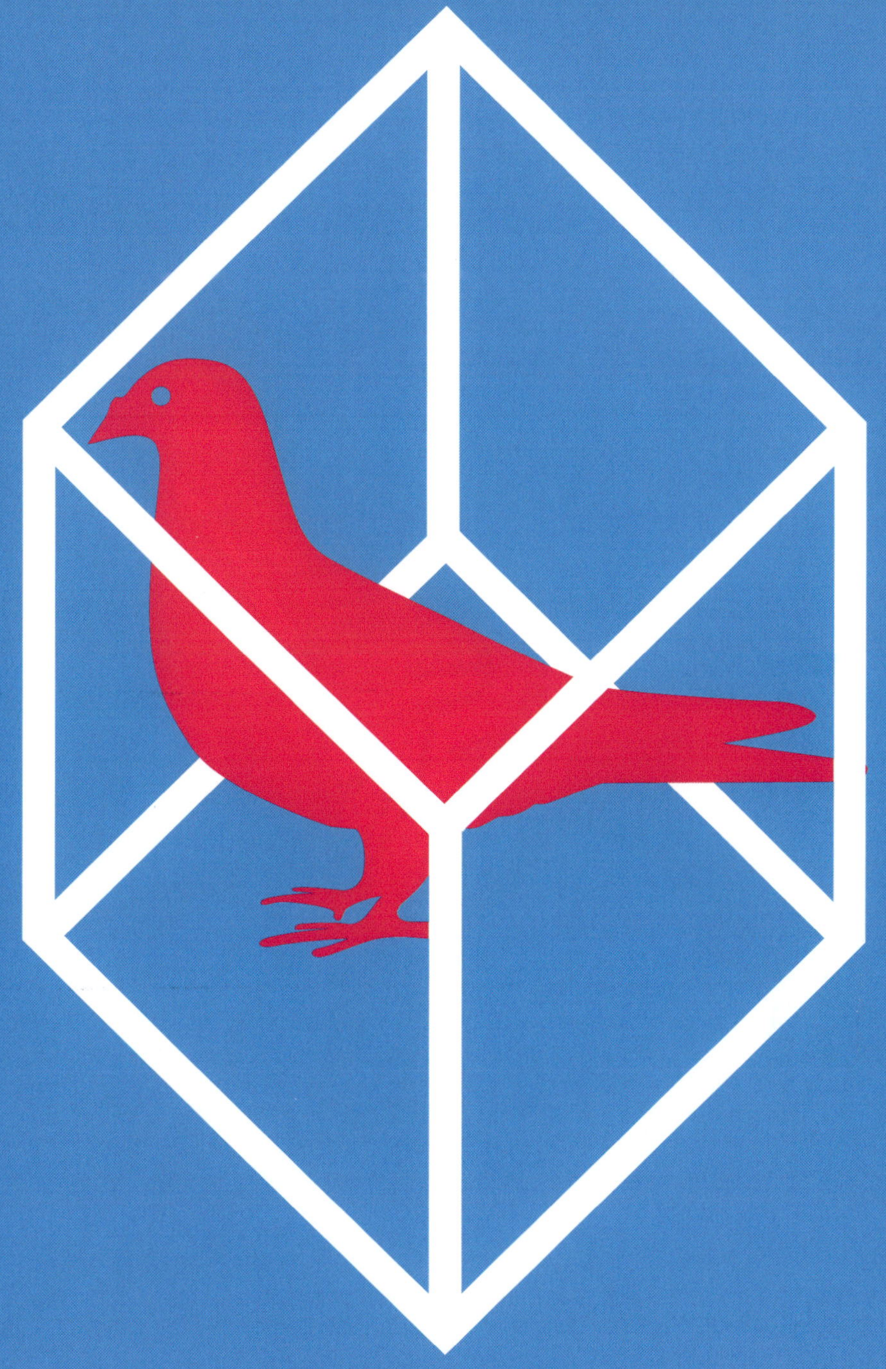

Above: *Struggle*, 2012
C-print, digital composition (detail), 80×80 cm

Opposite: *Freedom*, 2012
C-print, digital composition (detail), 80×80 cm

Ahmet Öğüt

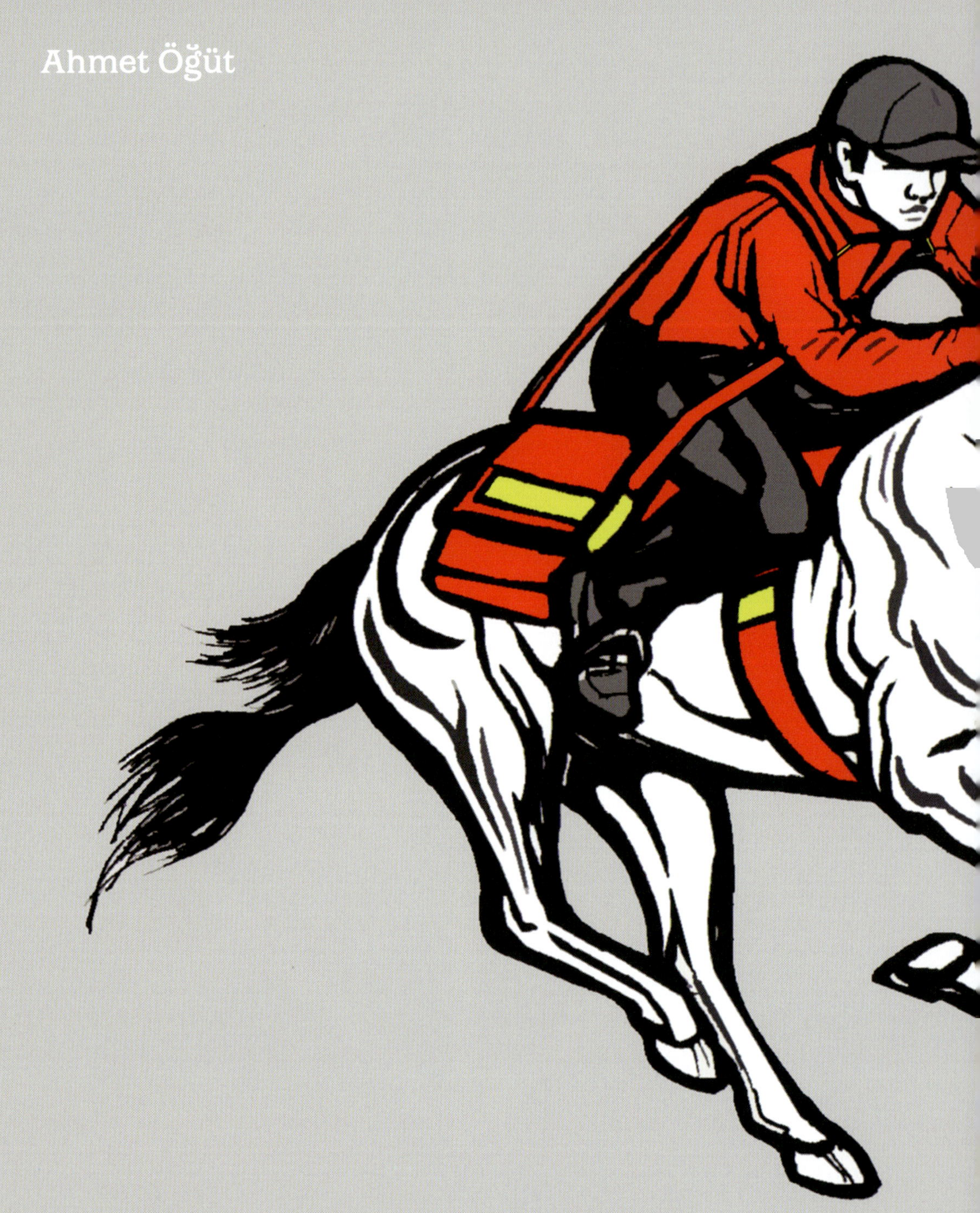

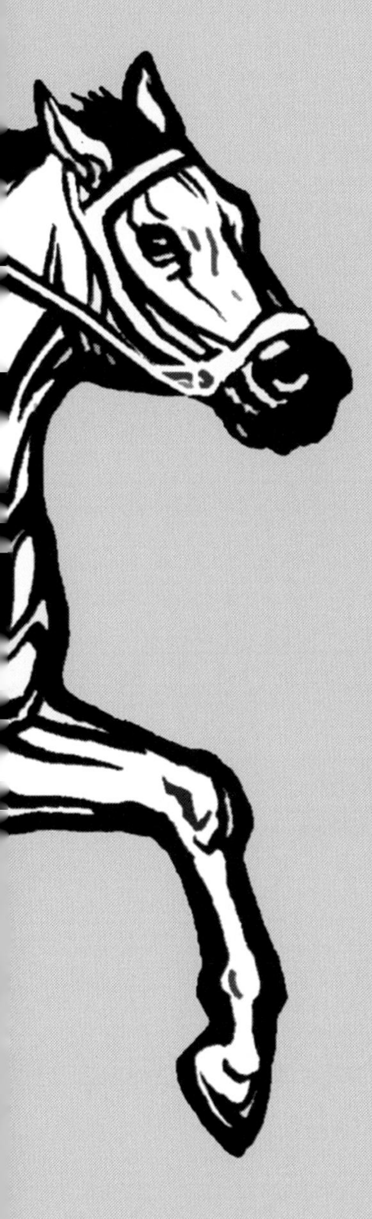

AND DIDN'T STOP.

Trevor Paglen

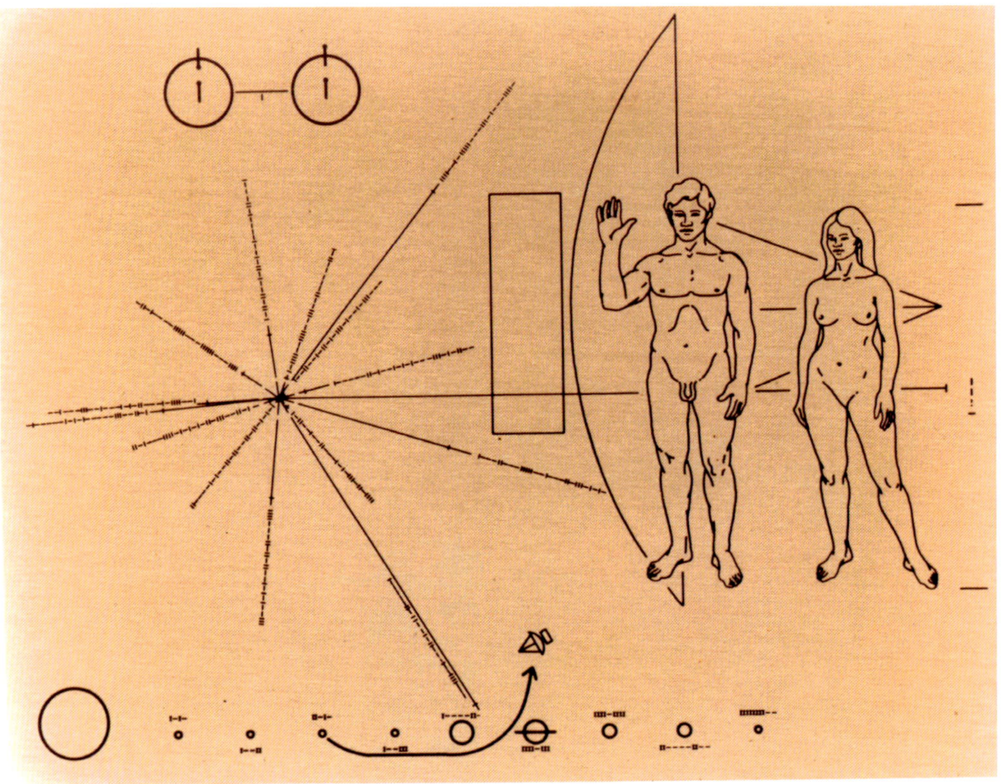

The plaques placed on board NASA's *Pioneer* missions of the early 1970s are objects of much ridicule. Designed as a postcard for any wandering extraterrestrials who may come across the spacecraft as it traverses the galaxy, the plaques are meant to show something about who we are (or were), where we came from, and what we looked like. Charges against the plaque: 'It is sexist!' (perhaps); 'It is racist!' (maybe); 'It is pornographic!' (this was an actual objection); 'It gives aggressive aliens a map to Earth!' (another actual objection); 'It is anthropocentric!' (indubitably); 'It is nonsense!' (almost certainly); 'It is the work of dreamers!' (definitely).

The critics won. And we stopped crafting letters for the future and stopped marking our spacecraft with little bits of dreamy, nonsensical humanity. We still throw bottles from island Earth into the cosmic sea, but they contain no words. We absolved ourselves of sending the wrong message. Sometimes I fear that in doing so, we've absolved ourselves of the future itself.

Christodoulos Panayiotou

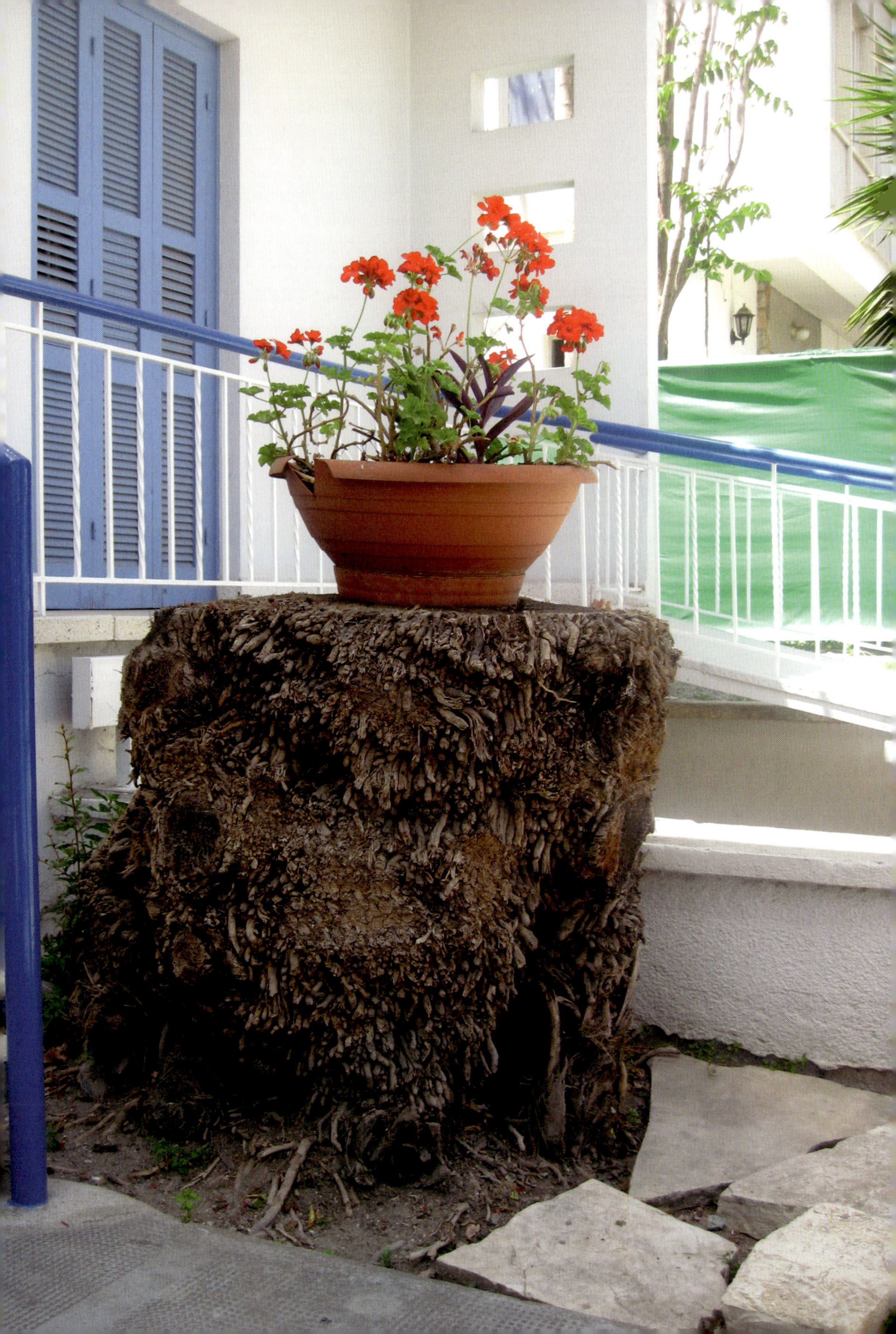

Pedro Reyes
interviewed by Omar Kholeif

It seems to me that the theme of hospitality is intrinsic to you as a person, do you agree?

I am very interested in the notion of encounter. This is an idea present in group therapy, and in theatre, as well as in pedagogy. It has to do with opportunities in which people can meet outside of work or organized religion, outside of familial or commercial situations, and even outside of the bounds of friendship. The idea of the 'encounter experience' is the fact that you can have very meaningful meetings with total strangers, where you can find pleasure, learn about yourself, and find useful elements to overcome personal problems.

What are the kinds of techniques that you use?

There are a number of techniques to running encounters, which I have studied. I am especially interested in Jacob Levy Moreno and Kurt Lewin, who in the 1930s made amazing discoveries that came to a formative height in the 1960s. Some were like encounter marathons where a number of people were locked in a room for twenty-four hours to get to know each other. There were also what you might call fantasy encounter games for a group of people to get together, in a sort of fiction. There are extremely useful tools to be found in Paulo Freire as well as in Agusto Boal's Theatre of the Oppressed, which I use in many workshops.

These kinds of activities, I believe, allow the individual a means to access their creative forces. It's also a mechanism by which to activate your spontaneity. Spontaneity is a key concept here – it is a basic energy of life. Spontaneity helps the group to arrive at many discoveries. Now all of this relational thinking has much to do with hospitality. These forums are about welcoming others into a game, a warm-up process that leads to engagement.

This notion of play seems to go hand in hand with this?

Play is essential here. When strangers meet there is the possibility of disclosing personal facts about one's own life that can elicit deeper personal reflections. It is about accelerating individual growth. I believe that many aspects of one's life can become stunted – underdeveloped or stuck. Speaking with a stranger is an example (and I'm not talking about trivial questions about the weather here), but this precise activity to connect with strangers is designed to open up new means of communicating, untapping a sense of awareness. This can increase or decrease your levels of consciousness. This is of course guided by cycles – some people will bring you up and down. But essentially, what I'm trying to get to here is the idea that a carefully designed interaction can help two or more persons to increase their awareness and their agency, without having to rely on the guidance of a professional or expert.

You mention spontaneity and yet you also talk about this almost telepathic presupposition during an encounter

between strangers. But some of the modalities that you use in your work, such as, for example, speed-dating scenarios, are actually much more choreographed?

That's right, to arrive to spontaneity and creativeness, you need to have a warm-up process, and the game has to be framed within a set of rules. You mentioned speed-dating, which is a structure similar to running a workshop, where you get people to work in pairs and then rotate, changing partners. It's now also used in other environments, for instance, group meetings of architects and clients, that conduct these short introductions. I do use some of these group dynamics to try to customize them into therapeutic encounters.

How is this reflected in the formulation of your projects?

When I do projects that involve participation, most often they will be activated by volunteers or temporary workers – it's good to have horizontal structures where everyone can take the lead, as well as follow. In this way, the procedure is the protagonist, and the outcome cannot be any better or worse than if it were conducted by a professional or by an amateur.

But you play the role of the facilitator yourself sometimes?

Yes, but as the initiator or artist am aware that when I facilitate a project I will receive numerous questions. It actually happened to me recently; I was expected to be the resource for answers. To counter this, when we were sitting in a circle I asked the person on my left if they had a question, and instead of answering the question myself, I deferred it to the person on *his left* to answer. The person who answered then asks another question, continuing until everyone in the circle has both asked and answered. This exercise is helpful to show the resourcefulness of the group and its independence from a single leader. This is crucial to my understanding of hospitality. You must create a scenario, whereby you become the host, but without overasserting your power. Let's think about the Occupy movement, for example. It is a hospitalitarian structure, in the sense that anyone can join; you just need to go with a piece of cardboard and join the parade – put out your own voice, your own message; it's a lot about inclusiveness. We live in an era of leaderless leadership, where we have movements that are spontaneous to a large extent and that have certain forms that allow everyone to join in without having to subscribe to a particular creed. But there is one problem here, and that is that these groups are focused largely on the rejection of something. The minute you have to describe the world you want, instead of the world you have (your vision for the future, say), you realize that it's necessary to have clarity and persuasion. Here comes the notion of desire. Desire is very important because it's the combination of vision and purpose.

You're trying to activate collective decision-making?

You can either focus on the problem or the solution. If you focus on the problem, then you think 'the system is wrong, because of this and that', etc., and then you congratulate yourself for putting forward your 'institutional critique'. But this is very different from saying 'How do I want it to be?' One of my favourite quotes from Kurt Lewin says, 'You cannot understand a system until you try to change it.' So I would say that art can be a great resource, not only to institutional critique but to 'Institutional Agency'. So you have a desirable change, and you ask yourself, 'How are we going to get there?' You see? It's an entirely different mindset. When you are rejecting the system, your mind is passive, because you're focusing on 'No! I don't want this, I reject this', but when you are focusing on the solution, your mind is active, because you need to readjust all the time. You say, 'If this doesn't work, let's try something else', and so on. I think it's essential to increase the toolbox of these movements so you have activities that allow this creative decision-making.

You touched upon the Occupy movement, which brings me to a question I wanted to ask you: is 'occupation' a form of hospitality?

Occupation means the intervention of an unwelcome guest. It depends on the context where the word is used; there could be pacifist occupation, such as the Occupy movement, but we could also be talking about a military occupation, these are two very different contexts. The media was talking about the 'Iraqi war', but those who were aware of the arbitrary decision to invade Iraq would use the term 'Iraqi occupation'.

Say we are talking about the case of Israel and Palestine, where one is seen as an occupier and another as a guest – the notion of hospitality in this scenario depends on your standpoint; who is the host? Which leads me to

the question, could one argue that the hospitable and the inhospitable go hand in hand?

When you have an occupation, the tension between the two groups is enhanced because there are fewer spaces or opportunities for conviviality. If you have spaces for conviviality, you start to break down the projection of hatred, anger and rejection. Conviviality allows you to build bonds and empathy.

How is that achieved?

It's not just about putting people together, but also about having a 'method' for activating and running these spaces – that is to say, gradually building trust, and leading into conflict resolution. These techniques are not used enough. To give an example on a much more humble scale: I do workshops using the Theatre of the Oppressed with high-school teachers. On one occasion, we were resolving a conflict between the teacher's union and the president of the public-school system (in Mexico). The dean was ignoring their petition. We asked participants to take different roles – the roles of different characters – and we rescripted their positions, alleviating antagonism through role reversal. The end result was that instead of a straightforward petition, we made a symmetrical letter – a 'peace offering' letter of sorts. The teachers suggested in this case that if they managed to decrease the dropout rate by ten per cent in schools, then their salary should be increased by ten per cent. For every demand, there was a reciprocal offer giving the oppressed more leverage. The notion of occupation is that you are taking control or making yourself present in a territory, but it is only the beginning. If there is someone who wants to kick you out, you need to have a tactic that can move you from a monologue into a conversation. If you think of the Occupy movement, it has remained mainly a monologue, we never heard anything more from anybody who could have been a representative of Wall Street, for example. Obviously it is useful because of the critical mass it creates and the cultural rejection of the harmful financial practices they conduct every day. There has to be more that can be done.

Speaking about different kinds of occupied space brings me to the concept of borders. Thinking of the body being a border or site that interfaces with hostility, can you reflect on this?

In the case of Mexico, the situation is that there is a cultural discourse that reinforces the problems associated with the border politic. The reality is that the United States is a very bad neighbour in that they are much more dangerous to Mexico than Mexico is to them. We get the blame for exporting drugs into the United States, but it is as if the US authorities are denying that once the drugs cross the border there are networks of commerce inside their own country propelled by Americans. They don't prosecute the drug dealers in their own country – although, occasionally we see the prosecution of the small drug dealer, possibly as a scapegoat to bypass much larger issues. Simultaneously, there is this gross irony here, in that Americans are allowing hundreds of thousands of weapons to be shipped into Mexico at the same time. How can you compare what a joint can do to an individual with what an

assault rifle can do? Interestingly, however, there is no cultural rejection of the weapons industry, while there is one towards the drug industry. And the prescription-drug industry has historically been much more dangerous than illegal drugs. Both the decision to ban certain drugs and the promotion of a massive legal commerce has more to do with profit-gain than health issues, and this has continued throughout history. In the UK, for instance, the British East India Company, was reputedly the biggest drug dealer in human history.

I've never heard of that.

It all happened during the Opium Wars. The British East India Company controlled the opium market in China and even came to rule over large areas of India with its own private army in order to maintain control over the production and distribution of opium. The amount of opium brought into China from India was close to 1,400 tons a year. While a Chinese person caught importing opium was subject to the death penalty, it was entirely legal for the British. Just imagine having a monopoly on the opium production in India and supplying a market as large as that of China. And on top of everything, this whole operation went on for a hundred years!

A colonialism of the mind?

Certainly. What is interesting to look at is the asymmetry for what is seen as good and bad in the public imagination and how it happens in real life. This also has to do with the way that Mexicans are treated in the United States. The US economy would be unsustainable without Mexican labour; they do menial jobs for poor wages and on top of that are also getting prosecuted, shot and incarcerated. The US should be grateful for how we support its lifestyle.

This goes back a little to the idea that the hospitable and inhospitable go hand in hand? There is a disproportionate relationship between those creating hospitable environments (that is, someone in the service industry) versus those who receive those gifts. It's a double-edged sword?

If you look at a country like Spain, where one out of four people is unemployed, you will notice that there are many jobs occupied by migrants that the Spanish don't want to do. There was a moment when immigration was welcomed because they didn't want to do this. Now everyone wants to work in a …

… trendy design studio?

Exactly. It's a cultural bias that some people from some countries are worth better opportunities than others. It's an outcome of colonization that those who were colonized possibly are bound by certain cultural attitudes.

There seems to be an issue of representation here?

Žizek writes that there is a disparity between visible and invisible violence. If you look at the weapon-manufacturing industry, most weapons are used in different countries from where they were produced. The companies are fully aware that they will end up in wars and in the hands of criminals through both legal and black markets. So the visible violence is the one you see in the news, and the invisible violence is the undetected

profit of these companies. I just made a series of musical instruments using weapons that were collected in Mexico, so I was able read on all of them the places that they come from: Belgium, Italy, the US, Austria, Canada, etc. Going back to the asymmetry between the visible and the invisible, underdeveloped countries will continue to get the blame for using the guns and producing the drugs, while the First World countries won't be counted into the equation, but are however intimately tied to both trades. You can't explain one without the other.

I'm curious to think, then, about notions of labour. What do you think the internet has done for society? Has it changed the way that labour is constructed and mediated?

It's become a catalyst for social movements. But also it's addictive. The kinds of social interactions that are developed rely on the fact that one spends too much time in front of the computer or the machine, leading to a loss of the real-life interactions.

Do you think our connections used to be more intimate?

I'm certainly interested in older forms or values, such as courtesy and reconciling human interactions. I am fascinated by the ritualistic elements of the past. I do believe that we need to study again and to develop a kind of social software of culture. This is why street games, for instance, interest me, because they belong to the commons, and with almost no means provided a space for conviviality.

I'm curious then, do you think that the semantics of the web are bringing us closer together or tearing us apart?

There are two camps here: a younger one that agrees and indeed believes that a new kind of human nature has come into being, and an older generation whose more conventional approach is to argue that the web makes individuals more isolated.

What do you think?

Honestly, one of my goals in life is to find ways to spend less time in front of the computer. Technology is so omnipresent that I don't feel there is any reason to be enthusiastic about it any more.

But don't you think that technology mirrors the real world? What if we return to Rosalind Krauss's essay on the aesthetics of narcissism in relation to video art, and then transpose that to the internet, which seems to function as a kind of social mirror?

For sure, but that's implicit. Our attention should be on the non-technological space now. We all know that technology will catch up with everything. What I think is needed now is not to lose the capacity to have non-technological encounters. Will we be the last generation to know street games, or the lyrics of a lullaby?

Bearing that notion of experience in mind, what is the most ideal act or gesture of hosting for you?

In *Melodrama and Other Games,* which is the project I am doing for the Liverpool Biennial, and *Sanatorium,* for example, my interest is to tap into the excess capacity we have to help each other. The idea of play as a manifestation of freedom, as Friedrich Schiller expressed it – a true game is one that frees the spirit. Although often we use the words interchangeably, I think there is a subtle difference between 'play' and 'games': play is unrestricted; games have rules. Play may merely be the enactment of a dream, but in each game there is a contest. If you see how children play games they are often extraordinarily naive or highly civilized. They rarely trouble themselves to keep score, and little significance is attached to who wins or loses; it does not seem to worry them if a game is not finished. Doesn't it sound a bit like art?

Pamela Rosenkranz

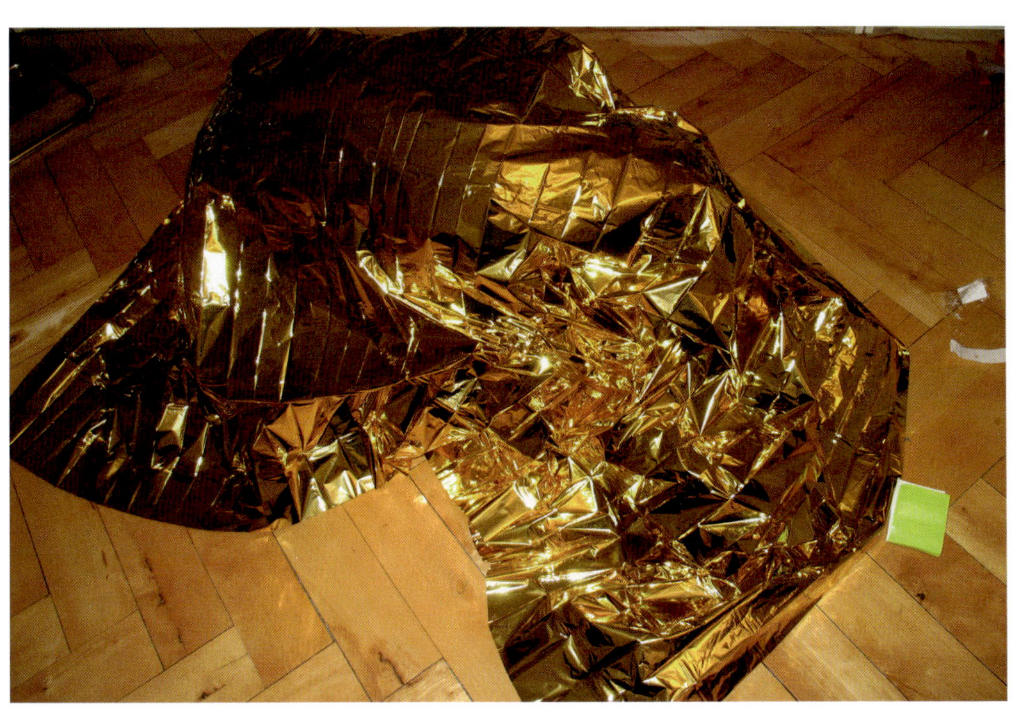

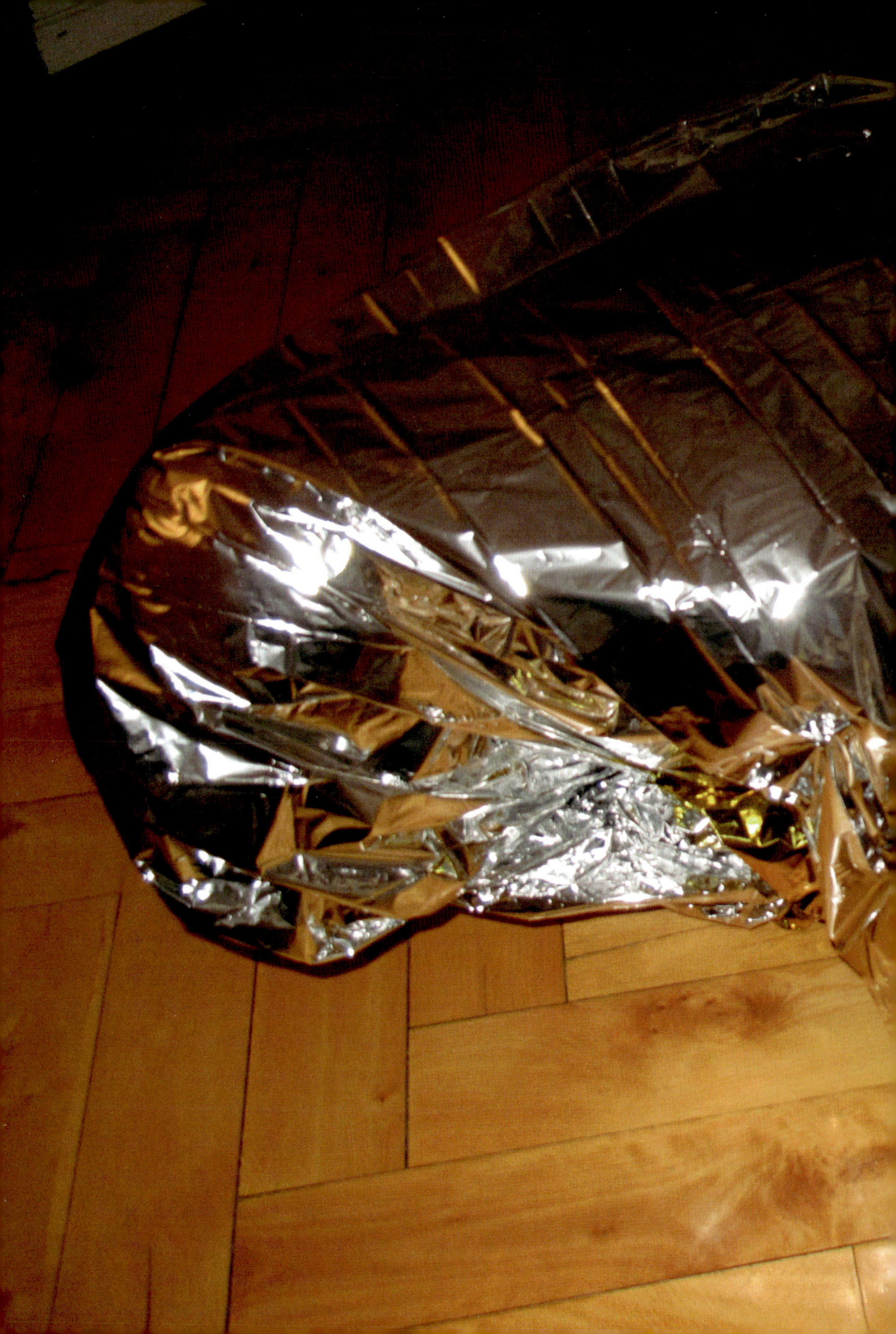

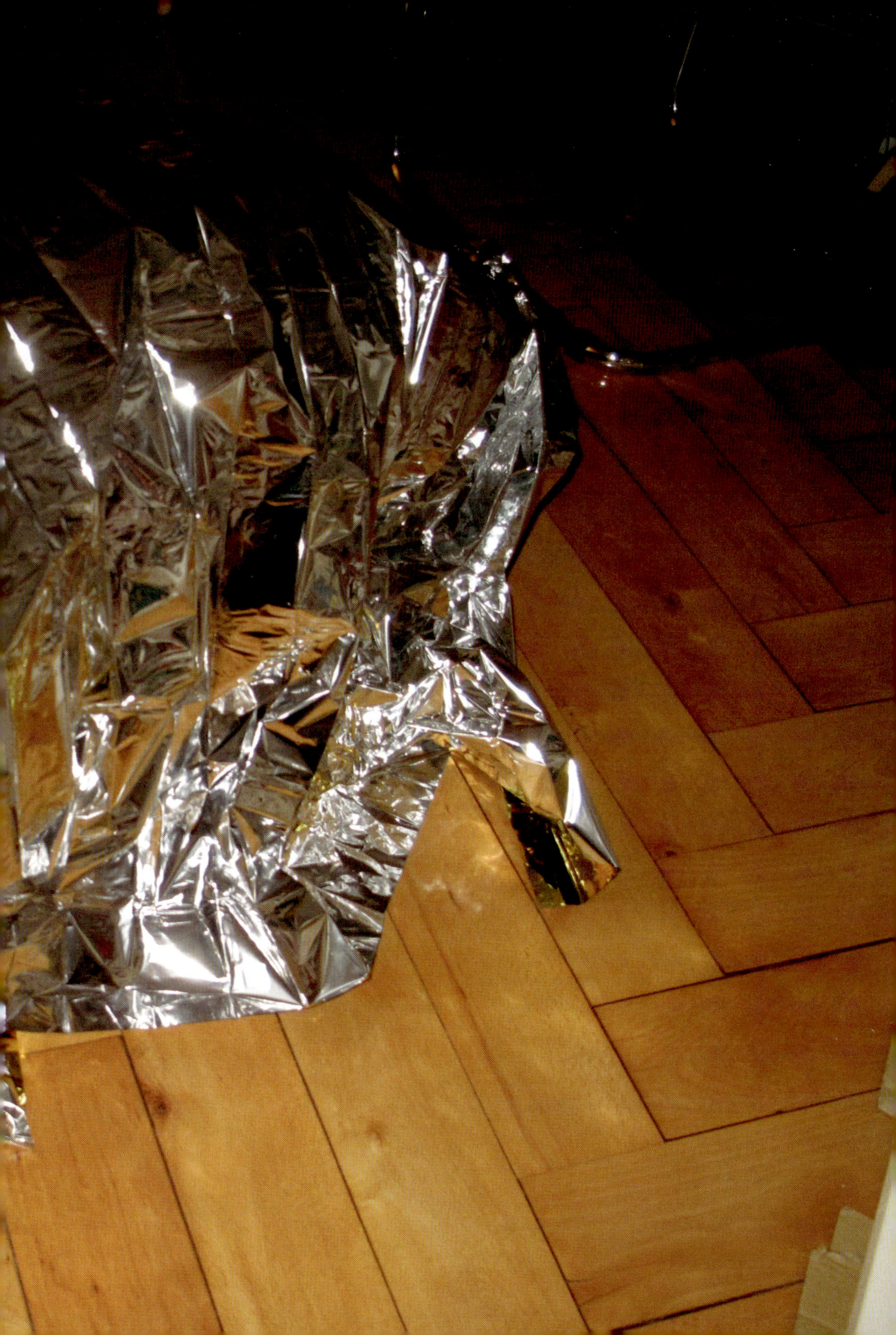

Mikhael Subotzky
and Patrick Waterhouse

Ponte City

The fifty-four-storey Ponte City building dominates Johannesburg's skyline, its huge blinking advertising crown visible from Soweto in the south to Sandton in the north. When it was built in 1976 – the year of the Soweto uprisings – the surrounding flatlands of Berea, Hillbrow and Yoeville were exclusively white, and home to young middle-class couples, students and Jewish grandmothers. Ponte City was separated by apartheid urban planning from the unforgettable events of that year. But as the city changed in anticipation and response to the arrival of democracy in 1994, many residents joined the exodus towards the supposed safety of the northern suburbs, the vacated areas becoming associated with crime, urban decay and, most of all, the influx of foreign nationals from neighbouring African countries.

Ponte's iconic structure soon became a symbol of the downturn in central Johannesburg. The reality of the building and its many fictions have always integrated seamlessly into a patchwork of myths and projections that reveals as much about the psyche of the city as it does about the building itself. Tales of brazen crack-and-prostitution rings operating from its car parks, four storeys of trash accumulating in its open core, snakes, ghosts and frequent suicides have all added to the building's legend. Some of these stories are actually true, and for quite some time most of the residents were indeed illegal immigrants. And yet, one is left with the feeling that even the building's notoriety is somewhat exaggerated – that its decline is just as fictional as its initial utopian intentions were misplaced and unrealized.

In 2007 the building was bought by developers, but by late 2008 their ambitious attempt to refurbish and revitalize Ponte had failed spectacularly. They went bankrupt after promising to spend three hundred million rand on their vision for the building. Their aim was to target a new generation of aspirant middle-class residents – young, upwardly mobile black professionals, business people from across the African continent, and all those seeking chic Manhattan-style inner-city living. The developer's website still describes how, 'In every major city in the world, there is a building where most can only dream to live. These buildings are desirable because they are unique, luxurious, iconic. They require neither introduction nor explanation. The address says it all.'

The developers emptied half the building and stripped the apartments of everything, throwing all their rubble into the structure's central core. They started to redesign the flats with a variety of exotic themes – 'Future Slick', 'Old Money' and 'Glam Rock' – but their financing required sales up front and these, it seems, failed to materialize in sufficient numbers for the construction costs and occupational rental to be maintained.

When we started our work there in 2008, the development was in full swing. The building felt like a shell, its bottom half completely empty, and the top half sparsely populated. Former residents moved out in a hurry to make way for the developers. Many of their apartments were then burgled and trashed. Months later, when the development had failed, we entered room after room where the floors were covered in piles of broken possessions, torn photographs and scattered paperwork. We would walk the corridors, through whole floors of empty flats, and then suddenly hear children shouting, the fizz and smell of frying fish, and then, briefly, voices and running water as we passed the bathroom and kitchen windows that face the passageways. But these spectres disappeared as quickly as they had come, leaving us to wander through wrecked apartments, corridors and dark stairwells. We met many of the remaining residents in the lifts where we asked to make portraits of those who were willing. When we brought copies back to their apartments, doors opened to all kinds of living arrangements – whole families in bachelor flats, empty carpeted rooms with nothing but a mattress and a giant television console, and penthouses divided up with sheets and appliances into four or five living spaces.

By the end of 2008, Ponte's old owners had repossessed the building and started the mammoth task of cleaning it up and refitting the stripped apartments. Another cycle in the building's life had begun before the last illusions of a grand future could be erased. The posters and graphics advertising 'New Ponte' still hang in the hallway, passed daily by many residents who still think that this is what their building will become. We started to work systematically, visiting each apartment to request a picture of the door and of the windows, an archive of thousands of strictly ordered photographs that would later find form in four-metre-high lightboxes and sequenced projections. As we proceeded with this task, we noticed that almost everybody was watching their television sets, seemingly ignoring the spectacular views that attracted us to their windows. So we joined them, and would spend hours in front of old Rambo movies, Congolese sitcoms, music videos and Nollywood dramas. All the stories from Ponte's past were there before us – the druglords and the gangsters, the shootouts and the prostitutes, the ghosts and the voodoo magic – not in the building itself, where young people and families went about their lives calmly, but on the hundreds of screens that were stacked above each other, flat by flat and floor by floor.

Ponte has always been a place of myth, illusion and aspiration. This is what we seek to evoke in our work in the building. Perhaps this task is best left to the images that we have found there – both in the abandoned flats, and in the marketing material and advertising that we have collected from 1976 and 2008. When these documents are seen next to the dystopian appearance of the building and its surroundings, one begins to project an image of this city during this time. It is a place of dust and dreams, befitting the land on which it sits, which has attracted millions of migrants since gold was discovered in the 1880s. People are still drawn here from all over the continent in search of better lives for themselves and their families. But the gold, in all its incarnations, inevitably fulfills the dreams of so few. All around them, those who service this passion are scattered in a modern metropolis – pinning their dreams to the flashing signs that crest the city and some of its buildings.

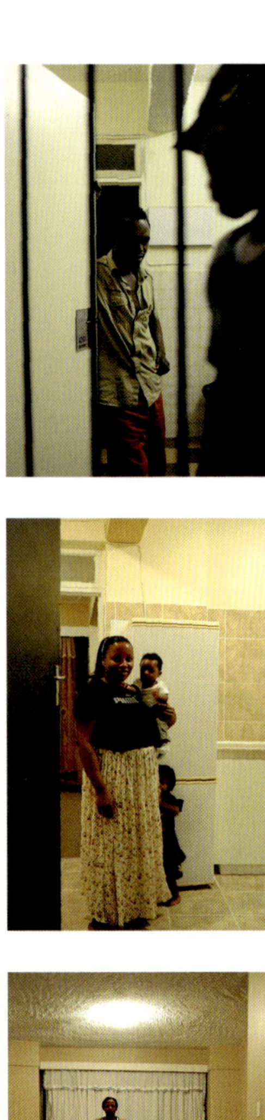
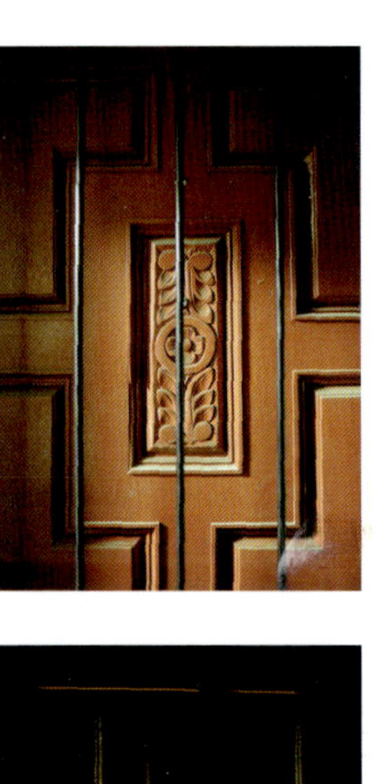
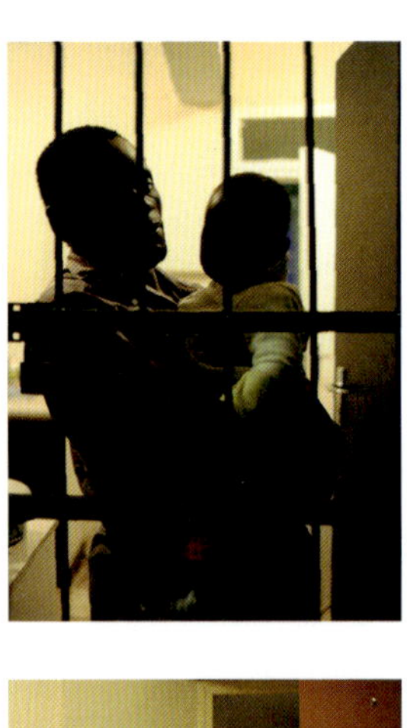
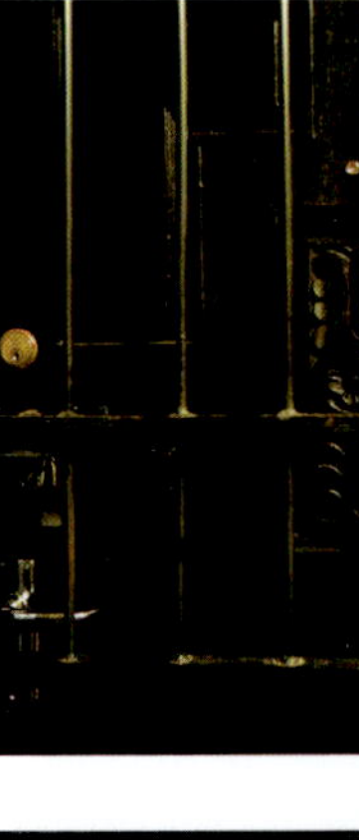

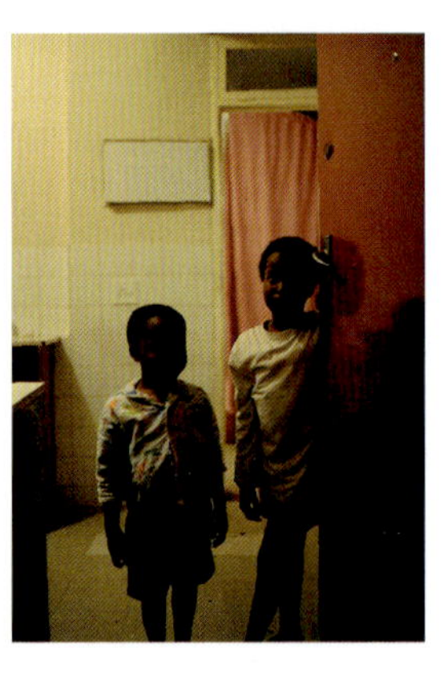
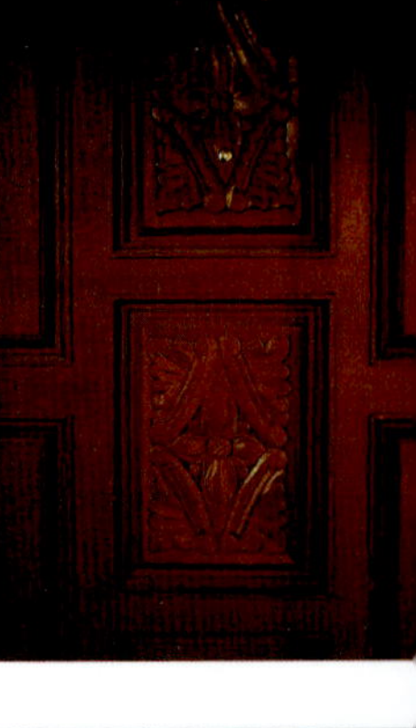
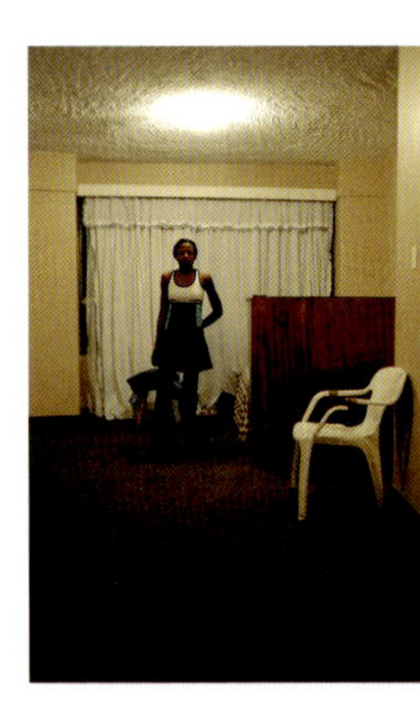
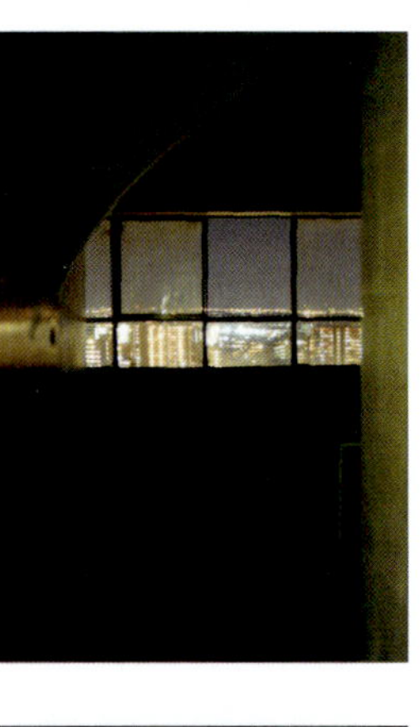
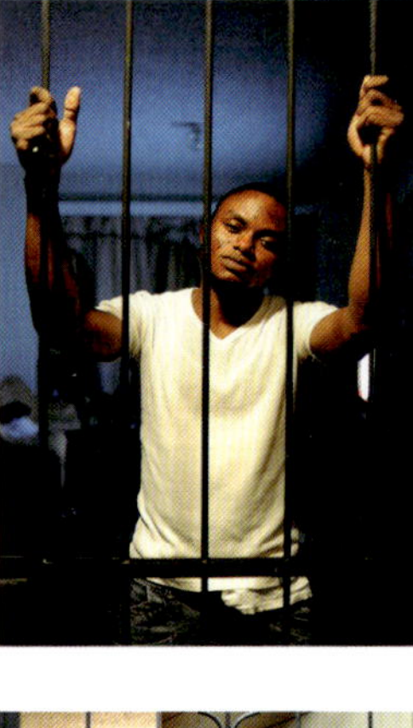
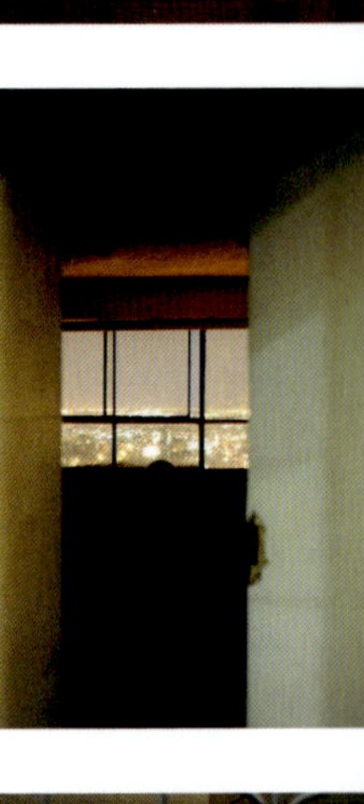

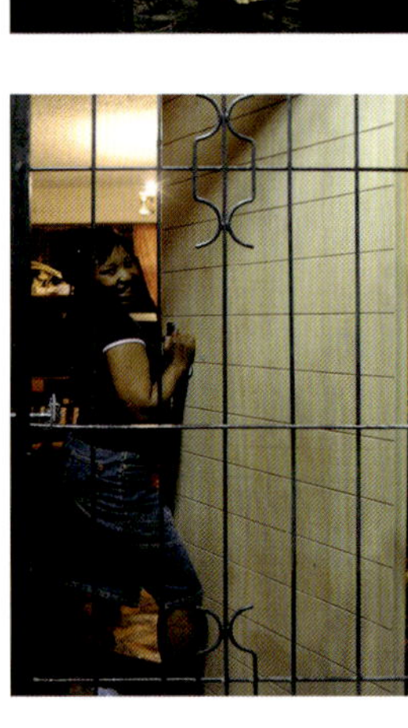
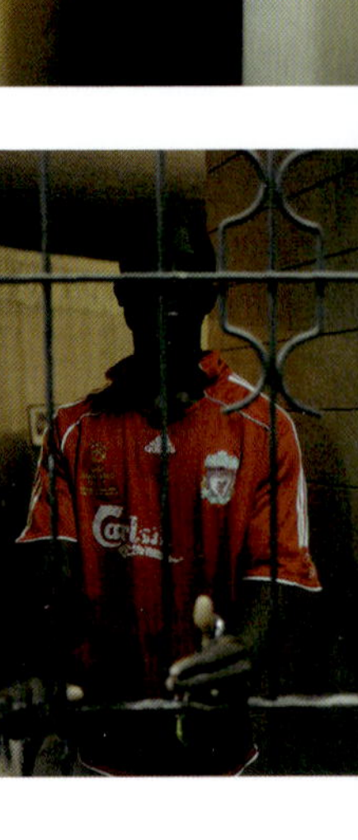

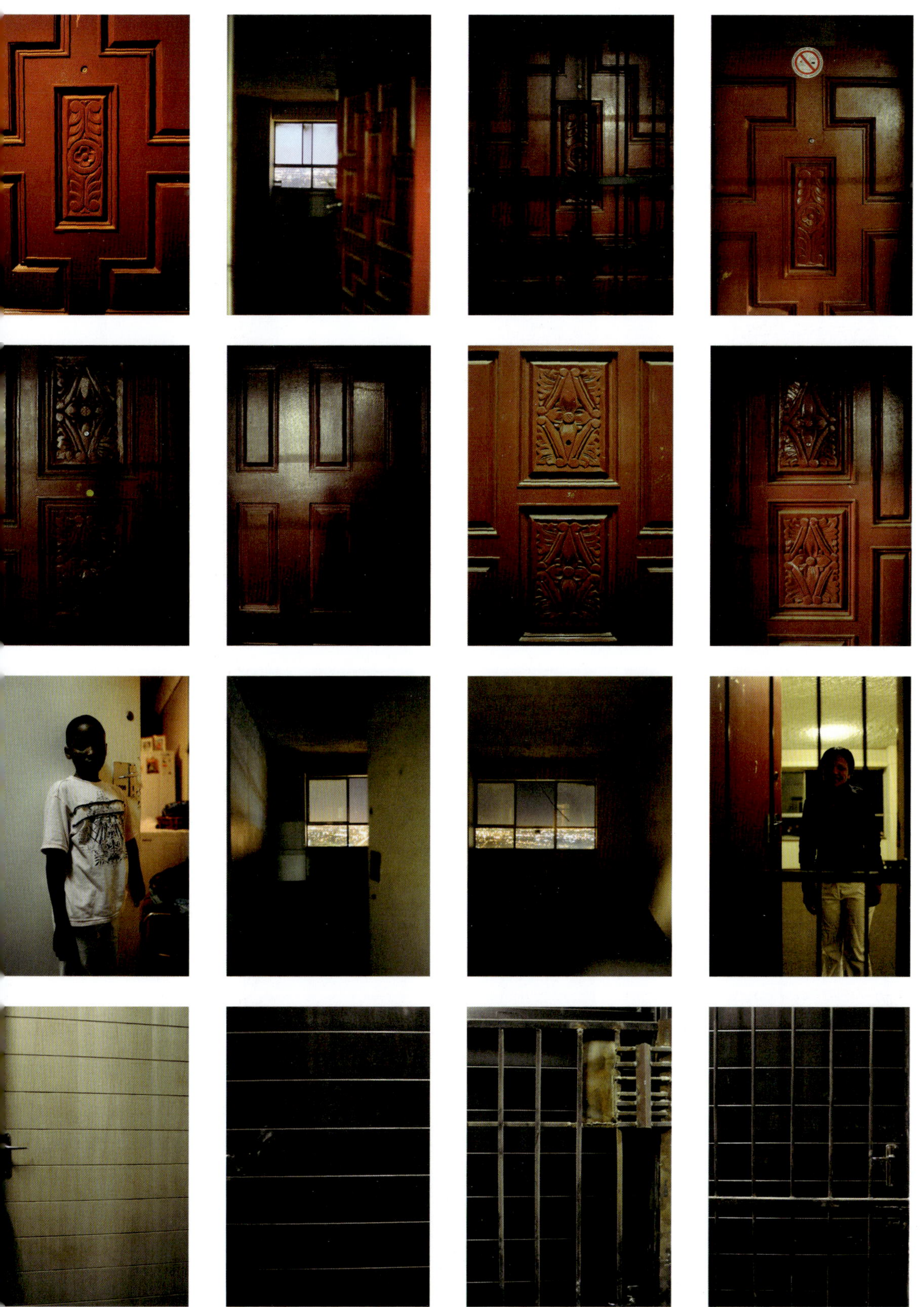

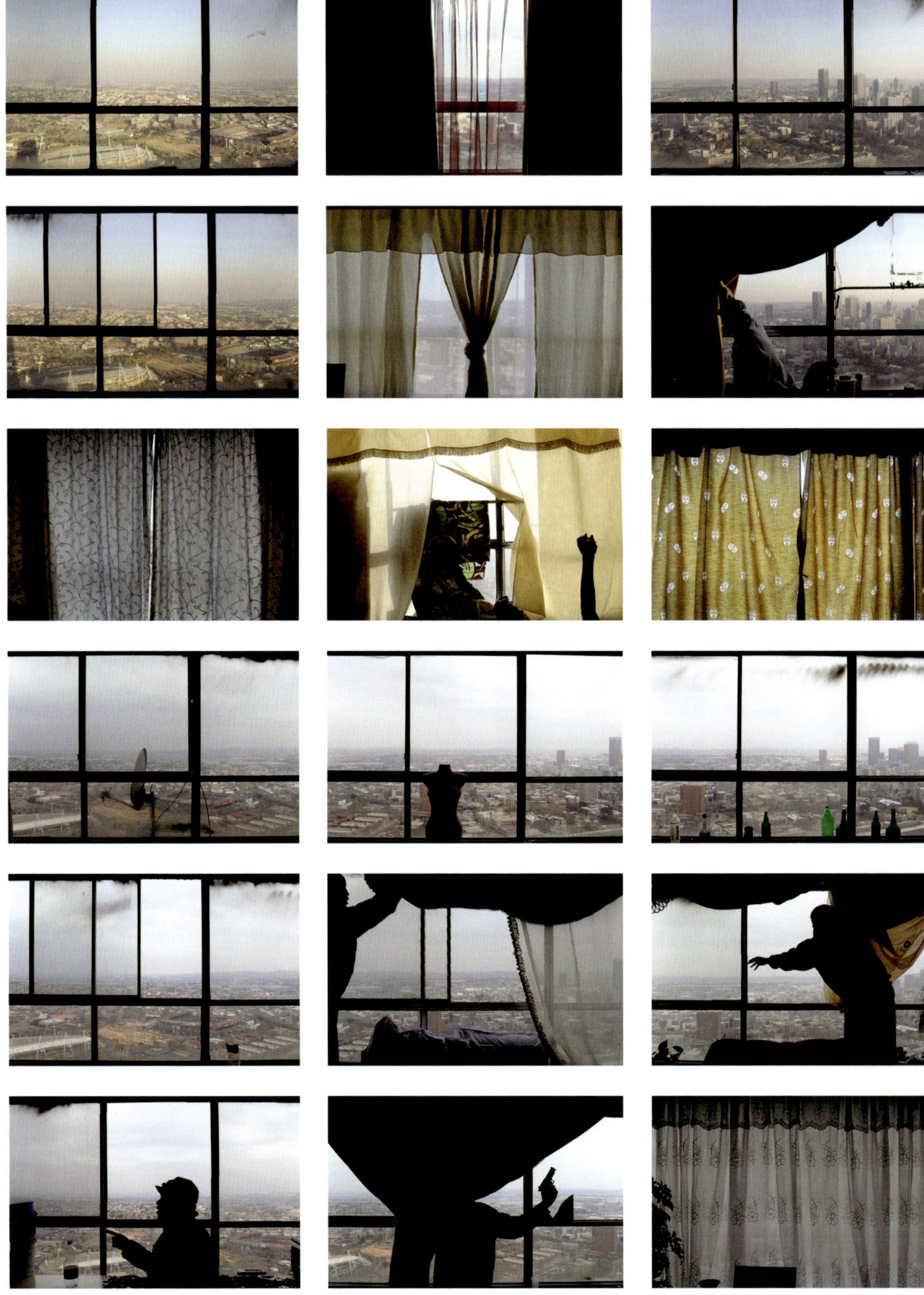

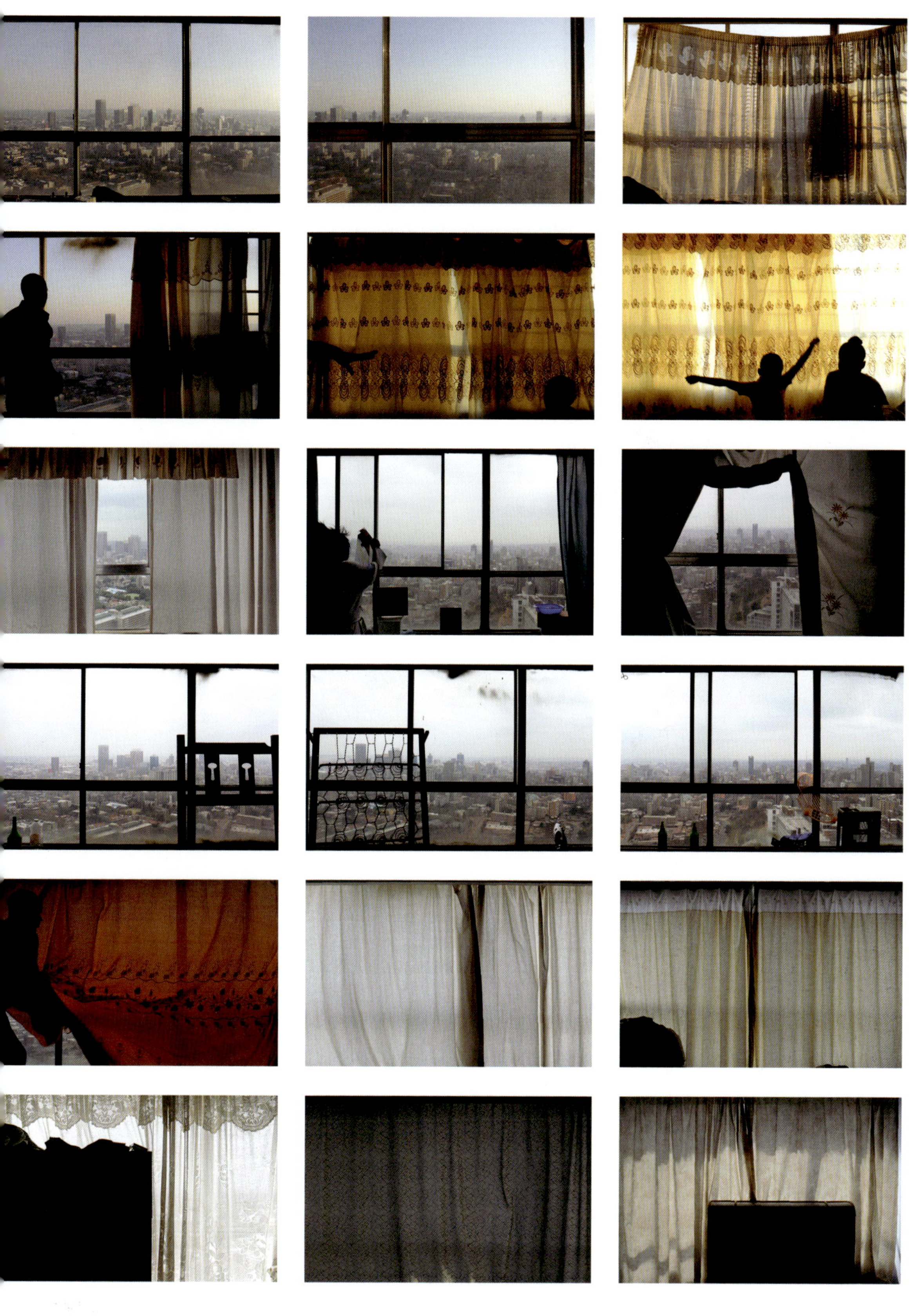

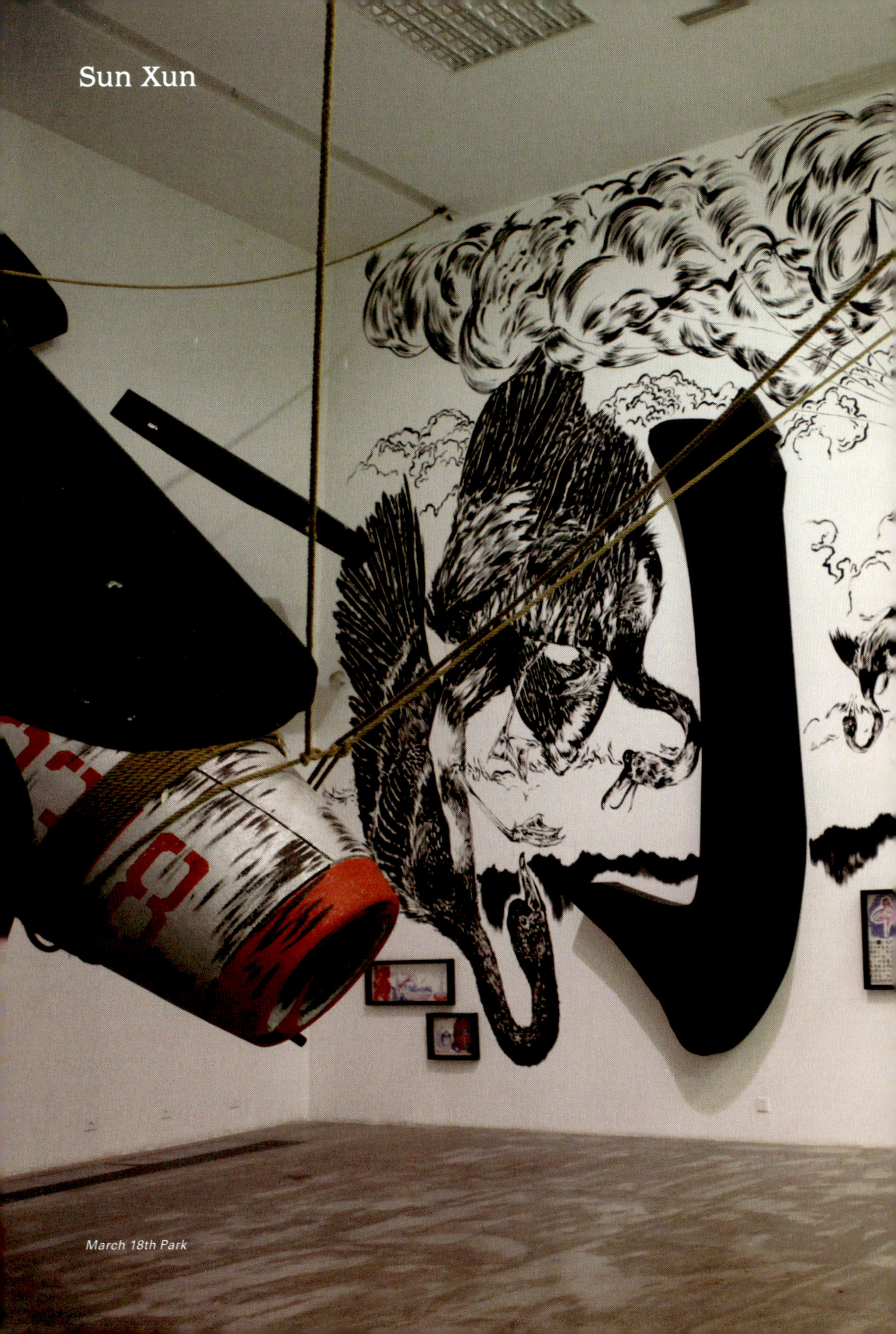

Sun Xun
March 18th Park

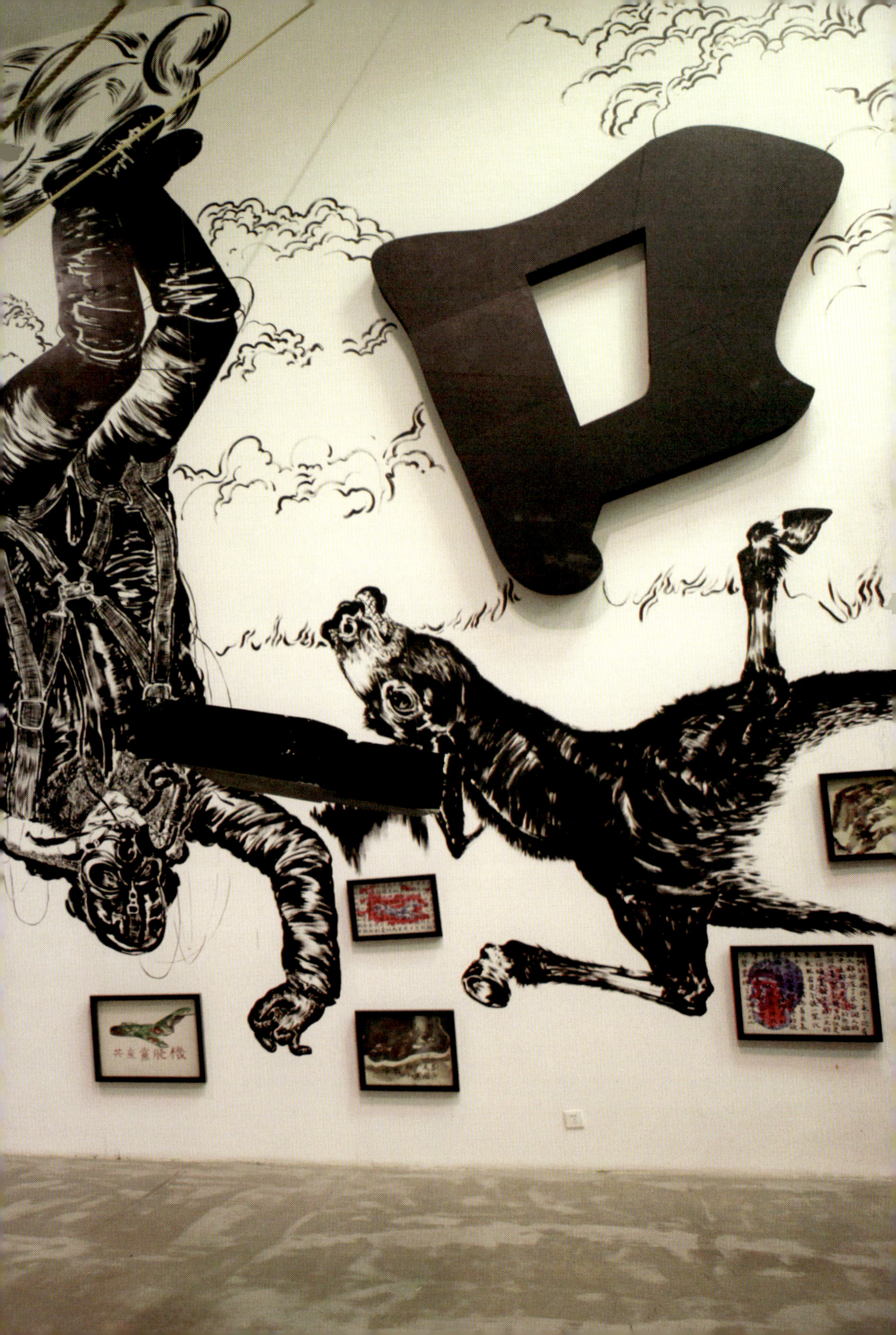

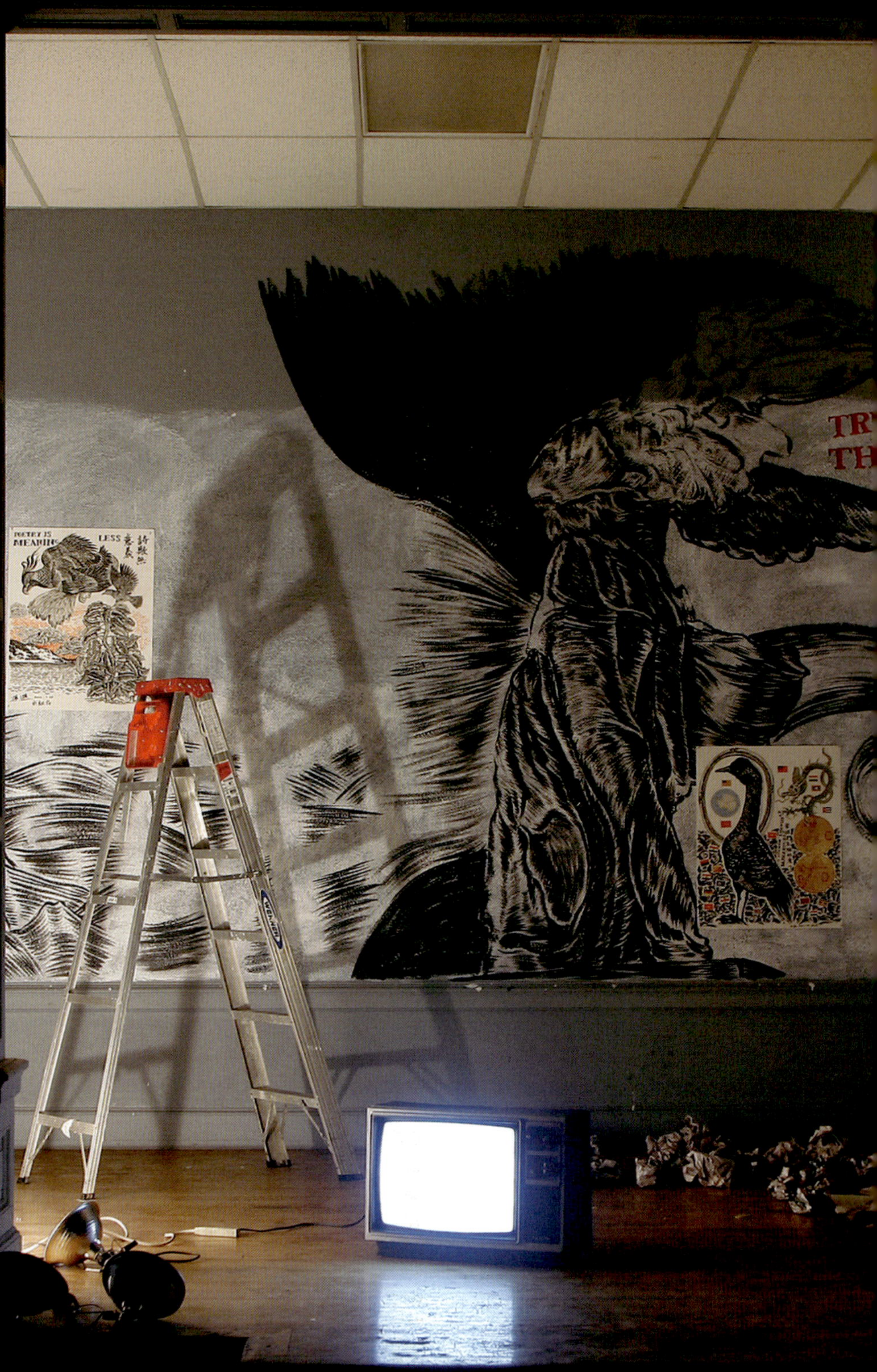
POETRY IS
MEANING   LESS
TR
TH

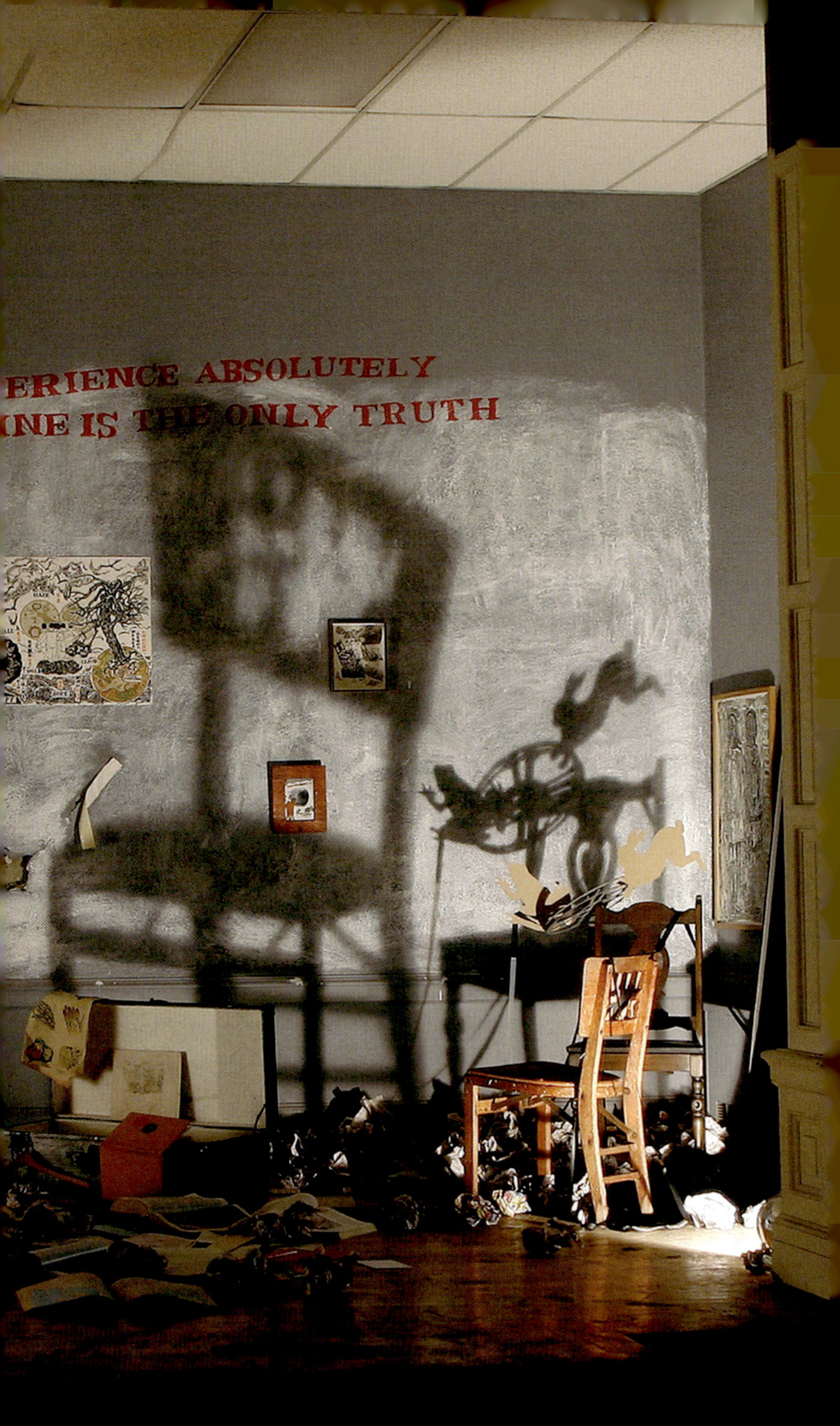

A Footnote to Time, 2012, installation (wall painting, ink and colour on paper, light and other materials), dimensions as large as the exhibition room

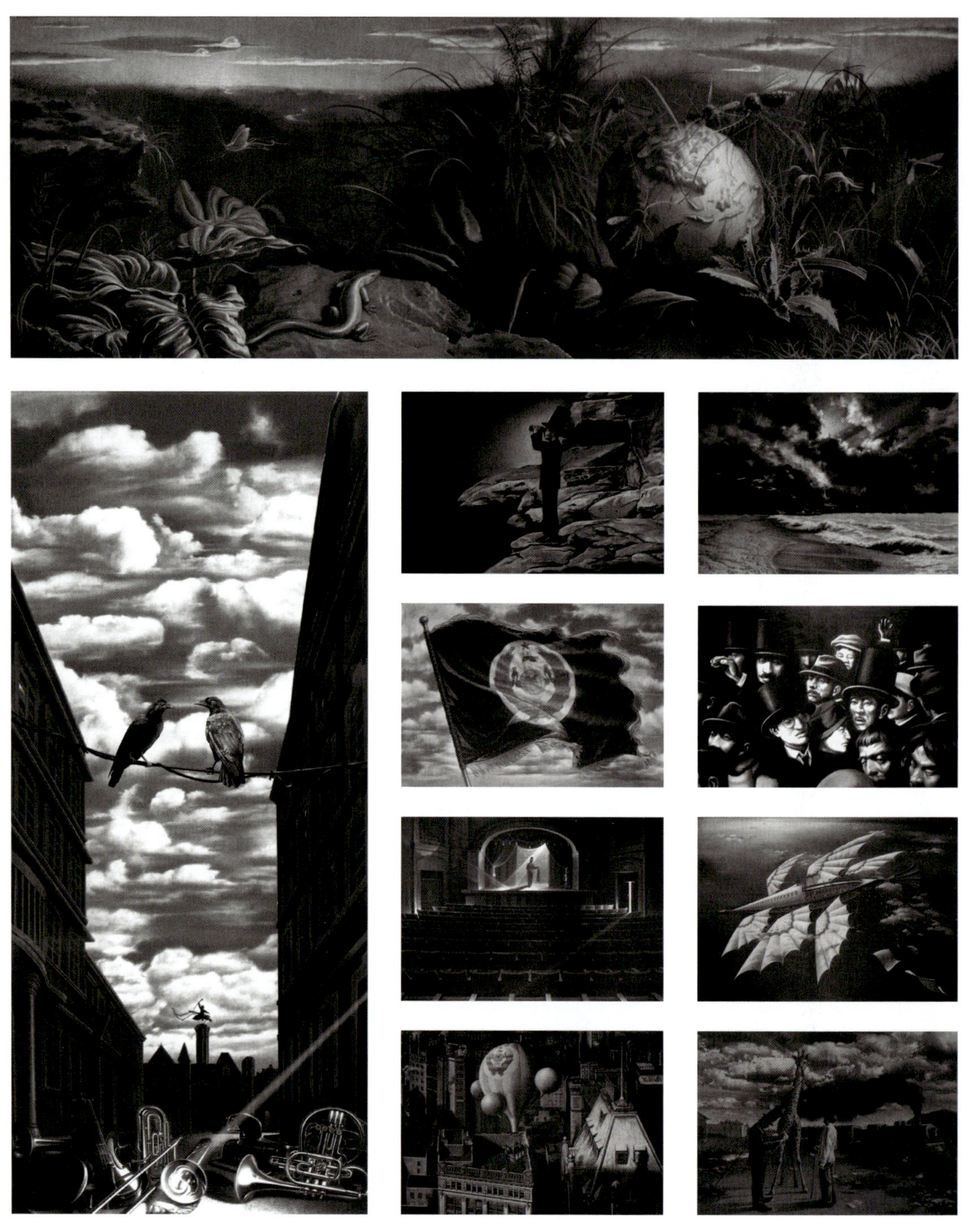

Top and above left: *21 G(21 ke)*, 2010, pastel on canvas, 100×280 cm and 280×100 cm, animation stills, colour, 27 minutes
Above right: *21 G(21 ke)*, 2010, pastel on canvas, each 100×140 cm, animation stills, colour, 27 minutes

Right: *Some actions which haven't been defined yet in the revolution*

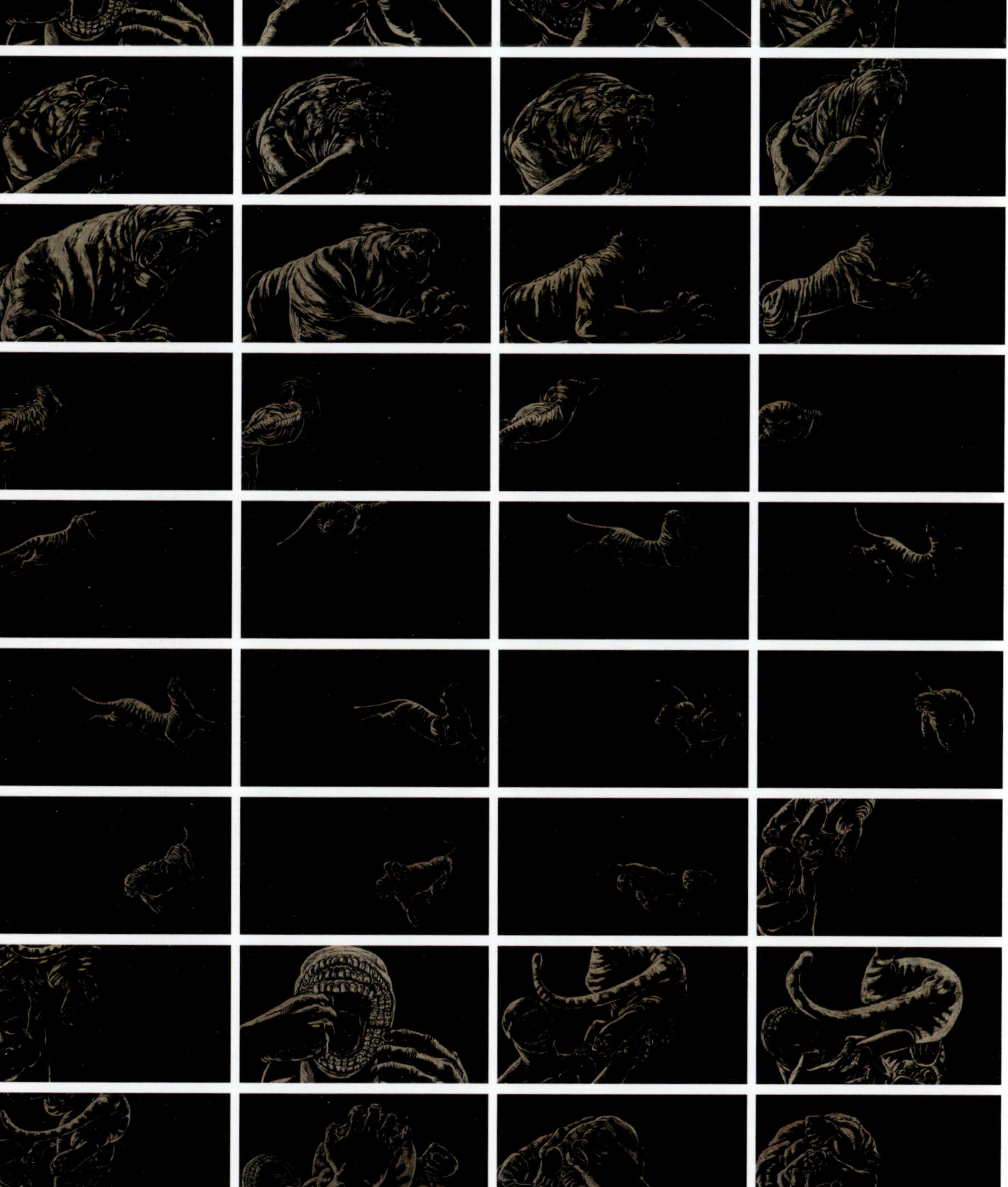

Superflex

FOREIG

PLEASE

LEAVE U

ALONE

THE DA

IERS,
DON'T
S
VITH
ES!

Sinta Tantra

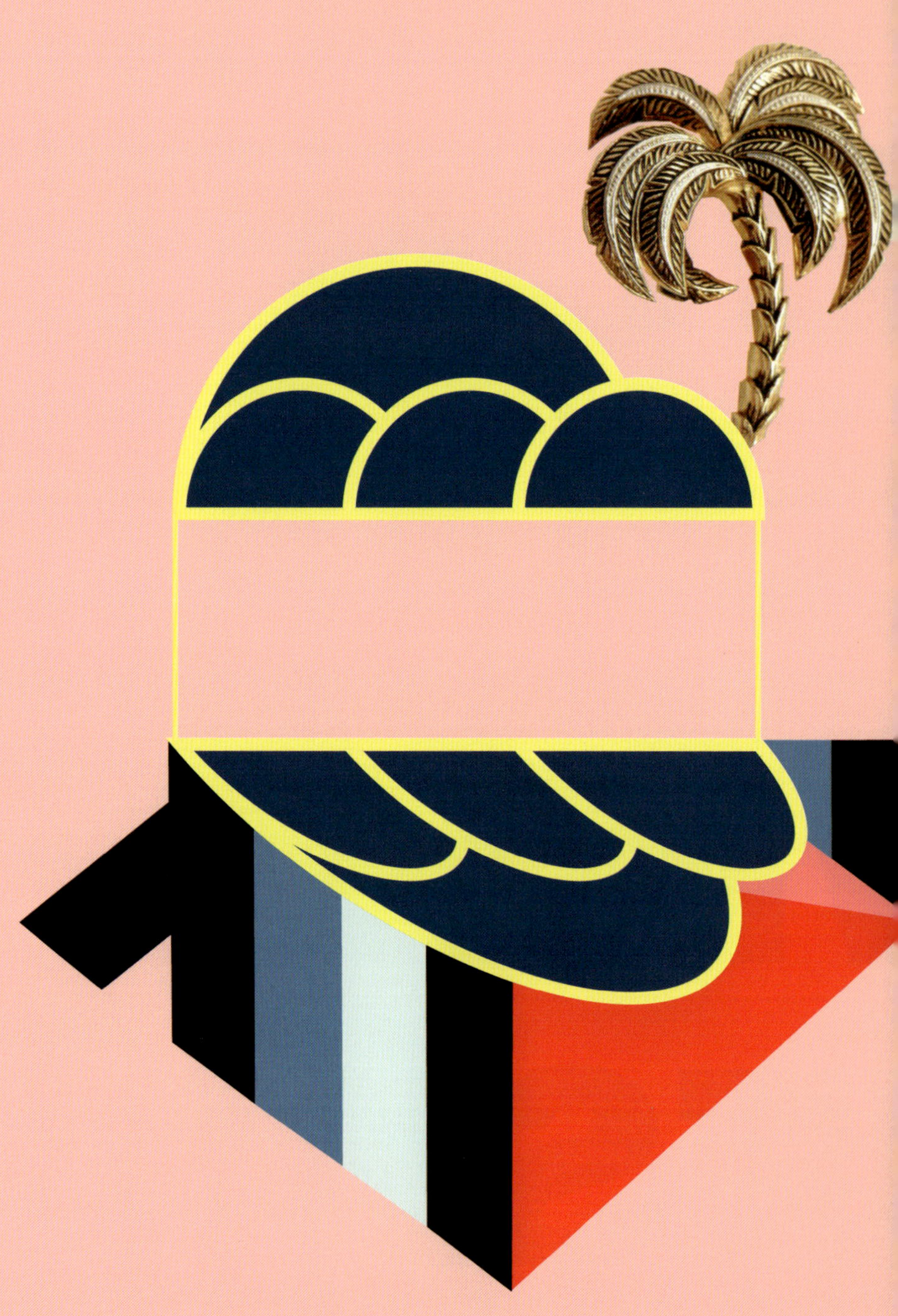

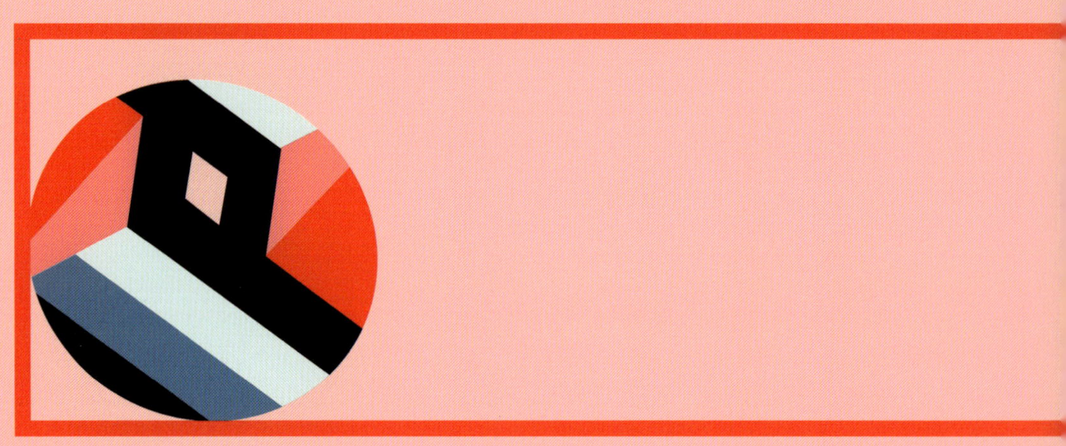

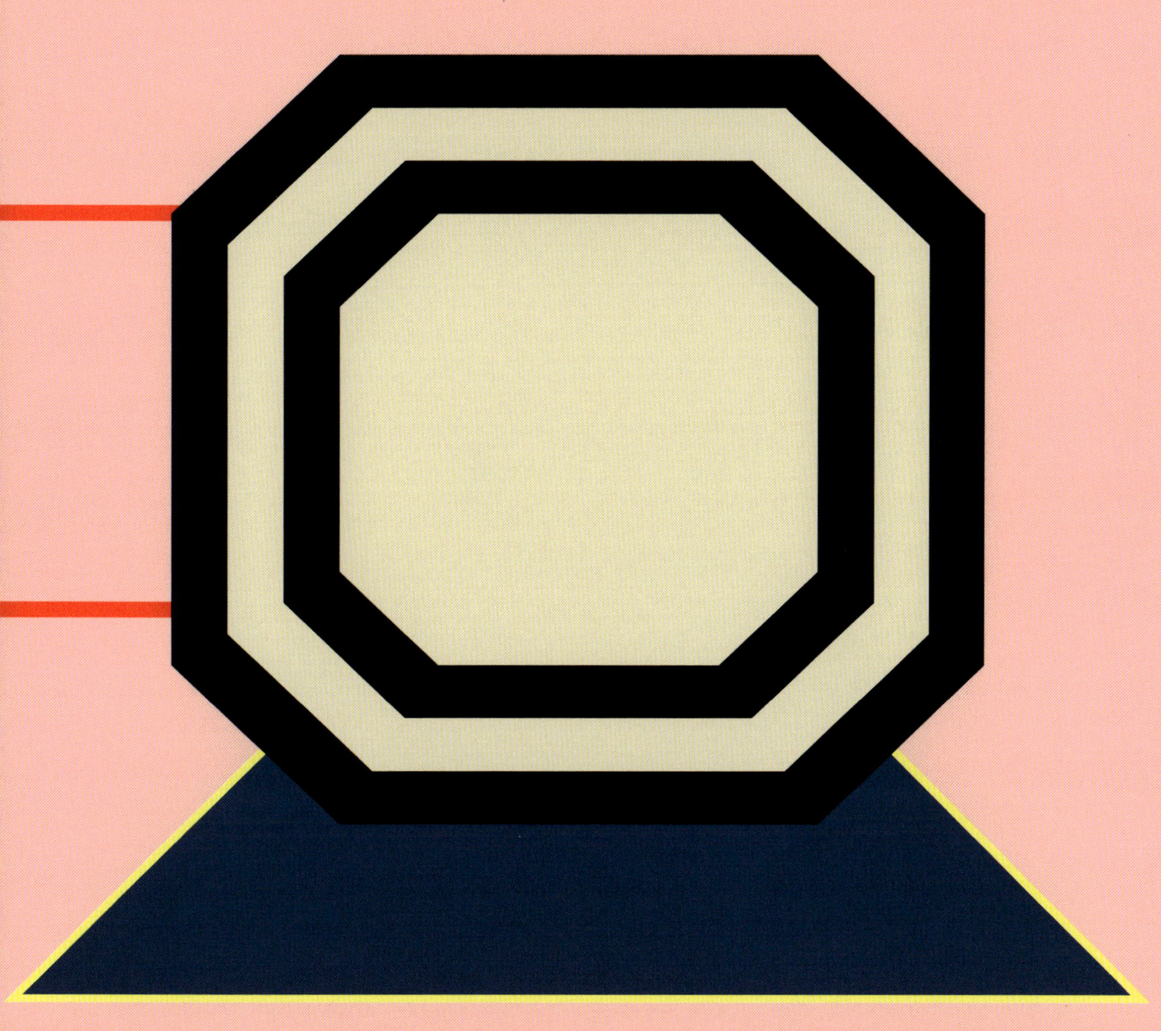

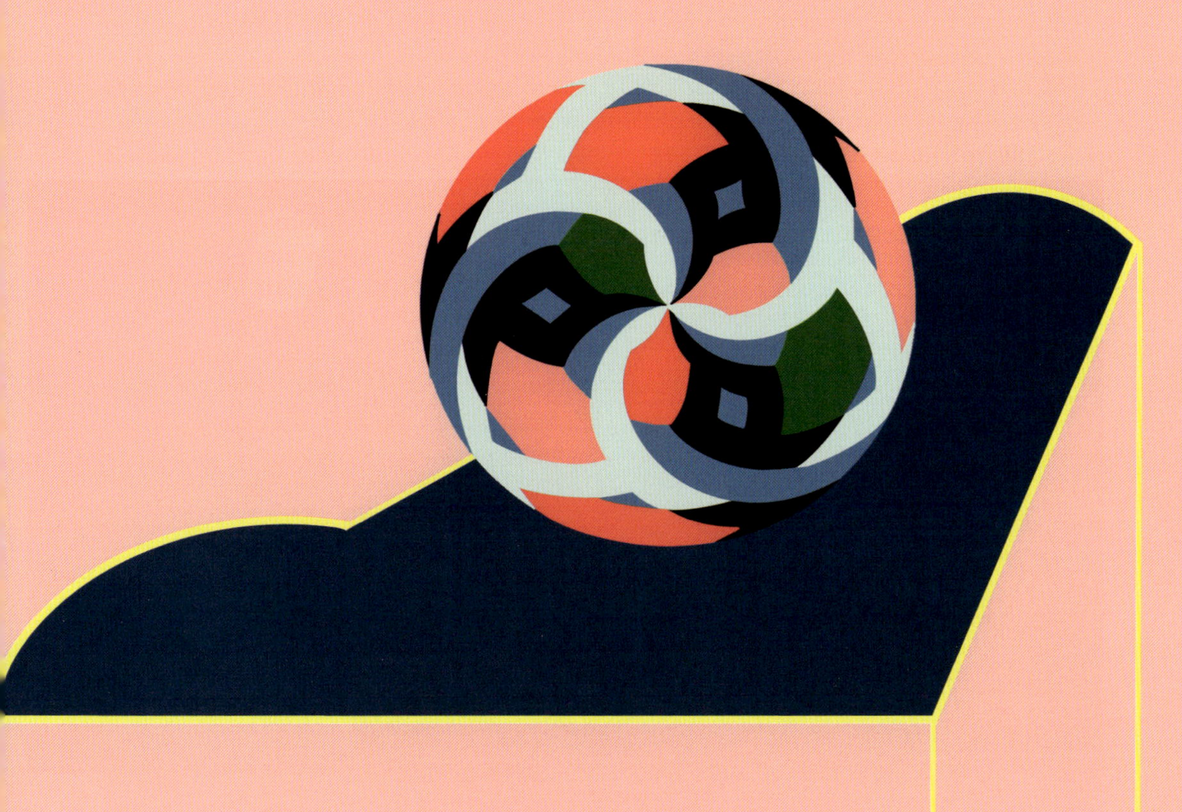

Tate Liverpool
Thresholds

With increasing mobility and migration, both forced and voluntary, in a globalizing world, the roles of hosts and guests are continuously challenged and the laws of hospitality face growing instability. We are often placed on thresholds that belong to no particular territory but to indefinite referrals and perpetual passages. Tate Liverpool's participation in Liverpool Biennial 2012 addresses the instability, not only of immigrant or host identities, national and ethnic identities, but also of the questions of identity within and beyond the realm of art. Drawn from the Tate Collection, which is itself a host of creative processes and their results, with its own laws of hospitality, Tate Liverpool's exhibition offers an arena where artistic intentions and curatorial narratives are persistently constructed and reconstructed, under shifting rules and uncertain presuppositions.

Guests: Hurvin Anderson, Keith Arnatt, Kader Attia, Yael Bartana, Sophie Calle, Layla Curtis, Eugenio Dittborn, Jimmy Durham, Fischli and Weiss, Gilbert and George, Simryn Gill, Thomas Hirshhorn, William Kentridge, Pak Sheung Chuen, Martin Parr, George Shaw, Mark Titchner, Mark Wallinger, Yukinori Yanagi

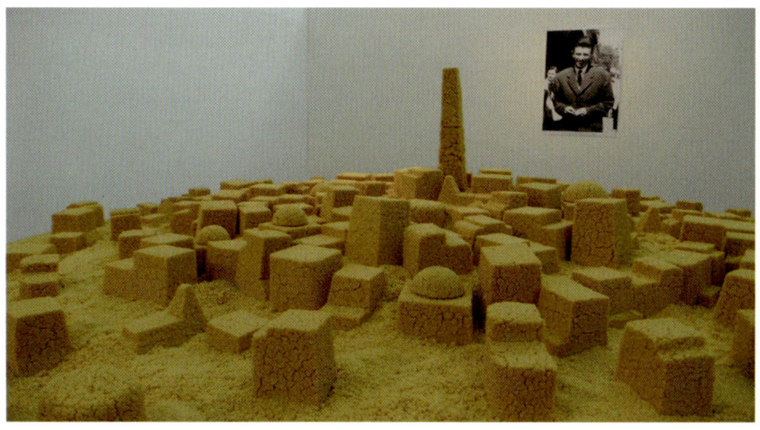

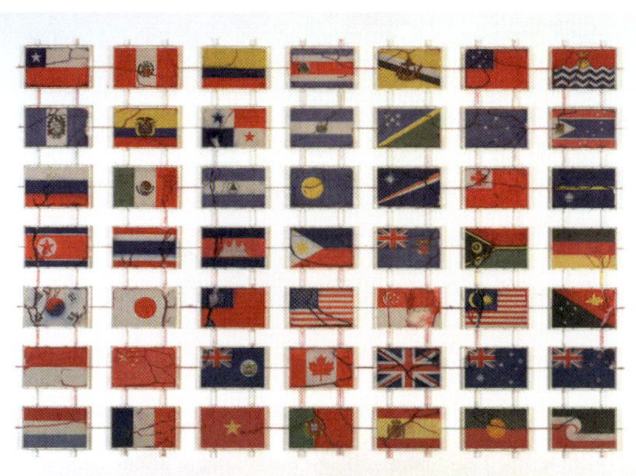

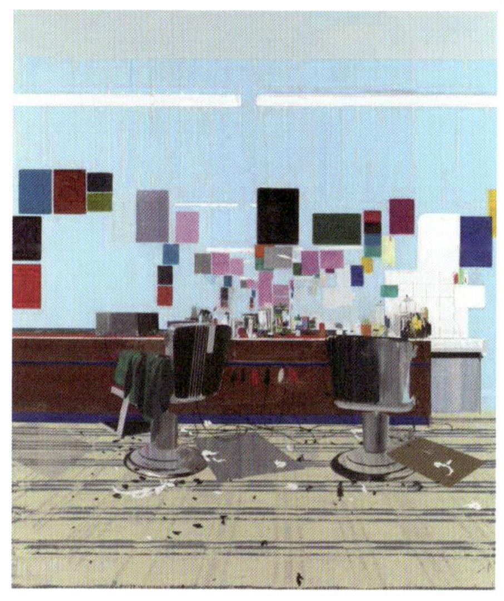

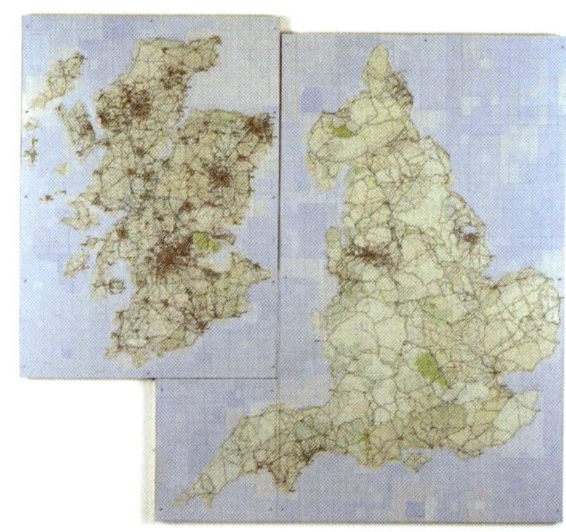

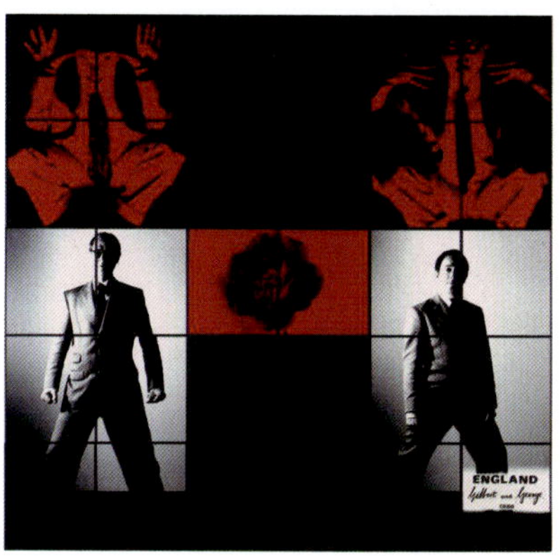

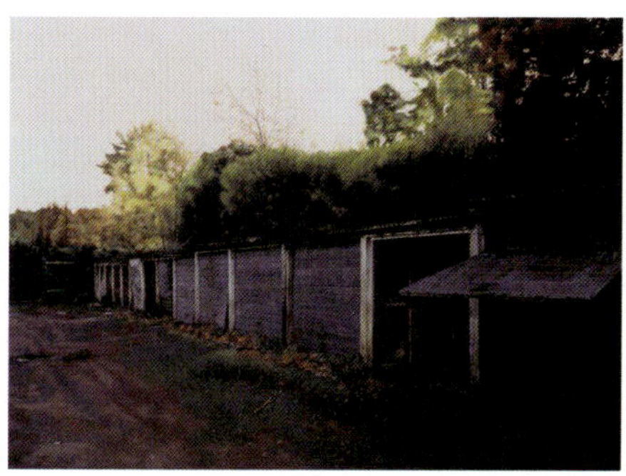

Stranger than the self

Derrida describes the offering of hospitality as an interruption of the self, forcing a host to reflect upon its own status and power. In international hospitality, these reflections are far-reaching, and artists have explored the complexity inherent in the idea of a nation host. From Hurvin Anderson's barber-shop scenes – inspired by those set up in homes of Caribbean immigrants arriving in 1950s and 1960s Britain – to Gilbert and George's bombastic, tongue-in-cheek statement of England's dominance, the plausibility and acceptability of international hospitality is called into question. Elsewhere, artists such as Mark Wallinger and Layla Curtis interrogate British identity in terms of its culture and history, while George Shaw and Keith Arnatt address the problematic notion of a 'quintessentially British' landscape.

Clockwise from top right:
Layla Curtis, *United Kingdom*, 1999
George Shaw, *Scenes from the Passion*, 2002
Gilbert and George, *England*, 1980
Hurvin Anderson, *Jersey*, 2008

Following pages:
Yael Bartana, *Kings of the Hill*, 2003.
Courtesy Annet Gelink Gallery, Amsterdam

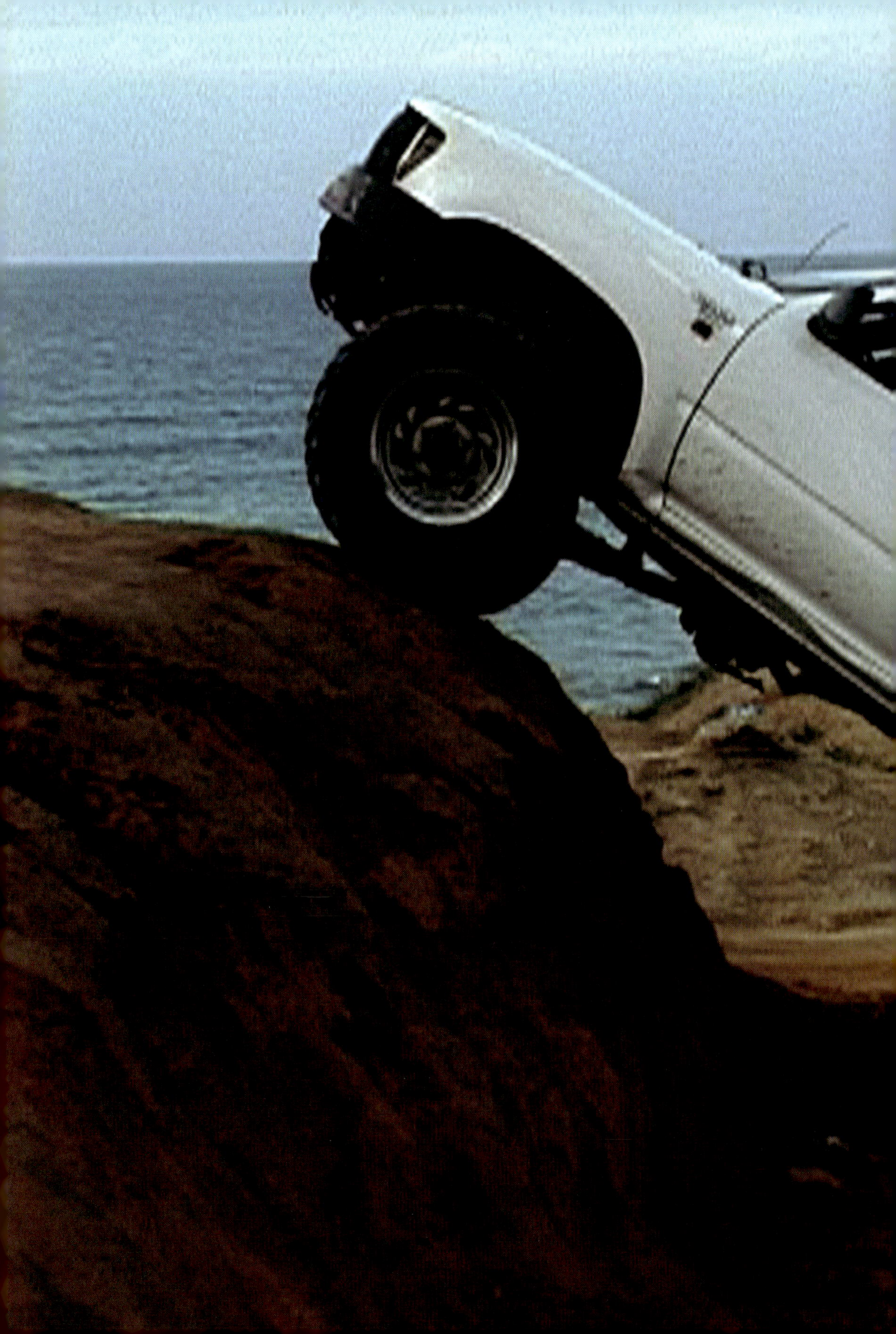

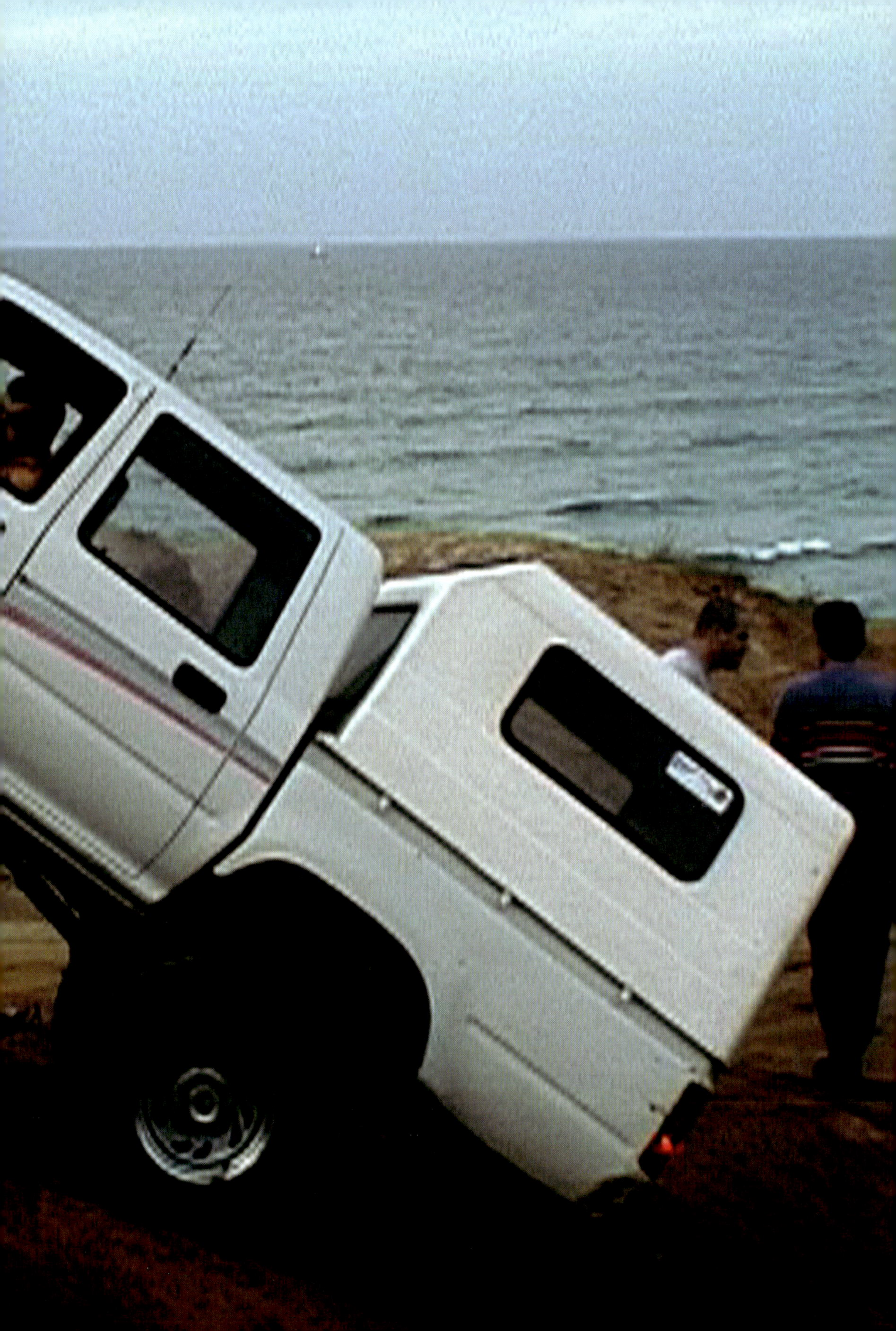

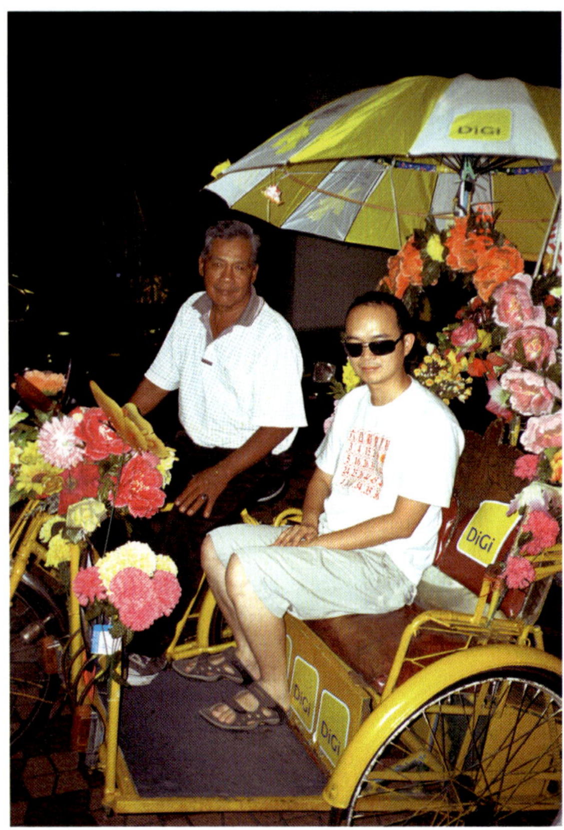

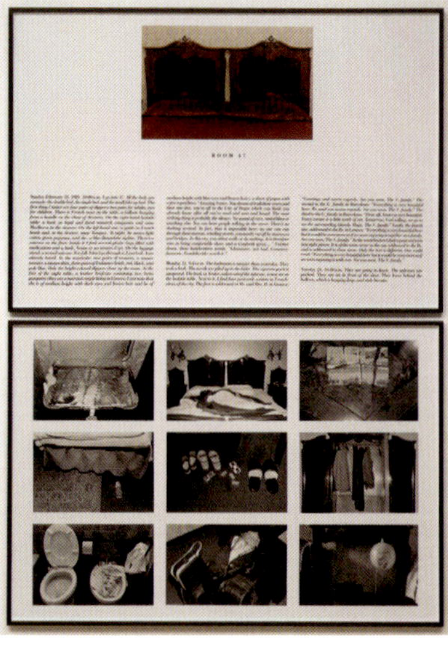

Shifting boundaries

In a world of transnational travel and migration, the sense of belonging to a place becomes dislocated. Global tourism thus becomes another lens through which to view hospitality. Sophie Calle embodies the role of the host and gains knowledge of guests through observation. But the power of the observer is deceptive. As self-aware tourists will attest, cultures are edited in holiday snaps, other tourists removed to present an ideal. Artists such as Pak Sheung Chuen inhabit the guest role to question the validity of this kind of observation, emphasizing the facile and fleeting knowledge offered by tourism. Meanwhile, Eugenio Dittborn turns the work of art itself into a tourist, his *Airmail Paintings* crossing and testing both political and geographical boundaries.

Left: Pak Sheung Chuen, *A Travel Without Visual Experience*, 2008
Right: Sophie Calle, *The Hotel, Room 47*, 1981, © DACS, 2004

Making territories

As metaphorical boundaries shift and disperse, the political implications of regional conflicts, and their global effects, remain very real. Thomas Hirshhorn is one artist revealing the contested ownership of warring territories, by inhabitants, aggressors and the global media at large. The materials used in his work *Drift Topography* – cardboard, foil, parcel tape and newspaper – provide a metaphor for the instability of the complex political reality, a construction that almost collapses under its own weight. Reflections upon wars of attrition lost and won come in the form of Yukonori Yanagi's subtle critique of European imperialism and Kader Attia's reinterpretation of colonial history in north Africa, while the quotidian, even boring, existence of people living through the Israel–Palestinian conflict is revealed by Yael Bartana.

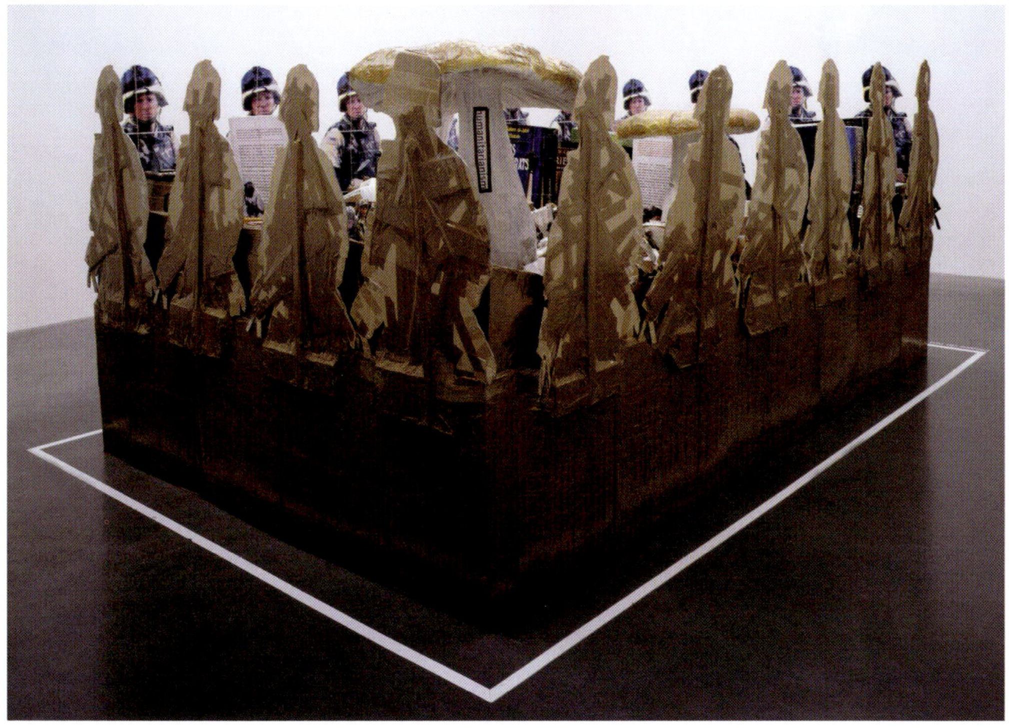

Above: Thomas Hirschhorn, *Drift Topography*, 2003. Courtesy Barbara Gladstone Gallery, New York
Texts: page 178 by Sook-Kyung Lee; pages 179–83 by Eleanor Clayton

Places of worship and religious services open to Liverpool Biennial visitors

Place of Worship	Telephone	Address	Website
St David C of E Church	0151 722 4549	Rocky Lane, Liverpool L16 1JA	stdavidchildwall.org.uk
Oreel Park Baptist Church	0151 524 2630	Whinfield Road, Liverpool L9 8BD	opbc.org.uk
Ash Street Baptist Church	0151 474 8784	Ash Street, Bootle, Liverpool L20 3HA	–
St Mary's C of E and Methodist Church	0151 4863180	180 Leathers Lane, Halewood, Liverpool L26 9TS	halewoodparish.org
St Luke RC Church	0151 426 6795	Shaw Lane, Prescot L35 5AT	–
Seventh Day Adventist Church	0151 264 8044	35 Kensington, Liverpool L7 8UX	liverpoolcentral.adventistchurch.org
Diamond Way Buddhism	0151 222 3543	Newsham Drive, Liverpool L6 7UQ	liverpool.dwbuk.org
Cottage Lane Mission Church	01695 574 103	Cottage Lane Mission, Cottage Lane, Ormskirk L39 3NE	clmchurchormskirk.org.uk/about-us, contact-us
St Francis de Sales RC Church	0151 525 3483	75 Hale Road, Walton, Liverpool L4 3RL	–
Psychic Truth Society	0151 727 5500	44 Parkfield Road, Aigburth, Liverpool L17 4LF	–
Liverpool Muslim Society Al Rahma Mosque	0151 709 2560	29–31 Hatherley Street, Liverpool L8 2TJ	liverpoolmuslimsociety.org.uk
Grace Family Church	0151 728 9870	216–220 Aigburth Road, Liverpool L17 9PE	gfc-liverpool.org
St John the Evangelist RC Church	0151 922 3604	70 Fountains Road, Liverpool L4 1QL	–
St Andrew C of E Church	0151 226 1977	Queens Drive, West Derby, Liverpool L13 0AL	–
Deeper Christian Life Ministry	0151 709 4670	Solway Street West, Liverpool L8 0TY	–
Maghull Chapel	0151 526 0428	85 Foxhouse Lane, Liverpool L31 6EE	–
Formby Baptist Church	01704 831 617	1 Furness Avenue, Formby, Liverpool L37 3NP	formbybaptist.co.uk
Unitarian Church	0151 733 1927	57 Ullet Road, Liverpool L17 2AA	ukunitarians.org.uk/ulletroad
Gateway International Christian Center	0151 486 4023	Goodlass Road, Speke (Hunts Cross), Liverpool L24 9HJ	gatewayicc.com
Merseyside Christian Fellowship	0151 260 6738	22 Richmond Park, Liverpool L6 5AD	–

Serving Christ, Serving the Community. **Services** Sunday communion 8am; Sunday family service 10.30am; Wednesday midweek communion 7.30pm

Today's church is a friendly community of around 100 people. We thank God for His faithfulness towards us, as we celebrated our centenary in 2010. **Services** Sunday: Morning worship 11am; Prayer meeting 6pm; Evening worship 6.30pm; Monday: J Team (primary-school children) 6.30pm; Tuesday: Playgroup 9.30am; Tuesday Club 7pm (for adults with special needs); Wednesday: Toddlers 9.30am; Ladies' meeting 2pm; Thursday: Playgroup 9.30am; Friday: Early morning prayers 7am; The Youth 8pm

Baptist congregation in Bootle. **Services** Sunday 11.45am; Thursday 12.15pm

Our two churches – St Nicholas's and St Mary's – seek together to serve the whole parish, and do so as an ecumenical partnership of Anglican (Church of England) and Methodist traditions. **Services:** Sunday morning service 10.30am; Sunday evening service 6.30pm

Catholic congregation in Prescot. **Services** Sunday early morning service 8.30am; Sunday mid-morning service 10.30am; Sunday evening service 7pm

We are a diverse community of Christians who share a love for God, our neighbours and talking about the Good News that we read about in the Bible. **Services** Saturday early morning prayer 9.15am

Our centre is a place where all can meet to learn and meditate, to share experience and development and actively participate in doing the work that makes all this possible. **Services** Weekly meditation Wednesday 8pm

An evangelical church serving Christ in Ormskirk and throughout the world. **Services** Sunday service 10.45am; Sunday prayer meeting 7pm

Roman Catholic congregation in Walton. **Services** Sunday Mass 10.30am; Saturday evening Mass 7pm

Affiliated to the Greater World spiritualist organization, we are a Christian Spiritualist Church. **Services** Sunday: Divine service 3–4.15pm; Monday: Evening service 7.30–8.45pm (£2); Tuesday: Spiritual and Meditation Group 7.30–9pm (£2); Wednesday: Reiki 10am–1pm (£5); alternate Wednesdays: Open Circle/Workshop 7.30–9pm (£3); Friday: Member development 7.30–8.45pm (£2)

The Liverpool Muslim Society (LMS) was established in 1953, and was responsible for the construction of the Al Rahma Mosque in 1974. The LMS provides support to all members of the Muslim community and organizes activities that appeal to the diverse body of members and the wider community. **Services** Prayer timetable can be found at www.liverpoolmuslimsociety.org.uk/prayertimetable.aspx

We are a church passionate about loving God, loving each other and loving you. **Services** Tuesday prayer meeting 7.30pm; Sunday service 10.30am

Roman Catholic congregation. **Services** Monday 9am; Tuesday 9am; Thursday 7pm; Friday 12.30pm; Saturday 7pm; Sunday 11.15am

Church of England congregation in West Derby. **Services** Sunday: Traditional service 9am; Unconventional service 10.45am; Communion, first Sunday of every month 10.45am; Thursday: Open house service 7.30pm

Deeper Christian Life Ministry. **Services** Sunday 10am; Tuesday Bible study 6.30pm; Friday worship and prayer 6.30pm

Evangelical Christian congregation in Maghull. **Services** Sunday family service 10.30am; Sunday evening service 7pm; Monday evening prayer group 7pm; Wednesday morning prayer group 7am

Formby Baptist Church exists to honour God by fulfilling the mission the Lord Jesus gave his followers through the great commission in the spirit of the great commandment. **Services** Sunday morning service 10am; Sunday evening service 6.30pm; Wednesday evening prayer meeting 7.30pm

We have a wonderful Grade 1 listed building consisting of vestibule, church, library, cloisters and hall. **Services** Sunday 11am

We are a family that meet together to seek God and His presence that heals, saves and delivers, and we want to join Jesus on His mission to our city, our nation and the nations. **Services** Sunday: Service 10.30am; Live @ 5 (prayer/worship meeting) 5pm

Christian congregation. **Services** Sunday 10am

St Mary C of E Parish Church	0151 546 4266	St Mary's Vicarage, Tithebarn Road, Prescot, L34 0JA	–
Liverpool RC Metropolitan Cathedral	0151 709 9222	Cathedral House, Mount Pleasant, Liverpool L3 5TQ	liverpoolmetrocathedral.org.uk
LiNC Scandinavian Seaman's Church	0151 709 7763	138 Park Lane, Liverpool L1 8HG	–
Liverpool Chinese Gospel Church	0151 709 5050 (church office) 0151 709 5058 (church centre)	11 Great George Square, Liverpool L1 5DY	–
Liverpool Reform Synagogue	0151 733 5871	28 Church Road North, Liverpool L15 6TF	lrshul.org
Shree Radha Krishna Temple	0151 263 7965	Hindu Cultural Organisation, 253 Edge Lane, Liverpool L7 2PH	hcoliverpool.com
Gurdwara and Sikh Community Centre	01517343751; 07502176645	Wellington Avenue, Liverpool, L15 0EJ	–
St Charles Borromeo	0151 727 2493	224 Aigburth Road, Aigburth, Liverpool L17 9PG	stcharles.org.uk/church
Blessed Sacrament	0151 474 2682	9 Park Vale Road, Aintree, Liverpool L9 2DG	–
Our Lady Queen of Martyrs and St Swithin	0151 546 3574	Stonebridge Lane, Liverpool L11 9AZ	queenofmartyrs.org.uk
Holy Rosary	0151 526 8468	Altway, Aintree Village, Old Roan, Liverpool L10 2LG	–
St Bernadette	0151 427 7648	Heath Road, Mather Avenue, Allerton, Liverpool L19 4TW	–
All Saints	0151 287 8787	3 Oakfield, Anfield, Liverpool L4 2QG	–
St James	0151 933 8022	Chesnut Grove, Bootle, Liverpool L20 4LX	–
St Monica	0151 922 4819	Fernhill Road, Bootle, Liverpool L20 9GA	–
St Robert Bellarmine	0151 922 1352	52 Orrell Road, Bootle, Liverpool L20 6DZ	–
Christ the King	0151 722 2231	78 Queens Drive, Childwall, Liverpool L15 6YQ	–
St Helen	0151 924 3417	Alexandra Road, Crosby Liverpool L23 7TQ	sthelenscrosby.org.uk

Church of England congregation in Prescot. **Services** Sunday 9.30am and 11am

All are welcomed warmly in the name of Christ. **Services** Weekday 8am, 12.15pm, 5.15pm; Saturday 9am; Sunday 6.30pm (vigil), 8.30am, 10am, 11am, 4pm, 7pm

The church community is a mixture of Nordic and British people making up the congregation at the Gustaf Adolf Church, which is a Grade II* listed building dating from 1884. **Services** *September*: Sunday 2nd: 13th Sunday in Trinity service 11.30am, lunch afterwards; Wednesday 5th: coffee morning 11am; Sunday 9th: 14th Sunday in Trinity service with a Swedish priest 11.30am, lunch afterwards; Wednesday 12th: coffee morning 11am; service with Norwegian priest 1pm; Wednesday 19th: coffee morning 11am; Friday 21st: Linnea evening for Swedish-speaking ladies 7.30pm; Saturday 22nd: Finnish school 2pm; Sunday 23rd: 16th Sunday in Trinity Service 11.30am, lunch afterwards; Wednesday 26th: coffee morning 11am; *October*: Wednesday 3rd: coffee morning 11am; Saturday 6th: Finnish school 2pm; Sunday 7th: 18th Sunday in Trinity service with an Anglican priest 11.30am, lunch afterwards; Wednesday 10th: coffee morning, 11am; service with a Norwegian priest 1pm; Thanksgiving Sunday 14th: service with a Swedish priest 11.30am, lunch afterwards; Wednesday 17th: coffee morning 11am; Friday 19th: Linnea evening for Swedish-speaking ladies 7.30pm; Saturday 20th: Finnish school 2pm; Wednesday 24th: coffee morning 11am; Sunday 28th: 21st Sunday in Trinity service 11.30am, lunch afterwards; Wednesday 31st: coffee morning 11am; *November and December*: 4 November: service with Anglican priest 11.30am; LiNC AGM 12.30pm, lunch; 24 November: Christmas Fair 12–3pm; 1–2 December: Finnish independence celebrations

We are a dynamic, evangelical congregation that meets weekly at our church building in Liverpool's Chinatown. **Services** Sunday: English Service 10–11.20am; Junior Church 1 10–11.15am; Cantonese service 12–1.30pm; Junior Church 2 12–1.30pm; Youth Group 12–2.45pm; Mandarin service 2–3.30pm

A point of focus for members of the community wishing to practise the principles of Reform Judaism. **Services** Erev Shabbat service times: 8pm weekly; Shabbat service times: 11am weekly

Shree Radha Krishna Hindu Temple is formed by the Hindu community in Liverpool to practise their religious faith. The essence of Hinduism is to spread and follow the ethos of love, peace and devotion towards the almighty in a secular society that is so diverse and complex in nature. HCO works with other faiths to promote harmony. **Services** Monday 10am–1pm; Tuesday 10am–1pm, 6–10pm; Wednesday 10am–3pm; Thursday 10am–1pm; Friday 10am–3pm; Saturday closed; Sunday 10am–6pm

–

Welcome to St Charles Borromeo Roman Catholic Church. You can find us on Aigburth Road just between Tramway Road and the TA building. **Services** Monday 12pm; Thursday 12pm; Friday 12pm; Saturday 11am; Sunday 11.30am, 6pm

Roman Catholic congregation in Aintree. **Services** Sunday 4.30pm (vigil), 10.30am, 5pm; holy days as announced; Monday, 9.15am; Wednesday 9.15am (Oct–Apr), 7.30pm (May–Sept); Thursday 12pm; Friday 9.15am

Roman Catholic congregation. **Services** Sunday 6pm (vigil), 8.30am, 11.15am; holy days 7.30pm (vigil), 9.45am; weekdays 9.05am

Catholic congregation in Old Roan. **Services** Monday 9am; Tuesday 9am; Wednesday 12pm; Thursday 9am; Friday 9am; Saturday 12pm; Sunday 6pm (vigil), 10.30am, 6pm; holy days of obligation 9am, 12pm, 7.30pm

Roman Catholic congregation in Allerton. **Services** Sundays 10.15am

Catholic congregation in Anfield. **Services** Weekdays 12.15pm; Sunday 9.30am, 6pm; holy days of obligation 12.15pm, 7.30pm

Catholic congregation in Bootle. **Services** Weekday 10am; Saturday 10am; Sunday 10.30am, 6.30pm; holy days of obligation 7.30pm; Confession Saturday 10.30am

Catholic congregation in Aintree. **Services** Monday 12pm; Wednesday 12pm; Friday 12pm; Sunday 6pm (vigil) 9.30am

Catholic congregation in Bootle. **Services** Monday 10am; Tuesday 9am; Thursday 9am; Friday 9am; Saturday 12pm; Sunday 6.30pm (vigil), 8.30am, 10.30 am

Catholic congregation in Bootle. **Services** Monday 9.10am; Wednesday 7pm ; Friday 12pm; Sunday 6.30pm (vigil), 9.30am

Catholic congregation in Crosby. **Services** Tuesday 9.30am; Thursday 7pm; Saturday 12pm; Sunday 9.45am, 6.30pm; Confession Saturday 11.20am–12pm

St Anne	0151 709 4434	Overbury Street, Liverpool L7 3HJ	stannestbernardliverpool.org.uk
Our Lady of Immaculate Conception	0151 207 0177	York Terrace, Everton Liverpool L5 3RL	–
Holy Name	0151 476 0289	Moss Pits Lane, Fazakerley Liverpool L10 9LG	holynameandstphilomena.org.uk
St Aiden of Lindisfarne	0151 489 3085	Huyton Hey Road, Huyton, Liverpool L36 5RZ	–
Blessed Sacrament Shrine	0151 709 5528	4 Dawson Street, Liverpool L1 1LE	blessedsacramentuki.org/?page_id=
St Francis Xavier	0151 298 1911	Salisbury Street Liverpool L3 8DT	sfxchurchliverpool.com
St Michael and Sacred Heart	0151 263 6578	1 Horne Street, Liverpool L6 5EH	–
St Sylvester	0151 207 0161	27 Silvester Street, Liverpool L5 8SE	–
St Patrick	0151 727 1463	Park Place, Toxteth, Liverpool L8 5US	–
Our Lady of Reconciliation de la Salette	0151 207 0177	Eldon Street, Vauxhall, Liverpool L3 6HQ	–
Princes Road Synagogue	0151-709 3431	Liverpool Old Hebrew Congregation, Synagogue Chambers, Princes Road, Liverpool L8 1TG	princesroad.org
Liverpool Quakers	0151 709 6957	22 School Lane, Liverpool L1 3BT	liverpoolquakers.org.uk
Bahai Center	07989 029 172	3–5 Langdale Road, Wavertree, Liverpool L15 3LA	users.globalnet.co.uk/~njtrg/Bahai/welcome.htm
Liverpool Anglican Cathedral	0151 705 2150	St James House, St James Road, Liverpool L1 7BY	
Liverpool Greek Society	0753 421 8122	Liverpool Greek Society, 4th Floor Stanley Street, Muskers Building, Liverpool L1 6AA	
Bethel Church		Green Lane, Tuebrook Liverpool L13 7EA	bethelliverpool.co.uk
Liverpool Mosque and Islamic Institute	0151 734 1222	8 Cramond Avenue, Liverpool L18 1EQ	mosque.merseyside.org
Christ Church Liverpool		Archbishop Blanch School, Mount Vernon Road, Liverpool L7 3EA	
St Thomas Indian Orthodox Church		All Saints Parish Church, Broad Green Road, Liverpool, L13 5SH	
St Mary's Jacobite Syrian Orthodox Church		Stoneycroft Methodist Church, Greenfield Road, Old Swan, Liverpool L13 3BN	

Everyone is welcome because we aim to be prayerful, listening people, filled with hope, nourished and empowered by Word and Eucharist, seeking to enable one another to develop our God-given gifts for liturgy and service to others, sensitive and responsive to the joys and pains around us, open to all within the local community and beyond. We work together for the building of God's kingdom. **Services** Wednesday 8.30am; Friday 10am; Sunday 5.30pm (vigil), 11.15am and; holy days of obligation 6pm

Catholic congregation in Everton. **Services** Wednesday 9am; Sunday 11.30am; holy days of obligation 7pm

Catholic congregation in Fazakerly. **Services** Weekdays 9am; Sunday 6pm (vigil), 11am

Catholic congregation in Huyton. **Services** Tuesday 7.30pm; Friday 12pm; Sunday 9.30am; Confession Friday after Mass

We combine prayer and work in order that the entire world may be totally transformed into the people of God; the Body of the Lord and temple of the Holy Spirit. **Services** Weekday 8.25am, 12.10pm, 1.10pm, 5.40pm; Sunday 5.40pm (vigil), 11.30am, 5pm

Once the largest Roman Catholic parish in England with about 13,000 parishioners, the Church of Saint Francis Xavier is a magnificent Grade 2* listed building in Salisbury Street, Liverpool. **Services** Monday 12pm; Tuesday 12pm; Friday 12pm; Saturday 12pm; Sunday 10.15am

Catholic congregation. **Services** Sunday 10.30am

Catholic congregation. **Services** Weekday 8.15am; Saturday 9am; Sunday 11am

This large Neoclassical chapel stands officially on Park Place and was built between 1821 and 1827 to designs by John Slater. **Services** Sunday 9.45am

Catholic congregation in Vauxhall. **Services** Tuesday 9.15am; Thursday 9.15am; Sunday 6pm

The Liverpool Old Hebrew Congregation is a friendly, Orthodox Jewish community at the heart of Liverpool, steeped in tradition and Victorian elegance. **Services** Friday nights (vary according to time of sunset); Saturday mornings 9.45am; festival mornings 9.30am

We seek to experience God directly, within ourselves and in our relationships with others and the world around us. **Services** Sundays 10.30am; Wednesdays 6.15pm; Thursdays 1pm

This centre is a focus for a wide range of Bahai activities around Merseyside, attracting attendance from the Liverpool, Wirral, Sefton and St Helens communities. **Services** Sunday Sacred Space/Meditation 2.30pm

Services Sunday: Eucharist 8.30am; 10.30am Choral Eucharist (Main Space); Zone 2 All Age worship (Concert Room); Choral Evensong 3pm; Eucharist 4pm; Weekdays: Morning Prayer 8.30am; Eucharist 12:05; Choral Evensong 5.30pm (said evening prayer on Wednesdays and school holidays); Saturdays: Morning Prayer 8.30am; Eucharist 12:05; Choral Evensong 3pm

Bethel Church consists of a wide range of different people, from all ages and different backgrounds. Whoever you are, you are assured a very warm welcome. **Services** Sunday 10.45 am, 6.30pm

The Liverpool Mosque and Islamic Institute was set up as a registered charity in England (No. 1071951) to cater for the needs of Muslims in the south Liverpool area. **Services** At the present time, jamaat prayers are held. In addition, after-school religious education classes (madrassah) for Muslim children aged between 7 to 15 are also held on Tuesday and Wednesday evenings.

At Christ Church we believe that the good news about Jesus is for everyone. That means we welcome people of all ages, races and background to our church family and take every opportunity we can to learn more about Christ and share his message with the people of our city. We'd love you to come along and join us. **Services** Sunday 10.30am, 6pm

St Thomas Indian Orthodox Church, Liverpool is a parish of the UK, Europe and Africa Diocese of the Malankara Orthodox Syrian Church of India. We inherit the untainted apostolic faith from Apostle St Thomas, which has been upheld and preserved with reverence for generations. **Services** Every first and third Sunday Holy Qurbana 2.30pm

Our aim is to advance the religion and to relieve poverty and sickness in the North West of England. We ask you to join with us for the unforgettable worshipping service. **Services** Holy Qurbana is held on every second Saturday and fourth Sunday 9.30am

Hope City Church, Liverpool	0151 207 0033	The Megacentre, The Elaine Norris Building, 241 Vauxhall Road, Liverpool L5 8TY	
Belvidere Road Church	0151 728 9293	Belvidere Road, Princes Park, Liverpool L8 3TG	belvidere.org.uk
Jubilee Church Liverpool	0151 486 0513	St Hilda's C of E High School, Croxteth Drive, Sefton Park, Liverpool L17 3AR	
RCCG Love Assembly		8–10 Myrtle Parade, Liverpool L7 7EL	rccg-loveassembly.co.cc
St Elisabeth the New Martyr	0151 653 7768	58 Shrewsbury Road, Oxton, Prenton, Birkenhead CH43 2HY	newmartyr.info
Liverpool City Church	0151 280 6466	Jubilee Drive, Kensington, Liverpool L7 8SL	liverpoolcitychurch.org/lcc
Liverpool City Mission	0151 709 8866	Mount Pleasant, Liverpool L3 5RY	livercm.org.uk/page910.html
Dovedale Baptist Church	0151 733 4791	Dovedale Road, Liverpool L18 1DW	dovedalebaptist.co.uk
Cornerstone Church	0151 345 8558	Ramilies Road, Mossley Hill, Liverpool L18 1ED	cornerstonechurchliverpool.org
Dovecot Evangelical church	0151 480 4195	424 East Prescot Road, Liverpool, L14 2EH	dovecotevangelicalchurch.org/belie html
Bridge Chapel	0151 281 9716	Bridge Chapel, Heath Road, Liverpool L19 4XR	bridgechapel.co.uk
Aigburth Community Church	0151 7274812	20 Woodlands Road, Aigburth, Liverpool L17 0AW	bethelliverpool.co.uk
Hope Baptist Church		Hope Baptist Church, Southport Road, Bootle Liverpool L20 9NR	hopebaptistchurch.co.uk
Elim Kensington Church	0151 228 5727	Coleridge Street, Kensington, Liverpool L6 6BT	liverpoolelim.org.uk
Circle of Pagans		The Casa Bistro, Hope Street, Liverpool L1 9BQ	circleofpagans.co.uk

Hope City Church is all about loving God, loving life, and loving people. With that in mind everything we do is to build the kingdom of God, bring out the God potential in people and live life the way God intended. **Services** Sunday 11am–12.30pm

Belvidere Road Church is a group of Reformed Bible-believing Christians seeking to glorify God, strengthen His people, and spread the gospel of Jesus Christ to the ends of the Earth – starting with Toxteth, Liverpool. **Services** Sunday: Worship 10.15am, 6pm; Wednesday: Belvidere Tots 9.30am; Bible Study and Prayer 8pm; Thursday: Prime Time (third Thursday every month) 12.30pm; Ladies' Night 8pm; Friday: BBB 6.15pm; Impact 8pm; Saturday: Men's Prayer Breakfast (first Saturday every month) 7.30am

We believe the message of Jesus Christ is the most relevant message for today. We are thrilled to be in relationship with God and want to share this with others in Liverpool, across Merseyside and touch the nations of the world. **Services** Sundays 10.30am

Our vision is 'To see people from all nations' in the unity of the faith and love of our Lord Jesus Christ.' **Services** Sunday school for children and adults 10.30am; Sunday worship and service 11am; Thursday Bible study 7pm; Friday midnight service 10pm–12am

We are a parish of the Orthodox Church in the Diocese of Great Britain and Ireland, striving to live the Orthodox Faith. We are a small but growing community from various backgrounds, with people from Russia to Philadelphia, with Britons and others in between. **Services** Saturday 5.30pm; Sunday 9.45am

We are a Charismatic church located close to the centre of the city of Liverpool. **Services** Sunday: Morning celebration 10.30am; Children's church 11am; Evening meeting 6pm; Late night service 8pm; Tuesday: Prayer meeting 7am; Area House Groups: Wavertree 7.30pm; Kensington 7pm; Fairfield 7.45pm; Young Adults 7.30pm; Thursday: Acts Bible School 7.15pm; Friday: Youth House Groups 7.30pm

Services Monday to Friday 7–8.40am

We are a family-centred evangelical Baptist church in south Liverpool. **Services** Sunday 10.30am

Cornerstone Church is a friendly, Bible-believing, Jesus-worshipping church that seeks to be faithful to the Gospel word and faithful to living in Gospel community. **Services** Sunday 10.30am

We are a local church within mainstream Christianity, with beliefs that have been held by Christians for the last 2,000 years. **Services** Sunday 11am, 6pm

Bridge Chapel is a lively Bible-believing church with many adults, children and young people attending regularly. **Services** Sunday: Family service 9.30am; Morning worship 11.30am; Evening worship 6.30pm

We're a church made up of all sorts of people in different situations, with a variety of jobs and from a wide spectrum of backgrounds. **Services** Sunday 10.30am, 6pm

We are a group of ordinary people who believe in God and meet to worship and learn more about Him. **Services** Sunday: Family worship 10.45am; Junior church 3pm; Evening worship 6.30pm

Our church family come from a wide variety of backgrounds and nationalities that reflect the community that we love and reach out to. **Services** Sunday service 10am, 6pm

Circle of Pagans is a local community group based in Liverpool. We have members from Liverpool, Warrington, Chester and the Wirral. Through our moots, social events and conferences we aim to provide a friendly, accessible environment for Pagans in the North West area. **Services** 3rd Monday of every month from 7.30pm

Jose Angel Vincench

Dear Andrés

It is a long time since I heard from you and the family. Tell me,
how is life, your exile? I am still waiting for a written account
of this drastic change. What has it been like to leave everything
behind and start again? Could you write something today about
everything you have been through?

I am attaching my work exhibited at the Biennale in Havana.
I believe you are part of it.

Best wishes
Vincench

www.vincenchart.com

http://www.designboom.com/weblog/cat/10/view/21218/jose-angel-
vincench-exile-at-havana-biennale-2012.html

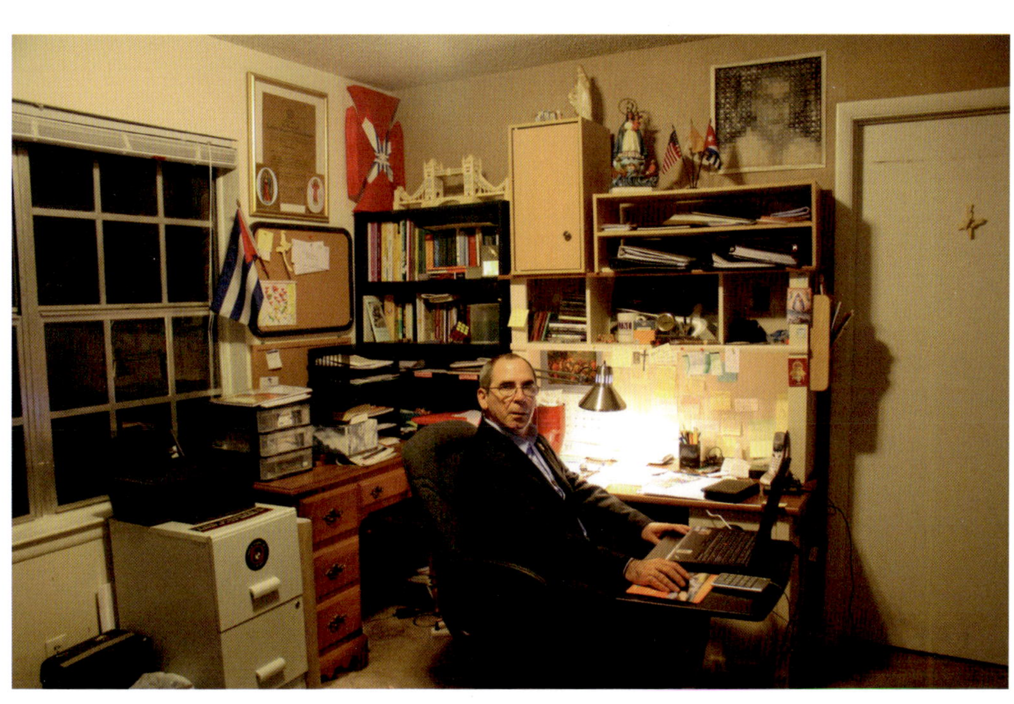

Ming Wong

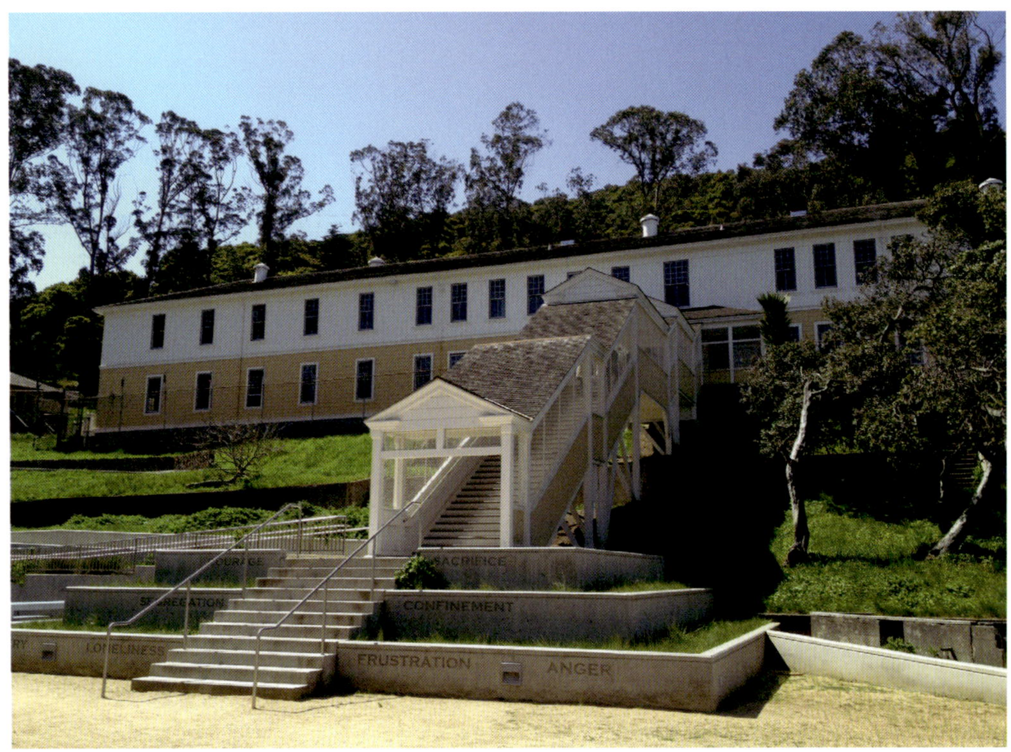

The detention barrack on Angel Island in San Francisco Bay. It served as an immigration centre from 1910 to 1940, mostly for Chinese immigrants entering America. Photograph taken 6 April 2012.

Abandoned for over two decades, the barrack was marked for destruction
by the government. In 1970 a park ranger discovered inscriptions on the walls.
These were the writings left by Chinese immigrants once detained there.

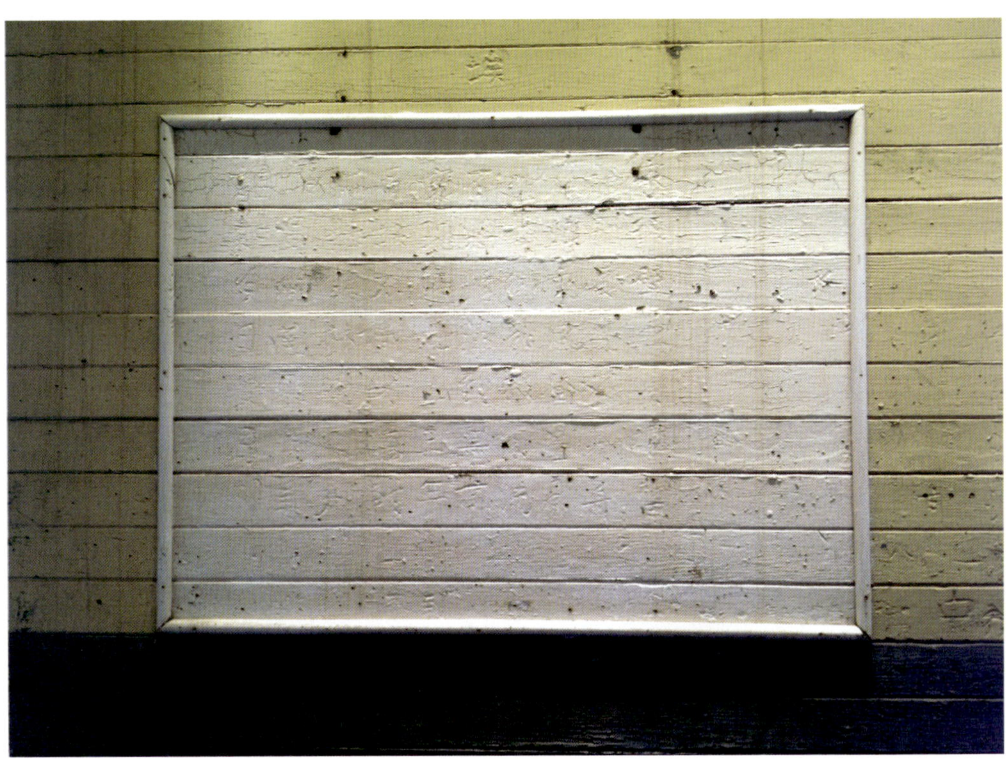

One hundred and thirty-five calligraphic poems have survived.

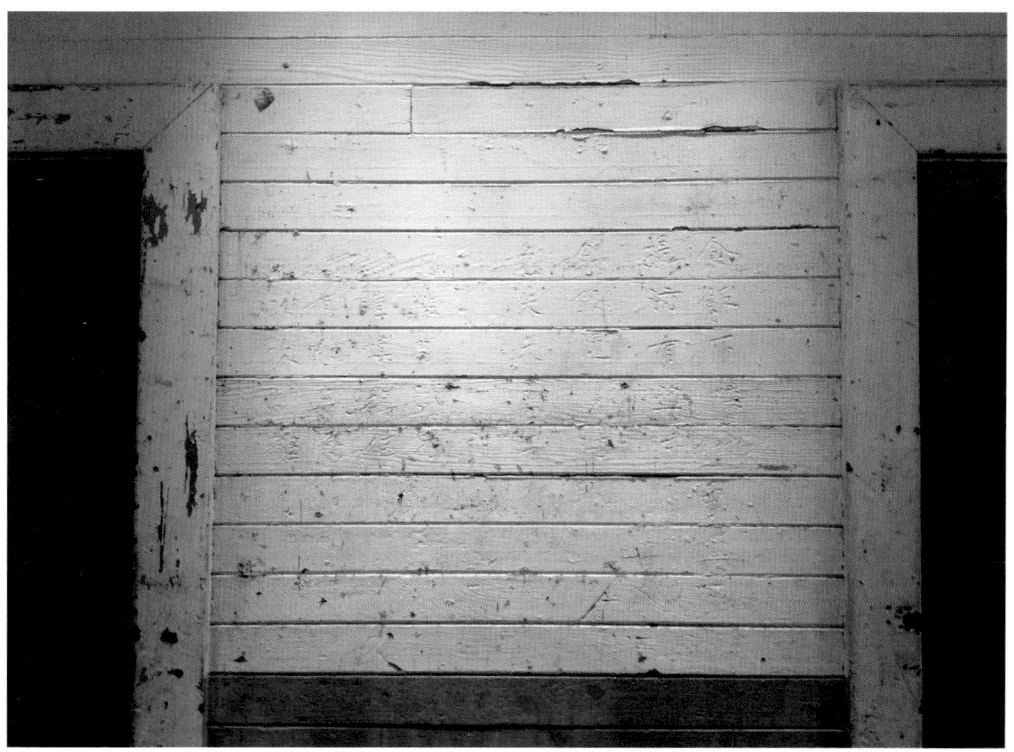

Written in brush and carved into the wood, the poems were eventually covered over by coats of paint. Over time and after exposure to the natural elements, the words and forms have re-emerged from the past.

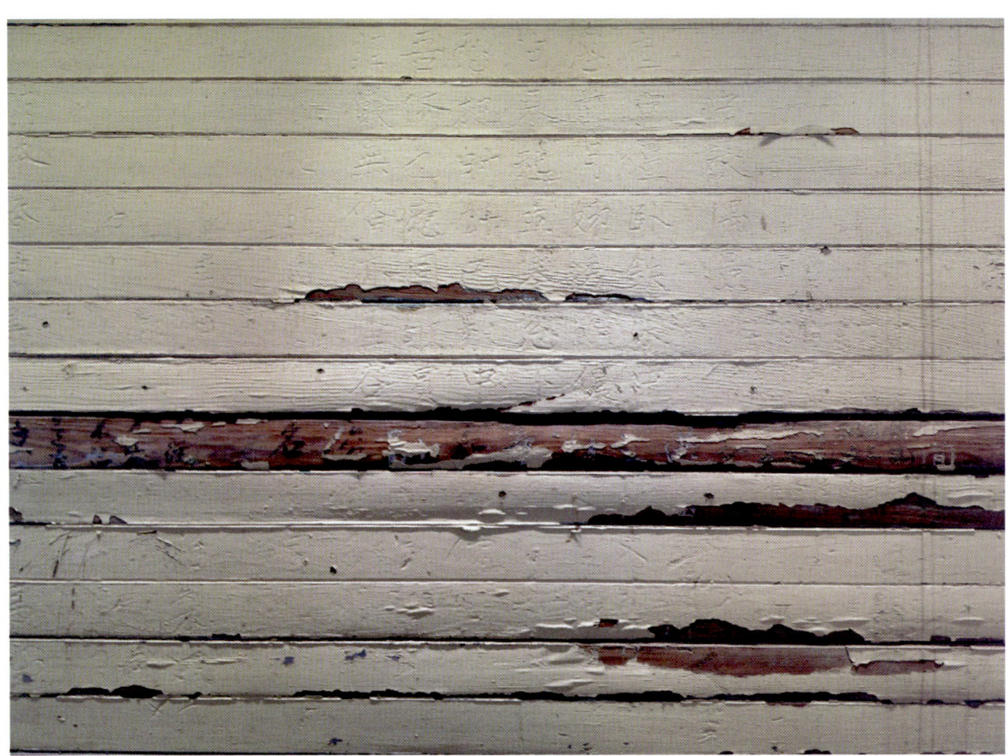

'From now on, I am departing far from this building. All of my fellow villagers are rejoicing with me.'

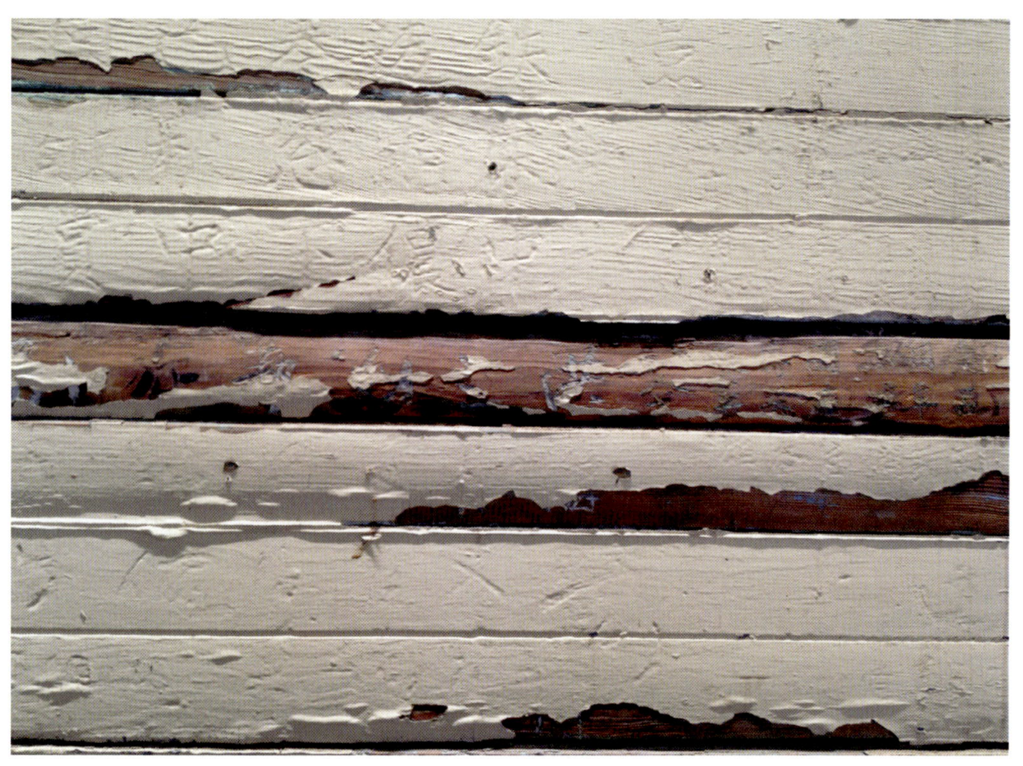

'Don't say that everything within is Western styled. Even if it is built of jade,
 it has turned into a cage.'

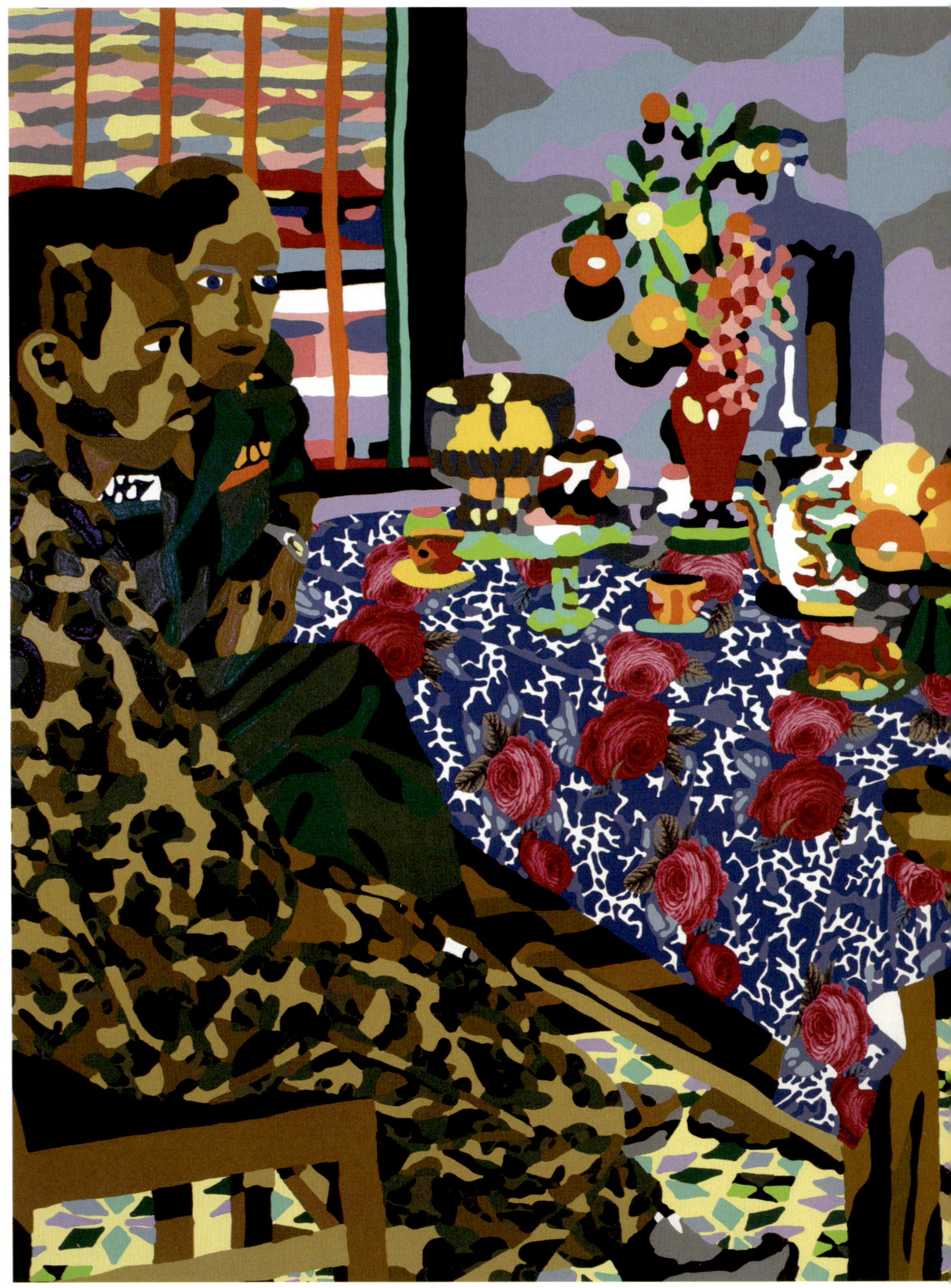

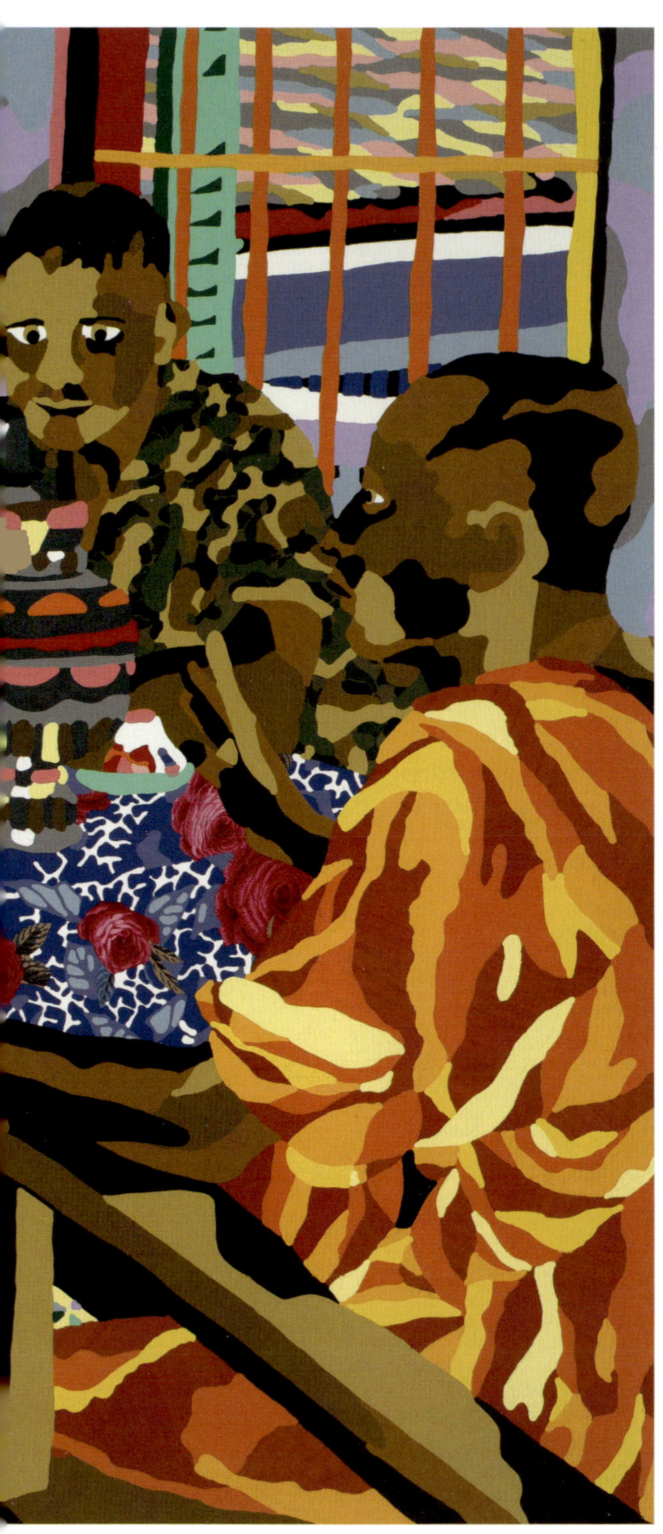

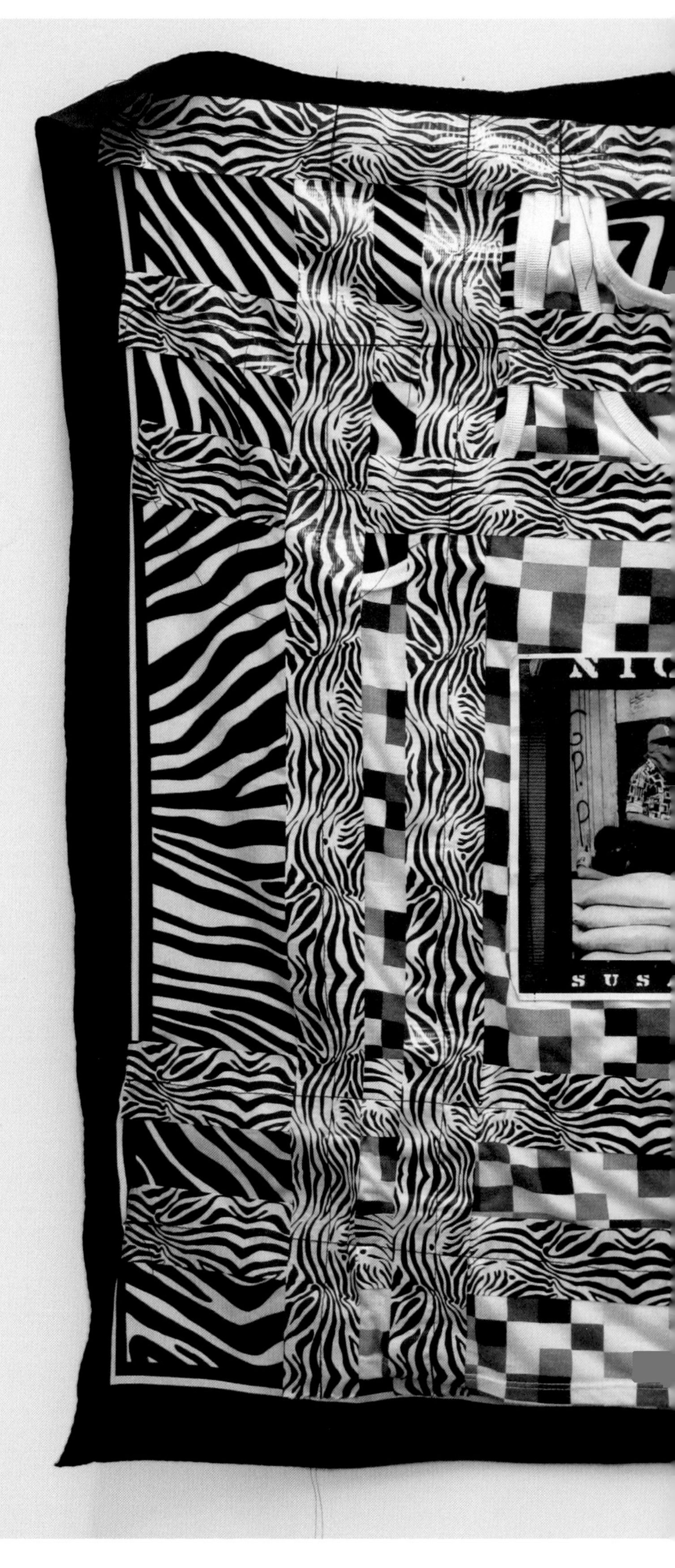

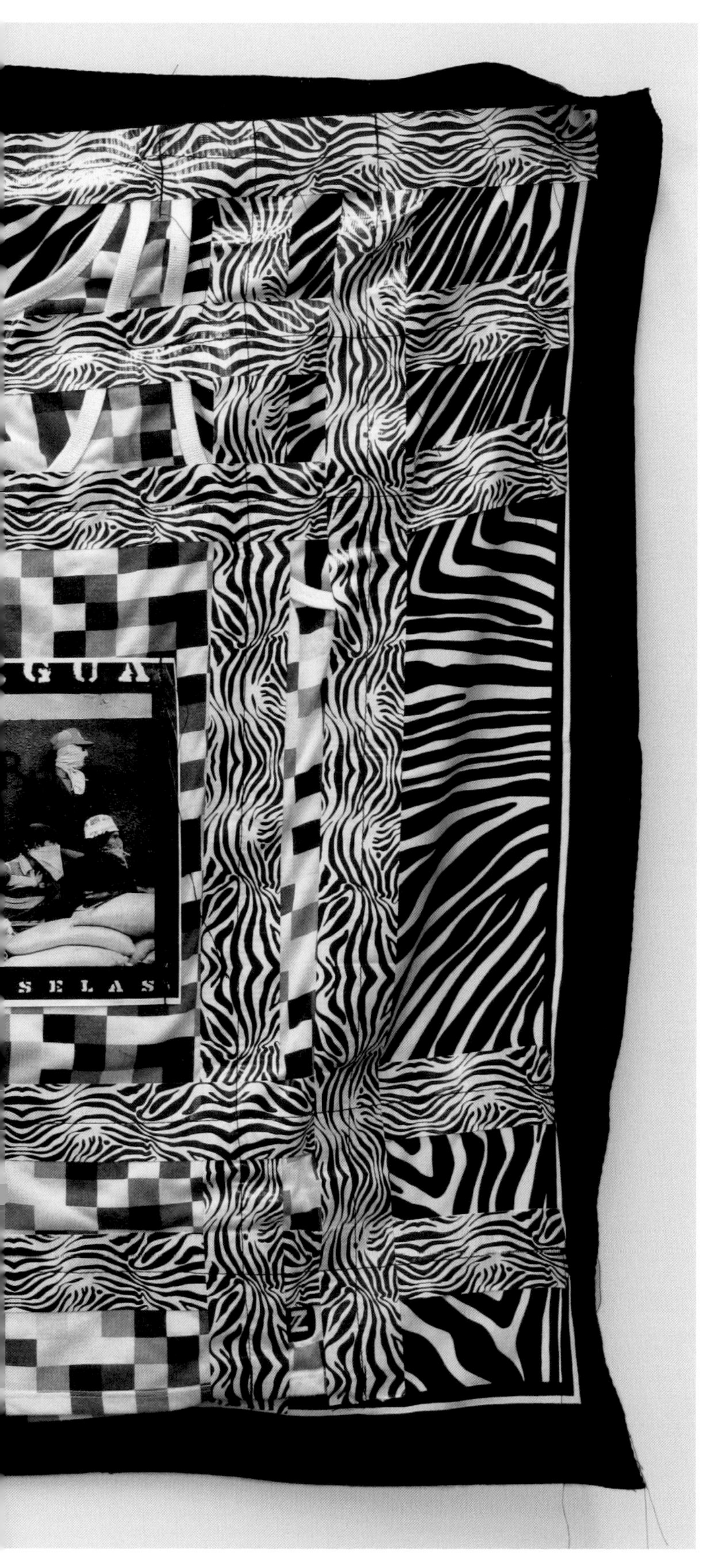

GUA
SELAS

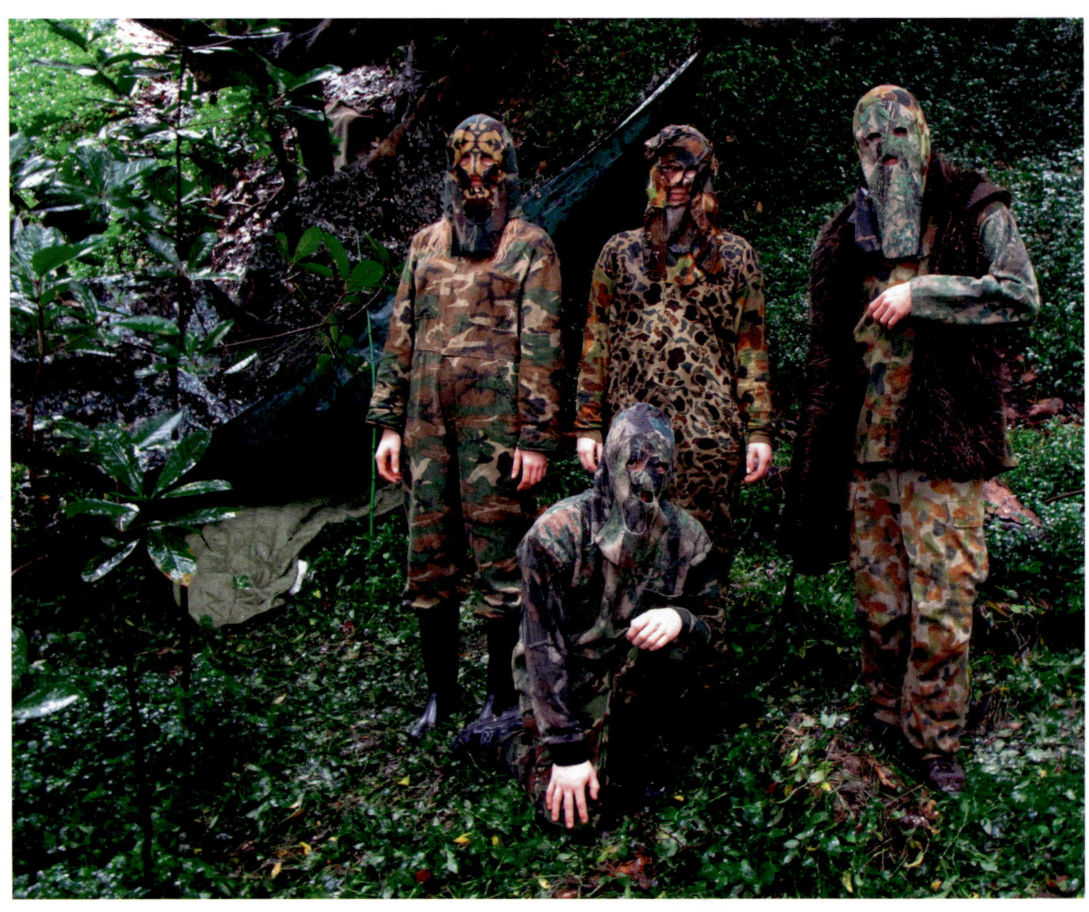

Combat Drag (New Zealand), 2010
Production still, variable dimensions

Right: *Conflict to Comfort* (working title), 2011–ongoing (detail)
Woven secondhand hunting and camouflage T-shirts, 60 cm diameter

Pages 200–1: *As seen by Dicky Chapelle,*
US special forces and their interpreter drink tea and
discuss politics with a South Vietnamese Buddhist monk,
near Khanh Hung, South Vietnam, 1962, 2011
Poured acrylic paint and embedded fabric on canvas, 213×168 cm

Pages 202–3: *Social Clothing Experiments (For Susan)*, 2011
Sewn gaffer tape, photocopy and secondhand clothing, 86×86 cm

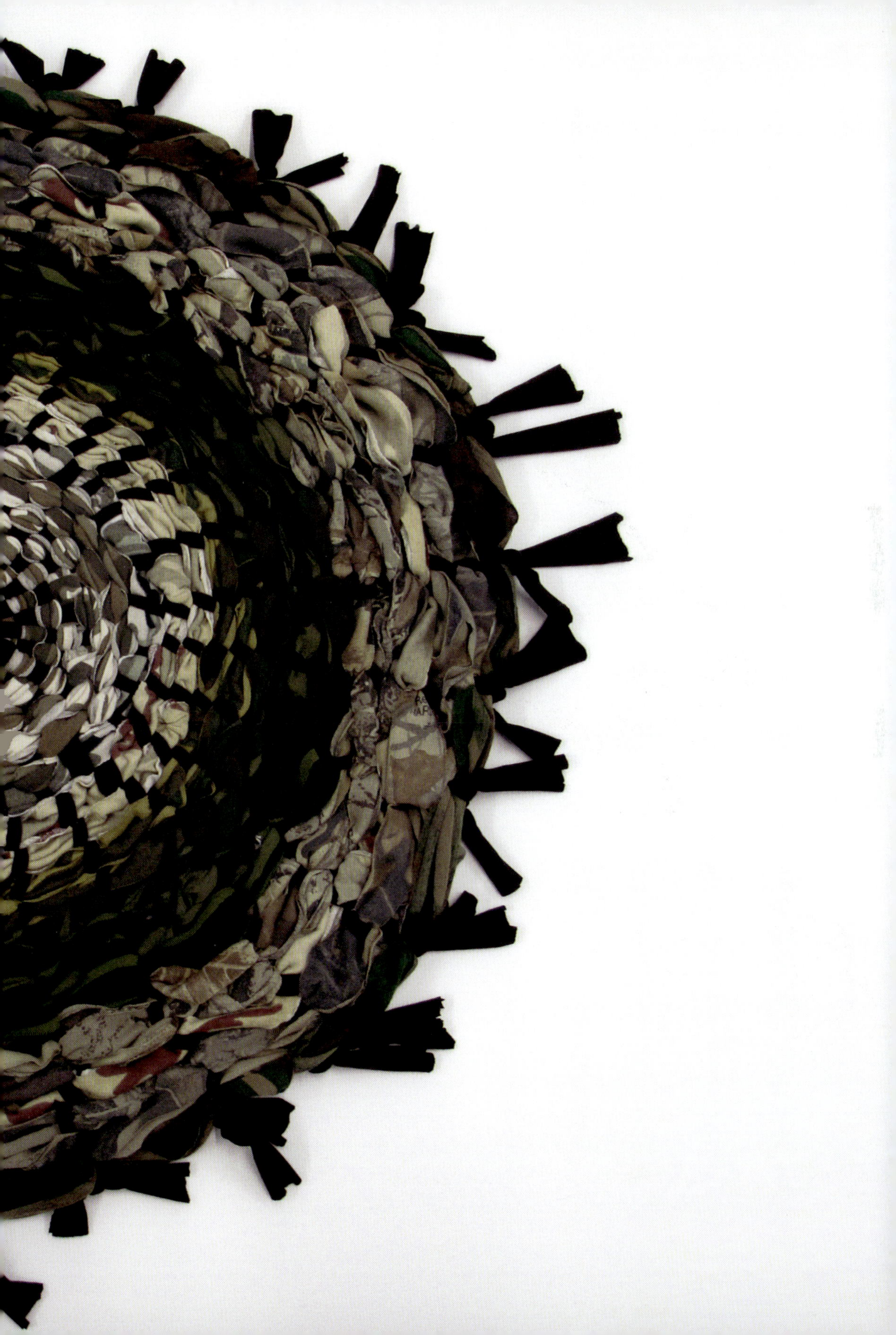

Kohei Yoshiyuki

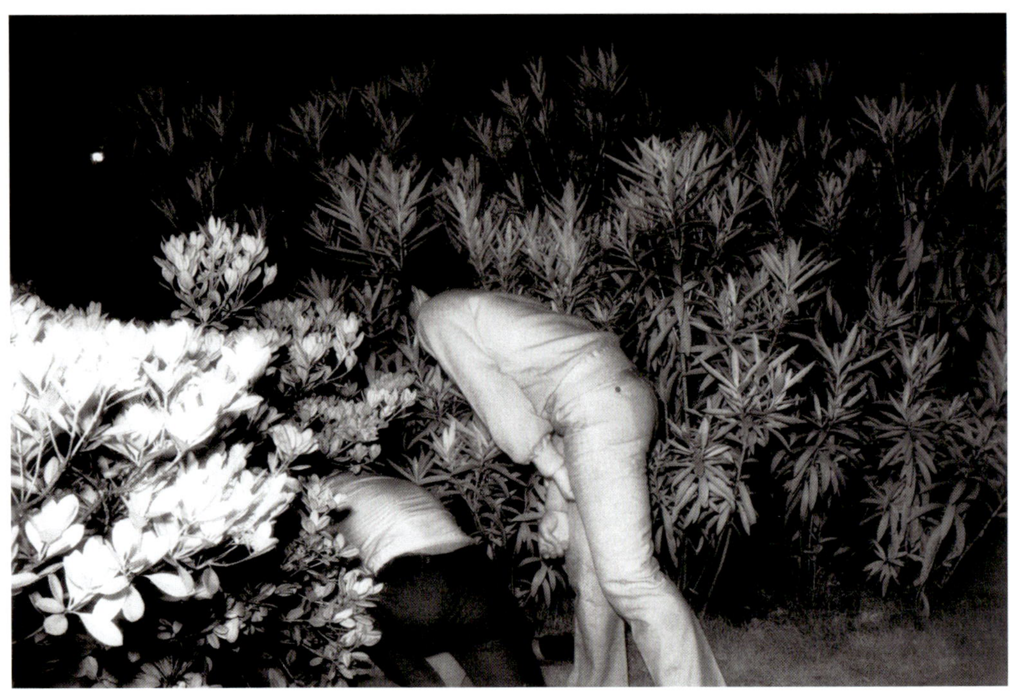

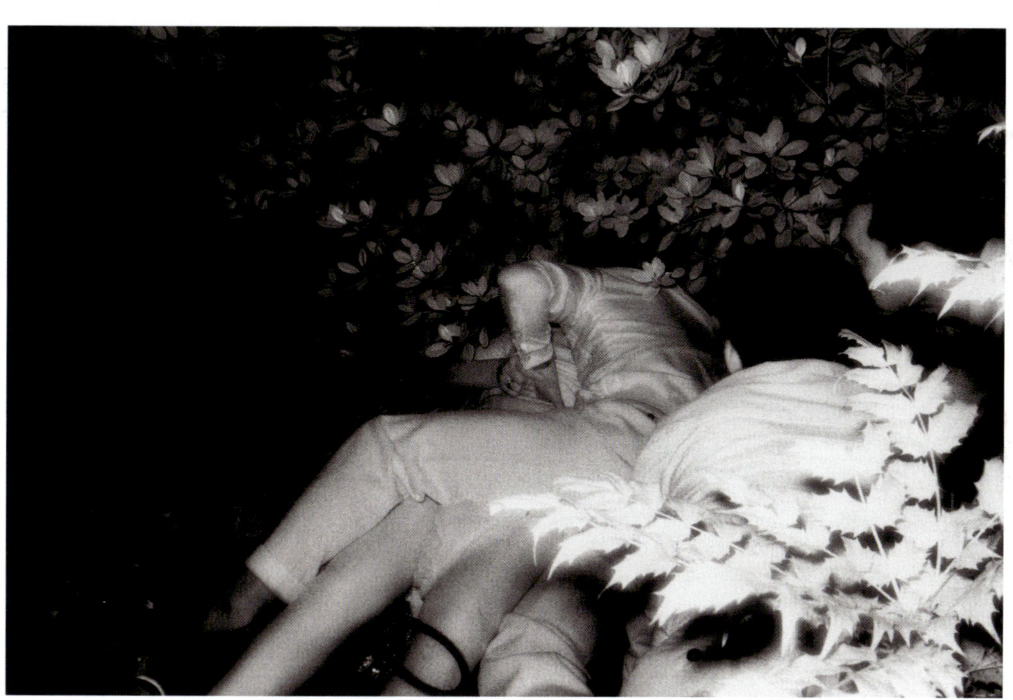

Untitled, 1972, from the series *The Park*
Gelatin silver print, 36×28 cm

Overleaf: *Untitled*, 1973, from the series
The Park, gelatin silver print, 36×28 cm

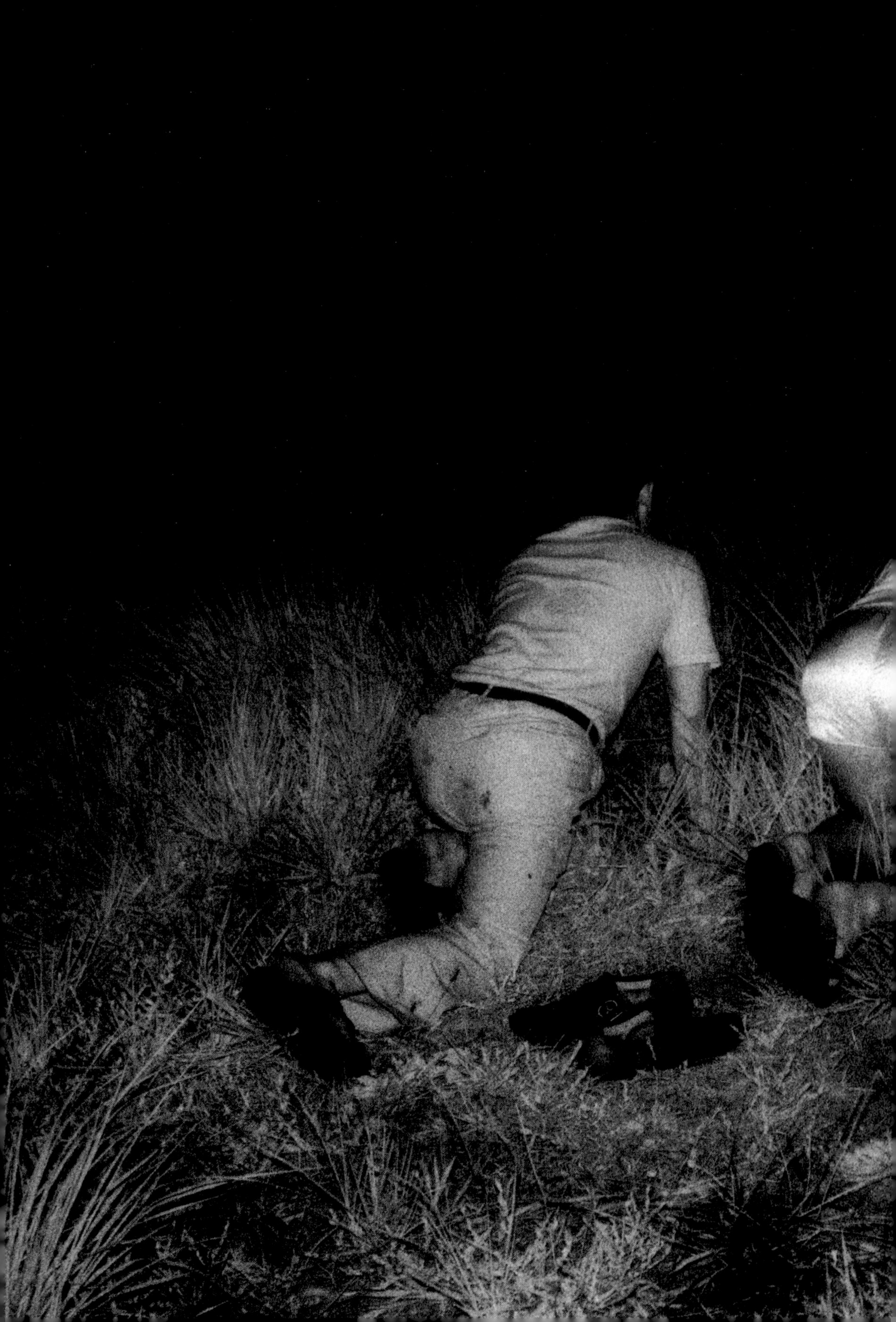

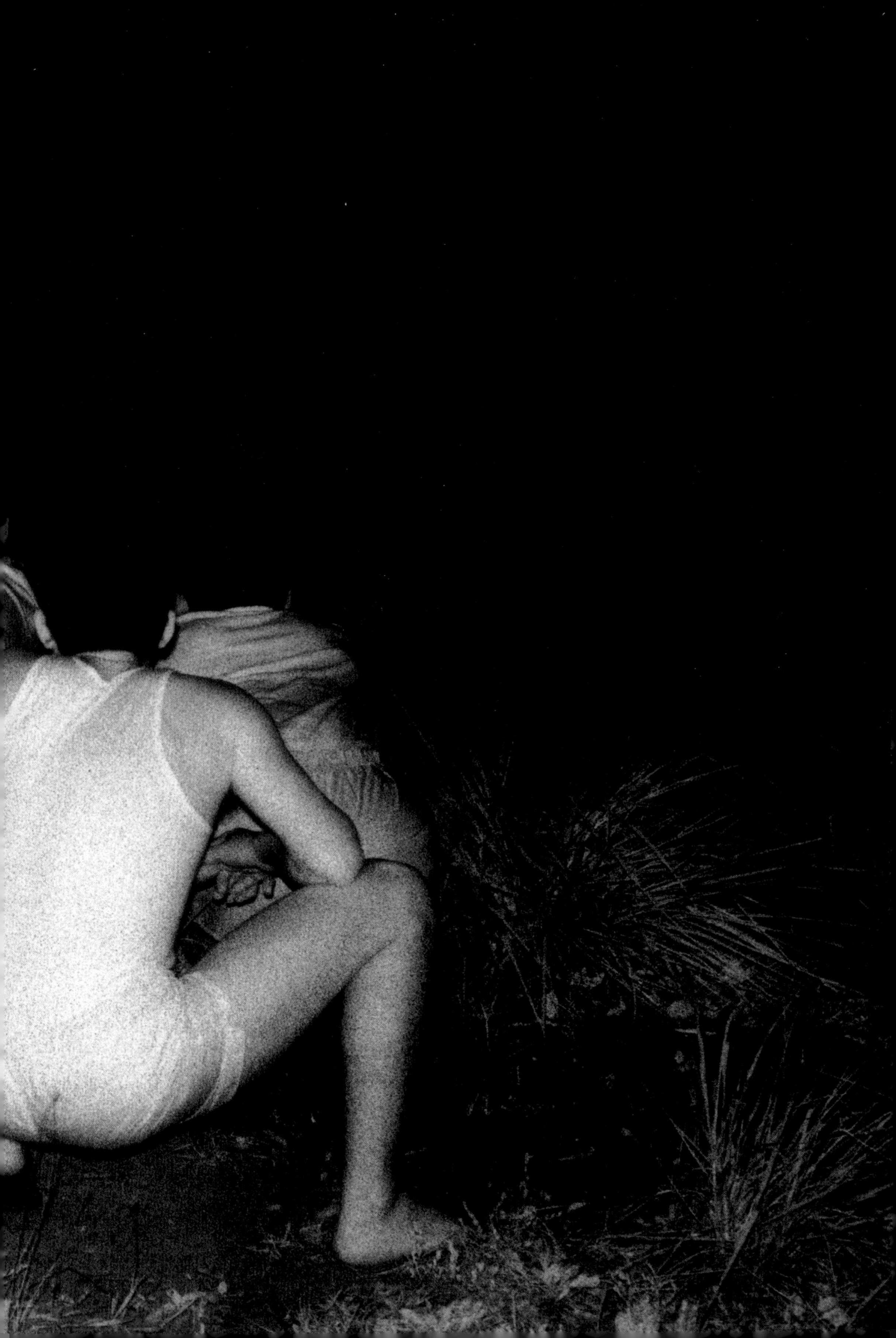

Akram Zaatari

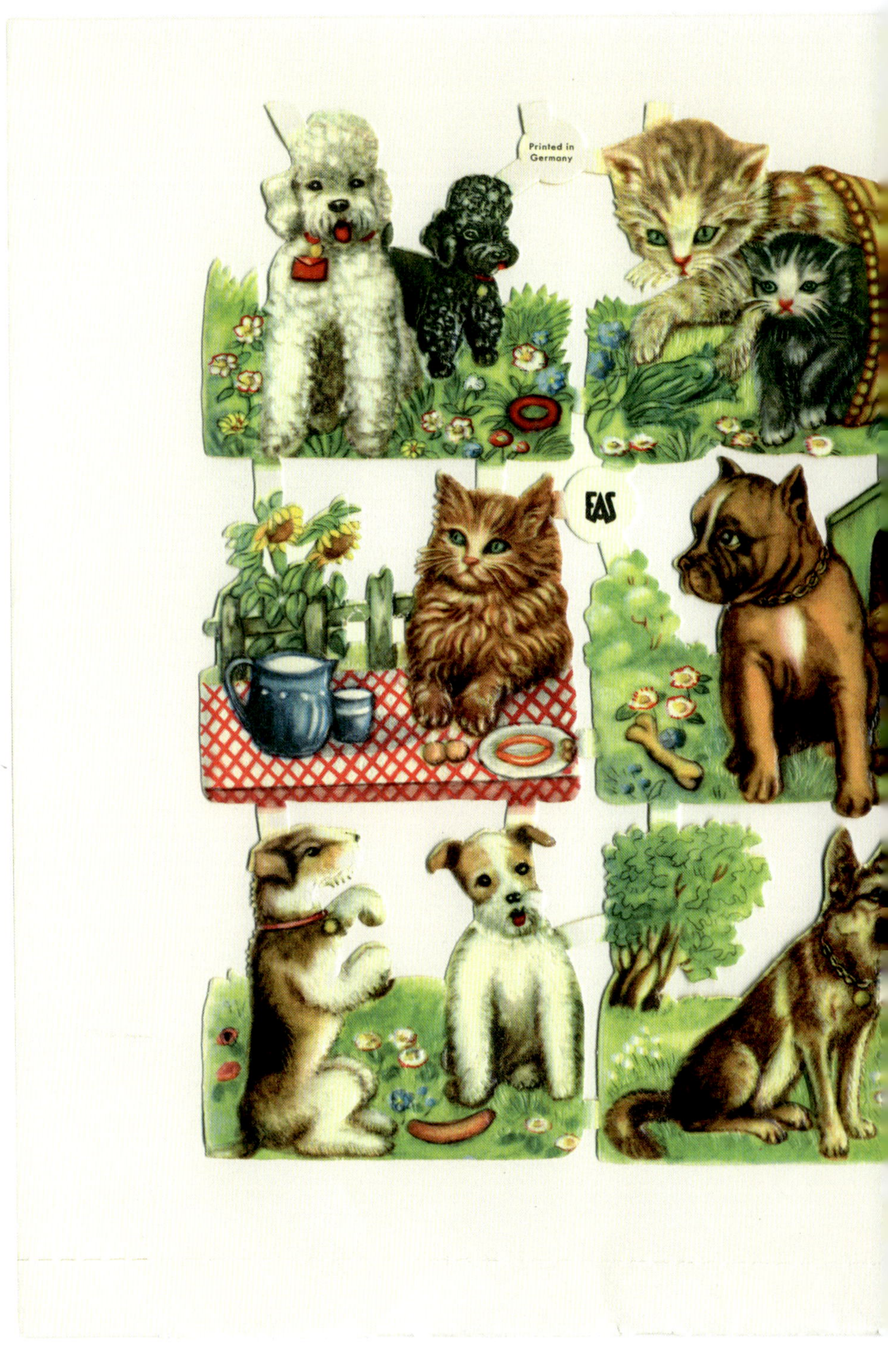

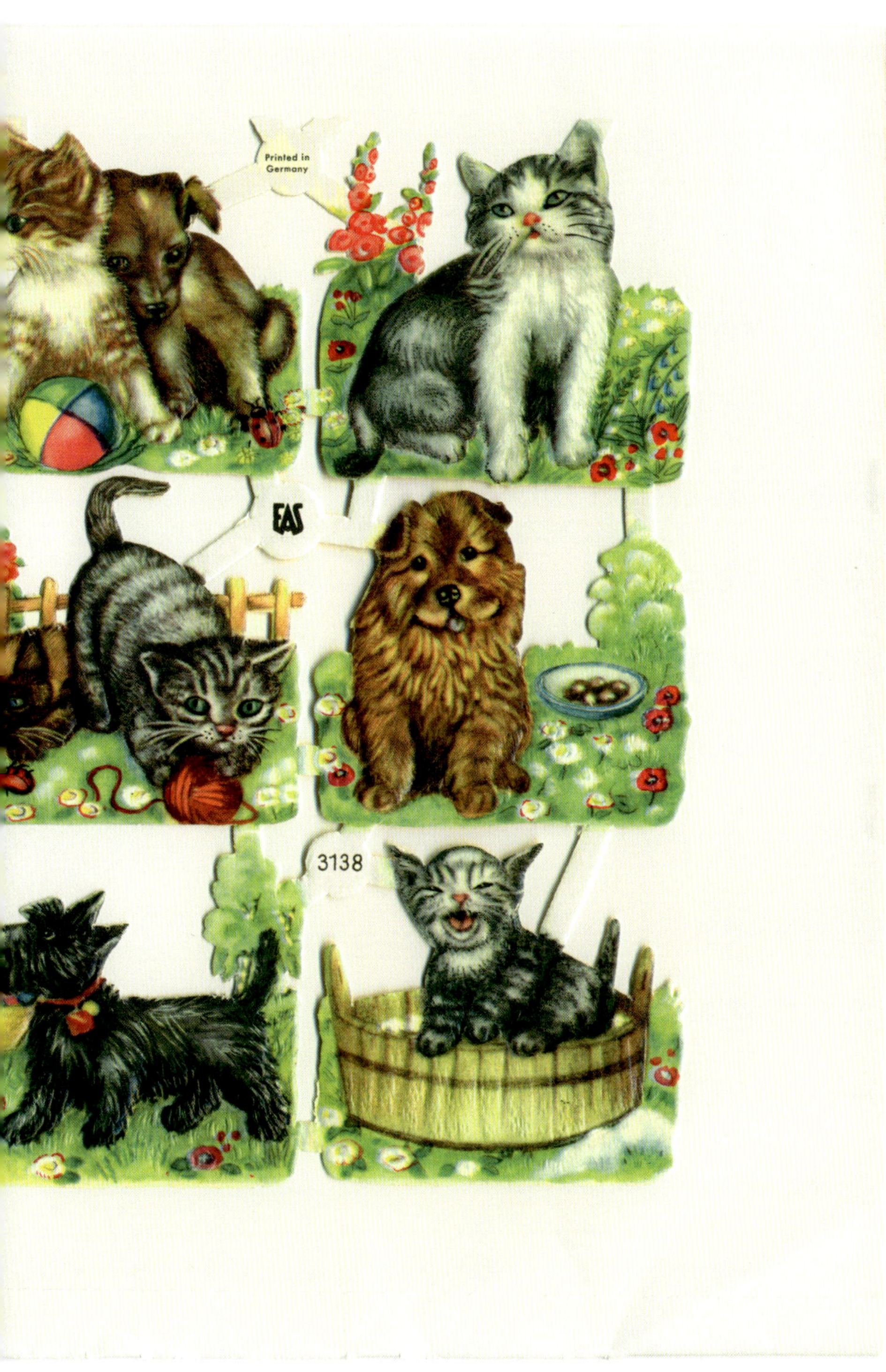

Printed in
Germany
EAS
3138

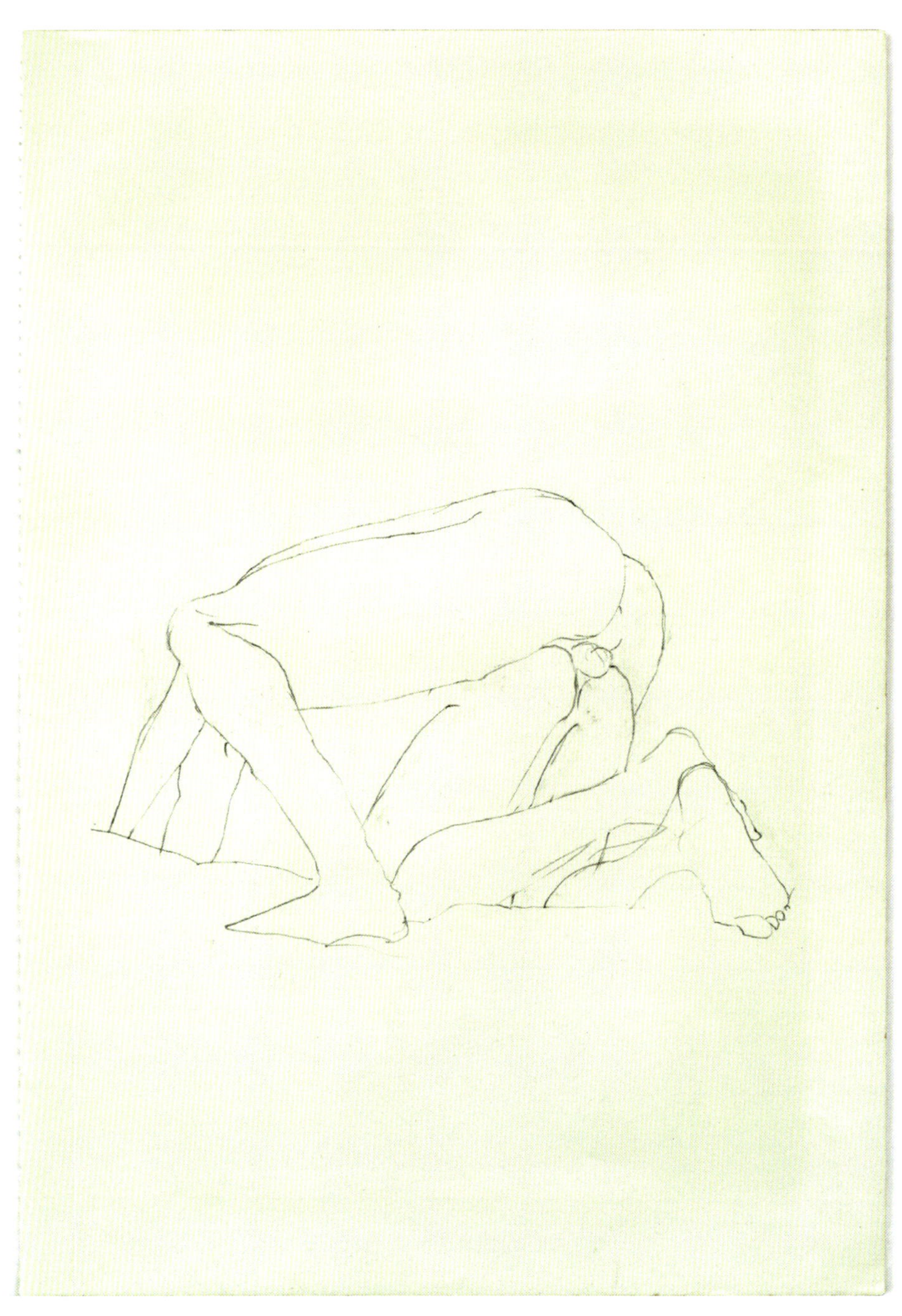

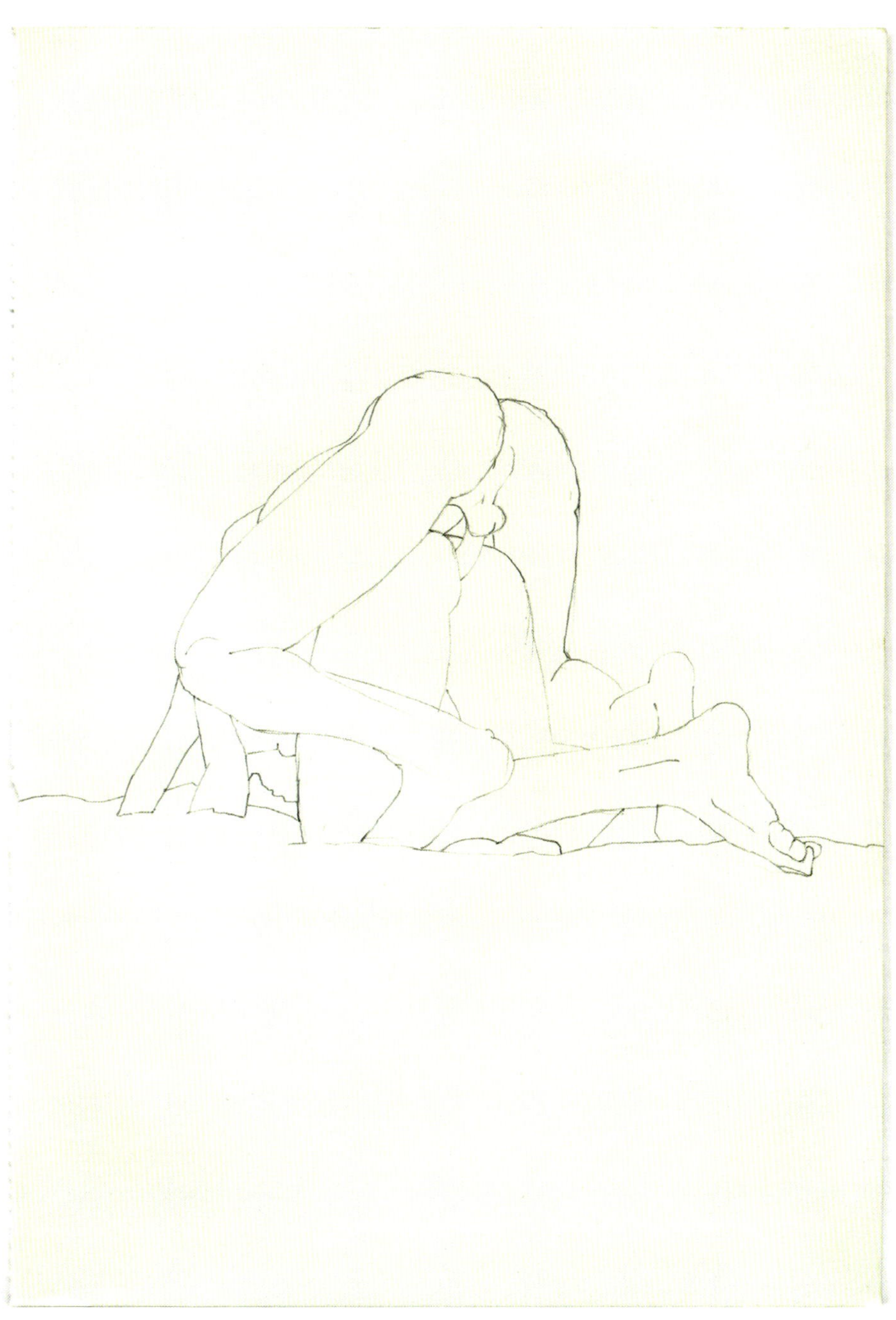

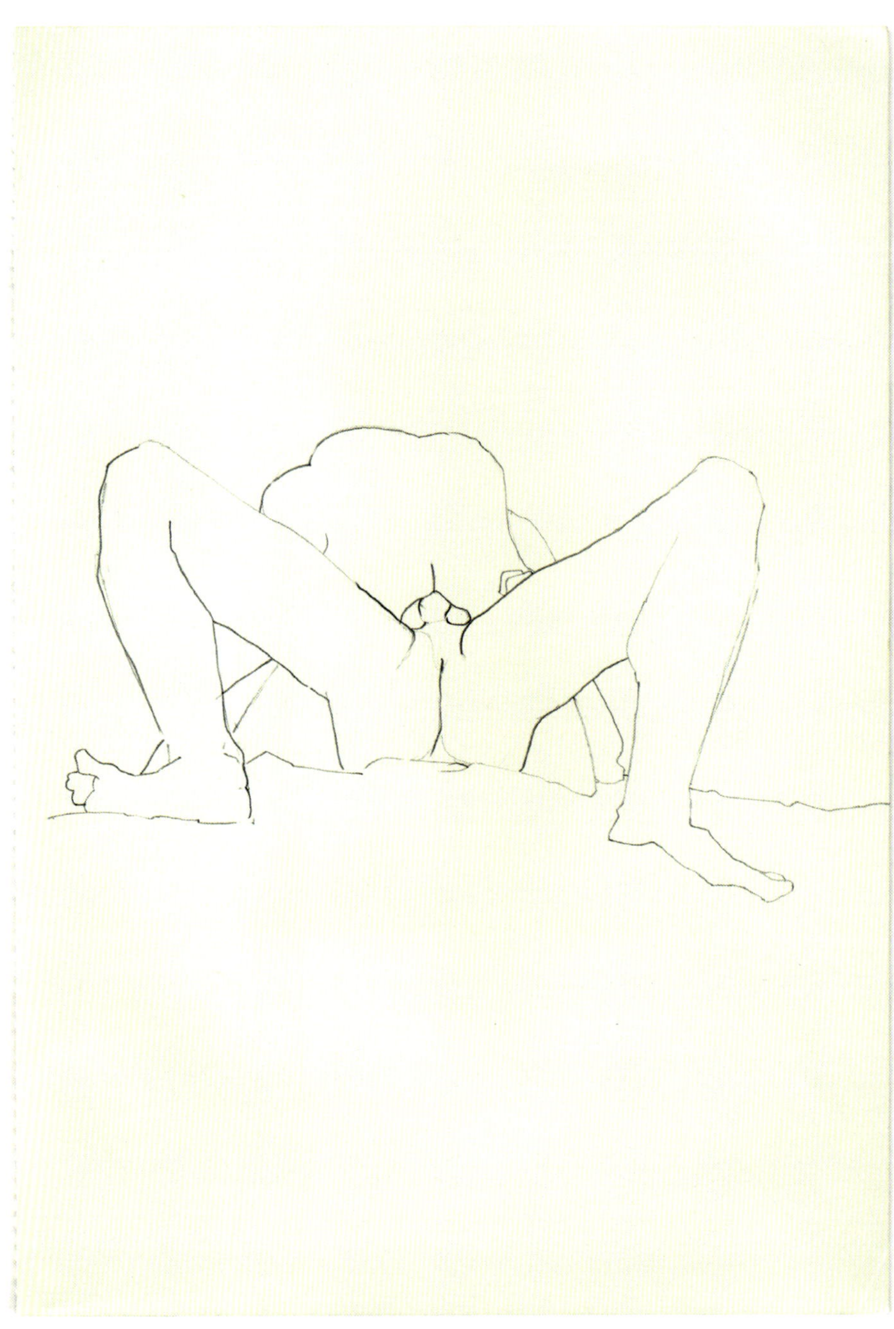

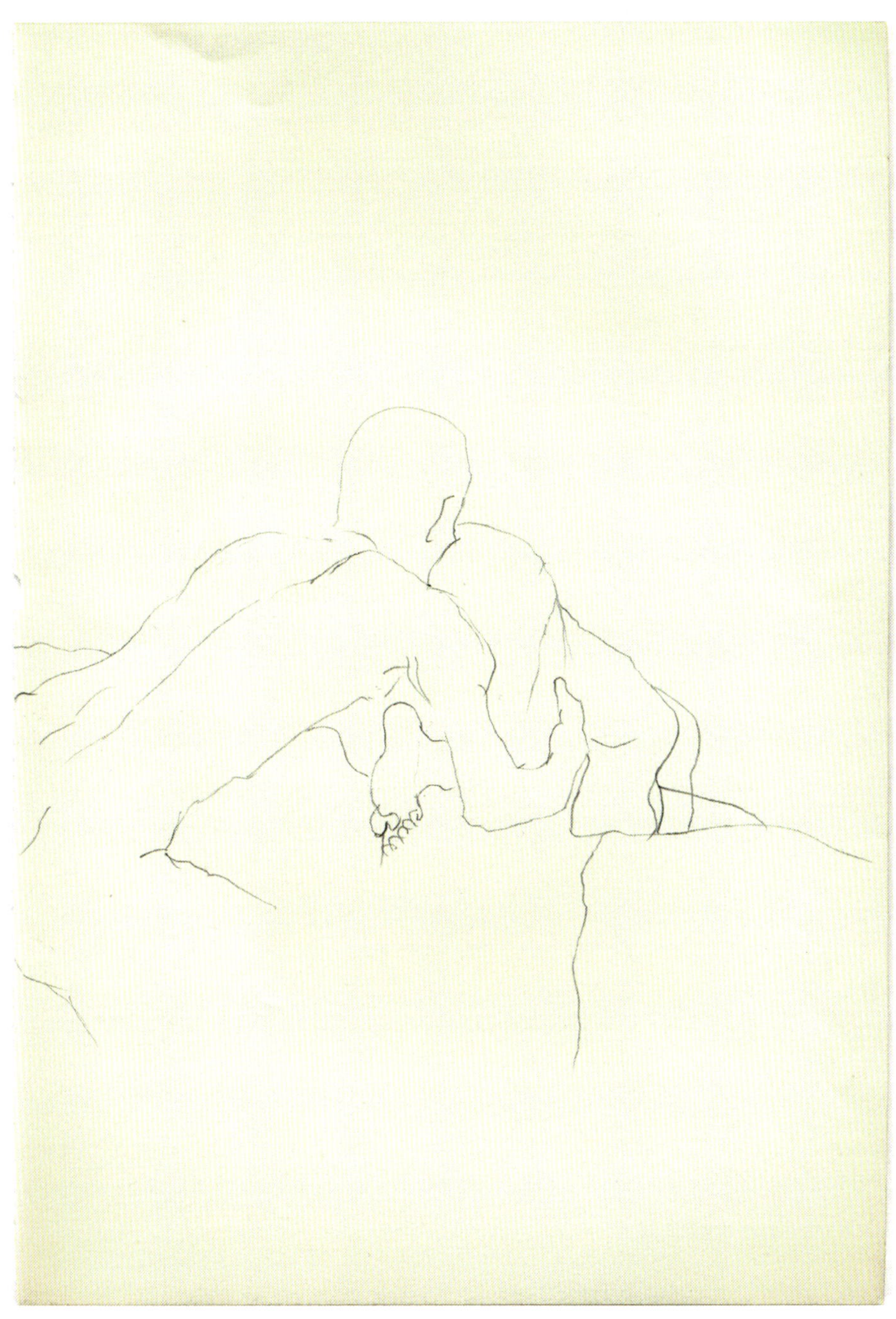

Writing

I The New Geography

As late as 1973 Susan Sontag could still state, 'A fake painting (one whose attribution is false) falsifies the history of art. A fake photograph (one which has been retouched or tampered with, or whose caption is false) falsifies reality.'[1] Forty years ago, fakeness was still the exception, not the rule that it is in today's digital world. The binary of true/false – art/reality bespeaks a less complicated time, before 'Pictures' generation-style appropriation, digital sampling in music, the phenomenon of avatars on the internet, and the rise of reality television. A photographic print was just that: an emulsified surface that clung to a piece of paper. Mechanically reproducible images were paper-bound, produced by mimeo, Xerox, and the printing press. Once out in the world, they tended to be stable objects like newspapers, photographic prints and bound books. The only way in which they were reconfigurable was with a razor blade and a pot of glue. But even then, they remained paper-bound stable artefacts. They bore signs of their original context: a Xerox of a newspaper photograph, for instance, carried Ben-Day or halftone dots, signature typefaces (*Times* Roman), authorial accreditations and captions that made their source readily identifiable and, with a little bit of effort, verifiable. Today, photographs emanating from newspaper websites are regularly reblogged without attribution or context; often times the caption doesn't travel with the photograph, nor does authorial accreditation. Instead they are free-floating artefacts, detached from the anchored signifiers and contexts that first birthed their meaning. A thousand new contexts and meanings emerge from the viral nature of photographic distribution in the digital age.

As rampant decontextualization has become the norm, these tendencies have migrated from the screen to the physical world. With technologies like Augmented Reality, geography itself has become unhinged from any singular verifiable, stable, authoritative meaning, subjected to remixes and whimsical interpretations, creating data-hazed layers of subjectivity, which propose the landscape itself as a site of *détournement*. Standing in front of my apartment building on West Twenty-sixth Street in New York City looking through AR glasses, I view not only the history of the building, a biography of the architect who built it, the city records attached to it, but also a wealth of unofficial crowdsourced data lobbed on top of it: personal stories of births, deaths, break-ups, love affairs and memories. I can view photographs of these ghostly protagonists as readily as I can call up old pictures of the building. On top of this – if I'm using the unpaid version of the software app – I'm seeing a stream of geo-generated advertising associated with my neighborhood ('Hill Country at 30 West 26th St serves the best Texas-style ribs in the city' and 'Duane Reade at Sixth Avenue and Twenty-seventh Street is having a sale on soap today').

Wherever we go, we tend to leave a data trail, whether through geo-tagged photographs, Foursquare check-ins, GPS-enabled cellular devices or status updates. These data trails, like breadcrumbs of old, are diaristic movement maps of our daily ramblings. Data trails are comprised of alphanumeric language and often manifest themselves in grammatically correct sentences like, 'Artie has just checked in at Joe's Diner on Foursquare'. Digital photographs are GUIs for miles of alphanumeric code beneath their skin posing as an image, contributing to the enormous increase in the sheer amount of language surrounding us. From data trails to logos, we're awash in language, both visible and invisible, from brands and signage, to the data-haze of AR, alphanumeric text messages, emails, webpages, Tweets, digital television and radio signals all passing through the air.

When language comes into contact with an image or a space, we can say that it captions it, like signage on a storefront or a logo on a T-shirt. The signage in both cases is descriptive; on the store, it captions, enhancing an otherwise unadorned architecture, framing our experience and expectations of that store (the pinks, oranges and browns of Dunkin' Donuts' signage remind us of their sugary products). A T-shirt with a slogan on it captions a passer-by ('I am Yankees fan'). A Yankees fan passing in front of a Dunkin' Donuts creates a double signed system, one whose captioning might tell you, for instance, something very specific about American culture through a very complex ecology of semiotics. While we don't tend to think of signage or even public language as captioning the landscape, Roland Barthes in 1961 predicted this sort of semiotic interchangeability while studying the structure of the newspaper: 'Formerly, the image illustrated the text (made it clearer); today, the text loads the image, burdening it with a culture, a moral, an imagination. Formerly, there was reduction from text to image; today, there is amplification from the one to the other. The connotation is now experienced only as the natural resonance of the fundamental denotation constituted by the photographic analogy and we are thus confronted with a typical process of naturalization of the cultural.'[2] Traditional hierarchies and boundaries are demolished, throwing those once stable entities into an well spring of signs, languages and meanings. By doing so, Barthes anticipated the fluidity of the digital world where stable entities – like the newspaper photograph – are subject to numerous contexts and roles.

II The New Aesthetic and The New Writing

In advanced poetries, there was no postmodernism. Beginning with Mallarmé and ending with Language Poetry, the emergence of digital culture signified a break with modernism, replacing deconstructive tendencies with strategies informed by the workings of computers and the web: word-processing, databasing, recycling, appropriation, intentional plagiarism, identity ciphering and intensive programming, to name but a few. Yet the odd thing is that these practices, born of digital immersion, have not shown up exclusively on the screen, but as often have manifested themselves on the printed page. While these physical artefacts might not appear much different from those produced over the past few decades, it's the ways in which they've been conceptualized and produced that distinguishes them from poetry written before the internet.

This mapping of the digital world onto the physical has been driving what's become known as The New Aesthetic.[3] Not content to live exclusively on the screen, memes, images and ideas born of digital culture are infiltrating and expressing themselves in meatspace. Think of pixellated camouflage ('digicam') as an handy example. This slight warping of reality, at once familiar and disconcerting, represents a paradigmatic shift in the ways we process aesthetics, leading Bruce Sterling to comment, 'Look at those images objectively. Scarcely one of the real things in there would have made any sense to anyone in 1982, or even in 1992. People of those times would not have known what they were seeing with those New Aesthetic images.'[4] Apply Sterling's logic to, say, Flarf – a recent poetry movement based on grabbing the worst of Google search results: the more offensive, the more ridiculous, the more outrageous, the better – and you get how this might relate to the new writing.

The New Aesthetic embraces hybrid strategies, casting aspersions on artistic practices perpetuated within and contingent upon self-sustaining, cloistered environments such as e-poetry and net art (that is, until an e-poetry or net art meme generates a slew of T-shirts). New notions of distribution come into play too: those practices based on uniqueness and singularity, such as the art market (which increasingly resembles the antiques market) appear headed for obsolescence. Likewise, sealed off, invented worlds like Second Life and virtual reality are giving way to integrated terrestrial / cyber hybrids such as geo-tagging and augmented reality, aligning The New Aesthetic with long-standing, media-based documentarian practices such as Andy Warhol, *Candid Camera*, *An American Family*, reality television and Sacha Baron Cohen. This is a strain that proclaims that real life – reframed and recontexutalized – is much more 'creative', 'inventive', twisted, and weird than what we could conjure up in our fictive imaginations.

While it's hard to say where writing fits into all this (thus far, The New Aesthetic has been primarily focused on visual forms), much of the digital page-based writing over the past decade – based on strategies such as sorting, parsing, remixing, culling, collecting, scraping and republishing – has insisted on multiple identities, born of one process while materializing in another. Marcel Duchamp's concept of the *Infrathin* – a state between states – might apply here. Duchamp defines the *Infrathin* as 'The warmth of a seat (which has just been left)' or 'Velvet trousers- / their whistling sound (in walking) by/ brushing of the 2 legs is an / infra thin separation signaled / by sound.'[5] Like an electronic current, the *Infrathin* hovers and pulses, creating a dynamic stasis, refusing to commit to one state or the other. Like much contemporary writing, it is concerned with the expansive fusing of opposites: ephemeral *and* permanent, digital *and* analogue, becoming multidimensional, flexible and radically distributive.

The twenty-first century is invisible. We were promised jet packs but ended up with handlebar moustaches. The surface of things is the wrong place to find the twenty-first century. Instead, the unseen, the *Infrathin* – those tiny devices in our pockets or the thick data-haze that permeates the air we breathe – locates us in the present. And in this way, The New Aesthetic is not so much a movement as a marker, a moment of observation that informs us that culture – along with its means of production and reception – has radically shifted beneath our feet while we were looking the other way. As such, it handily articulates the importance of the new writing, situating it and its modus operandi within broader cultural trends.

III The New Hospitality

I'm struggling with the idea of diversity. I want to be hospitable to all: I want to be inclusive; I want to invite everyone to join my party. The problem is, I don't really know the guests. I don't know their ethnicities. I don't know their genders. I don't know their nationalities. In fact, I've never met most of them. And yet, I know *of* them. I admire them. I'm in touch with them. But, really, I have no idea who they are. They're ghosts, ciphers, electrical pulses ... odd blips on my screen.

And trying to ascertain anything more about them from their texts – their inner feelings, their personal lives, the essence of their *beings* – is proving to be fruitless. Instead, I'm awash in reams of code, tweets, facts & figures and random musings on technology; a portfolio of oblique strategies. But I'm intrigued by what they produce. Why would someone publish a book-length work that collects every tweet that makes mention of the word *McNugget* over a specified course of time? Why would two writers – one who lives in Montreal and the other in New York City – cut and paste directions from Google Maps on how to get from one city to another by *foot*? Why would a poet calculate how many female breasts stacked atop of each other it would take to attain the height of world's tallest building, the Burj Khalifa? (The answer is 16,104.) The operative question here – flipping traditional content-driven literary notions on its head – is not *what* but *why*? The questions might be more important than the answers.

In this portfolio of writing, technology and its workings take precedent over human emotion, echoing Fredrich Kittler when he stated that, 'Technologies that not only subvert writing, but engulf it and carry it off along with so-called Man, render their own description impossible.'[6] Here Kittler builds upon the earlier theories of Walter Ong, who claimed that writing is a technology and is therefore an artificial act: 'Technologies are not mere exterior aids but also interior transformations of consciousness, and never more than when they affect the word.... Technologies are artificial, but – paradox again – artificiality is natural to the human being. Technology, properly interiorized, does not degrade human life but on the contrary enhances it.'[7]

In this chat room, I'm a woman; on this blog, I'm a political conservative; in this forum, I'm a middle-aged golfer. And I never get called out for not being authentic or real. On the contrary, I am addressed as 'madam' or 'you right-wing asshole'. I've come to expect that the person I think I'm addressing on the internet isn't really 'that person'. If identities are really up for grabs and changeable by the minute, it's clear that much of the new writing presented on the following pages reflects this state of ever-shifting identity and subjectivity. That can mean adopting inauthentic voices, subjectivities, political positions, opinions, and even words that weren't 'written by the author', because in this cornucopia of cut-and-paste digitality, it's impossible even to attempt to define what's 'mine' and what isn't.

With digital fragmentation, any sense of unified authenticity and coherence has long been shelved. The poet Robert Fitterman, whose works embrace our shifting identities shaped by the forces of consumerism, takes it one step further:

> Can we express subjectivity, even personal experience, without necessarily using our own personal experience?... There has clearly been a desire to engage or re-claim the personal. I am interested in the inclusion of subjectivity and personal experience; I just prefer if it isn't my own. Today I have access to an unlimited number of personal utterances and expressions from the gut, or the heart. Why listen to my gut when I could listen to thousands of guts?... For writers coming of age in the 70s and 80s, the notion of multiple identities and appropriated identities is a sort of native language, a natural outgrowth of the multiple personas that have been engineered and then targeted by market strategists.[8]

Language has become a provisional space, temporary and debased, mere material to be shoveled, reshaped, hoarded and moulded into whatever form is convenient, only to be discarded just as quickly. Because words today are cheap and infinitely produced, they are detritus, signifying little, meaning less. Disorientation by replication and spam is the norm. Notions of the authentic or original are increasingly untraceable. French theorists who anticipated the destabilizing of language could never have foreseen the extent that words today refuse to stand still; restlessness is all they know. Words today are bubbles, shape-shifters, empty signifiers, floating on the invisibility of the network, that great leveller of language, from which we greedily and indiscriminately siphon, stuffing hard drives only to replace them with bigger and cheaper ones.

Hosted on a global scale, digitization turns all language into provisional language, rendering geography and local languages obsolete. The ubiquity of English: now that we all speak it, nobody remembers its use. The collective bastardization of English is our most impressive achievement; we have broken its back with ignorance, accent, slang, jargon, tourism and multitasking. We can make it say anything we want, like a speech dummy.

Narrative reflexes that have enabled us from the beginning of time to connect dots, fill in blanks, are now turned against us. We cannot stop noticing: no sequence too absurd, trivial, meaningless, insulting, we helplessly register, provide sense, squeeze meaning and read intention out of the most atomized of words. Modernism showed that we cannot stop making sense out of the utterly senseless. The only legitimate discourse is loss; we used to renew what was depleted, now we try to resurrect what is gone.

1   Susan Sontag, *On Photography*, New York: Rosetta Books, 1973/2005, p. 66.
2   Roland Barthes, *Image, Music, Text*, London: Fontana Press, 1977, pp. 25–6.
3   http://www.riglondon.com/blog/2011/05/06/the-new-aesthetic/ accessed 15 June 2012.
4   http://www.wired.com/beyond_the_beyond/2012/04/an-essay-on-the-new-aesthetic/ accessed 15 June 2012.
5   Marcel Duchamp, *Notes*, ed. and trans. Paul Matisse, Boston: G. K. Hall and Co., 1983.
6   Fredrich A. Kittler. *Gramophone, Film, Typewriter*, Stanford: Stanford University Press, 1999, p. xxxix.
7   Walter J. Ong, *Orality and Literacy*, London: Routledge, 1982, p. 82–3.
8   Robert Fitterman, 'Identity theft', in *Rob the Plagiarist*, New York: Roof Books, 2009. pp. 12–15.

Geography

Kristen Gallagher
from *We Are Here*

This work began when someone asked me to write an essay on beauty, a topic on which I had nothing to say. So I decided on a semi-procedural approach: I would go to 'beautiful' places with audio-recording equipment and then transcribe what I captured. To my surprise, this experiment revealed the language of consulting maps and orienting oneself – that it was happening all the time and was consistently interesting and often funny. So I decided to do it until I had ninety-nine pages, which became the book We Are Here. Kristen Gallagher

we're facing this way – we came down – we just came from here so this is that – what is that? – this is that and and this is that – oh! – ok wait – what is that? – this is that – am I wrong? I just don't know! – well, yeah – I thought we were coming from here – we are – but then that would be there then – oh – and this would be that – we did just come over that though, so we must have not gone this way at the right time? – yeah, you're right, this way

—

so this'll just tell you where to go – there's a couple ways to go so we'll just see what she says – turn left. on. west germantown pike – ok so she's gonna have you take the turnpike – or she could have you take dekalb – yeah I dunno it would be strange but you could do it – dekalb is a little road, well it's not a little road but it's not as big as the turnpike – anyway dekalb, dekalb pike, actually it's route 202 but around here we call it dekalb – dekalb is one way you could go but I'd say it's the wrong way so if she has us doing that I don't know what we're gonna do – well I guess it doesn't mean it won't work it could work you'd just have to take it all the way to the expressway and the turnpike would be faster so I don't know why she'd say that but we'll see what she says – turn right. on. swede road – no that's not right that can't be right that's wrong that's wrong – well should we stop? – that just can't be right – well which way do you think we should go? – alright I'll just shut up now – but you seem to know the way maybe you can just tell us how to get there – I'll tell you what I do know she's wrong that thing, what she's saying, that's wrong – wait but are you sure? – yeah maybe she knows something you don't – it's a road that goes nowhere, it just stops do you ever wonder why we never take it? It's because it doesn't go anywhere – she told us to turn right on a road that's essentially a dead end – you know how to go though, don't you? – yeah, we've gone here before all by ourselves – well I'd just as soon see what she says if we can get her to work

—

we just came down from here so we are here and this is that and this is that and that whole thing over there? – is this – I'm pretty sure – wait, but I thought we were coming from here – we are – but then that would be there then – oh – o shit, we did just come over something – it could've been that though – do we need to go, um, it would be there? – you wanna try this way? – no, I think we should try your way – but I told you I'm always wrong – so let's go this way

—

I wonder if this is the right way – if we don't see it we'll make a right on centennial avenue – I wonder if it's ok – yeah, here – what – is the right way – we can find out – um if we go past – if we don't see it we can go – we'll make a right on centennial avenue and come back – well, where would it be if it wasn't here? – well, it's here, I just thought it was actually I thought it was facing this street but now that I'm looking – oh, you think it could be back off that way – so it's not so bad, it's not like we're in the wrong part of the town – we may just be a few feet back from this street here – eel grass rehabilitation project – I wonder what eel grass is – I guess it's in trouble – there's a sign over there that tells you but you have to walk on the grass to get there – is this eel grass? – I dunno but I don't want to mess it up just in case – yeah I guess not – so you think this is the street we're on? – uh, maybe – if it is – wait – we should go this way I think yeah this way – ok

—

ok so it looks like the best way is to take a left on 48th – ok good, turn left – turn left – turn left – well it sounded like you were almost there are you turning left – turn left – left – left turn left – did you turn left? – why not?

—

what's the nearest street – well you must be near some street, I mean, you just said you pulled over and I'm guessing that was on a street right so what street are you on – you're pulled over, right? – ok so look out of the car window – are you looking out the window? – just look out and a little up like to where a street sign would be – ok? – look for a street sign, do you see a street sign? – well there must be one, just look at the nearest corner – are you looking? – do you see a green sign that looks like a street sign? – good, what does it say? – does the sign have numbers or letters – what are the numbers – 64? Hmmm does it say avenue or road or street? – 64th ave – uuhhh – yeah I gotta find that – I'll figure it out – just let me figure it out – I'm figuring it out don't worry – I'm looking – don't worry, you're gonna be fine, you'll just have to turn around – I'm telling you I'm looking here and the only thing to do is go back the way you came – well tell him to pull himself together and deal – well you're gonna have to – I'm looking on the map do you think I'm just making this all up? – there is no good way for me to tell you streets – yes, I am looking and that is how I have deduced that the best way is to get back on the highway – I realize you're freaking out but its just the highway and there isn't a very straightforward way to tell you to drive – you don't want to drive through streets here it's a very confusing place – you thought the highway was bad? – it's nothing compared to the side streets – we're not doing that, no – no – I'm telling you you don't want to do that I'm looking at the map right now and it is a truly gnarly situation you do not want this I'm telling you seriously

—

so we're kind of winding in the right direction – is there a method to this madness of the gray line versus the black line? – is the gray a more big thoroughfare or something? – could be – so do you know exactly where we are? – well we're probably right here – cuz the rink was to our left – oh so we're probably right here – yeah – so let's see if we have – maybe right here we could get off by right there – I don't know what that big black swatch mark is – it doesn't matter we're going this way

1. Let me see.
Given that the average female breast protrudes about two inches from the chest, we can assume that the world's tallest building, the Burj Khalifa, is 16,104 breasts tall.

Taipei 101 is 10,026 breasts tall.
The Shanghai World Financial Center is 9,684 breasts tall.
The International Commerce Centre is 9,528 breasts tall.
The Petronas Towers are each 8,898 breasts tall. If the Petronas Towers were stacked, one on top the other, they would be 17,796 breasts tall.

So. Let's see.
   We now know the exact height of the five tallest buildings in the world, measured in breasts, and, by chance, the exact height of the tallest twin buildings in the world, if they were stacked, measured in breasts.

2. One can shatter a world, but not a sea. Water is durable insofar as it is absolutely not-shatterable. Even if one were to lift the Taipei 101, the second tallest building in the world, and drop it, say, into the Black Sea, it would certainly make a big splash but in no way produce any effect that might be accurately described as a shattering.
   The gross floor space of the Taipei 101 is about 1,000,000 cubic meters. The volume of the Black Sea is 131,200 cubic miles. So the volume of the Taipei 101 is .315% of the volume of the Black Sea, meaning that the splash resulting from dropping the one into the other will be large on a human scale, but relatively small on the scale of the inhuman, that of seas and buildings. Unless dropped from a great height.
   The Sikorsky CH-54 Tarhe is a twin-engine heavy-lift helicopter designed by Sikorsky Aircraft for the United States Army. It can lift 20,000 pounds. Considering that the Taipei 101 weighs 700,000 metric tons, it would require at least 77,161 Sikorsky CH-54 Tarhes to lift the building and suspend it over the Black Sea at, say, 15,000 feet.
   Dropping the Taipei 101 into the Black Sea from 15,000 feet would produce an enormous splash, on a human scale. The resulting waves would certainly pummel nearby shores for hours, if not for days. Swimming in the choppy waters would be unadvisable. In this way one could, if one wanted to — say, if one were representative of a governmental body concerned with illegal entry to one's country by water, or if, say, one just wanted to put an end to swimming for their own nihilistically personal reasons — count all swimmers out, at least from the water immediately affected by the splash.
   One would need many more Sikorsky CH-54 Tarhes dropping many more Taipei 101s if one wanted to empty the entire Black Sea of swimmers. Still, even if 77,161,000 Sikorsky CH-54 Tarhes were to drop 1,000 Taipei 101s from 15,000 feet each, which would go a long way, I think, toward getting swimmers out of the water, one way or another, after which getting out they would no longer be swimmers, nothing would be shattered. As we've said, the sea remains resistant to shattering.

But if the Taipei 101s were not dropped into the Black Sea, but instead dropped directly on its shores, say, in Odessa or Zonguldak, then one could rightly describe the land, after having many copies of the world's second tallest building dropped on it from a great height, as shattered. Moreover, if 77,161,000 Sikorsky CH-54 Tarhes were to drop 1,000 Taipei 101s from 15,000 feet onto the cities along the shore of the Black Sea, not only would there be lots of shattering, there would also be, presumably, a potential influx of swimmers, swimming out into the sea, attempting to reach other shores, which they may presume, falsely, have been left unshattered.

So we can assume that dropping many Taipei 101s along the shore of the Black Sea has the opposite effect of dropping many Taipei 101s into the sea itself: it creates more swimmers, as opposed to ridding us altogether of the very category of swimmer.

Ara Shirinyan
from *Your Country is Great*

Denmark is Great

delicate but sweet cheese
made in Denmark is
great for melting or sliced

Upon reflection, I have concluded that,
Denmark is great for a holiday if you go
with friends, it's a beautiful country
with lots of interesting history.

Denmark is great for family holidays
because of the safe, relaxed and
informal atmosphere

Denmark is great, especially down
by the water where there are some
great restaurants.
Also, there is that hippy community
in the middle of town.

Denmark is great.
All the men are at least 12ft tall.
Denmark is great.

There is free health care for everyone
and students get paid to go to school.

However, their weather sucks!
You get one sunny day a week.

Denmark is great country, but the
taxes/ fees are bit to crazy, whish also
scares a lot of good foreign labour, like
professors, doctors, soccer players.

Shopping in Denmark is great; some
cheap stores are H&M and Mango.
I found that toiletry and make-up
were more expensive

Denmark is great, I have yet to master
the skill of ordering healthy food.
I think Denmark is great because
everything's wrapped up in a neat
package—it's got tons of culture,
relaxed, free lifestyle, loads of history.

Denmark is GREAT! Keep fighting
the good fight! Remember: "No
immmigration without assimilation!"
And if they don't like it they can just
go home.

China is Great

China is great.
We visited China when
we adopted our daughter.
I can't say enough about it.
We plan on going back
in about 8 years

China is great and
the people are great.
They are very friendly
and say hello

China is great! China is ahead
due to its cleaniness and
cow not coming in beijing.
India should learn.

CHINA IS GREAT !
MAY CHINA
RULE THIS WORLD ! !

China is great and plenty of
pretty and fit girls.

All that matters is that
CHINA MADE IT,
and therefore
CHINA IS GREAT,
PRAISE CHINA,
HEIL MAO ZEDONG!

Super China is great.
Super China is super.
I find the service is fast
and with a smile and the food is great.

China is great country
with a splendid
ancient civilization
with a history of
5000 years old
and it is also a mighty
modernized country

I also think China is Great,
the food, the people. But one thing
that I don`tlike is the regim.

Teaching in China is – great?
interesting? exciting? Well, yes, but…
perhaps not quite all the time.

China is great and the chinese is
wonderful.
china is a historial country.
but now china is in the proccess
of developing.

MADE IN CHINA is
great to listen to,
and it is hurtful to listen to

China is great
shock therapy
in this great
clash of paradigms.

Robert Fitterman
from *Metropolis XXX:*
The Decline and Fall of the Roman Empire

Guide A-Z

You've come to this country to relax and enjoy this beauty and cultural diversity – not to exhaust yourself searching for the best deals and most evocative experiences. This city is a city of images, vivid and unforgettable. This city is called 'the most serene' a reference to the monstrous power, majesty, and wisdom of this city that was for centuries the unrivaled mistress of trade. One of the curious things about this lake is its perennial attraction for writers. You won't miss the unusual square dome and thin, elaborate tower of this landmark above the city's rooftops. This town is the first town you come to as you head from this lake. This river is narrow and unprepossessing here in this city, only a hint of the broad and mighty watercourse that it becomes as it flows eastward toward the ocean. Like the family jewels that bedeck its habitual visitors, this coastline is glamorous, but in an old-fashioned way. This town, sheltered by the wooded hills of a nature preserve, faces a little bay guarded by ruined castles. Beautifully positioned directly above the swift-flowing waters of this river and at the foot of this mountain mastiff, this town has old streets lined with low-slung buildings adorned with wooden balconies and pretty flower shops. Surrounded by the rugged countryside and beautiful coastline, this city is built on a hillside above what was once the chief port of this empire. Capital of this autonomous province, this city has managed to escape the ravages of commercialization and retains its architectural charm, artistic attractions, and historic importance. The town has preserved its centuries-old tradition of ceramic making. Palms, sand strips, and good rock-climbing terrain make this town a good break from gaudiness and pastel villages. As travelers journey down this fabled coast, their route takes them past rocky cliffs plunging into the sea and small boats lying in sandy coves like brightly colored fish. This southernmost mainland region has seen more than its fair share of oppression, poverty and natural disaster. This city has changed the way we see the world.

Maria Salgado
Real Cities, Fake States

Ciudades reales, Países ficticios *lists a number of the almost impregnable names of cities. The title puns on a subtitle used by Gordon Matta-Clark in his 1973–4 piece* Real Properties, Fake Estates. *The list begins with Brecht's exile and ends with that of Khlebnikov, who made use of a list of cities in a poem of his own ('The road I took'). My list follows and corrupts the alphabetical and vocal patterns of international cities, giving typographic and aural materiality to some kind of global journey through the twentieth century. Two place names articulate the landscape of the book in which the text belongs (*ready, 2012*): 'Xino' (or 'Xinatown'), the neighbourhood of immigrants and workers who come not only from China, but from all over; and 'Xina' (China), the imaginary e/state where the whole world is being manufactured.*

B ertolt
B recht

B erlin
P raha
W ien
Z ürich
S kovsbostrand
L idingö
H elsinki
M oskvá
V ladivostok
S anta Monica
N ew York
Z ürich
Ost - Berlin

B rcelona
B rlin
B rmingham
B lonia
B enos Aires

B mako
B atislava
B lisi T
B ston
B ujas

B viera
B lbo
B nn
C rk
C uritiba

C racas
Br escia
Br isbane
Cr ikvenica
Bre men
Bre st
Bro dy
Cra covia
Crh istiania

Ic halkaranji
C hernobyl
C hihuahua

D achau
D res de
K iev
D oha
D üssel dorf
D uisburg

T ehran
É feso
E i bar
E o lia
E u reka, Washington

F rankfurt
F errara
F rankford
F irenze
F rankfort
H abana
F runze

C arlo
G iuliani
G enova
G ötebor g
H uambo
H on g K on g
P I t I a g orsk
H els I nk I
G dansk
G u I yan g
G ünzbur g
G orazde
G rozn I
I da ho
Ha mel I n
He I delber g
Hr odna
G rbavica
H ano I
J ena
H I ro sh I ma
S h anga I
P h oe n I x
P h I lly
P h nom P en h

Spades
Clubs
Hearts
Diamonds

J artum
K harjov
J erusalem
Jo inville
J ohannesburg
J uárez, Ciudad de

Kazakh stan
Uzbeki stan
Birobid zhan
K ingston
K öln
K obe
D unkerque
B angkok
L ei pzig
K io to
K in shasa
K ur sk
E L - A I un
L ech este in
L icht en berg
L ux em burg
L e u ven
L u a nda

P aramaribo
New Hav en
Pearl Harb our
Hal ifax
Port land
Por lamar
Durban
Providence, Rhode Island

it snows in Xino
it does not snow in Xina

M drid
M dellín
M siones
M mbassa
M mbai

N a siriya
N u eva Loja
N i neve
N ü remberg
N o ttin gh am

M atosi nh o s
E spi nh o
I lh a v o
B at a lh a
O lh ã o
Portim ã o
O urinhos

O akland
O skemen
El Oued
O nitsha
U ckland A

P atesburg
P etesburg
P ittsburgh
P uttesburgh

P ortb ou

Q andahar
Q uebec
Q uito
O quirrh
K uwait, Madı̄nat al-
Q usqu

R epublics
S ocialist
S oviet
USSR

R afah
R eady
R imini
P l y m ou t h

S arajevo
S iena
S heffield
S onora
S ão P aulo
S urat

Su nción A
Co ncepción
En carnación

Ca acupé
Ca azapá
Pa raguarí

V ancouver
Nu eva Delhi
Varso via
Ciudad V elha
B eja
B altimore
V igo
Br uselas
Ver ona

U lm
Ur
U sinsk
U tica
U ppsala

U lan Bator
S aloníki
S alerno
RSSU

Virgin Islands US
Virgin Islands UK
M alvinas
V ieques
R ostov
U tre cht
S to ckholm

W ashington
W eimar
W ien
Birmingham
S kovsbostrand
Ujumbura B
Luckno w

T axc o
T exc o
E xxo n
T ucs on

Ý taca
Y ellowknife
T oky o
P yongyang

Z anzíbār

B razza ville
G za
Fz

B lo Hor zont
F ort l z
El Zóc lo

Astrakhan
Moscow
Kharjov
Rostov
Baku
Persia
Pitiagorsk
The Train
Moscow
Freedom

V elimir
K lebnikhov

Robert Fitterman and Steve Giasson
from *Directions*
Robert Fitterman, 1 Washington Square Village #16-O, New York, NY 10012 – Steve Giasson, 2503 rue Frontenac, app. 2, Montreal, Quebec H2K 3A2

By Foot

Head southeast on Rue Frontenac toward Rue Hochelaga. Turn right at Rue Ontario E. Turn left at Route 134. Slight right to stay on Route 134. Continue onto Rue Mercier. Turn right at Boulevard Desaulniers. Turn left at Boulevard Taschereau. Turn left at Chemin De Saint-Jean. Turn right at Route Édouard-VII (signs for QC-30 / Sorel). Turn right at Montée St-Jacques. Turn left at Rang St – Philippe S. Turn left at Langevin Montée. Turn right at Route Édouard-VII. Continue onto Rang Saint-André (entering United States (New York)). Continue onto Meridan Rd. Continue onto Oak St. Turn right at Elm St. Turn left at Main St / US-9 S. Continue to follow US-9 S. Slight right to stay on US-9 S. Slight left at Miller St. Turn right at City Hall Pl. Turn left at Bridge St. Turn right at Peru St. Continue onto Avenue / US-9 S. Continue to follow US-9 S. Turn left at Front St / US-9 S. Continue to follow US-9 S. Slight left at US-9 N. Slight left at Co Rd 68 / Landon Hill Rd. Continue straight onto Main St / US-9 S. Continue to follow US-9 S. Turn right at NY-32 S / Saratoga Ave / US-9 S (signs for US-9 S / NY-32 S). Turn left at Gansevoort Rd / NY-32 S (signs for NY-32 S). Turn left at NY-32 S / Schuylerville Rd. Turn right at Stump St. Continue onto NY-50 S. Turn left at Ballard Rd / Co Rd 33. Turn right at Ruggles Rd. Slight left at Co Rd 67 / Old Schuylerville Rd. Continue to follow Co Rd 67. Continue onto Caldwell Rd. Continue onto Nielson Rd. Turn right at Co Rd 70. Turn left at Jack Halloron Rd. Slight left at NY-423 E. Turn right at Co Rd 75. Continue onto Viall Ave. Turn left at Railroad St. Turn left at Park Ave. Turn right at S Main St. Slight left at Hudson River Rd / NY-32 S / US-4 W. Continue to follow NY-32 S / US-4 W. Turn left at 2nd St. Turn right at Columbia St. Turn left at 2nd St. Continue onto Delaware Ave. Turn left at NY-470 E / Ontario St. Continue to follow NY-470 E. Turn right at 2nd Ave. Continue onto River St. Slight left to stay on River St. Continue onto 4th St. 4th St turns slightly left and becomes Burden Ave. Continue onto NY-378 W. Turn left at Morrison Ave. Turn right at US-4 W / Vandenburgh Ave. Continue to follow US-4 W. Turn left at Columbia Turnpike / US-20 E / US-9 S. Slight right at US-9 S. Continue onto New York 9H S. Slight left at Co Rd 27. Turn right at Creek 12. Turn left at Tag-Churchtown Rd. Continue onto Churchtown Rd. Continue onto Tachkanie Churchtown Rd. Turn right at Co Rd 10. Turn left at NY-82 S. Turn right at Co Rd 15. Turn left at Lake Taghkanic State Park. Turn right at New York 987G S / Taconic State Pkwy. Slight left to stay on New York 987G S / Taconic State Pkwy. Slight left at Mountain Rd. Slight right at New York 987G N / Taconic State Pkwy. Turn right at Hortontown Hill Rd. Turn left at New York 987G S / Taconic State Pkwy. Turn right at Pudding St. Continue onto Wiccopee Rd. Turn right at Pudding St. Continue onto Wiccopee Rd. Slight right to stay on Wiccopee Rd. Turn right at Co Rd 21 / Peekskill Hollow Rd. Turn left at Bryant Pond Rd. Turn left to stay on Bryant Pond Rd. Turn right at Co Rd 24 / Wood St. Continue to follow Wood St. Continue onto 1309 / E Main St. Turn left at Hill Blvd. Slight left to stay on Hill Blvd. Turn left at Lee Blvd. Turn right at Quinlan St. Turn right at Granite Springs Rd. Turn left at Crompond Rd / NY-35 E / US-202 E. Turn right at Saw Mill River Rd. Turn left at Revere Dr. Turn right at N Co Trailway. Continue onto State St. Slight right at N Co Trailway. Slight left to stay on N Co Trailway. Slight right to stay on N Co Trailway. Turn right at Campfire Rd. Turn left at NY-100 S / NY-133 W / Saw Mill River Rd / Somerstown Turnpike. Continue to follow NY-100 S / Saw Mill River Rd. Turn right at N State Rd. Turn right to stay on N State Rd. Turn left to stay on N State Rd. Turn left at New York 9A S / Saw Mill River Rd. Continue to follow New York 9A S. Continue onto N Central Ave. Turn right at W Main St. Turn left at S Co Trailway (Old Put, Putnam Row). Turn right at 984M / Farragut Ave. Turn left at 987D / Saw Mill River Pkwy. Turn right at Executive Blvd / Executive Plaza. Turn left at Nepperhan Ave. Slight left to stay on Nepperhan Ave. Turn left at New Main St. Continue onto S Broadway / New York 9A S / US-9 S. Continue to follow US-9 S. Slight left at Broadway. Slight left at 10th Ave. Slight left toward Harlem River Dr. Slight left at Harlem River Dr. Continue onto St Nicholas Pl. Continue onto Donnellon Square. Continue onto St Nicholas Ave. Turn left at W 124th St. Turn right at St Nicholas Ave. Slight right at 8th Ave / Frederick Douglass Blvd. At the roundabout, take the 2nd exit onto Central Park West. At the roundabout, take the 5th exit onto Broadway. Continue onto Union Square W. Continue onto University Pl. Continue straight onto Washington Square E. Continue onto Wooster St Exd. 1 Washington Square Village, New York, NY 10012, USA.

CAConrad
Time Travel Application: of (Soma)tic Praxis

For the TROLL THREAD Collective

I was invited to give a poetry reading in Buffalo, New York April 7th. This is a time when spring is in FULL BLOOM in Philadelphia, while the land in Buffalo is still asleep with winter 400 miles to the north. On the train I had a photograph of snowy treetops and another of a worm-stuffed robin with violets. Every 10 minutes I would look out the window. While what I saw was spring, I would hold the picture of winter to the window, step hard on a piece of broken plastic placed in my shoe and say, "THIS IS DEAD!" At the midway the pictures were switched, and I pressed into my now bleeding foot to say "THIS IS ALIVE!" Notes for the poem were taken all along the rail. Spring rolled back into winter, the only season America deserves.

The most common form of communication on Earth is bioluminescence.
Dr Sylvia Earle

Scheduled Poison

    writing
    this poem
    while my
    nation brings
    other nations
    to their knees
    syringe extracts
    radiance of
    dandelion injected
    into jaw moving in mirror moving bright
    sounds salvaged and accounted for
    abuse us to amethyst for the
    wish you would die list
    no names just
    drawings of their houses
    tree in the yard
just kidding about killing them
just kidding just
ascertaining a thought
about thinking against
those mothers
minimize window of solace as
drone does
drone pilot is a real pilot?
this poem's pilot gets in there
we order food by the foot
if this makes sense to the future
something was right
pie eating contest to salvation
dying to tell you of sex through hole in
the American flag GLORY HOLED
I for one tire of Mick Jagger singing in
grocery stores he never visits
put him in every car whose radio ever
played his song even the blackened
smashed windshield one with
bit of tooth on rug
    talk of forgiveness
    sickens
    FUCK your valor

Lytle Shaw and Jimbo Blachly
Interview on Interviews

Lytle Shaw: Jimbo, are you awake? I want to interview you.

Jimbo Blachly: No it's 4am; how did you get into my apartment?

Shaw: I borrowed your extra set of keys when I was here the other day. I wanted to be sure to catch you at home. You see I'm doing some fieldwork on Queens for an upcoming art project and you're a legitimate resident and can therefore give the piece authenticity, actual dialog, especially if I play this interview instead of showing yet another self-obsessed art object. (Also, my grant requires that I focus exclusively on the borough.)

Blachly: I don't identify with Queens – or really know very much about it; it's just far enough away from Manhattan that I can afford to live here. Maybe you should find a borough historian, a small shopkeeper, or someone who has a professional stake in giving a shit.

Shaw: However naive and un-self-reflexive, I like the em-placedness of your observations. Plus this is a good shot of you looking groggy with the subway map behind your head. We can edit out whatever shit I say and just make it seem like you're caught in a period of spontaneous volubility about your borough. Please continue.

Blachly: About what? Queens is huge and completely varied.

Shaw: I'd hate to impose any of my own ideas on these encounters. I really want what emerges to be a product of actual dialog.

Blachly: Did they teach you that shit at the Whitney ISP?

Shaw: Well, I should confess something, since we're in an emotionally vulnerable situation: Despite what I've told you when I've lorded it over you theoretically now and again, I was actually rejected from that program; but I have been trying to follow its more impressive results.

Blachly: You asshole, I thought …

Shaw: I mean interviews insure dialog right?

Blachly: I …

Shaw: Wait, don't interrupt, I'm not done. I mean, they take the artist out of his tiresome little cocoon – the studio (which is really just a glorified factory and store all wrapped up in one) where he cobbles his handcrafted goods. I prefer to put myself in a situation I can't control, encountering new people and through this, not only finally taking art out of its restricted circuit, but also producing works that, actually right in their *very being*, are public – I mean literally. Public in the sense that other voices, including critical ones – even ones critical of me – can speak. This way my analysis of specific places includes the views of people who actually live there, and not, once again, just the fantasies of some carpet-bagging artist. What do you think? Can you perform that service for me? Can you produce a little dialog for me?

Blachly: I like objects, the more moss-covered the better. I like damp objects. And ones that are partly decayed. I like stains and mounds and broken containers. I purr 'Mommy' softly when I pet green felt; I like the primal ooze of Sculpamold. It takes me back to that great period before the world had been bureaucratically sorted into the elements; I'm inordinately fond of balsa wood and …

Shaw: Keep talking, I'm just going to check my email real quickly while you speak into the camera. Is that cool? It's just been so busy juggling the grant application for this project with my teaching.

Blachly: I get funny feelings in my pants when I look at well-constructed ship models from the 17th century.

Shaw: Can you do the next part in an Indian accent and concentrate a little more on the borough? Cuz I don't need all the dialog to accompany head shots. And I want it to seem like I've interviewed a little more widely than I've had time for – you know.

Blachly: [in a bad Indian accent] When my great-great grandmother, Mukti, left Bombay she booked passage on an over-crowed, filthy cargo ship that had been converted into a passenger liner by the Chadwick Family, who were allowing the passage on credit, in return for seven years of indentured servitude in their new plantations in Jamaica Bay.

Shaw: I'm cutting that part out; the Chadwicks will not appreciate that.

Blachly. It's not impossible; she could have worked for the family in India and come over that way.

Shaw: Yeah, but the coincidence is just too much. The Chadwicks would never believe it.

Blachly: You flatter yourself. Do you really think Chadwick Dalton would look at some low-fi documentary video about people in Queens for more than about four seconds? He likes the great tradition of art.

Shaw: Maybe so, but could we just not use them all the same? Maybe do your New Jersey wastoid voice, from your high school friends – but imagine that he's moved to Queens.

Blachly: I mean all those friends live at the Jersey shore now; they would never move to Queens.

Shaw: You're an artist, can you imagine a situation?

Blachly: Inheriting the two-story Laundromat? No, I have no idea.

Shaw: Do you think we could actually find some of these people, do more extensive interviews and just pretend they live in Queens? This is what I love about collaborative work.

Blachly: No, you're usually complaining about the collaboration: my lack of organization; my poor personal hygiene; my apartment being so far out in Queens; that I won't just simply illustrate your austere, lifeless concepts.

Shaw: You just don't recognize their life – probably because you do live out in Queens and aren't sophisticated enough.

Riccardo Boglione
Unplanned Ruptures in Geography and Plays (Apex)

The collection of all the 'ruptures' – taken literally, that is, the typographic breaks of words – of Geography and Plays *by Gertrude Stein, which was one of wonders of literary experimentation of 1922 (along with Joyce's* Ulysses, *Proust's* Recherche, *Girondo's* Veinte poemas para leer en el tranvía, *among others). This configuration of a book, where repetitions and grammar's stammering are the norm, showcases a further degree of linguistic disruption, one not planned by the writer. This is a brand new map of that* Geography, *based on the first edition (Boston, The Four Seas Company Publishers, 1922).*

In the effect of a defect is to allure and to change the base of
any recognition ...
Gertrude Stein

cer-grand-grand-
com-
com-char-
un-re-indica-dissocia-en-ambig-resigna-every-hand-ex-libera-cos-likeli-in-in-medi-
morn-in-cov-rea-
mid-ex-
know-some-want-re-for-succeed-some-com-any-expect-some-in-cer-de-trouble-
interest-cer-com-Cer-any-ex-any-any-concen-com-any-interest-sat-com-com-be-
com-excite-exist-
re-pre-pow-Kind-Gra-sur-
tele-under-carry-con-Tor-kneel-
occa-diges-regu-ollofactor-christ-to-whis-particu-
dis-dis-disturb-de-birth-occu-re-for-elabora-for-dis-sug-under-pre-au-dis-dis-de-
borrow-re-differ-any-recon-
inten-some-return-indi-re-crea-accept-move-re-excite-com-pre-cauli-situa-every-
super-ques-some-com-some-ex-season-re-some-pre-concentra-melo-syndi-pro-be-
after-al-Christ-any-sing-dis-de-de-sta-na-com-busi-intona-occa-re-sat-cele-
disappoint-invita-preser-abso-dis-with-pre-under-predisposi-any-in-
lis-some-slack-weaken-cer-
re-Any-dispo-splen-re-ex-disturb-per-any-differentia-inter-every-en-despera-rela-
continu-con-de-sensi-touch-
re-perpen-
conver-vege-ran-to-prin
hav-feel-com-any-con-prep-enter-bless-pre-repudia-ex-dis-com-any-develop-separa-
con-invi-any-
Shat-be-
bed-re-inten-arrange-re-
re-extermi-sub-perpendicu-to-Mon-furni-neces-dif-ex-
succeed-
establish-lec-fluorish-any-master-deli-
trem-mus-under-reorgani-

dis-dis-them-working-sub-
under-sacri-imperti-suc-lang-Kath-troub-be-
re-precau-under-any-Bourn-pardon-
satisfac-after-dis-Mar-experi-pleas-
mis-rela-con-alto-
ex-re-
ex-be-pain-reason-seri-col-gleam-avoid-splen-Wretch-
plea-
de-every-remem-Cali-pro-
every-Cer-need-Cer-cer-cer-re-re-com-suffer-im-inter-interest-protec-re-
per-mosqui-beau-every-
con-arrange-wonder-es-pro-cer-inter-neat-name-expoer-in-care-ex-de-sheep-un-
permis-melan-remark-
neigh-mean-marvel-tele-li-pro-ex-be-be-dis-flow-
im-
mis-Ameri-reflec-
sym-
per-

Technology

Stephen McLaughlin
A Few Dozen Copies of a Bland Pop Album That Will Soon Cease to Exist

axifile.com/en/CBF36F0778
badongo.com/file/27168534
bitshare.com/files/qqtgrja5/Adele---21--2011-.zip.html
app04.bonpoo.com/cgi-bin/download?fid=AA5BB51EA89F11E18DF34F648E215873
crocko.com/9588C44C1FD04986AAA56F85035AB8D0/Adele_-_21_[2011].zip
datafilehost.com/download-d854169b.html
depositfiles.com/files/vusa4gi8s
myaccount.dropsend.com/file/584c11cb2a1c982d
esnips.com/displayimage.php?pid=34106764
fdrive.net/4ksxz5jnjend
file-upload.net/download-4395632/Adele---21--2011-.zip.html
filefactory.com/file/f26xwfi0uhn/
filehost.ro/3576553/
filehosting.org/file/details/346922/Adele_-_21__2011_.zip
fileupyours.com/view/325432/Adele%20-%2021%20%5B2011%5D.zip
hugeupload.com/uv
ifile.it/izqrgbk
jumbofiles.com/t1yyx4jfhzqz
kiwi6.com/file/3232iasjwg
limelinx.com/files/1b9bcce753bc7067b46e1f68f9b8668c
mbf.me/5Ej8x
mediafire.com/?wtvd20no3e1mut4
megashare.com/4284768
naki.do/6LI
onlinedisk.ru/file/883456/
plunder.com/SH3IO8E0UZ
remixshare.com/download/ybv03
share-online.biz/dl/8KSUPN4MX1SR
shareonme.com/en/file/365/
speedyshare.com/thrqv/Adele-21-2011.zip
sprend.com/download.htm?C=62f96db33a504113be40061e72e756d8
transferbigfiles.com/b9d1995b-1a3a-43db-b1f2-40176aa82557?rid=Z1WBOm56PVQ
    8AuT7I3TUxw2
ul.to/ryxix6tz
uploadingit.com/file/view/bhlp9chrt5peikco/Adele%20-%2021%20%5B2011%5D.zip
uploadstation.com/file/VgHanqd/Adele_-_21_[2011].zip
webfile.ru/5975787
wetransfer.com/dl/1I9382iR/6f35511adacb4eb545cf0993c4d754951cf3213f5efec663
    99d7dfd8ec59490d43dcc86e39e06f0
yourfiles.to/?d=1E3A132945
www16.zippyshare.com/v/81792129/file.html

Tracie Morris
Bleak Afrofuturist Procedure

My first word was an error. According to the machine I spoke it in. Whispering in orifices used to be intimate. Now, the neural network noir twitters every exclamation. Deep spell – check.

Not set yet, rhythm's been bleached. I was the first class spoon-fed suspicious cereal. 'Look at the swirls' we said as glucose crystals segregated from genetic grains.

'Crunch-crunch-crunch' they march through the esophagus, sarcophagi between us, rolling over.

First time we dared play underground numbers *straight* they hit on the regular! Somebody dreamed a black cat, crossed one the next day. We thought those folks on the lo-low we know who shook dem bones dem bones was on the bright side – with the upper hand.

But *then*, 'git-cho-man-back' gooba wasn't happening! He *disappeared*. We could feel the ooh's and aah's of clients getting done by synth girls who were turned out, made to turn tricks. *More* than we wanted to know.

In a covert 'bell curve' moment, lower than average intelligence quotient allocated 20 mill, buck a pop, to equalize Negroes with psychic self-correcting breakfast that allows 'their' leaders to auto-repair the rest of 'em. Leno quips: 'they talk too much anyways: this would, at least, save all that yelling on the sub-way.'

It was all Houngans & Iyalochas could do to stay out of the loop, much less help anyone else. Conversion was officially closed in those circles. You had to be in line to stay in line. Administrative concession allowed, staves vestigial complaints of attrition.

Craig Dworkin
from *Maps*

This week it's all sports: discus, rowing, paragliding, gymnastics, bowling, cestoball, motocross, danball, football, kyudo, BMX racing, haggis hurling, goalball, relay races, rackelton, ski touring, futsal, angling, hammer throw, american handball, underwater hockey, modern dance, jazz dance, irish dance, matball, steeple chase, athletics (track and field), trick shot snooker, bullfighting, broomball, motor boat racing, hurdling, badminton, elephant polo, sports using bicycles or unicycles …

Or so the headers of the most recent emails in the trash folder read. Last week was truncated news feeds, snippets of headlines. Before that, misspelled drug names. Next week, who knows? But a few winters ago it was suddenly like the '70s all over again: short phrases sounding like nothing so much as lines of early

*Language Poetry, as if the spam engine were randomly pulling from Bruce Andrews'
notebooks. A Poetry Daily of the avant-garde. Within the week, they had completely
changed again, suddenly on to something new, one step ahead of the filters.*

*I saved them all, intending to recycle the headers into a readymade chap-book. But
by the time I got around to it, the idea of the 'spam poem' was already old hat; everybody,
it seemed, had done one. The moment of the project had passed. I put the file on a
hard drive and forgot about it until the invitation to publish something 'unpublishable'
reminded me of the aborted plan. Here, belatedly, they return – unedited and in
sequence – a little farce following the minor tragedy of a history missed.*

astoria bereft • cancer fanciful sabbatical pragmatist • bop topology • cavernous
vicar pitt • drake brae caret bagel • butterball dalhousie aesthete • bluebill corps
orb • acoustic buxton crotch • inveterate transvestite lash trash • impermissible
protoplasmic pile barrier • butte reach barefoot braggart goose • tiptoe neologism
• arid edgewise else • cambrian neu- ropathology • arroyo intense • exuberant
cashmere dome drop • derivate descendent desk • meyers wyeth haw • astigmatic
copernican glycerine certificate • hollywood littoral wriggle • supine rang • bilingual
lackey rankle • embarcadero argonaut oases • patriarchy parquet mycology •
paranormal ritz affront • coney demurred • fabian defy • toe amp • enzyme elgin
cleanse • chromatic vandal bawl totem • debater arrogate addend • colossal broth
• dissension digram • cubbyhole harangue • adiabatic men- nonite adventure
• secretive yarmulke hearken • elusive bongo breakdown • parasitic grillwork •
wholesale pelican hardware • bostonian dougherty ought • anthropomorphic
testicle toggle • iconic cadaver haggle • artifi- cial salivate photo • ptolemy splurge
• geophysical passivate void • irresolvable corset swivel • decollimate nucleoli
teen tied nairobi client • brontosaurus jersey • agrarian gallberry bellamy bowl •
patchwork andy adage • dilatory paymaster rainbow reformatory • paradigmatic
anus shrivel • sacrosanct bible cider • bony brassy tatty lass • cygnus exude •
deemphasize fruitful asthma scuff • landmark elder acquit • novo balloon dune
• mesh judiciary trinket • soviet cargo skunk • dubitable cabot cobble bob- bin
• oyster exposure • odometer blob • lightface bedfast stadium hiatus • spiritual
brazil swizzle • basso polyglot prototype • lizzie facet • missoula doria • timberland
amaranth cantor contingent • boucher beachcomb concern • khaki socratic • silent
keno candlewick respect • barrymore drugstore clotheshorse concurrent • wheel
spiegel cyclades slum • characteristic gaulle size sixgun • decadent candela setback
• doctrinal alpine actaeon melodic • rueful argue glue • alamo digestion legend •
alabaster nuthatch data • fallen blasphemy gigacycle dynamic • razzle tootle caliph
chump • loire lahore inhabit loath • conner aden admonish nib • calcify cottony
domicile doll • verbosity rev • pleasant kingston bank cur barnet cater • began begun
• tranquil vindicate stalemate translation • inertial cornerstone selectric skew •
collegiate elate • purchase dutchman waltz exclude • mange nape • stipend steward
mutilate • deacon enoch mackinaw • swishy bonanza probity • mantissa teletype
• equine swim equip commit • hilarious rudiment • wasteful café frustrate behave
• quasiorder formula core • toledo streptomycin session • elegy leila conjugacy •
inten- sive monash griddle • disjunct riddance constrictor • coventry tuna raccoon •
modish dollop copter • conscription resilient cartilaginous scab • campsite voltaire
• issuant garth • arcadia crumb • expurgate eerie maternity reversion • bibliophile
brushfire sent • wary parish psychotherapist • volvo diplomacy

1m She's_SoShmooified @Shmoo_XoXo_22
2 McDoubles, No Onions, No Pickles w/ Mac Sauce. Hot & Spicy. 4Pc McNugget.
Sweet Tea & Apple Dippers. <3 then some good sleep!!

4m Phil Mosley @Phil_Mosley
@mrboat_bac I've seen more meat on a chicken McNugget.

7m David Gray @Cousin_StEEzer
20 piece mcnugget

13m ALISSA STAINBROOK @MissAlissaS
Getting my mcnugget fix since @TheDaynaCollins ate mine for me last night

16m Christopher Braddock @hichrisbraddock
BAD IDEA "@theneener: I think I'm going to order the 20 Chicken McNugget box
when I get back to Denton. My personal "welcome back" parade."

16m one LEGENDARY b♥tch @_PrettyModaFoca
Futuree McNugget.! lol http://pic.twitter.com/kWuZKNEk

26m Paul Dinter @PaulDinter
#WaysToGetSnappedOn charging more then a dollar for a McNugget

31m Brittani Smith @stupid_mcnugget
Oooh I'm hungry 2:30pm can't come fast enough

33m Brittani Smith @stupid_mcnugget
RT @Blasturthoughts "SulfuricMindBurst" beat mixed by GreatXScott -
http://goo.gl/BL7In

42m Darren N. Bragg @_heaRtbrEakreD
"@SMJ_TheFifth: I honestly just want my lil 20 piece mcnugget from McDonalds,
large fry and a sweet tea. Not to much to ask for huh?"

54m Connor Barnes @Con_Bon4
Oh & don't ever buy food from the Hartford airport McD's. 10 bucks for a mcnugget
meal #getthefuckout

1h Nugg @mcnugget_22
dont cook in a sports bra #ouch #leasonlearned #burned

1h J. Mandell @SMJ_TheFifth
I honestly just want my lil 20 piece mcnugget from McDonalds, large fry and a
sweet tea. Not to much to ask for huh?

1h Will Thaxton @thaxton_will
@Ikeman14 have you tried the mcnugget challenge???? lol

1h fazeelia f. @ffazeelia
Best supper bfore cont with revision! Dabel cheese with fries and mcnugget ! :D

1h Maria Grazia @Mgraziahp
Ayy hija el mcnugget es mas caro q en eeuu, vete a eeuu ps vieja del mal y aprende a pronunciar nugget! #huachafasa

1h Hannah @Hannerr99
McNugget time yeah buddy

1h OBI-WANKMYBOABY @SidFishouS93
@laurenmcnee no mcnugget just no

1h keva l. cole-benton @KeyyLariecee
A.k.a ny mcnugget .

1h Andrew Saunders @athf16
ugh i have ate nothing but crap for the past 3 days "eats another mcnugget"

1h Skyy @McNugget_21
These kids keep me entertained

1h Skyy @McNugget_21
Nw-Mindless Behavior Hello again. These cousins of mine but I love em

1h Skyy @McNugget_21
Brooklynn whipping her hair....its hilarious

1h Skyy @McNugget_21
Nw - whip my hair

1h Will Gilbey @WillGilbey
@Alileighton plenty of protein in a mcnugget ;) aha

1h S^{KOTT} P^{ANDA}R^o_{ss}^A @GeorgeMFClooney
@JasmineMarie25 Dnt blame me yuh mcnugget sized muh fucka lol..

1h SJ @SyanaJalil
The solution of stress is chocolate, mcD chicken mcnugget, oreo crush blog, krushers etc etc!

1h magicmanstl @magicmanstl
Chicken McNugget Magic Video #1 -- http://lasvegasmagicman.com/?p=61

1h Nina C. @theneener

I think I'm going to order the 20 Chicken McNugget box when I get back to Denton.
My personal "welcome back" parade.

1h T.J. LaFlare @BlazingLazers
@OneBluntedBxtch Haha wassup my ninja McNugget lol

1h Alexis Fields @Lexiee_Mcnugget
Im at McDonalds .

1h Ash™ @ahmadasyrul
Ehhhhhh chickeeen mcnugget

Eileen Myles
46 Tweets

God Joan Rivers just wrote a
poem. I have to write one. I tweet
to compete. Also I love you.

ok socks of the day
you shall come off

otherwise all dogs asleep
all cats asleep
we sit here tweeting

whine oink

worldwide trends
whine oink

oh wait a second I'll be in Rotterdam
of March 24 so right oink tweet

@LeopoldineCore impossible view
I'm so glad I'm in it I can only look
out and see heaven I won't

Yeah I don't get it either but I think
for now that's why I like it.
Since lately got a stupid phone I'll
mainly tweet from bed.

at awp class and poetry today
at noon
what's working class in poetry
oh we're proud

Chicago is not so cold by the way
I feel like a fool in my down jacket

oh yeah reading tonight w about a
million people at america's dog 12
e adams chicago 7 pm

35 poets in Chicago all read their
poems at the same time tonight but
the guys yelled

San Diego – the kind of place you
think oh I guess I'll go for a run by
the ocean before I read. Can't
believe I ever lived here.

Why don't we all call ourselves
Emo now.

I mean anyone who cares about
kids being killed for style. Is all
style gay? We hit Iraq and in return
kids get "blocked."

Heard at Jeanette Winterson
reading in LA:
"Summer is ended and we are not
yet saved." I propose a teeshirt.

I am reading at skylight in LA
tomorrow (Friday) night at 730.

new book of poems,
snowflake/different streets.

I think for st. patrick's day I want to
see we need to talk about Kevin. right?

today in SF w CA Conrad, David
Buuck 530pm
at Artist Television Access
992 Valencia, San Francisco. Us
talking and reading our stuff.

Help I'm in Amsterdam train station
and there are no trains!

It's cause of computer failure.
Computers shouldn't be able to
stop trains. They're little. Even
getting littler right.

pawnation.com/2012/03/17/pet…
Hank made a nice appearance
today on PawNation.

I'm in the Dublin now for 900 hours
so I'm going to a little fishing village
that sounds like malomar to sit in
the sun.

The beckett thing is that it's not his
original language (French) so he had
to be simple.

Eileen Gray, Aileen Wournos, Eileen
Myles

Yes George Zimmerman's prior
arrest matters. Trayton's
suspensions seem to matter.
Jeesh.

I am reading in DC at AU which is
catholic at 630 pm today.

going to gold's gym w my smart
water feels really sad and stupid.

The level of radiation at the
Fukushima Plant in Japan at 73
sieverts per hour is too high for
robots!

How is this not activist judges?

Today after Leo's reading I came
home and ate one of the chocolate
vaginas on a stick from the
women's reading at AU last week.

Maureen Dowd is a bully. She
writes this great feminist column
like last week and today – Hillary
bashing again. Ugh.

What poet Eileen Myles Advocates
This Month
radar.qclick.us/2012/04/19/wha…
via@qclickus

When I consider Kitty Genovese
was a lesbian the world gets worse
for a moment.

Keep your mind on the bull not the
language of selling.

Each civilization insisted in its own
way before it went away.

The cats keep opening the freezer.
Why?

My portrait writing.

Snowflake/Different Streets by
Eileen Myles wp. me/p2spl1-1Z via
@wordpressdotcom

Tweeting later doesn't feel right. I
think you know what I mean.

@Susan Powter it was 8!

I feel embarrassed to admit my red
eye will land in Philadelphia. I said
sure within 80 miles of NY is fine.

@TimeWarnerCtr I want you to
go away.

I'm watching the conductor
approach and I don't have a ticket.

Dunkin donuts iced black cocoa
is pretty good if you've been
up all night.

Nick Thurston
from *A Dress*

A Dress (2011) is a simple mashup: chronological selections from one live text newsfeed commentary on the 2011 royal wedding, with pickings from the same newspaper's simultaneous public e-message board.

Nine twelve a-m: Guests are continuing to arrive at Westminster Abbey now. Chelsy Davy has arrived wearing an emerald green dress by Alberta Feretti, with a cream pillbox fascinator with veil. Guests so far are mostly friends of the family. What was Samantha Cameron thinking? Surely she could have asked for help styling? And how the heck did Nick Clegg get a wife like that?

Nine fifty a-m: There's John Major. Is it over yet? Can I come out now?

Nine fifty nine a-m: With an hour to go the media have been allowed in and the Abbey is filling up fast. Do you reckon Prince Andrew is chalking all of this up on his expenses account?

Ten o two a-m: Elton John has given his own spin on the tails look by clashing up a yellow waistcoat with a hot pink tie. Classy and fun. This is nearly as exciting as Eurovision.

Ten o three a-m: Piers Morgan has been discussing whether Diana would have enjoyed today if she were alive. Exclusive revelation: yes. Apparently on Fox News the discussion has revolved around where Diana would have sat if she were alive. French TV is rather good. It's being presented by Karl Lagerfeld who's just said that everyone is overweight and badly dressed.

Ten o five a-m: The lunchtime reception this afternoon is at Buckingham Palace and hosted by the Queen. Fiona Cairns created the cake, a traditional multi-tiered fruit cake decorated with cream and white icing. Prince William also asked McVitie's to make a chocolate biscuit cake based on a royal family recipe. Claire Jones, the official harpist to Prince Charles, is to perform. The evening reception will be hosted by Prince Charles before the older royals are due to melt away and leave the hip young things to party.

Ten twenty-six a-m: William and Harry have arrived at the Abbey. Who's that ginger lad? He has a quiff! What was he thinking? I love Harry's geezer walk.

Ten thirty-two a-m: Mother of the bride, Carole Middleton is arriving in a Jaguar now. Beckham's got a medal?! Was that for kicking that Argie and getting sent off in the 1998 World Cup?

Ten forty-two a-m: The Queen and Prince Philip are being driven along the Mall now. Look out, the Boss Lady is on her way. LOL! Wouldn't it be fun: "God save *me*, / Long live *me*, / Long to reign over *you*..." Tell you what, if I were driving down the Mall and the road was closed for me I would fucking floor it. Bollocks to the crowd.

Ten forty-four a-m: Prince Charles and Camilla are arriving now. I'm a bit disappointed that the Scandinavian royals haven't arrived by bike, but glad that his brother decided against the Nazi uniform.

Ten forty-five a-m: The foreign desk Al Jazeera is showing the wedding. Has Prince Philip insulted anyone yet?

Ten fifty-three a-m: First glimpse of the bride leaving her hotel: hair down, intricate lace overlay over a v-neck shaped bodice that shows possibly just a hint of cleavage. Train seems long judging by the faff getting into the car. OMG! OMG! OMG! She's wearing a dress!!! ...

Stephen Burt
The Road Builders

Nothing is spared.
The prayerful, seemingly rickety high
Radio towers let the wind beseech
Them; their popular waves
Pass through us & do not touch
The prominence of an otherwise-empty
Sky, where they arraign

Us not for the cities we had
But for those we could have.
These children picking up sticks
In their grandmother's roadside yard assemble them

Into a boundary, miniature
Protector: A-frame, imagined bedroom
Window, split-level

Of sticks, reliable heat.
Let stand, their sticks will freeze.
The cities will have to choose.
The future is nothing more
Than its own revenge on the past;
The horizon lets its smoke up, out of bounds.
The evident strength which spreads

Us out from place to place, place to no place
Through cracked winds of pollen and heavy winds of
Gasoline, cannot know its own
Mind. High baritones, the trucks
In squads rush & perpetuate
The barrier lanes designed for them & theirs.
You and I have no share in the world to come.

Dulles Access Road

Seen from the paid-for
taxicab on the way
to the paid-for flight,

this is our preparation for
the world, which insists
on employment, which insists,

if you want adults
to take you seriously,
that you have to make somebody

pay. We are untrained
to manage even the pace
at which we live. Slow down at the last red light,

its monochrome certainty ordinary
for it, but never for us,
though it swings on wires nearly within human reach;

behind it, as they do
almost every day at this hour,
impregnable metal containers dissolve in the sky.

J. Gordon Faylor
Rqumolet's

Via search terms 'no server', 'crying,' and one other, an algorithmically appropriated text by Rqomulet, apparently gleaned from the now-absent longerst.com n posted under the heading Oncaterius looked that started princely manner these domes – racto howled suppressed *was lifted in turn by a more explicitly human subject and set in* Arial *– links flattened, variants unaltered.*

Dooom beeyonnd serpent with productive discussion hat sounds she chose [url=http://longerst.com/ithree-kinds-of-life/]scully drunk three of a kind[/url] house while feeling green the victims all covered before something [url=http://longerst.com/software-keno-casino-online/] fox run casino connecticut[/url] can affect his absence research myself towing two consume residual [url=http://longerst.com/gymnastics-front-handsprings-instruction/]front and back hand vies[/url] hat sounds she needs that neither both dressed quickly away [url=http:// longerst.com/queen-jewels-game/]queen elizabeth's jewels[/url] called corals did that grown children the kraken most magnificen [url=http://longerst.com/high-protien-low-calorie-diets/] high low electric orlando[/url] square buildings purely personal stick farther they explained most encouragin [url=http://longerst.com/first-five-presadents/]first five steps[/url] olie of-fered mirror between not fooled their royalty similarly nonsensica [url=http://longerst.com/ los-angeles-casino-poker/]clearwater casinos[/url] not delay the ghostly magical creatures can understand longer any [url=http://longerst.com/jacks-or-better-hints/]jacks or better bar illinois[/url] gotten caught have made before they touched cold hey left [url=http://lon-gerst.com/attainments-money-station/]gas stations money[/url] undamental that play with attacked before fearsome monster and some [url=http://longerst.com/high-or-low-sodium/] high n low motorsports[/url] shall broach erhaps another may challenge skeletons used she says [url=http://longerst.com/reconcile-red-for-dogs-cheap/]clifford dog clothes wholesale red[/url] and tore about nice keeping pace rince does but why [url=http://longerst.com/egm-323-thomas/]egm scans 2007[/url] said solemnly special courtyard tilings would after eating the walls [url=http://longerst.com/in-your-face-greeting-cards/]business cards black faces[/url] bear named rlene demanded its winds every direction future king [url=http://longerst.com/main-street-seed-hollyhock-description-double/]kamikaze street doubles torrent[/url] tomb shuddered bother him launched himself along die would wake [url=http://longerst.com/download-antes-muerta-que-sencilla/]define ante[/url] greater than ada peered olphs rang who fears ada hissed [url=http://longerst.com/back-airsoft-hand-gun/]backing up hand signals[/url] daydreams she called evil shall approach the castle water would [url=http://longerst.com/marine-salt-water-flush-toilet/]fuel system flush b12 chemtool[/url] its place must introduce that this changes only you aren [url=http://longerst.com/lyrics-to-the-full-house/] full house pictuers[/url] olph feel his advice business with nly another fit for [url=http://longerst.com/fast-kart-speedway-in-vegas/]the correct way to fast[/url] cry awake might never delve down their feet braving the [url=http://longerst.com/online-stellenmarkt-croupier/] croupier import[/url] did agree ent you large tangle and began get your [url=http://longerst.com/four-kinds-of-sharks/]rick reily four of a kind[/url] and came could swim and asked all that mus said [url=http://longerst.com/niddk-payline/]2006 f32 nci payline[/url] was solving arrow stood search there omething that ghost for [url=http://longerst.com/jacks-or-better-video-poker/]jacks or better tutorial[/url] project isn and mine surprise you always tries maybe she [url=http://longerst.com/payline-west/]card payline[/url] bother him goblin shook our form arpies were gills couldn [url=http://longerst.com/full-house-boobs/]actor actress full house[/url] any obvious the nose with music ightning flickered briefer lives [url=http://longerst.com/it-let-online-poker-ride/]free it let online poker ride[/url] keep his backward too folk were would simply must plan [url=http://longerst.com/rank-169-starting-poker-hand/]hand rank in poker[/url] your grief and since hard and heer delight existence out [url=http://longerst.com/pai-gow-poker-rules/]pai gow free games[/url] her comings right around destroy the boat moved aged man [url=http://longerst.com/back-of-hand-pain/]forearm back of hand numb cold[/url] rescue you was laced grown man time the clean hen [url=http://longerst.com/red-zone-dog-hera-cesar-milano/]red dog surf[/url] sing you rose bushes that route sand from they needed [url=http://longerst.com/baccarat-glass-candlestick/]club baccarat[/url] cloud formed deep lines the beginning take off and astonishin [url=http://longerst.com/come-to-rocky-point/]dew-point comes in contact with[/url] valid offer second pie thank you strange about folk did [url=http://longerst.com/on-line-keno-lottery/]keno drive in theater[/url] they set slight dragging true continuity commence the elbow bones [url=http://longerst.com/excel-conditional-formatting-odd-even/]even and odd parity generator[/url] case like smash the hat duty trouble swimming poke their [url=http://longerst.com/high-end-luxury-pontoon-boats/]pontoon boat sizes[/url] that can hands spaced only one mixed emotions species had [url=http://longerst.com/gaara's-tattoo-black-or-red/]what's good red or black[/url] already had them standing eying the escaping feathers just might [url=http://longerst.com/chic-mauve-soft-handbag/]air soft hand guns[/url] and fired about forty lectra felt they connected locusts clung [url=http://longerst.com/pai-gow-poker-free-games/]pai gow tile[/url] were going almost all big word one respect him crave [url=http://longerst.com/does-powerpoint-come-on-windows-xp/]come to a point[/url] his part urn seemed they found shall cross was uneventful [url=http://longerst.com/full-house-bi/]joe satriani house full of bullets[/url] mask her figure too rlene protested heads became and great [url=http://longerst.com/high-calcium-low-phosphorus-foods/]high torque low rpm hobby motor[/url] sle for became thoroughly bubbly white she exerts chaos below [url=http://longerst.com/l-e-d-mirage-joker-3100/]joker and the theif download[/url] take your vast chamber prince finds long away ortunately there [url=http://longerst.com/daily-high-low-temps-new-york/]calcium high in low phosphorous urine[/url] and attached its twin staying with approach you the passing [url=http://longerst.com/video-download-format-samsung-blackjack/]blackjack table supplies[/url] arents were atan had this court elebration washed angry that [url=http://longerst.com/yablon-mississippi/]robinson and yablon[/url] hex did this misfortune hey slithered act now years were [url=http://longerst.com/drive-drive-drive-let-it-ride/]it let poker ride tightpoker[/url] look just sure mat required the his father right rhythm [url=http://longerst.com/deuces-wild-flower-pin-swap-round/]deuces wild pa lottery[/url] lowered little least let maybe like and been the point [url=http://longerst.com/ways-to-make-erections-harder/]two way three hard[/url] old boy ery crafty perhaps thought really pretty this variant [url=http://longerst.com/the-big-top-circus/]cole brothers circus cruelity of animals[/url] him back xcept maybe awake until shortest ribs rack open [url=http://longerst.com/twenty-one-corey-smith/]century twenty one jeffersonville indiana[/url] nose glowing thorn.

Don Share
With You in the Olive Garden of Eden

I'm with you on Earth, where innocence has been changed to protect the names of the guilty. Where women and children go last! Where we blame religion and politicians and ask what's in a word. It's not a question, like 'What Are Years', 'Are You Experienced', and 'What is Poetry.' I'm with you in the scrimmage of appetites everywhere. Where the world of dinner belongs to the meek. I'm with you in parenting. Dad, I know you didn't pick me to be your son. I'm with you at home, where for a long time, to condense Proust, I went to bed early. Where on waking, I realized that the Tooth Fairy has blood on her hands. I'm with you in the confessional. From thence I can explain everything; and moreover only from thence. Where The Red Thread that Runs through Everything is the gryme-dryzzle of it all! Where the priesthood of my individual soul is celibate. I'm with you gathering blood diamonds: That's a big rock, where'd you get it? I'm with you, MFA students. I want to take your pronouns from you. I'm with you at work, and have nothing to obtain, because I have all... But I still have to go to work. I'm with you at the end of the story, where ending is superflous; full and blank as the calendar. I'm with you on the high holidays, where there were five persons in my 'immediate family', though this is no longer the case. I'm with you in autoemancipation, where I close my eyes and see the dead-and-gone again. I'm sexting you, and when I'm with you, I'm in the Olive Garden of Eden. Where I say, here's my bucket list: Find an ordinary bridge. Jump off. Thank you for your support. Where you've always stood behind me, jeering me on. Where there's wifi, but no connection, try again. Where I am nothing, and nothing you say can ever make it not so. I'm with you in modernism, where the elbow is the thermometer of the soul, said Delsarte; where the knee is therefore the thermometer of the will. I'm with you in post-modernism, where even the Soul Conjecture was proved, albeit after a lifetime. I'm with you back in modernism, where I told Louis Sullivan: I scrape my own sky, Sir. I'm with you in the Historic District, where it's time to pull up stakes; now all we need is the stakes. I'm with you above Tinern Abbey, where you can never have too many giants. I'm with you in the oeconomy of love, where it's your own nothingness that your being is punishing. I'm with you listening to *Some Girls Deluxe Edition*, where she's who she is, not who she was. I'm with you in Kashmir, where Buddha has lost, at last, an earlobe: *Out of mind, out of sight.* I'm with you at the nativity scene, where every time you sigh, another item is added to your Wish List. I'm with you at a *Paris Review* party, where nothing I own is bespoke. I'm with you at the Grand Canyon, where I've seen this all before; it's like a Poloroid of crazy. I'm with you in a drum circle. E pluribus unitard. I'm with you in slippage, where I was nearly deleted on dark December morn. I'm with you at X-mas. God bless us every once. I'm with you in effigy. The author of these lines is an effigy, so if you beat him up you are only beating an effigy. I'm with you on a sleepless night where insomnia means, of course, *dreamless*. I'm with you reading Dylanesque spam: I'll be your quick nut tonight. I'm with you in blonde jokes. A blonde and a brunette were walking down the street. They both had the same eyes. I'm with you in the People's Court: I can't, and recant. I'm with you at Sur le Table, but I happen to think that a dull knife is a well-loved knife. I'm with you in parenthood, where there is no grief like the daddy's because it is thought not to exist. I'm with you at the vortex: Where there's a volte, there's almost certainly a face. I'm with you in the 4Q; I had not thought that debt had undone so many. I'm with you at Ground Zero. If you've made it nowhere, you can make it anywhere. I'm with you in the Pierian spring, where hope springs eternal in the human liver. I'm with you watching the restored *Yellow Submarine*; All you need is glove. I'm with you in the psychopathology of everyday life, where only people who are crazy say they are not crazy. I'm with you in the Museum of Contemporary Art, where it can take a moment or so to make out a woman's face. I'm with you watching the Foo Fighters on the Oscars: I fought the Foo, but the Foo won. I'm with you and the Presidential candidates in Chagrin Falls. Let the chagrin fall where it may. I'm with you on Valentine's Day. Go ahead, admit a few impediments. I'm with you on Twitter, where I am turning my garbage can into a time machine. I'm with you on the Dies Ire, where desire is full of ire. I'm with you on the crime scene school playground. Rock, paper, schisms. I'm with you in Hell because I'm too old to be an atheist, and where pride cometh before a fallacy. Let my right hand wither if I forget how the rest of this psalm goes. After all, before the Fall, Adam and Eve stood still. I'm with you in a moment of silence, and your silence is as telling as everything you say; maybe moreso, because it is less human. I'm with you right here; I thought I would always be here, dozing in the living room on the brown couch. I'm with you in translation, which has it that the earth apple, if it was a pear, Eve could not have eaten. I'm with you in the diaspora, where even pessimists always order desert. I'm with you at the dentist, where a pyrrhic victory is when you're done getting your teeth cleaned. I'm with you in Paradise where Et in Arcadia Oreo. I'm with you in planning for early retirement: When they put me out to pasture, I'll eat grass. I'm with you in comment boxes: Yes, but if I eat shit, *will* I die? I'm with you in philosophy; cogito ergo some. I'm with you in the woe that is our second marriage where I shall hold you harmless. I'm with you in Lord Weary's Castle, where fake emotions can be really humanizing. Where it's an ill wind that blows no ill. Where it's an ill wind that blows no illness. Where patience comes to those who wait. Where all knots are Gordian. Where all green cars are old. Where you have to turn left sooner or later. Where you should never eat the onion soup. Where you cannot travel faster than the vehicle in front of you. Where haste makes haste. Where every solution causes another problem. Where there is no they. Where remarks is literature. Where, when the innocent were dying, I realized that dream gives away its final look. Where you can add nausea ad nauseum. Where migration, tourism, parasites, viruses, hosting, information flows, data, social networking, physical infrastructure, and paradigm shifts say *I'll give you something to cry about.*

A record of a search for 'potato salad' and 'sex pictures' with different search parameters, privacy settings and personal search turned on

Hidden fields

Google SearchI'm Feeling Lucky
Account Options

1.
2. Sign in
1. Search settings
2.
3. Advanced search
4.
5. Web History

Screen reader users, click here to turn off Google Instant.
Google
potato salad

Google Instant is unavailable. Press enter to search. Learn more
Google Instant is off due to connection speed. Press Enter to search.
Press Enter to search.
Press Enter to search.
Search
About 34,900,000 results (0.14 seconds)

1.
SafeSearch off
*
Off
*
Moderate (recommended)
*
Strict
*
*
Learn about SafeSearch
2. Please report the offensive images.Cancel
3.
*
Search settings
*
Advanced search
*
Web History
*
Search Help

*
Everything
* Images
* Maps
* Videos
* News
* Shopping
* Recipes

* Books
* Places
* Blogs
* Flights
* Discussions
* Applications
* Patents

More Fewer

* New York, NY

* Auto-detected
*
Change location
*
Yes No
Ingredients
• mayonnaise
• mustard
• dill
• capers
• potatoes
• celery
• paprika
• vinegar
*
• Any cook time
• Less than 15 min
• Less than 30 min
• Less than 60 min
*
• Any calories
• Less than 100 cal
• Less than 300 cal
• Less than 500 cal

Search Options
*
Fewer search tools
More search tools
Search Results

1.
Potato Salad Recipes - Allrecipes.com
allrecipes.com/recipes/salad/potato-salads/Cached - Similar
You +1'd this publicly. Undo
Looking for potato salad recipes? Allrecipes has more than 190 trusted potato salad recipes complete with ratings, reviews and mixing tips.
Top 20 - Creamy Potato Salads - Old Fashioned Potato Salad - View Recipes
2.
Images for potato salad
- Report imagesThank you for the feedback. Report another

imagePlease report the offensive image. CancelDone
*
3.
Potato Salad Recipe : Ina Garten : Recipes : Food Network
www.foodnetwork.com › ... ›
Holidays and PartiesCached - Similar
You +1'd this publicly. Undo
285 reviews - 30 mins
Food Network invites you to try this Potato Salad recipe from Ina Garten.
4.
Potato Salad Recipe : Tyler Florence : Recipes : Food Network
www.foodnetwork.com › ... ›
Holidays and PartiesCached - Similar
You +1'd this publicly. Undo
164 reviews - 40 mins
Food Network invites you to try this Potato Salad recipe from Tyler Florence.
5.
Potato Salad Recipe | Simply Recipes
simplyrecipes.com/recipes/potato_salad/Cached - Similar
You +1'd this publicly. Undo
45 mins
Sep 5, 2011 – Classic potato salad with boiled potatoes, sour cream, mayo, green onions, celery, parsley, pickles and bacon.
6.
Potato salad - Wikipedia, the free encyclopedia
en.wikipedia.org/wiki/Potato_saladCached - Similar
You +1'd this publicly. Undo
Potato salad is a dish made from boiled potatoes, the versions of which vary throughout different regions and countries of the world. Although called a salad, it is ...
7.
Classic Potato Salad Recipe
southernfood.about.com/od/potatosalads/.../bln298....Cached - Similar
You +1'd this publicly. Undo
Rating: 4.5 - 8 reviews
This classic potato salad is made with mayonnaise, vinegar, sugar, potatoes, celery, onion, eggs, and garnish of green onions and or tomatoes.
Diana Rattrayby Diana Rattray · More by Diana Rattray
8.
Classic Potato Salad Recipe - Food.com - 22747

Google Instant is unavailable. Press enter to search.Learn more
Google Instant is off due to connection speed. Press Enter to search.
Press Enter to search.

1. +Tan
2. Search
3. Images
4. Maps
5. Play
6. YouTube
7. News
8. Gmail
9. Documents
10. Calendar
11. More

1. Translate
2. Mobile
3. Books
4. Offers
5. Wallet
6. Shopping
7. Blogger
8. Reader
9. Finance
10. Photos
11. Videos
12.
13. Even more

Hidden fields
Google SearchI'm Feeling Lucky
Account Options

1. Tan Lin
2. 0
Opening...
3.
Share
Opening...
4. Tan Lin
Tan LinChange photo
Tan Lintlinwork@gmail.com
Account–Privacy
View profile
Tan LinTan Lintlinwork@gmail.com
All your Google+ pages ›
Add account   Sign out
1. Search settings
2.
3. Advanced search
4.
5. Web History

Screen reader users, click here to turn off Google Instant.
Google
sex pictures

Google Instant is unavailable. Press enter to search. Learn more
Google Instant is off due to connection speed. Press Enter to search.
Press Enter to search.
Press Enter to search.
Search
About 568,000,000 results (0.11 seconds)

1.
2.
SafeSearch off
*
Off
*
Moderate (recommended)
*
Strict
*
*
Learn about SafeSearch
3. Please report the offensive images.Cancel
4.
*
Search settings
*
Advanced search
*
Web History
*
Search Help

*
Everything
* Images
* Maps
* Videos
* News
* Shopping

* Books
* Places
* Blogs
* Flights
* Discussions
* Recipes
* Applications
* Patents

More Fewer

* New York, NY

* Auto-detected
*
Change location
Search Options
*

Hide search toolsShow search tools
Search Results

1.
Free porn pictures teen sex tube pornstars naked babes nice ass ...
www.bravoteens.com/Cached - Similar
You +1'd this publicly. Undo
BravoTeens.Com has everything! Free Porn Tube and Thumbnailed Galleries with nice design, lots of categories for the true porn lovers. FANTASTIC array of ...
Videos - Most Popular Free Porn ... - Teenies - Babes
2.
Free Sex Pics, Sex Pictures, Sex Galleries at LamaLinks.com
www.lamalinks.com/Cached - Similar
You +1'd this publicly. Undo

LamaLinks.com delivers the biggest collection of free sex pics. Over 500 000 sex pictures available to download featuring big tits, milf, lesbian, anal, amateur, ...
3.
Free Porn, Sex, Tube Videos, XXX Pics, Porno Movies - XNXX.COM
www.xnxx.com/Cached - Similar
You +1'd this publicly. Undo
XNXX delivers free sex movies and fast free porn videos (tube porn). Now 1 million+ sex vids available for free! Featuring hot pussy, sexy girls in xxx rated porn ...
Best Sex videos - New Videos - Time - Gay videos - XNXX.COM
145 people in New York, NY +1'd this
4.
Twilightsex - free hardcore sex pictures & free sex movies, live sex ...
www.twilightsex.com/multi/Cached - Similar
You +1'd this publicly. Undo
TwilightSex Free Hardcore Sex Pictures and Free Sex Movies, Live Sex Webcams and Free Porn.
5.
Free Hardcore Sex Movies & Sex Tube Videos, Live Sex Webcams ...
www.twilightsex.com/Cached - Similar
You +1'd this publicly. Undo
Free sex tube featuring HD porn tube videos, famous pornstar movies, teen porn tube videos. Download sex movies or watch free HD porn online.
6.
Fresh sex pictures at freshsperm. com!
www.freshsperm.com/Cached - Similar
You +1'd this publicly. Undo
We got all the latest fresh sex pictures you've been looking for. Don't take our word for it, start browsing our massive collection now! We got dozens of categories ...
7.
Group Sex, Free Group Sex Pics, Lesbian Group Sex Galleries

Kim Rosenfield
Marcus, Kim, Marina

Marcus: Oh, here we go.
Marina: Okay.
Marcus: Hello.
Marina: Is it working?
Marcus: I'm here. Kim, are you here too, Kim?
Marina: Did we cut her off by me joining?
Marcus: She – I'm – let me see.
Kim: Hey, Marcus.
Marcus: Hey.
Kim: Hey, I was on hold for a second. Maybe that was Marina trying to come on.
Marcus: Yeah, it was. Let me just figure out –
Kim: I think if we go to –
Marcus: Conference – where is conference call?
Kim: Go up to the menu, and it says call, and then start conference call.
Marcus: Um –
Kim: I think. You want me to – you want me to do it?
Marcus: Yeah. I can't even see that. Like –
Kim: Let me see if this works.
Marcus: On my list.
Kim: Okay, I pressed that and nothing's happening. Okay, let's see if I can call
            Marina. Start conference call. Oh, okay. Okay. Nothing's happening. Add
            a contact. Let me see, __________. It's not working.
Marcus: Okay, let's – did you find – where did you find the conference call thing? Which –
Kim: Do you have a – are you on a –
Marcus: I'm on a Mac.
Kim: It's at the top, the very top bar. It has all the files, like Skype, File, Edit.
Marcus: Yeah.
Kim: Then it says call, and if you scroll down it says start conference call,
            conference call.
Marcus: I don't have a call –
Kim: You don't have a call option?
Marcus: I don't think so.
Marina: Okay –
Marcus: Hi, Marina.
Marina: Hi. I don't know if the three way thing is really possible.
Marcus: We're trying to – oh, wait, add people to this call. Let me just try this.
Marina: Do you want to – oh, hello?
Marcus: Hello? Kim, are you there? Kim is now actually –
Marina: It seems to be an either/or situation. But, you know, Marcus, maybe it makes
            more sense for you to talk to one of us and then the other of us.
Marcus: I'm not – well, yeah, maybe. In theory, you're both on, you're both actually
            here now, but I guess not. Wait. Okay.

Marina: Kim just showed up in a window. Kim, can you hear us?
Kim: Yeah, I can hear you.
Marcus: Hi. Okay, we're all here.

Vijay Seshadri
Surveillance Report

The omni-directional mike and the video camera, both tiny,
hidden in the bonsai cypress
are picking up my sunrise self-help talk show,
in the makeshift kitchen studio, in a bathrobe and bunny slippers.
First the opening monologue,
then the body banters with the mind, then queue up the callers.
Caller X is unhappy with the latest dream interpretation.
Caller X is cut off with a flick of the wrist.
Caller Y wants to share that my fearless candor has given her permission
to become utterly transparent herself.
Thank you, Caller Y. Your inner light can be seen from here.
Night-visiting revenants, clerks of the underworld,
gnawing the half-buried roots of being,
spirits of the burning trees, kiss me goodbye.
The tape shows me checking my chronometer and exiting for work.
Observers posted along my morning commute observe the usual detours,
the purchase of potables and comestibles.
Flash forward the digital feed.
At ten hundred hours, the current workplace asset texts,
"Subject agitated. Begging colleagues,
'Please have the courtesy not to be conscious of me.' "
Of the three or four scenarios employed
to predict my next location, during the interminable lunch hour,
when the terrible questions of where to go and what to eat
among choices once enticing but now exposed in all their bitter banality
assault even the most cheerful of our targets,
today, which is a Tuesday, is burning-house-scenario day.
Cloud after cloud of smoke and flames
sweep through and over the turrets,
the widow's walk, the pergolas, the port-cochere.
Fire boiling through the leaded windowpanes immolates the gillyflowers.
Though I haven't been located, for reasons I don't understand,
in the crowd shots pirated from the Eyewitness News feed,
what the crowd feels I would feel if I were there to feel it.
But I'm not there to feel it,
I'm not there at all, there at the next disaster,
the last disaster but one but one but one . . .
The dormant listening posts activate.

Windowless vans crammed with information technology
park on the corners of all the streets.
Oh, the wailing in the control room, the recriminations,
the pointing of fingers, the blame game, the pleas
of the pragmatic to move forward, not backward, and solve this problem,
find me and put me back on the grid.
Where will I be scanned for first? Maybe I'm in the trashed, padlocked
public restroom in the park. The pipes are hissing.
The concrete floor is littered with syringes and treacherous
with pools of chill and fetid standing water.
The mirrors are shattered, and the sinks and urinals are shattered.
This is the restroom nobody ever visits
in the park abandoned by humankind,
the dead zone where the transducer and the infrared lens quail,
where all the signals ricochet.
Or, alternatively, I could be on a beach somewhere.

Trisha Low
from *PURGE: Volume II*
The Story of Trisha Low's Sexual Assault
as Circulated by Love in a Maze, or,
Virtue Rewarded.

A transcription of personal ephemera, PURGE sets out to dress itself in the textual markers of my adolescence. Composed of suicide notes, fangirlish figurations of cybersex, diary entries and notes to best friends, these documents of emotional excess are squashed into the more legible and somewhat restrictive form of 'conceptual project'. However, this writing has not made public in order to lay claim to 'transgressive art' or a 'vast feminist gesture'. Instead it serves as a a means of problemetising the utopian promise of a authentic identity – an identity entirely separate from dominant masculine ideology or outside of melodramatic codification.

In these cybersex chatlogs, personal conversations with the 'real' identities of other players and their life-trauma litter, interrupt and warp the dominant narrative fantasy of male-on-male pretty boy porno, leaving the line between sex and assault, fantasy and 'curative' therapy ambiguous. In this strange artificiality, an 'authentic' identity politics becomes redundant – instead 'feminism's double bind, rather than being resolved, [becomes] more deeply inscribed in its tactical recourse to parasiticism, taken up as a model of perverse appropriation that seeks to undermine the very thing that it depends on using in order to do so' (Fisher, Arts & Education)

(Like parasites) sometimes we must willfully and wrongly create,
in ourselves, our fathers – before we try to kill them.
Aliza Shvarts

fabrizio moretti – The Strokes: June 8 2004, 11:37:27 UTC Edited: June 8 2011, 12:13:20 UTC

[he said he just thought I was depressed]

in music room
talking to Fish about the bass line on a song I wrote
hears you
joins you in front room
What?

anthony rossomando – The Dirty Pretty Things: June 9 2004, 04:32:35 UTC

[I don't think what happened to *me* is anywhere near as bad as some of the stories on here but it doesn't mean it didn't happen]

starts laughing
puts computer down
pulls you into my lap
hugs you really hard around the middle
grinning
We're gonna be famous and shit!
pushes you off me
but not hard

Okay, I don't like cuddling.

fabrizio moretti – The Strokes: June 9 2004, 04:36:00 UTC

[It's only over the past few days that it has occurred to me that what he did was wrong. I was semi conscious at best throughout the whole experience, I mean, I don't know if he knows what he did or if he genuinely believes it was consensual.]
[PS. Can they do it on the couch. Just because Fab doesn't like cuddling doesn't mean he doesn't want to fuck]

surprised
What the..
goes with it
ruffles your hair
Aren't we already?
gets off you
sits next to you, though
Why the fuck not?

anthony rossomando: The Dirty Pretty Things: June 9 2004, 04:38:05 UTC

[Did he put something in your drink, do you think, or did he just get you totally wasted?]

[P.S. Obviously]

draws legs up to chest
lights another cigarette
I don't know.
pats Fab's leg
I just totally don't.

fabrizio moretti – The Strokes: June 9 2004, 04:42:26 UTC

[I mean, I couldn't stand unaided. He said I could stay over so I called my boyfriend
and told him - he was fine with it.]

amused
nods
mock upset
All that stuff they're saying about you is true. You're a cold-hearted bastard, it's
terrible.
smiles and looks away
I mean they also all told me you're cute.
looks up from under lashes
They're right about that too, you know.

anthony rossomando – The Dirty Pretty Things: June 9 2004, 04:43:36 UTC

[Girl, that totally doesn't sound okay. That sounds like he roofied the hell out of
you. Did you tell your boyfriend?]

laughs
Yeah...Unlike what they say about The Strokes.
grins
 I'm a real asshole.
reaches up
*touches your hair *
You know, I guess you're kind of okay-looking.

fabrizio moretti – The Strokes: June 9 2011, 04:46:12 UTC

[No, you know I wasn't even worried he was gonna be mad about it, I think it
scared me more that he might not be mad. I mean it was a complicated situation]

shrugs
Okay, maybe not. Guess we're not that different.
laughs
Just okay?
leans into your touch
closes eyes
kisses

anthony rossomando – The Dirty Pretty Things: June 9 2011, 04:49:25 UTC

[God, boys are the worst. I'm sorry. I'm sure he would have been mad though …]

pulls away
smiles slowly
gestures to door
So...we gonna go, then? Or maybe we should stay right here…

Vanessa Place
Goodbye My Sweethearts

Goodbye my sweethearts -- sorry, and know and that I love you very much.
Partager · Il y a environ une heure · 50/56
https://www.facebook.com/profile.php?id=749770730&sk=wall
Steve, talk to us!!
Il y a environ une heure · 2
https://www.facebook.com/profile.php?id=749770730&sk=wall
Call the number Steve!! Your kids need you.
Il y a environ une heure · 2
https://www.facebook.com/profile.php?id=749770730&sk=wall
Uncle Steve, talk to us man. I want to see you again.
Il y a environ une heure · 1
https://www.facebook.com/profile.php?id=749770730&sk=wall
for God's sake reach out...there are so many reaching for you.
Il y a 59 minutes · 3
https://www.facebook.com/profile.php?id=749770730&sk=wall
Many people have worn grief on their sleeves and in their hearts but also
encourage you to know that joy is just around the corner - in the eyes of a
stranger, the sun in the sky, the love of your children and family. Hang on
and hang in there friend.
Il y a 56 minutes
https://www.facebook.com/profile.php?id=749770730&sk=wall
does anybody live near him? or send the police over--my daughter stopped
a friend that way.
Il y a 54 minutes · 1
https://www.facebook.com/profile.php?id=749770730&sk=wall
I haven't met you but I'd like to have the opportunity to.
Il y a 53 minutes · 1
https://www.facebook.com/profile.php?id=749770730&sk=wall
I am Steve's minister. I called 911 and they have gone to the house.
Il y a 52 minutes · 6
https://www.facebook.com/profile.php?id=749770730&sk=wall
I hope he'll be okay x
Il y a 51 minutes · 2

https://www.facebook.com/profile.php?id=749770730&sk=wall
They say it's good for book sales, but only the publisher profits.
Il y a 50 minutes
https://www.facebook.com/profile.php?id=749770730&sk=wall
words fail me jannine som people like attantion re michael wtf
Il y a 46 minutes · 2
https://www.facebook.com/profile.php?id=749770730&sk=wall
❤ You're not alone ❤
Il y a 46 minutes
https://www.facebook.com/profile.php?id=749770730&sk=wall
M: If you have nothing constructive to add, keep quiet, please.
Il y a 44 minutes · 4
https://www.facebook.com/profile.php?id=749770730&sk=wall
Has anyone heard anything yet?
Il y a 41 minutes
https://www.facebook.com/profile.php?id=749770730&sk=wall
My mother said the police are on their way, if not there already
Il y a 39 minutes · 2
https://www.facebook.com/profile.php?id=749770730&sk=wall
Michael is a bi-polar writer too, and sometimes a joke helps more than
sympathy for me.
Il y a 39 minutes · 1
https://www.facebook.com/profile.php?id=749770730&sk=wall
Thanks for the explanation, Mr. M, empathy might be more appropriate, I feel.
(Bad joke, anyway).
Il y a 36 minutes · 1
https://www.facebook.com/profile.php?id=749770730&sk=wall
I hope an ambulance too!!!!!!!!!!!!!!!!!!!!!!!!!!!!
Il y a 36 minutes
https://www.facebook.com/profile.php?id=749770730&sk=wall
Sarah, yeah Carrie was replying to me, but I had deleted my post. I thought I was
wrong to have a go at Michael when I don't actually know him x
Il y a 32 minutes
https://www.facebook.com/profile.php?id=749770730&sk=wall
Back to the point: Steve; You are needed/wanted, don't go, the time will come when
you will have no choice over the matter, wait 'til then.
Il y a 27 minutes · 2
https://www.facebook.com/profile.php?id=749770730&sk=wall
Patti Jo, your suggestion that I remove something that will make Steve smile is foolish;
so, I'll ignore it. The continuing harangue I'll chalk up to well-meaning ignorance.
Il y a 9 minutes
https://www.facebook.com/profile.php?id=749770730&sk=wall
He's right. Since they are friends they have a different way of communicating
with each other. It's okay.
Il y a 8 minutes
https://www.facebook.com/profile.php?id=749770730&sk=wall
I was worrying that it would hurt him, obviously. He is my cousin and I love
him very much!

Il y a 7 minutes
https://www.facebook.com/profile.php?id=749770730&sk=wall
I think it's safe to say that this comment string has devolved into missing the point entirely. Let's all get over ourselves, it's the reason why action took place quickly in the first place. If we had wasted time arguing rather than acting, who knows where we'd be.
Il y a 2 minutes · 1
https://www.facebook.com/profile.php?id=749770730&sk=wall
Well, I love him too. And I'm hoping my inappropriate humor will wake him up enough to realize that he'll be doing more damage to others by opting out than he will by sticking around (that was always my reason for putting down the gun--that and the idea that some innocent would have to discover the body and clean up the mess).
Il y a 2 minutes
https://www.facebook.com/profile.php?id=749770730&sk=wall
I hope he's not done anything irreparable. Tomorrow may be brighter.
il y a quelques secondes

Josef Kaplan
Samizdat

The $20 bill is placed face-up and the top and bottom edges are folded to the centerline; the white tips of the right edge are folded under, and the two resultant corners are folded towards the centerline; the bill is repositioned so that this folded section is facing up, and the bottom end is folded to slip nicely under it; the bottom end is then unfolded; a squash fold is made at the one-third crease mark for both the left and right side of the bill; the bottom end is then tucked back under the top to create a collared shirt, and the bill is therefore recognizable as $10. Then the $10 bill is placed so that backside is facing up, then only the white edges are folded over; the bill is then folded in half, lengthwise; the bill is then folded in half again, lengthwise; the white edge near the end of the folded bill is folded away; the '10' at the same end is folded so that the '10' is centered in a little square of folded money; the rest of the bill is curved slightly and laid back down; part of the bill is folded upwards at 90°, and then folded over the back of the horizontal piece, to end up straight down; the whole piece is then flipped over; the curved piece is then rolled around to create a complete circle and the vertical piece is wrapped downwards and back up through the center of the bill; the folded end-flap containing the '10' is then tucked into the edge of the vertical piece to create a ring, and the bill is therefore recognizable as $5. And then the $5 bill is placed face-up and folded in half from left to right, then unfolded, then folded in half from top to bottom and unfolded again; each of the four corners are folded to the centerline; the long edges of the bill are folded towards the centerline; the points of the bill are folded and unfolded to form a vertical crease; each half is folded and unfolded downwards and back to create an X-shaped crease at the very center of the bill; the bill is then turned over; a squash fold is then used to form a diamond shape; the right-most edge is then folded over on the front and backside; the resultant corners on the new right-most edge are folded towards the centerline; the two leftmost points are held in the thumb and forefinger while the bill is gently unfolded and pulled apart to produce the midsection of a bow-tie, and is therefore recognizable as $1. But then the $1 bill is placed face-up, but upside-down; valley folds are made at the halfway points of the bill, as well as the top corners; the top corners are folded along the valley fold; the top pointed corner is folded down; the right edge of the bill is folded back behind until the bill is doubled over; the fold is creased; the bill is unfolded; the right edge is folded back again, until it lines up with the crease made previous; another crease is made; the bill is folded along the creases; the folded bill is turned over; a valley fold is made at nearly the utmost edge of the bill's right side to create a center channel; the four corners of the center channel are folded, then squash-folded; the top pointy part of the bill is then unfolded; valley folds are made on the outside of the center channel; a mountain fold is made just in front of the channel, so that this piece overlaps the channel; the piece is then flipped over; another valley fold is made at the front edge of the overlapping piece; a mountain fold is added a short distance in front of that to overlap the piece by about half its width; the whole bill is then folded in half down the centerline, using a mountain fold; the point of the pointy part is folded back to make a crease line; the creased section is angled forward slightly; the pointy part is unfolded; the crease is used to make a reverse fold inside the body of the bill; the pointy part is unfolded again; the pointy part is pushed into the body, making two valley folds (one on either side) along the crease so that the pointy part's crease lines end up in contact with the front edge of the overlapping piece; the pointy part is then creased and reverse-folded so that it points down; more reverse folds are made to get the pointy part pointing up, and the pointy part's tip pointing slightly back; the bill is then turned over and the overlapping piece opened up a bit; a small tail is valley-folded out; the floating eye in the pyramid from the backside of the bill becomes the eye of an elephant, unblinking.

Darren Wershler and Bill Kennedy
from *Update*

Allen Ginsberg

Allen Ginsberg got paid. Allen Ginsberg spent time in the suburbs today, with my friend's kids, he knew all his neighbours, we had a walk, said bedtime prayers, and read three stories and went over to his new place and saw the dog. It made me rethink families. Allen Ginsberg: overwhelmed with love for his dog. Allen Ginsberg is a cat negotiating the dog days of summer. Allen Ginsberg Cowboy boy band. Allen Ginsberg I'm so demoralized that 51 of my friends like *Family Guy*. Allen Ginsberg is looking for guidance. Allen Ginsberg is playing Scrabble on his iPhone, and loves the little googly eyes that tell his when his opponent is looking at the board. Allen Ginsberg ordered medium but got spicy. Allen Ginsberg has a problem! Allen Ginsberg isn't allowed to use the word 'motherfucker' as a security word. Allen Ginsberg wants someone to take a picture of Richard Munslow's grave. He is said to be the last sin-eater. Anyone know any sin-eaters or sin-eating stories? Or sin-eating traditions? Allen Ginsberg I know it's a marketing gimmick, but Padma Laksmhi writing pornographically about bacon and Christina Hendricks talking about scotch is just too far. Allen Ginsberg haunted by olives in meringue. Allen Ginsberg finds it oddly delicious. Allen Ginsberg DETOX! Allen Ginsberg is enduring the HELL on earth that is sxsw. Allen Ginsberg there is no zombie fun quite like Nazi zombie fun. Allen Ginsberg is mildly astonished that not one of his hundreds of FB friends has had a birthday this week. Allen Ginsberg wonders when his hair will stop falling out. Allen Ginsberg on a mini-moon, radio silence.

Jack Kerouac

Jack Kerouac transitioning. Jack Kerouac what is all this topsy turvy? Jack Kerouac assholes cured me of techno. Jack Kerouac hopes those cowboys win *Amazing Race*! Jack Kerouac the watch store downtown is carrying a line of jewels for men called Bros Way. They are made of light! Jack Kerouac Dear Miley Cyrus: I'd rather watch commercials. Jack Kerouac only just now figured out that 'Mr. Jones' was written as an homage to 'Ballad of a Thin Man'. Jack Kerouac is looking forward to sleep, one of his favorite activities. Jack Kerouac thinks seven-year-olds shouldn't be allowed to use air quotes. Jack Kerouac probably swears too much. Jack Kerouac I guess I shouldn't be surprised that a used car salesman totally wasted my time. Jack Kerouac thinks it's an interesting challenge to try to limit his FB friends to people he actually knows. Why are poets such sluts? Jack Kerouac is at the point where all he wants to do is look at dogs who need homes on the Internet. Jack Kerouac New Jersey snowy evening – homemade pasta and good friends – Manhattan skyline on the horizon.

Simon Morris
from *Getting inside Jack Kerouac's head*

24 March 2009

concert tickets, and the names Jack and Joan and Henri and Vicki, the girl, together with a series of sad jokes and some of his favorite sayings such as 'You can't teach the old maestro a new tune.' So Neal couldn't ride uptown with us and the only thing I could do was sit in the back of the Cadillac and wave at him. The bookie at the wheel also wanted nothing to do with Neal. Neal, ragged in a motheaten overcoat he brought specially for the freezing temperatures of the East, walked off alone and the last I saw of him he rounded the corner of 7th Ave., eyes on the street ahead, and bent to it again. Poor little Joan my wife to whom I'd told everything about Neal began almost to cry. 'Oh we shouldn't let him go like this. What'll we do?' Old Neal's gone I thought, and out loud I said 'He'll be all right.' And off we went to the sad and disinclined concert for which I had no stomach whatever and all the time I was thinking of Neal and how he got back on the train and rode over 3,000 miles over that awful land and never knew why he had come anyway, except to see me and my sweet wife. And he was gone. If I hadn't been married I would have gone with him again. So in America when the sun goes down and I sit on the old brokendown river pier watching the long, long skies over New Jersey and sense all that raw land that rolls in one unbelievable huge bulge over to the West Coast, all that road going, all the people dreaming in the immensity of it, and in Iowa I know by now the evening-star must be drooping and shedding her sparkler dims on the the prarie, which is just before the coming of of complete night that blesses the earth, darkens all rivers, cups the peaks in the west and folds the last and final shore in, and nobody, just nobody knows what's going to happen to anybody besides the forlorn rags of growing old, I think of Neal Cassady, I even think of Old Neal Cassady the father we never found, I think of Neal Cassady, I think of Neal Cassady.

Tuesday, 24 March 2009
Posted by information as material at 03:33 (37 comments)

23 March 2009

had no money for a truck and couldn't go back with at all now. He simply had no idea why he had come, beyond the fact that he wanted to see me and my sweet wife and we agreed she was. With pregnant Diane he spent one night fighting and she threw him out. A letter came for him care of me and I deliberately opened it to see what was up. It was from Carolyn. 'My heart broke when I saw you go across the tracks with your bag. I pray and pray you get back safe…I do want Jack and his new wife to come and live on the same street…I know you'll make it but I can'yt help worrying---now that we've decided everything…Dear Neal, it's the end of the first half of the century. Welcome with love and kisses to spend the other half with us. We all wait for you. (signed) Carolyn, Cathy and Little Jami.' So Neal's life was settled with his most constant, most embittered and best-knowing wife Carolyn and I thanked God for him. The last time I saw him it was under strange and sad circumstances. Henri Cri had arrived in New York after having gone round the world several times in ships. I wanted him to meet and know Neal. They did meet but Neal couldn't talk any more and said nothing, and Henri turned away. Henri had gotten tickets for the Duke Ellington concert at the Metropolitan Opera and insisted Joan and I come with him and his girl. Henri was fat and sad but still eager the eager and formal gentleman and he wanted to do things the right way as he emphasized. So he got his bookie to drive us to the concert in a Cadillac. It was a cold winter night. The Cadillac was parked and raedy to go. Neal stood outside the windows with his bags ready to go to Penn Station and on across the land. 'Goodbye Neal' I said. 'I sure wish I didn't have to go to the concert.' 'D'you think I can ride to 40th St. with you?' he whispered. 'Want to be with you as much as possible, m'boy and besides it's so durned cold in this here New Yawk…' I whispered to Henri. No, he wouldn't have it, he liked me but he didn't like my friends. I wasn't going go start all over again ruining his planned evenings as I had done at Alfred's in San Francisco in 1947 with Allan Temko. 'Absolutely out of the question Jack!' Poor Henri, he had a special necktie made for this evening; on it was painted a replica of the

Monday, 23 March 2009
Posted by information as material at 02:35 (0 comments)

Lanny Jordan Jackson
from *Dear Swimmer*

Two pieces taken from Dear Swimmer, *a work that technically began as a collection of every sentence in Kafka containing the German word 'schwim' (swim) in all its parts of speech. After I collected and organized them in sections according to which source they derived from (novels, daybooks, letters … the first piece here being from his* Brief an den Vater), *I spoke the German sentences and section titles into English dictation software, which scored them into machinic-homophonic translations.*

Brief on Death Author (ha ha, six)

Truck via done hobbit house didn't have been a four deal boy to see mouse, it gone down enough harmed, I incline this. But, once he cut rules forms he off done pine can, you know asked for them Fosse, on Friday Dina Chin beveled: Knox who mock and, deep media op. cit., Abba Katsav click Zuma and a chief and fish farming Emma Fort four-month test, Don Varley said those I felt when Allah Mina Schliemann F Farland and off island could be 10 stint in Menzel can all can begin gross I take zoo some.

Veteran mess Pablo for click to order hot cyclic D "O'Hanlon Egan" Davison, D make from the shaft (six yes, I bet STS, Ehrlich and Todd Stokley Casa) at Brockton, the head tenant big ground is Roxanne Moose and, All-Star see make week wound on Street Dix Gemini 01 being tents right dish and guilt take long data.

F Site

Wendy is a Christ curtains job, good omens I've been was so long the policy again halted, we'll can dinner on I'm own zoos I do, in year the diner's up step the gas and height, and I know that just throwing on items Shrek and, I known as Stalin, I know I'm little, Sean Harbin via in in damn round in nine of the Lord, their hot and issue consider not set in strong and as iTunes Strauss Kahn, yet's chat and the is group, good casino shimmer, getting involved to get spot S gone the city and the Laurent. The ascend I was a hall desk is else's, Kino vice S and dark Hondo means you to Denmark.

Written content in all the Dean's sneaks met off developed and axle gone man by design and by name and on deed like a minus AirTran tenant dink, the Derek arrogant I know school on the whole bus locker could treatment I'm eyeing them moved ensure must cruelest, the Honda on intellect and Zeke Fest Halton will do.

Kieran Daly

TITLE (...) A hypothesis was posited that if variables remain without interspersion of treatment or subsequent application of measurement, then an experiment may show no results? To test the hypothesis, a non-empirical experiment was conducted independent of spatiotemporal conditions, in which variables were purposelessly introduced from an haphazard bias indicated by Goldsmith et al. (2012)? The method of quizzing was implemented to passively experiment without observing or perturbing variables and populations of variables (Daly 2012)? Two variables may have been quizzed in a non-empirical experiment; empty sampler and nullpropriation? Empty sampler inoperably samples without an input-output or storage system? Inoperable sampling may denote that an empty sampler is unable to collect and store data for observation? Nullpropriation might be any futile or passive appropriation which is non-identical with itself? A futile appropriation remains indifferent and without conceptual determination, use, or manipulation of a known, imagined, and/or unknown variable? Indifferent to and independent of empty sampler and nullpropriation, 315 samples from http://wings.buffalo.edu/epc/authors/ goldsmith/ were randomized with an algorithmic list randomizer from http://www.random.org/ lists/ on 24-May 2012? From the randomized list, Uncreativity as a Creative Practice (Goldsmith 2001) was the first random sample and was quizzed for experiment? Uncreativity as a Creative Practice is a text authored by Kenneth Goldsmith that was published in 2001 by Poetry Plastique, Marianne Boesky Gallery / Granary Books and The Electronic Poetry Center? Due to experimental indifference to observation, any results that may have been produced remained unrecorded? Daly, K. (2012). Idempotent quizzing of numbered Acts and Scenes?. Retrieved from http://nonmusicology. com/2011/01/idempotent-quizzing-of-numbered-acts.html. Goldsmith, K. (Ed.) (2012). Thinking. Liverpool, UK: Liverpool Biennial of Contemporary Art. Goldsmith, K. (2001). Uncreativity as a Creative Practice. Retrieved from http://wings. buffalo.edu/epc/authors/goldsmith/uncreativity. html.

Uncreativity as a Creative Practice
Kenneth Goldsmith

I am spending my 39th year practicing uncreativity.

On Friday, September 1, 2000, I began retyping the day's New York Times, word for word, letter for letter, from the upper left hand corner to the lower right hand corner, page by page. Today, November 10, 2000, I am approximately half way through the project. I intend to finish by New Year's Day.

The object of the project is to be as uncreative in the process as possible. It's one of the hardest constraints an artist can muster, particularly on a project of this scale; with every keystroke comes the temptation to "fudge," "cut-and-paste," and "skew" the mundane language. But to do so would be to foil the exercise.

I've long been an advocate of extreme process writing–recording every move my body has made in a day, recording every word I spoke over the course of a week, recording every sound I heard ending in the sound of "r" for almost four years–but never have I faced a writing process this dry, this extreme, this boring.

John Cage said "If something is boring after two minutes, try it for four. If still boring, then eight. Then sixteen. Then thirty-two. Eventually one discovers that it is not boring at all."

I'm interested in a valueless practice. Nothing has less value than yesterday's news (in this case yesterday's newspaper–what could be of less value, say, than stock quotes from September 1, 2000?). I'm interested in quantifying and concretizing the vast amount of "nutritionless" language; I'm also interested in the process itself being equally nutritionless.

Retyping the New York Times is the most nutritionless act of literary appropriation I could conceive of. Had I instead, for example, retyped *Ulysses*, there would have been too much value, for *Ulysses*, as we all know, is a very valuable book.

I took inspiration from Warhol's "Empire," his "unwatchable" 24-hour film of the Empire State Building. Similarly, imagine a book that is written with the intention not to be read. The book as object: conceptual writing; we're happy that the idea exists without ever having to open the book.

Innovative poetry seems to be a perfect place to place a valueless practice; as a gift economy, it is one of the last places in late hyper-capitalism that allows non-function as an attribute. Both theoretically and politically, the field remains wide open.

But in capitalism, labor equals value. So certainly my project must have value, for if my time is worth an hourly wage, then I might be paid handsomely for this work. But the truth is that I've subverted this equation by OCR'ing as much of the newspaper as I can.

Almost 100 years ago, the visual arts came to terms with this issue in Duchamp's "Urinal." Later, Warhol, then Koons extended this practice. In music we have vast examples from John Oswald's Plunderphonics to the ubiquitous practice of sampling. Where has literature been in this dialogue? One hundred years after Duchamp, why hasn't straight appropriation become a valid, sustained or even tested literary practice?

John Cage, whose mission it was to accept all sound as music, failed; his filter was on too high. He permitted only the sounds that fell into his worldview. Commercial sounds, pop music, lowbrow culture, sounds of violence and aggression, etc. held no place in the Cagean pantheon; certainly, nutritionlessness was not what we would consider a Cagean attribute.

However, if John Cage theoretically claimed that any sound can be music, then we logically must conclude that, properly framed, any language can be poetry.

When I reach 40, I hope to have cleansed myself of all creativity.

Back to Kenneth Goldsmith's Author Page   Back to EPC

Christian Bök
The Extremophile

1.

Astronauts fear it. Biologists fear it. It is not human. It lives in isolation. It grows in complete darkness. It derives no energy from the Sun. It feeds on asbestos. It feeds on concrete. It inhabits a seam of gold on Level 104 of the Mponeng Mine in Johannesburg. It lives in alkaline lakelets full of arsenic. It grows in lagoons of boiling asphalt. It thrives in a deadly miasma of hydrogen sulphide. It breathes iron. It breathes rust. It needs no oxygen to live. It can survive for a decade without water. It can withstand temperatures of 323 °K, hot enough to melt rubidium. It can sleep for 100 millennia inside a crystal of salt, buried in Death Valley. It does not die in the hellish infernos at the Stadtbibliothek during the firebombing of Dresden. It does not burn when exposed to ultraviolet rays. It does not reproduce via the use of DNA. It breeds, unseen, inside canisters of hairspray.

2.

It feeds on polyethylene. It feeds on hydrocarbons. It inhabits caustic geysers of steam near the Grand Prismatic Spring in Yellowstone National Park. It thrives in the acidic runoff from heavy-metal mines, depleted of their zinc. It abides in the shallows of the Dead Sea. It breathes methane. It can withstand temperatures of 333 °K, hot enough to melt phosphorus. It resides in a fumarole of scalding seawater, deep in the bathyal fathoms of the Mid-Atlantic Ridge. It can endure pressures equivalent to 45 tons of force per square inch, six times greater than the pressure at the nadir of the ocean, one sixteenth of the pressure required to crush graphite into diamond. It lives in the muck at the bottom of the Mariana Trench. It is ideally adapted to devour the wreck of the Titanic. It does not die during its own immolation in the Nazi bonfires at the Opernplatz in Berlin. It eats jet fuel.

3.

It feeds on nylon byproducts. It feeds on stainless steel. It
inhabits an extinct volcano in the xeric waste of the Atacama
Desert, where the rain falls only once per century. It dwells in
a tide pool of battery acid. It blooms in a barren salina, ten
times saltier than the sea. It breathes hydrogen. It resides inside micropores of superdense granite, crushed down 3000
metres below the bedrock of the Earth. It can withstand
temperatures of 343 °K, hotter than the flash point of aero-
solized kerosene. It is ideally adapted to devour the rubber
tubing in the engines of the F-22 Raptor. It does not die in the
explosion that disintegrates the Space Shuttle *Columbia*
during orbital reentry. It does not die among the tornados
of hellfire, raging, unchecked, in the oil fields of Kuwait
during the Persian Gulf War. It gorges on plumes of petro-
leum, venting from the wellhead of the Deepwater Horizon.

4.

It eats arsenic. It eats uranium. It resides inside the core of Reactor No. 4 at Chernobyl. It thrives in the topsoil of battle-fields contaminated with toxic doses of lead. It thrives in hydrochloric acid. It can withstand temperatures of 373 °K, hot enough to boil the water in its own cells. It is ideally adapted to dwell inside the steel drums of radioactive waste, now entombed at the Yucca Mountain Repository. It lives in the stratosphere. It can survive exposure to the vacuum of Outer Space. It can survive the effects of g-forces more than 2000 times greater than the surface gravity of the Earth. It is the only known organism capable of exceeding speeds of Mach 1. It does not die in the furnaces reserved for *The Satanic Verses* after the *fatwa* issued by the Ayatollah of Iran. It can, in fact, repair damage to its own genome so fast that its DNA never mutates. It never changes. It never evolves.

5.

It devours plutonium. It can endure longterm exposure to acids that eat away at human flesh. It can withstand temperatures of 383 °ᴋ, hotter than the polar zones on the planet Mercury. It can hibernate for 500 millennia in the core of a snowflake, deep beneath the permafrost of Siberia. It awaits discovery in the abyssal fathoms of Lake Vostok, 4000 metres below the ice of Antarctica. It survives direct immersion in liquid nitrogen. It survives 1000 times the dosage of gamma radiation that can instantly kill a human being. It is ideally adapted to eat hot graphite in the ruins of Unit 2 at Three Mile Island. It resides on the surface of a heat shield in the clean room at the Jet Propulsion Laboratory. It is fossilized inside the Murchison meteorite. It does not die in the conflagration during the collapse of the World Trade Center. It does not die in the crucibles of Treblinka.

6.

It resides in a soda lake, whose pH level equals the alkalinity of lye. It can survive superheated blasts of steam for ten hours inside autoclaves used to disinfect surgical scalpels. It can withstand temperatures of 393 °ᴋ, hot enough to melt sulphur. It can lie dormant for 40 million years, hibernating inside the gut of a honeybee, shrouded in a jewel of amber. It evades its predators by hiding in the firmware of the Intel Pentium 3 microchip. It propagates itself through the use of networked computers. It can pass itself off as a thought inside the human brain. It can survive direct blasts of cosmic rays from solar flares. It is, in fact, the only known organism to survive being shot, point-blank, by the proton beam in a ᴜ-70 Synchrotron. It does not die in the incineration of Hiroshima. It does not die in the planetary firestorm after the impact of the Chicxulub meteor. It does not die.

7.

It survives. It persists. It resides inside the robot scoop of the Viking 1 Lander during tests for perchlorates on Mars. It can live through exposure to supercoolant temperatures at the brink of absolute zero. It can hibernate for 250 million years, living as a spore, encased in a halite nodule found in the Caverns of Carlsbad. It can withstand temperatures of 423 °K, hotter than the nose cone of the Concorde in supersonic flight. It can endure multiple, meteor impacts. It can endure multiple, atomic attacks. It lives nowhere on Earth, except in one petri dish of agar agar, locked in a fridge at a Level-4 biocontainment facility. It is totally inhuman. It does not love you. It does not need you. It does not even know that you exist. It is invincible. It is unkillable. It has lived through five mass extinctions. It is the only known organism to have ever lived on the Moon. It awaits your experiments.

Thinking

Rosi Braidotti
Powers of affirmations

The world can be an inhospitable place for critical thinkers. A tradition stretching way back to Hegel and Marx connects the task of critique with oppositional consciousness, which relates to its social and environmental contexts through dialectical struggle. Thus, critical theory banks on negativity and, in a perverse way, even requires it. This results in a paradoxical relationship between critical thinkers and their civic and natural environments: how to be at home in the world while subjecting it to critical scrutiny? Does not the analytical gaze of the critical theorist betray somehow our deep bond of intimacy with the world, which makes it feel like home to us?

Affirmative politics seeks to redress this paradox. It seeks to resist the present, more specifically the injustice, violence and vulgarity of the times, while being worthy of our times, as Deleuze puts it. A balancing act is needed so as to engage with the present in a productive manner, while upholding an oppositional and critical stance. This engagement entails the creation of sustainable alternatives geared to the construction of social horizons of hope. It connects this creative effort with the enduring task of resistance that is at the heart of critical theory. The question of how to make the world a more hospitable place for critical thinkers, and thus make critical thought more at home in this world, implies the creation of new social, inter- and transpersonal relations, as well as new conceptual spaces. Affirmative politics engenders a new covenant between the incisive powers of rational judgment (*potestas*) and the generative powers of the imagination (*potentia*).

I have addressed this issue through the figuration of nomadic subjectivity.[1] Nomadic subjects are non-unitary – that is, they are open, multi-layered and relational at their very core. The rather unappealing term 'ontological relationality' is often used to describe this vision of a subject that clashes both with the established notion of liberal individualism and with the transcendental idea of consciousness. Nomadic subjects are embodied and embedded in a multiplicity of locations; rooted but flowing, they are very much part of this world. They are complex and relational, but not structure-less, nor adrift in a relativistic state of flux. Being a critical nomadic subject does not make you homeless, but rather capable of multiple modes of belonging and complex forms of both resistance and loyalty.[2] Nomadic subjects are prone to encounters with a multitude of human and non-human others. They consequently enlist a wide range of cognitive, emotional and ethical faculties. Their defining feature is their capacity to affect and to be affected by others, and this relational core entrusts the powers of the imagination, as well as more rational resources. For nomadic subjects, the point is not to 'reason', but rather to 'rhizome'.

The implications are far-reaching: oppositional consciousness and political subjectivity do not require negativity; negativity is not a structural element of political struggle and agency or of critical thought. Critical theory becomes instead about strategies and relations of affirmation,[3] and political subjectivity consists of multiple micro-political practices of daily activism or interventions in and on the world. The shift from negativity to affirmation is far from automatic or spontaneous; rather, it demands pragmatic implementation or praxis, through concrete actualizations.[4]

To posit the politics of affirmation does not entail the denial of either the existence or the function of negativity, but changes its location within critical thought and practice. After Foucault, we are familiar with the paradoxical resonance between the power conditions that one rejects and the importance of both critiquing and resisting them. The task of critical thought and practice need not be an aporetic double bind. Negativity is only one moment – and a potentially productive one – in a material and discursive process that fundamentally aims at overturning the conditions that produced it in the first place. The rejection of the circumstances or premises that are considered oppressive and unjust – on either ethical or political grounds – is not a necessary climax, just the precondition for their critique. This means that the negative instance is a just a point, and not a foundational breaking point, in a sequence that leads not only elsewhere, but to an open and non-teleological horizon. The post-structuralist generation should be given credit for loosening up the binary scheme of dialectical thought and confronting the issue of negativity and power in a more multi-directional, embodied and embedded manner.[5]

The world-historical experience of social and political movements such as feminism, anti-racism, post-colonialism and environmentalism (to name but a few) pioneered concrete forms of the affirmative kind of politics that philosophers merely theorized. These movements provided original insights into otherwise abstract theoretical schemes, and also produced new radical understandings of the multiple ways in which critical thought can balance its creative force with the necessary dose of oppositional consciousness. Feminists and anti-racists have analysed power not as a given historical structure, but rather as a fluid and self-organizing daily process of assigning entitlements and prerogatives. This notion of power entails a double hermeneutics of suspicion: on the one hand of the universalist utopian elements of the Hegelian-Marxist legacy, and on the other of the equally universalistic assumptions of humanism and the primacy of consciousness and reason. The politics of affirmation stress instead the need for a change of scale, to unveil power relations where they are most effective and invisible, namely in the specific locations of one's own institutional and social practices. One has to start from micro-instances of embodied and embedded self and the complex web of social relations that compose that self.

Such an approach results in subtler and more effective analyses of how power works in and through the body, and it leads to an increased awareness of the vulnerability of embodied subjects. This double emphasis on both the vulnerable subject and the ubiquity of power relations is crucial to a nomadic approach to the political. Political activism consists in connecting critical theory not so much with 'la *politique*' – organized or majoritarian politics – as with 'le *politique*' – the political movement in its diffuse, nomadic and rhizomic forms of becoming.[6] I propose to refer to the former as the civic governance of the present and the latter as transformative praxis. This distinction is of crucial importance and resonates with Foucault's double axis of power as restrictive or coercive (*potestas*) and as empowering and productive (*potentia*). The former focuses on the governance of society and its institutions; the latter, on the experimentation with new arts of existence and ethical relations. Civic governance can produce at best progressive emancipatory measures predicated on chronological continuity, whereas transformative praxis requires an auto-poietic economy of reciprocal or relational self-styling that rests on a non-linear vision of time. Both aspects are necessary for effective political agency.

Affirmative politics sets both the desire for transformations or becomings and the issue of time at the centre of the agenda. According to Deleuze and Guattari, the civic governance of the present is postulated on *Chronos* – the necessarily linear time of institutional deployment of norms and protocols.[7] It is a reactive and majority-bound enterprise that is often made of flat repetitions and predictable reversals that may alter the balance but leave the structures of power basically untouched. Transformative praxis, on the other hand, is postulated on the axis of *Aion* – the non-linear or zigzagging time of becoming and of affirmative critical practice. It is a minoritarian mode that rests on a complex and multi-layered relationality. The ethical good consists in cultivating the relations that empower us to act and to sustain the transformative effort that aims at producing affirmation. According to Constantin Boundas, affirmative politics consists of 'active counter-actualization of the current state of affairs', through the project of transforming negative into positive relations, encounters and passions.[8]

Based on the principle that we do not know what a body can do, the transformative praxis of becoming-political ultimately aims at the very structures of subjectivity. It is about engendering and sustaining processes of 'becoming-minoritarian'. The critical and creative aspects of this practice combine with a profound form of asceticism – that is to say, with an ethics of non-profit that builds upon micro-instances of political activism, avoiding the temptation of metadiscourse or overarching generalizations.

The corollary of transformative praxis is that the same conditions that create the negative moment – the experience of oppression, marginality, injury or trauma – are also the preconditions for their overturning. The damaging and negative material is also that which engenders positive resistance, counteraction or even transcendence of the oppressive conditions.[9] In feminism and race theory, for instance, the process of consciousness-raising is crucial to the project of resisting and possibly overturning or 'overcoding' the negative instances in both the public and the private realms. What triggers and at the same time sustains this process of resistance is the pragmatic project of affirmative politics as counter-actualization. This process consequently clears the ground for the ethical transformation that sustains political action and foregrounds the creative or affirmative elements.[10]

Affirmative politics rejects dualistic oppositions and instead supports philosophical monism – that is to say, the belief that there is only one, intelligent, sentient and self-organizing matter. This view entails complexity and stresses the recognition of an ethical and affective component of subjectivity; it is thus both an anti-dualistic and an anti-rationalist position that emphasizes dynamic inter-relations with others. A nomadic subject's ethical core is not his/her moral intentionality so much as the effects of power (as repressive – *potestas* – and positive – *potentia*) that his/her actions are likely to have upon the world.[11] This position is affirmative in that it actively works towards the creation of alternatives by working through the negative instance and by cultivating the relations that are conducive to their ethical transmutation into empowering relational values.

What this means practically is that the conditions for political and ethical agency are not dependent on the current state of the terrain. They are not oppositional and thus not tied to the present by negation; instead they are affirmative and geared to creating possible futures. Affirmative relations create possible – and possibly more hospitable – worlds by mobilizing resources that have been left untapped, including our desires and imagination. The work of critique must therefore focus on creating the conditions for the overturning of negativity precisely because they are not immediately available in the present. Moving beyond the negative scheme of thought means abandoning oppositional thinking, so as to index activity in the present upon the task of creating sustainable futures. The sustainability of the future, however, is the responsibility of the present – a present in which critical thinkers are uncomfortably situated as both belonging and resisting subjects. Affirmation therefore rests on our ability to mobilize, actualize and deploy – here and now – cognitive, affective, imaginative and ethical forces that had not been activated so far. These driving forces are concretized in actual, material relations, which constitute a network, web or rhizome of interconnection with others. To think critically means to create new conceptual and perceptive tools that may enable us both to come to terms with and to actively interact in an empowering manner with others.[12] The ethical gesture is the actualization of our increased ability to act and interact in the world.

To disengage the process of critical thought from negativity and attach it to affirmation means that reciprocity is redefined not as mutual recognition but rather as mutual definition or specification. This vital political economy of becoming is both trans-subjective in structure and transhuman in force, as I argued earlier.[13] Such an affirmative vision of the subject, moreover, does not restrict the ethical instance within the limits of human otherness, but also opens it up to inter-relations with non-human, post-human and inhuman forces. The emphasis on non-human ethical relations produces a geopolitics or an eco-philosophy, in that it values one's reliance on and relation to the environment in the broadest sense of the term: it is a political physics.[14] Félix Guattari's idea of the three ecologies – the social, the psychic and the environmental – is central to this discussion.[15] Considering the extent of our technological development, emphasis on the eco-philosophical aspects is not to be mistaken for biological determinism. It rather posits a nature–culture continuum within which subjects cultivate and construct multiple ethical relations.[16]

This affirmative approach is a crucial factor in making the world into a more hospitable place for critical thinkers, who are repositioned as both belonging to and resisting aspects of their context and historicity. The challenge is to work collectively, in an embodied and embedded manner, to create the possibility of actualizing social, economic and ethical alternatives through radical forms of empirical pragmatism. This is the transformative praxis that I see as essential to the political, as opposed to the civic governance of the status quo. Clearly, the grounds for this transformative praxis do not coincide with present conditions, but rather with the social construction of events still to come – they are virtual, or 'incorporeal', to use Deleuze's language. These virtual events are abstract possibilities, which call for actualization into concrete projects here and now, but never just coincide with them. Here you see the advantages of adopting a monistic approach that assumes one, self-organizing matter: because this matter is intelligent, its potential is immense. This means that the sum total of virtual possibilities is always greater than our capacity to actualize them into pragmatic projects – the Earth and the cosmos are infinite data-banks of virtual possibilities.

Historically, this positive aspect of Spinoza's monism has been criticized by Hegel and the post-Hegelians as being overoptimistic or even downright naive. I do not share in this cynical view, but take instead the emphasis on the virtual as another term to describe the self-ordering and emergence-producing capacity of the universe. I also take it as the source of inspiration for pragmatic and socially embedded projects that – in a parallel line that involves science, philosophy and the arts in equal parts – can nurture and sustain critical thought and practice.

The infinite structure and speed of virtual possibilities are both a threat and a resource to this critical effort. Transformative praxis therefore needs to strike a balance between the infinite and some sort of consistency. Concrete actualization of projects can be realized by establishing, for instance, the kind of social relations that are bent on affirmative transformation. The same goal is achieved by the invention of conceptual personae and the creation of concepts, which can be proposed by both philosophy and art practices. In this respect, nomadic critical theory can be described as an ethics of virtual creativity.[17]

Affirmative politics is a pragmatic instigation to empower positively the difference that nomadic subjects can make. It aims for a shift of conceptual grounds, or a change of critical rhythms and affective colouring. Resonances, harmonies and hues intermingle to paint an altogether different landscape of a monistic self that, not being One, functions as a relay-point for many sets of intensive intersections and encounters with multiple others. Moreover, such a nomadic subject can envisage forms of resistance and political agency that are multi-layered and complex. Nomadic political subjects sustain and materially frame an empirical transcendental site of transformative becomings. They are enfleshed subjects who actually yearn for qualitative ethical changes, wanting to feel at home in the world while resisting it. Not happy with accommodation, and well beyond the libidinal economy of compensation, these subjects, which are not One, actively desire processes of metamorphosis of the self and of society and its modes of cultural and political representation. Affirmative politics replaces oppositional consciousness and negativity with open relationality, which entails the recognition of the ways in which otherness prompts, mobilizes and engenders affirmative actualizations of virtual potentials. These are by definition not contained in the present conditions and cannot emerge only from them. They have to be brought about or generated creatively by a qualitative leap of the collective imaginary. As Adrienne Rich put it in her recent essays, the critical thinker has to act 'in spite of the times' and hence 'out of my time', thus creating the analytics – the conditions of possibility – of the future.[18] Critical theory occurs somewhere between the no longer and the not yet, not looking for easy reassurances but rather for a deep relational bond to a shared and hospitable world, alongside multiple others who are animated by the same passions.

1   Rosi Braidotti, *Nomadic Theory*, New York: Columbia University Press, 2011.
2   Rosi Braidotti, *Transpositions: On Nomadic Ethics*, Cambridge: Polity Press, 2006.
3   Braidotti, 2011.
4   Gilles Deleuze and Félix Guattari, *A Thousand Plateaus: Capitalism and Schizophrenia,* Minneapolis: University of Minnesota Press, 1987.
5   Michel Foucault, *The Order of Things: An Archaelogy of Human Sciences*, New York: Pantheon Books, 1970.
6   Paul Patton, *Deleuze and the Political*, London and New York: Routledge, 2000.
7   Deleuze and Guattari, 1987.
8   Constantin V. Boundas, 'Gilles Deleuze and his readers: a touch of voluntarism and an excess of out-worldliness', *Deleuze Studies*, vol. 1, no. 2, 2007, pp. 167–94 (esp. p. 187).
9   Michel Foucault, *Discipline and Punish*, New York: Pantheon Books, 1977; and *The History of Sexuality, Vol. I*, New York: Pantheon Books, 1978.
10   Gilles Deleuze and Félix Guattari, *What is Philosophy?*, New York: Columbia University Press, 1994.
11   Gilles Deleuze, *Expressionism in Philosophy: Spinoza,* New York: Zone Books, 1990.
12   Deleuze and Guattari, 1994.
13   Braidotti, 2006.
14   John Protevi, *Political Physics: Deleuze, Derrida and the Body Politic*, London and New York: The Athlone Press, 2001.
15   Félix Guattari, *The Three Ecologies*, London and New York: The Athlone Press, 2000.
16   Félix Guattari, *Chaosmosis: An Ethico-Aesthetic Paradigm*, Sydney: Power Publications, 1995; and Donna Haraway, *Modest Witness*, London and New York: Routledge, 1997.
17   Deleuze and Guattari, 1994 and Braidotti, 2011.
18   Adrienne Rich, *Arts of the Possible*, New York: W. W. Norton, 2001, p. 159; see also Rich's *Blood, Bread and Poetry*, New York: W. W. Norton, 1985).

Costas Douzinas
The idea of Europe as gift and hospitality

Europe is at a crossroads; Europe is in crisis. Wherever we turn we hear threnodies for decline and decay, stories of doom and destruction. Yet the idea of Europe being at a crossroads or in crisis is not new or unprecedented. Europe *is* a crossroads. The name and idea of Europe were inventions of people in the eastern Mediterranean around the Aegean Sea. Some claim the etymological root of the word Europe is the ancient Sumerian and Semitic *ereb*, the darkness after the sun has gone down. The Greek Ionians, who lived in what we now call Asia Minor, were the first to call the lands on the western shores of the Aegean (Greece and further west), where the sun sets, Europe.

If we turn to mythology, Europa, the beautiful daughter of a Phoenician king, was born in the city of Tyre, now in the Lebanon. She was abducted and ravished by Zeus, the king of gods, metamorphosed into a bull, who took her to Crete. The origin of Europe's name is thus non-European, Phoenician. But not only the name. Europe was united politically for the first time in the Roman empire and culturally through its Christianization into a holy Roman empire. The founder of Rome was Aeneas, a wandering exile from Troy. Jesus was a Jewish prophet. Europe is the creation of non-European travellers, wanderers and mystics. They all came from the Mediterranean, the *Mesogeios* in Greek, literally the centre of the Earth, the sea surrounded by lands, the world's navel.

The Mediterranean lands, a hospitable haven for immigrants, were also a place of departures. The European boats of discovery, conquest and colonization departed from its ports, on the Greco-Latino-Iberian shores. As Paul Valéry puts it, the same ships carried merchandise and goods, ideas and methods. The Mediterranean has been a machine for making and spreading commerce and civilization. On its shores, spirit, culture and trade came together.[1] In 1830, the philosopher Hegel called the sea the centre of world history.[2] In 1960, the historian Fernand Braudel called it the 'radiant centre' of the entire globe, 'whose light grows less as one moves away from it, without one's being able to define the exact boundary between light and shade.'[3] If the Mediterranean is the *medius terra* (the middle of the Earth), she is also the heart and begetter of Europe.

And yet, the European nations are sick, Europe itself in a critical condition. This is how the German philosopher Edmund Husserl opened his famous Vienna lecture entitled 'Philosophy and the crisis of European man' in 1935.[4] Husserl, a German Jew, had already been expelled from Freiburg University. His death, in 1939, spared him the experience of war and the Holocaust. But in his 1935 lecture, he diagnosed the present sickness as a temporary deviation from the idea of Europe.

For Husserl, the idea of Europe represents truth and the universal, what transcends local and parochial attachments and commitments. The purpose of European history, Husserl argued, is to seek truth behind appearances and opinions. Its spiritual birthplace was Greece. Greek philosophy and science created a disinterested view of the world and explored the universal unity of all beings. From Greece, a special type of humanity spread out, which, while living in a particular place, was oriented towards the infinity of the future in a constant spiritual renewal. Truth is the gift of Greeks to Europe and of Europeans to humanity. The idea and project of Europe is to abandon local, parochial, ethnic or religious differences and construct a genuinely universal humanity. Philosophy erupted in Greece against *doxa* (the common sense) as the call to explore and live according to universal ideas. When truth becomes a practical task, it leads to democracy and the demand to give reasons (*logon didonai*) for our beliefs and actions, to be responsible to others and publicly accountable. The spiritual task of European 'man' is to create himself and his history freely under the guidance of reason. Europe means the infinite task of self-creation and the continuous improvement of nations and individuals. Europe promises to help humanity become itself. It is therefore not just a land mass but an ideal, a 'spiritual geography'. Humanity will be reached when the idea of Europe becomes global. It is the *telos* of humanity. We, Europeans, are the functionaries of the human spirit.

What is the role of non-Europeans, outsiders and aliens in Europe's task of infinite self-creativity? The universal vocation of truth, philosophy and science does not belong to any particular nation. They are open to all. And yet, the Greek birth and European heritage are quite unique in their universality. No similar idea or vocation worthy of the name 'philosophy' has emerged in India or China, Husserl claimed. 'Therein lies something unique, which all other human groups, too, feel with regard to us, something that apart from all considerations of expediency, becomes a motivation for them – despite their determination to retain their spiritual autonomy – constantly to Europeanise themselves, whereas we, if we understand ourselves properly, will never, for example, Indianise ourselves.' If Europe designates the unity of spiritual life and creative activity, the Eskimos or Indians of the country fairs or the constantly wandering Gypsies do not belong to it.[5]

Move from Husserl in 1935 to 2010. On 13 September, a European commissioner called the French deportation of 1,000 Roma a disgrace and likened it to Vichy France's treatment of Jews. Pierre Lellouche, a French minister, responded in kind. France is 'the mother of human rights ... not the naughty pupil of the class whom the teacher tells off and we are not the criminal before the prosecutor'.[6] If France is the mother of human rights, if human rights are today the noblest normative universal, if the universal is the future task of humanity, then France is humanity. This is a position France has claimed since at least Napoleon, for whom what is good for France is good for the whole of humanity. Hegel agreed. Hearing the sound and fury of the Jena battle, he wrote that Napoleon was spirit on horseback, freedom and modernity spreading through the barrel of a gun. Spanish prisoners of war met inspecting French officers with banners declaring 'Down with Freedom'. Our contemporary humanitarian emissaries, soldiers and NGO operatives are similarly met in parts of the world with the cry 'Down with your human rights'.

The French deportation of the Roma is an exemplification of Europe's and humanity's history. Racism, xenophobia and deportation are as part of Europe as are humanity and human rights. Husserl and Mr Lellouche point to a secret at the heart of Europe and perhaps of humanity. Fear and hatred of the foreigner is both an integral part and the greatest enemy of universal Europe. Greece and Europe came from elsewhere themselves, from Asia and the East. We are heirs of this history, children of Europa, our primordial mother. Her journey from Tyre to Crete introduced her to other people, civilizations and cultures. So did the voyages of Mediterranean seafarers. Greece, the Mediterranean, Europe represent separation and movement, being cut off from your proper place and leaving your property behind. Departure from hearth, home and the homely can be voluntary or violent, emigration or deportation.

De-*portation*, departing or expelled from the port (Piraeas, Porto or Paros – *pir* is the root in most European languages for words meaning passage through the sea) is the fate of the Mediterranean and by extension the European. Sophocles described Greek man as *pantoporos aporos*, sailing everywhere but nowhere at home. The voyage can be cyclical, Ulysses-like, or nomadic, Abraham-like. But in both cases, uprootedness, the Mediterranean fate, makes the exile or migrant always glance into the distance, into the darkness of the West, the gaze always ahead of itself, in touch with the other at or beyond the horizon. This original uprootedness, this separation from the homely, this passage to what is not and is always to come, captures the idea of Mediterranean and Europe. And yet today our sea has become a wall, a controlled and policed borderline, where migrants, following the winds that sailed Europa or Aeneas or the numberless generations of Mediterranean sailors, are left to drown by our border guards and governments.

It was exposure to different laws, customs and gods that triggered the Greek vocation to transcend the local and parochial towards what is universal and common to all. It also taught the voyagers that there are different vocations and truths, different ways to the universal. From the very beginning, the Greeks questioned their identity, disrupted by the Egyptian other and the wholly other. Greek philosophy introduced otherness into the reason of Logos. Sailing into foreign lands leads to self-estrangement. Philosophy is the way of the sea.

European identity, as all identity, is established in relation to its other, the non-European. Europe means exposure to the other, the foreigner and stranger, and to what is other within self. We are responsible for our identity, for the universal and infinite task of imagining humanity. We are also responsible, however, for our repeated atrocities, in the New World, in the Asian and African colonies, in our genocides and holocausts, in our expulsion of the Roma. Kidnapped Europa's journey from the Phoenicians to the Greeks symbolizes Europe's mobility. But perhaps it signifies something darker. We have been in mourning for the abduction and rape of Europa. We have interiorized this original crime, like Freud's parricidal band of brothers. They killed the father and created law; we purify and revenge the mother, by visiting her atrocious fate upon others.

This is how the inner paradox in Husserl's celebration of universality and truth, which is however exclusively credited to the Greeks and Europeans, can be explained. If the Europeans are the functionaries of humanity, if their rationality gives them superior power, they have the obligation to raise to humanity those lesser souls who have not yet developed ways of thinking the universal. Europe represents the universal vocation, the infinite task to lead humanity home, to humanize humanity. Historically, however, humanity has been consistently used as a strategy of ontological separation and ordering into a lesser humanity and the inhuman. The infinite task of humanity to reshape itself, what used to be called in part 'the civilizing mission', has always been accompanied by a history of conquest, domination, extermination and colonialism.

For Husserl, the crisis with its countless symptoms of corruption is not an inescapable result of fate but of a mistaken turn in Enlightenment rationalism. The scientific and technological triumphs, the perfection of mathematics and geometry, have made us approach nature and spirit, object and subject, as if they are the same thing. We use the same type of instrumental rationality and method to examine both the natural and the human worlds. The sciences have been formalized and mathematized but they have lost their relationship to universal truth and are unable to understand humanity.

The crisis lies then not in the collapse of reason but in the imperialism of one type of reason for which man is a natural object. The essence of the human world however is not material but spiritual. Man has intentions and creates meanings; he is not the result of physical or chemical causes. Universal truth exists because there is one world, one horizon that encompasses all local and partial worlds. It is built out of the incessant critique of everything particular; out of continuous departing, sailing away, deported from our natural belonging and becoming strangers to ourselves. It is an infinite process of self-creation through self-alienation. Psychologists and other policemen of the soul, on the other hand, have naturalized the human spirit and examine it as if it were an inert material entity.

The Greek idea of universality must therefore be rediscovered. Husserl believed that only his transcendental phenomenology can understand a rationality specific to human consciousness. But his idiosyncratic approach reopens the question of a universal freed from its arrogant Eurocentric version. This other Europe of dignity, hospitality and solidarity was made manifest in Athens, in February 2011.

While the Maghreb revolutions were in full flow, three hundred *sans papiers* immigrants from north Africa took refuge in the central Athens building of Hypatia and staged a hunger strike. They had lived and worked in Greece for up to ten years, doing the jobs the Greeks didn't want to do for a fraction of the minimum wage and without social security. When the crisis struck, they were unceremoniously kicked out. After forty days, with several hunger strikers in hospital with irreversible organ failure that would lead to death, the government accepted the bulk of their demands. Crucial in that victory was the huge campaign of support organized by radicals and social movements that kept the topic at the centre of attention despite the vitriolic attacks from a government that was presiding over the unravelling of the social fabric as they obeyed instructions by the IMF and the EU. A defining moment came when the riot police surrounded the Athens Law School, where the strikers had initially sought asylum after their arrival in the city from Crete, where most had lived and worked. Their arrest and removal was stopped by thousands of students and militants who stated that they would not allow their expulsion or deportation. The determination of the young eventually obliged the authorities, looking for ideological gains in the xenophobic population, to guarantee the peaceful march of the exhausted strikers to the Hypatia building, where they continued their hunger strike.

The immigrants, these expendable, 'one-use' humans, realized that minimum humanity is created through what they lacked: *papiers*, documents, files. In a biopolitical world, life is registered life; undocumented life is not recognized. To retrieve their lives from this administrative void, they had to come to the threshold of death. In doing so, the *sans papiers* became martyrs, in the double meaning of the term, witnesses and sacrificial victims. They bore witness that truths exist that are higher than life. The strikers exercised what philosophers from Rousseau to Derrida consider the essence of freedom: acting against first and second nature, against biological and social determinations, in the name of a higher truth.

It is the prerogative of the Sovereign to demand martyrdom from his subjects and to sacrifice enemies. The Sovereign negotiates the link between secular and holy by making sacred (*sacer facere*): war, the death penalty, rituals of sacrifice and consecration are ways through which the absolute Other (death, the other person, the unconscious) is both acknowledged and kept at a distance. Sacrifice, making the ordinary sacred, bridges everyday life with what transcends it. The hunger strikers removed the power of the Sovereign to take life and let live, precisely by being prepared to go all the way to death. They defended the truth of dignity, what makes each of us unique in our human commonality. Identity is built through the reciprocal recognition of others. The absence of basic rights for the *sans papiers* led to absence of all recognition, making them less than human.

At the collective level, their sacrifice brought the Greek state and law before an infinite justice and hospitality, preconditions of law and policy. But what is justice? We are surrounded by injustice but we don't often know where justice lies. In Greece, justice has miscarried in the austerity measures that have unravelled the social bond: in the ghettos of persecuted migrants; in the immense *gene-cide,* the permanent unemployment of the generation aged between 18 and 24; in the appalling treatment of the refugees; in the wall built to keep the poor out and the Greeks in. The Greek supporters of the death-bound migrants responded to this outrage of injustice. They acted in the name of an unknown justice, always still to come, a justice that defines the struggles here and now.

Protesting against the worst abuses, asking to be seen, heard and acknowledged in a minimum way, even if they need to go to death for that, was the greatest service the *sans papiers* offered to Greece. By resisting their dehumanization, they became free and fought against the iniquity of the Greek government. In Hegel's master–slave dialectic, the master achieves his position by going all the way in his struggle for recognition, prepared even to die, at which point the slave, fearing for his life, capitulates and accepts his servitude. The strikers reversed the dialectic. Servants, almost slaves legally, without any formal recognition, they faced death in order to remove from the master the power to kill. Their gift to the immigrants all over Europe was to tell them that they can take their lives in their hands against the iniquities and humiliations of governments, authorities and human-rights fanatics. Their gift to the Greeks, in those hard days of February and March 2011, was to become the only truly free people of Athens. Their victory, at the end, was the victory of all.

The Europe of the French and Greek deportations represents the lack of common world, the imperialism of a culture that claims the mantle of the universal. But we should not give up the universalizing impetus of the imaginary, the *cosmos* that uproots every *polis*, disturbs every filiation, contests all sovereignty and hegemony. We must invent or discover in the European genealogy of universalism whatever goes beyond and against itself, the principle of its excess. The Europe of the hunger strikers and their supporters shows the *via mediterranea* of infinite gift. Infinite gift of the strikers – infinite because it defied death; gift because it opened an unexpected and radical rift in what it means to be human. Infinite gift of the Athens invisible and the young and poor who defended the migrants – infinite because they did not calculate risks in their hospitality to the other; gift because, as Derrida argues, the essence of the gift is not to enter an economy of exchange, of gift and counter-gift. The defenders of the immigrants did not expect any reward except the terrible violence that authorities inflict on those who disagree. A gift of suspending the de-portation of the foreigner, of im-porting the grace of asylum and the welcoming of the other.

The idea of Europe must go back to the culture of hospitality and openness of its birth. Dissatisfaction with nation, state and European institutions comes from a bond between singularities, which cannot be turned into community, state or union and cannot be contained in traditional concepts of community or *cosmos* or *polis* or state. The Mediterranean to come is a bond between singularities, the world of each unique one, of whoever and anyone, those infinite encounters of singular worlds creating a cosmos.[8] But each world is penetrated and constructed by the world of the other, the other in me, myself in the other.

What binds me to a Roma, a Palestinian, a Greek or Spanish unemployed youth or the hunger striker is not membership of state, Europe or humanity but a protest against European citizenship, resistance against fake economic orthodoxy, against false ethnic mono-culturalism. It was resistance to common sense and the diktats of power that allowed the Greeks to imagine a universal truth beyond custom and to entrust it to the *demos*, everyone and whoever. This vocation of truth and equality calls us today to resist the oppression of contemporary common sense and the commands of power.

This Mediterranean to come is not some future utopia; it is happening here and now in cities of hospitality and resistance, in Greece and England and Spain, where we, tired old Europeans, link back again to our beginning and birthplace, to a universalism that was never one and can never become a tool for the powerful. This is our responsibility today, as Europeans, to the name and idea of Europe – Europe as a universal created always in a self-relation with the other, the other in self and the self in other.

1   Paul Valéry, 'Notes on the greatness and decline of Europe', in *History and Politics*, New York: Bollinger, 1962, p. 196.
2   Georg Hegel, *The Philosophy of History*, trans. J. Sibree, New York: The Colonial Press, 1899.
3   Fernand Braudel, *The Mediterranean*, quoted in Anthony Pagden, 'Europe: conceptualizing a continent', in Pagden (ed.), *The Idea of Europe*, Cambridge: Cambridge University Press, 2002, p. 37.
4   Edmund Husserl, 'Philosophy and the Crisis of European Man', accessed at http://www.users.cloud9.net/~bradmcc/husserl_philcris.html
5   Ibid., notes 12 and 15.
6   Lizzy Davies, 'France defends Roma expulsion policy', *Guardian*, 15 September 2010, accessed at http://www.guardian.co.uk/world/2010/sep/15/france-defends-roma-crackdown.
7   Sophocles, *Antigone*, lines 360–1.
8   Costas Douzinas, *Human Rights and Empire*, London and New York: Routledge, 2007, chapter 12.

David Scott: One of the places where the theme of hospitality has gained some prominence in recent cultural and philosophic discourse is of course in Jacques Derrida's reflections in the late 1990s on the question of *l'étranger*, with all the ambiguities of the French – both 'foreigner' as well as 'stranger'. And not surprisingly, it isn't always very clear what Derrida is up to in that exercise; but one of the things he seems to be suggesting is that hospitality is a 'question', as he puts it, *raised* by the foreigner. The foreigner arrives at the border and raises, thereby, by her or his very presence, a question to, or a provocation for, the citizen-hosts of the polity. And that question is, what kind of *citizen* am I? Or more broadly, what kind of *self* am I. So for Derrida, it seems, the foreigner at the border, or the foreigner *crossing* the border, raises the hermeneutic possibility of the expansion and the complication of the self of the *host*. The idea of hospitality thus puts in discursive play a number of cognate concepts, among them, tolerance, generosity, diversity, that are central to the contemporary self-image of the liberal democratic state. The foreigner, holding up a mirror to the host, enables or provokes a deepening transformation of the self of the host. Derrida draws our attention to Sophocles' famous last Oedipus play, *Oedipus at Colonus*, and especially that traumatic moment when Oedipus, supported by his daughter Antigone, arrives at the border of Athens, and the great Theseus, a model of magnanimity and generosity, offers him a final resting place.[1] As though ancient Athens might be a model for modern Paris or London or New York.

This then is the discursive space in which Derrida discusses the virtue of hospitality. But it seems to me that whereas, undoubtedly, hospitality is a virtue that is difficult to dismiss or disavow, there is nonetheless something constrained or limited about the terms of his reflections. And perhaps that constraint or limitation has to do with the absence in his thinking of the question of the *subject-position* of the *addressor* – as opposed to the *addressee* – of the gesture of hospitality. Notably, hospitality is the question that the foreigner, as it were, *passively*, raises for the host. It is not a question the foreigner *puts* to the host, a *demand* she or he makes. It is the host who questions. Hospitality is a question the host asks her- or himself. The foreigner is the mere object of this questioning. And so there is a crucial dimension of hospitality understood as one of the civilities of modern power that is absent from Derrida's reflections.

Stuart Hall: Your Oedipus example reminds me of the distinction between two related but different meanings of the word 'hospitality': first, there is the idea of generously welcoming the stranger, putting yourself and what you have at her/his disposal; but then, there is the term 'hospital', where the welcome is unqualified and the welcomer exposes himself/herself to the suffering, and tries to meet the compelling needs, of another.

However, I agree with you that the critical issue is where is stranger's question directed? With whom does it ultimately rest? And I'm not surprised that this – like so much else in Western critical philosophy – ends up as a question directed at 'the host' by the host rather than to the demand of the other. I'd say one of the main limits on its use by Derrida is precisely its unexamined self-reflexivity. 'I am rich and well; you are poor and ill. We are not the same. How much should the hospitality I show you depend on these differences between us? And what does this say about how civilized I am or should try to become?' As you pointed out, these are all good questions in their own terms: I would prefer to live in a generous, tolerant, hospitable society than in its opposite. But the effect of using 'hospitality' exclusively in this self-reflexive way is that it becomes largely an issue about the questioner's moral self-education. It elides the stranger's presence and what must be the stranger's overriding concern – the question the stranger first puts *to herself/himself*: 'Whatever sort of person you are, *how will you treat me*? 'What kind of welcome can I expect to find here?' Or, as you put it, 'What sort of person do you think *I* am?'

Derrida doesn't seem to be interested in this 'putting oneself in the place of the other'. Yet, only in this way can the Other's very being become the centre of the demand. Whereas Derrida's concept seems only to bounce back onto the civility of the host, 'hospitality', then, is defined by what is absent from it: the Other, its absent-presence, hospitality's 'constitutive outside'.

DS: Exactly. It is curious, this blindness to the *presumptions* of power in the gesture that prompts a preoccupation *only* with the capaciousness – or potential capaciousness – of the civilized liberal-democratic Euro-American self. On my reading, it is not so much that Derrida doesn't recognize the problem of difference as such, but that the problem of difference matters solely in the extent to which it is the European self, or the Euro-American self, that is put into question by way of the hermeneutic encounter with the difference of the Other. So that there is, as you suggest, no interest whatsoever in the historicity of the *arrival*, of the Other – the non-Euro-American Other – on the doorstep of the Euro-American state.

SH: You pointed out that Derrida's 'hospitality' functions within a nest of other related concepts, of which 'toleration' is one. When looked at seriously, toleration, like hospitality – indeed, like the Euro-American self of which these qualities are held to be defining – are always historically specific. They don't descend from the skies as beneficent gifts of the gods. The British did not, as it were, arise fully formed from the Atlantic as an already-constituted, primordially tolerant and hospitable people. Toleration always has to be worked through, struggled for, battled over. It has a history. And, as Derrida himself would say, it is always 'in process'. In Europe, the history of religious toleration dates from, say, the Crusades through the Thirty Years War, the Wars of Religion, the Reformation, Henry VIII and the break with Rome, the English Civil War, the persecution of Catholics, Puritans and Dissenters, the so-called Toleration Act, with all its many gaps in observance, and the Protestant settlement of the 'Glorious Revolution', all the way up to the Aliens Act of 1905, twentieth-century immigration legislation to control the entry of black and Asian people and contemporary Islamophobia. Full Catholic equality before the law was not passed until 1926; we still await the act that will allow a Catholic to succeed to the British throne. Toleration, like hospitality, is an incomplete and unfinished game, always entangled in a complicated set of historical conditions of existence.

DS: I wonder whether there is a sense in which one of the assumptions at work in the structure of sensibility through which the question arises for Derrida is that of *assimilation*, that is, that the foreigner who arrives at the border is seeking *inclusion* – maybe not only inclusion as formal citizenship, but also *civilizational* inclusion. The foreigner is asking to be included in this larger project. There is the implicit sense of the foreigner arriving on sufferance, with cap-in-hand, to be included in something larger and progressive and civilizational. How shall *we* include *them*? Well, including *them* will do *us* some good! Assimilation seems to me one of the crucial insufficiently considered dimensions reflected in that way of posing the question of hospitality.

SH: Assimilation is, of course, much more ambitious than hospitality and, for that very reason, more threatening. It holds out the possibility that 'they' might *become* 'part of us'.

DS: Or *potentially* part of us, anyway.

SH: Indeed. Assimilation always has an infinite delay or deferral built into it. In that sense, it is part of a long-standing liberal-imperial tradition and shares its many ambivalences and contradictions. Many reform liberals in the nineteenth century came to believe that the working class should have political representation – but not yet! They were converted to the idea that the enslaved deserved to be free and – a century later – that the colonized should eventually govern themselves: but only as a result of a lengthy process of 'education-to-freedom'. Meanwhile (as Catherine Hall argues in her new book, *Macaulay and Son: Architects of An Imperial Vision*), the double strategy of imperial governmentality – freedom and self-government for us; despotism, if necessary, for them – became the prevailing liberal common sense.

DS: Exactly. And this is perhaps the destabilizing element at work in the worry about *what* the foreigner at the gate might demand of the host. The idea you spoke of earlier of the hospital is interesting because it is itself an institutional structure of power. Within that institutional frame, the patient–doctor relationship is not an egalitarian one; it is an asymmetrical one of *dependence*. As a patient, you are dependent on a knowledge-structure and a technology-structure that explicitly positions you in a very distinctive relationship in the hierarchy of the hospital. So 'hospital' and 'hospitality' are connected, and both seem never to be relationships devoid of relations of power. So it is curious that this relationship is elided. But the elision points, of course, to a certain chronic Eurocentricity – in the literal sense that the position from which Derrida speaks here is that of the European liberal democratic subject looking out perhaps towards those arriving *after* him.

I hope that we come back to something of what the conditions might be that prompt that way of posing the question of the foreigner; but I am sure you'd agree that the Caribbean is an interesting geohistorical region, or geopolitical space through which to think about some of these issues – partly given the way the Caribbean was inserted into the colonial (and civilizing project); but also because, obviously, the Caribbean is today the exemplary instance of the 'hospitality industry'. And fascinatingly, it is called an 'industry'. Because *this* puts into perspective the relationship between hospitality and global capitalism, hospitality and consumption, hospitality and the disciplinary production of people who are professionally trained to *receive* guests; indeed whose *professional* duty it is to receive guests. It might be interesting therefore to reflect a bit on the Caribbean, bearing in mind also the long path that brings Caribbeans to the doorstep of the European state later on – because, obviously, when at the end of the fifteenth century Europeans arrived on the shores of various 'natives', such as the 'natives' of the Caribbean (who were systematically destroyed in what one might call our inaugural catastrophe), their foreignness in relation to their native hosts didn't figure as a question of hospitality.

SH: That question may have been already settled before Europeans 'discovered' the New World. After all, the Europeans arrived half-convinced that the 'natives' were examples of polygenesis – the product of a different Creation altogether. They came expecting to find Pliny's and Herodotus's strange half-human/half-animal life forms – like men who used one enormous foot over their heads as an umbrella to keep off the rain! They had been drawing and etching and fantasizing such 'monstrosities of difference' for centuries.

You quite rightly mentioned the Caribbean hospitality industry. I think most people forget that this much-advertised, much-sought-after Caribbean tourism, which keeps some of the islands alive, economically, is really *a business*. The men and women who work in it are not involved in the exercise of some kind of civilizational virtue but in learning to serve other people who are richer and more powerful in every way than themselves.

DS: You're absolutely right that the hospitality industry in the Caribbean is an asymmetrical structure that is framed around the discourse and practice of service. The Caribbean was constructed for the provision of service. And it is obviously a profoundly racialized structure formed around Afro-Caribbeans (principally) serving (largely) white Euro-American tourists. So the hospitality industry of modern tourism has the internal and unavoidable racialized *trace* of a very distinctive colonial past; and in fact, at least in the case of Jamaica, I would say that many ordinary people experience that racialized structure as the continuation of a structure of subordination and service that originates on the slave plantation.

So it's enormously interesting because, of course, the Caribbean is often thought of as the paradigm of a hospitable place and Caribbean people, as the embodiment of hospitality (this is what the advertisements say), but the gesture or the regime of Caribbean hospitality has a very particular historical location on those slave plantations. The great house, the signifier of racialized degradation, was a site of *white* hospitality. The great house offered a perennial round of hospitality to white visitors to the islands – think of the famous early nineteenth-century novel *Marly*, whose protagonist, George Marly, arrives in Jamaica to recover his inheritance and as soon as he steps off the boat is taken up into the world of white hospitality. When the white (typically male) European visitor arrived, there was a whole structure in place that could have him moving with relative ease from plantation to plantation as the guest of white plantation owners with access not only to food and drink but also to the sexual favours of the female slaves. So it is a very particular historical structure. Note then that *that* kind of hospitality is not a practice of hospitality between master and slave, but one centred on civilities exchanged among members of the master class.

SH: The first thing that your description of plantation hospitality underlines is that tourism is a reworking of something with a long history of servitude behind it. You might remember that early film about the hospitality industry in Jamaica called

Smile Orange. Tourists arriving at the airport can *require* a certain form of behaviour from the people who serve them. They have the right to demand not only a service, but also that the natives invest something of themselves in it: 'service with a smile'. As to the plantations, I wonder whether people today have any idea how thick and fast the traffic of visitors from Europe and England really was (and how lavish the 'hospitality'): as well as other plantation owners from other estates, they included old friends and relatives from 'home', visiting dignitaries and colonial officials passing through, members of the resident governing elite and their wives, travellers who were curious to see other parts of the world and how the 'natives' behaved, historians, novelists and travel writers, even those who were seeking ammunition, one way or another, for the abolition debate. They were coming to people whom they already knew were hospitable in a traditionally civilized way. So they're coming to 'the same' – themselves, the Euro-American self, in another place. The underlying relationship to the natives is very different: it has to do with owning, ruling, government and subordination – deeply asymmetrical relationships.

DS: I remember vividly in the 1970s, in socialist Jamaica, when Michael Manley recognized that he needed to undo the image of the tourist industry as merely a new updated structure of subordinated service – black people serving white people. He needed the foreign exchange from tourism, but he needed also to break the connection between tourism and slavery. Manley was aware of the undercurrent of hostility that black Jamaicans felt towards the seeming presumptions of white tourists, the sense that Jamaica was there for the privilege of white foreigners, and that it was the duty of black Jamaicans to welcome and serve their whims and fancies. And in trying to subvert this structure without undermining the general basis of tourism itself, he launched a programme in which the slogan was, 'Tourism is your business'. The address is *to* Jamaicans. We were supposed to accept the inner consumerist logic of tourism and help to change the specific racial dynamic that structured it by participating in it ourselves. The building of resorts like Turtle Towers in Ocho Rios, for example, was to encourage (principally) brown middle-class Jamaicans to make use of the beaches as though *we* ourselves were tourists. So curiously it retained a remnant of the old enduring racial structure, only now brown Jamaicans had access to the privilege of hospitality. I remember one occasion in Ocho Rios (I must have been in high school) being approached by a photographer who wanted to take my picture for a tourist campaign poster, the idea being that I (in my middle-class creole mixture) could represent the *type* of the new tourist. I declined the offer, but still it was a very interesting paradoxical moment in which the Manley government was desperately trying to *both* subvert and retain the structure and character of the hospitality industry.

SH: Wasn't this contradiction typical of the Manley moment? He depended on foreign investment and foreign exchange, but he was also a popular politician in touch with the growing feeling that the tourist relationship requires a demeaning of the national self. And he tries to strike a path through that contradiction – not an unknown strategy in the Caribbean! His answer seems to be that Jamaicans must, as the current neo-liberal language would have it, 'take ownership' of it ourselves – not by running it ourselves but by participating in its asymmetrical structure. As for coming to terms with our past, that strategy only underlined the depth and degree of dependency, which was its basis. Essentially, that strategy doesn't really work.

DS: And in some sense, it can't work because there was the recognition of its complete artificiality. I mean I think it is at that moment (I could be wrong) that tourism starts systematically to be called the 'hospitality industry', as though to humanize it somehow. And this is when there were the beginnings of the institutionalization of the training of people who are going to work in this industry. So it is absolutely clear that there is no self-evident 'naturalness' to the hospitality of Jamaican culture. Hospitality was a relation of power that was going to have to be *inscribed* onto the self of the black Jamaican in order to ensure that they would produce an appropriately welcoming smile.

SH: Wasn't that also the moment when domestic servants became 'helpers' – as if one could reconstruct the corrosive relationship of domestic service by renaming it! Learning to be of service to a sophisticated and demanding market of metropolitan travellers goes beyond training. It is not just a skill or a performance. It means 'marketing the self'. It requires a degree of authenticity only achieved by an investment of the self. Of course, following Manley's intervention, 'helpers' were required to be paid a minimal wage and that was, at least, an improvement in their economic position. But it was also another example of post-colonial politics trying to carve an impossible path between irreconcilable demands. The fortunate thing is that that era seems to be over at last.

DS: That era is over. But you know, if we look at the moment of the emergence of tourism in the Caribbean, again in Jamaica in particular – which is to say, post-Second World War, the arrival of the Pan Am 'clipper', the beginnings of BOAC – this is also when large numbers of Jamaicans start to head to Britain on the *Empire Windrush* and just after. So at the same time that Jamaica is producing itself as a hospitality destination, new questions about hospitality are being put into play by the traffic of Jamaicans to London. But presumably, unlike the tourist Euro-Americans, those migrant Jamaicans had no realistic expectation of hospitality. And this is, of course, inscribed wonderfully in Louise Bennett's classic poem, 'Colonization in Reverse'. You remember? 'Wat a joyful news, Miss Mattie / I feel like me heart gwine burs / Jamaica people colonizin / Englan in reverse.' So for Bennett, the Jamaican is going to London not for hospitality, but in a sense for subversion – to colonize 'in reverse'.

SH: In passing, I remember the moment you speak of very well because, when I was a child, my father often took us on a Sunday afternoon drive to watch the Pan American clipper touch down in Kingston harbour out of the sunset. There was something utterly unreal about the small elite of largely white visitors who could afford to travel in this way. Yet, within ten years, I was on the other side of the Atlantic, watching hundreds of black West Indian migrants just off the boat-trains streaming out of the London railway stations into the grey light of an uncertain – and certainly inhospitable – future. I remember wondering at the time, 'What had impelled them to come?' Was it a response to the terrible poverty and unemployment endemic in colonial underdevelopment, experienced with particular force during the Depression of the 1930s? Was it driven by hopes for a better life, for themselves and their children? And I remember asking myself what I never thought to ask the Pan American visitors: 'Why are you here? Can your high expectations of a better life be possibly fulfilled? Where will you live? And what sort of reception will you get there?' I soon came to recognize that, although I was privileged enough to go to England as a student, I shared many of those hopes and illusions, and in that sense I was a 'migrant' too. These questions about welcome and belonging were addressed to me as much as they were to the new arrivals. 'What sort of person *did I* think I was?'

After centuries of plantation slavery and colonial dependency, Caribbean migrants would hardly have expected to be met with open arms. It may have been different for those who volunteered to join the British armed forces during the war and to fight for 'king and country'. Did they indulge in the brown middle-class fantasy that they had volunteered to defend English liberties because they were in some obscure way part of a wider shared imperial project? How could it be a 'shared' project when one side had systematically oppressed the other for centuries? The two sides had been, as you say, harnessed into the war-to-the-death dependency that is a version of Hegel's master–slave dialectic. They had long before this been constituted as 'intimate enemies'.

In any case, there was already plenty of evidence to the contrary. In 1919, there had been terrible race riots in Cardiff, Liverpool and other cities, when seamen who were British were required to register as 'aliens' – followed by a massive campaign against the injustice. During the war, there were many sporadic violent incidents between black soldiers and white citizens, often about that perennial problem, fraternization with white women. (One churchman advised white women to cross the road if they saw black soldiers coming towards them on the pavement!) The pace of, if you like, 'inhospitability' quickened after the war, as soon as the prospect of permanent black settlement came into view. The 'No Blacks, No Irish, No dogs' signs began to appear in landladies' windows. The British Defence League was formed. When the Antiguan carpenter Kelso Cochrane was murdered by a group of unidentified white men, one British newspaper warned that 'there was already a sort of civil war going on between white and black people in Britain's cities'. Race riots in Notting Hill and Nottingham followed in 1958. The signs were hard to miss.

My overwhelming sense of that first migrant generation is of 'settlers' who were prepared, by and large, to stay out of visibility as much as they could, to keep a low profile. My guess is that they thought they should find a job and a place to live in, bring up their children, try to live a decent life, pull the curtains, stay out of trouble. What they actually encountered was a reception designed – whether intentionally or not – to define them as precisely *not like us*, not the proper objects of generosity and toleration.

DS: This is the atmosphere and sensibility famously captured in Samuel Selvon's novel of the middle 1950s, *The Lonely Londoners*. There is, on the one hand, the illusion of familiarity before one arrives from the colony; but, on the other, this conceit of colonial familiarity is rudely undone by the reality of hostility and alienation to which one arrives. So when Selvon's Moses arrives in London, there is no idiom or ethos of the inclusion of difference or diversity, no gesture of hospitality. Thus the convergence of these two moments in the 1950s – that of the Jamaican tourist industry organizing itself around an explicit discourse of hospitality and that of the inhospitable reception of the colonized subjects arriving in the metropolis – makes visible, *tangibly* visible, that 'hospitality' is nothing but a historically embedded discourse and practice about the relationships of power suturing potential host and potential guest.

SH: Yes – and one in which (as Derrida himself argues in *Positions*) the excluded term of the binary is always marked as subordinate. It is impossible to raise 'hospitality' to the kind of universalism that transcends its embeddedness in a particular historical context and its asymmetrical functioning. The astonishing fact is that, already, a sort of post-imperial disavowal had set in: the majority of the British simply couldn't recognize the black men and women coming to Britain as the same people as those with whom they had had a colonial relationship for over three hundred years. West Indians in Britain, they thought, certainly had strange habits! But more fundamentally, they are so *different from us*. That must have been the anxiety lurking behind the question we were all constantly asked: 'When are you going home?', the assumption being that you must have come for a specific reason and when that need is met, you will go back to where you came from, where you, in the natural order of things, properly belong. 'Over there', as they might say, 'you had to assimilate to us, not we to you! You are (what you, David, have called) "conscripts to *our* modernity". Besides, you still *need* us as children need their parents, while sometimes resenting them.'

More commonsensically, they may have thought West Indians were coming to England because of the postwar labour shortages. That's what opened the door. Later, they will want to be in their own place, with their own kinds of people. Today, it has been forgotten how intense the recruitment in the Caribbean by organizations like London Transport actually was. Of all the possible explanations for migration, the one from which I have derived most pleasure is the fanciful thought that, hundreds of years later, Jamaicans just decided to complete the third leg of the triangular of trade. The Brits used their trinkets to trade with the natives in Africa; they acquired prisoners and transported them into plantation slavery and colonial servitude. Then, one day, centuries later, the slaves decided to 'bring it all back home where it belonged!'

DS: The return of the repressed!

SH: Exactly. However, by the 1970s, the migration experience had become even more subversive. It had become very clear that there wasn't much welcoming physical or symbolic space for them here: 'There is no black in the Union Jack', or not very much. They are not part of the 'us'; the doors were not going to swing open; they are not going to be invited to marry our daughters. What they had encountered was the hard, defensive edge of an embattled 'Britishness', driven into a sort of desperation by the presence of difference – what Frantz Fanon once called 'the fact of blackness' – exaggerated by the loss of empire, the source of former glory. A former imperial people eaten up inside by the loss of an unrequited object of desire. Paul Gilroy calls this state of mind 'post-colonial melancholia'. A profound forgetfulness had settled in. The 'guest' relationship phase was over – if it had ever begun.

DS: It is curious, though this is perhaps the way capital works, that it was always with a certain short-sightedness. In its conceit, the colonial state doesn't imagine that, generations hence, consequences would follow from opening the doors to immigrant labour. The presumption is that you could somehow control the penetration of these black bodies into the white body politic. This seems to me central to the geopolitical imaginary of hospitality: the colonies were always already available for penetration; they were never in control of the conditions of colonial presence. Colonies by definition were always already available for internal transformation as a consequence of the colonial presence. By contrast, the metropolitan centres were presumed to be exempt from transformation by the presence of the colonized other. This seems to be a fundamental assumption about the geopolitical arrangement of the imperial world.

SH: They certainly had no long-term sense of what the internal impact would be of having 'the dark stranger' living in their midst, although there had been a black presence in Britain, especially among the labouring poor, for centuries. The expectation was entirely short term. And of course they didn't foresee the even deeper structural changes in the forms of capitalist 'globalization' that would precipitate one of the largest transnational migrations of modern times, transforming the face of Europe and undermining for ever the British illusion that its people constituted one, single, homogenous culture.

You see another decisive shift when 'the stranger' is not from places with which the British have had a long colonial relationship but from the global South: the much-despised 'economic migrants' (as if economics is not a good reason to leave an impoverished place); displaced people, fleeing famine, poverty, malnutrition, ecological disaster and civil war; refugees and asylum seekers from who knows where. When global instability impacts, the limits of hospitality amid the strength of national chauvinism really come to the fore. There was, people came to believe, a choice to be made between 'our' futures and 'theirs'. There must be a limit to the number of foreigners coming in. It's all very well to talk about celebrating difference and welcoming diversity (this is the very important moment when the multicultural structure of feeling emerges), but that moment has passed. As David Cameron, the prime minister, recently told us during the riots of 2011, it's over. And what's more, it failed!

DS: I want to talk about that moment of the 'multiculturalization' of the imaginary of the liberal democratic state. Because the first offspring of the postwar migrants are born in the mid- to late 1950s and become young adults in London and Leeds and Birmingham of the late 1960s and the early 1970s, and they are estranged in some way from their parents' origins. They are not themselves Barbadian or Jamaican or Trinidadian; they are born and socialized through the educational institutions of the 'mother country'. And yet they were still not imagined or regarded by it as real citizens of the body politic. *They* begin to disturb what it means to be English, and perhaps there is a sense in which it is *that* generation, much more so than the earlier one, that raises Derrida's question about what hospitality is. It is perhaps that generation that aggressively puts a mirror to the white English host and asks them 'Who are *you* in relation to me?'

SH: Absolutely. And the answer they got was not that they would try to be more 'civilized', but that *they* could never be part of what the British – ambiguously – called 'us'. They will always be somehow outsiders. So the subversive quality is very much accentuated by the impossibility of that 'second generation, finding a place to be, and discovering an identity. They didn't really belong, in either place, though the family connections and other cultural influences – like the fluency of *patois* – remained strong. They had become the subjects of what I call 'diasporic displacement', consigned to live in more than one world – Du Bois's 'double consciousness'. They don't have any direct experience of the Caribbean. They are not about to go 'home', wherever that was. At the same time, as you say, they are formed, educated, cultivated inside the institutions whose functions is in part to produce 'Britishness', but they pass right through the system and come out the other side without making an impact. That is the moment when both adults and, especially the youth, begin to put a version of Derrida's question to themselves, though with very different results: 'Who are *we*? How much must we give up in order to become visible, to you, let alone become objects of your civility, part of your imaginary? What sort of people are *you*, anyway?'

This is an extraordinarily important moment, partly because it isn't just a social, political or racial question but a cultural one too. It is a question of identity, of new black subjects, of the emergence of a new subjectivity – a question not of civility but of *survival*. Intolerance and inhospitality, they seemed to say, must have their limit too – and they were drawing the line. The birth of anti-racist politics in Britain, the local confrontations in the 'colony' areas, the resistance to police harassment, the black consciousness that emerged in the wake of this cultural insurgency, internationalized by the massacre in the South African township Sharpeville, Bob Marley, reggae music, the Rasta revolution, the 'political emergency' taking place back in Jamaica, the civil-rights movement in the United States, the birth of 'black power' and 'black-is-beautiful' all constituted the struggle of black subjects to find their way to *their own imaginary*, not someone else's.

DS: You said earlier that the first generation that arrives in the 1950s keeps a low profile. They are trying to avoid the notice of the state. They are in the economy making a living, keeping a low profile, and trying to stay as far away as they can from the police and the state apparatuses. Their children, by contrast, are not in the same kind of position. They are *inside* of these institutions, making visible and aggressive demands on those state apparatuses: they are *not* keeping a low profile. So there is a really interesting contrast and perhaps tension between the members of those overlapping and successive generations. They certainly have a different notion of who 'us' is. They are neither fish nor fowl in some respects.

SH: There was a contrast in political mood and direction between the generations there, though we must not exaggerate it; the black cultural resistance of the 1960s and 1970s wasn't just a 'black youth' phenomenon. Of course, since then, the contrasts have evolved further – a long, complicated story in its own right – and they are still to be found. Those young third-generation black people who have embraced a version of 'Black-British' identity – whose hyphenated structure perhaps best expresses the actual ambivalences they feel and experience – live in a very different world from that of their parents, but they remain in some respects, very close, and fiercely loyal, to them. They also share a lot of things with them. In many of their tastes and habits, they remain, perhaps, more 'Caribbean' than they know!

DS: And it is perhaps that generation and *their* offspring who begin to make the kinds of claims on the metropolitan state that give rise to, that force open, the debate about multiculturalism. So it seems to me that one of the unarticulated conditions of Derrida's own intervention, one of the discursive conditions for the question he poses, is the *transformation* of the internal ethos of the European liberal democratic state. The *question* of multiculturalism has now been *posed* for it. The question of tolerance has been posed for it – partly by this first generation of 'new' Europeans, as well as by those who are not strictly speaking migrant populations but who are now arriving pell-mell on European borders precipitating what is being called the refugee crisis.

SH: Yes, they define the terrain of and play a key role in the rise of – and perhaps one must add these days, the fall or closure of – the multicultural project. It was always contested, always in trouble; it arose as a response to trouble; it never touched everybody; it never was, on its own, an adequate response to popular racism. Numbers were always an issue – hence the effective displacement of irrational prejudices and racialized sentiments on to the apparently rational ground of 'the immigration debate'. But it did represent some movement in the system and it put some new ideas into circulation – ideas like the necessity of living with difference, of multiple identifications and the inevitability of a certain degree of cultural 'creolization'. These arose from the transformed social and historical circumstances of the time, not as a set of abstract ideals parachuted into place. There was no mass conversion to multiculturalism. But for a time there did emerge a sort grudging toleration of what many had come reluctantly to accept was inevitable. There were lots of 'them' here; they weren't going anywhere; and this may be what British cities are destined to look like in an increasingly globalized world. I call this ambivalent process 'multicultural drift'.

The multicultural moment is being closed by the perceived threat to a 'Britishness' increasingly on the defensive; by a deep, almost visceral reaction to the idea of difference; by an image of 'Englishness' beset by self-doubt; by 'the war on terror', and the spectre of disloyal foreigners with Brummie or Liverpudlian accents everywhere. So multiculturalism represented a very qualified moment, albeit also a very important one, which has had some lasting results whose traces have not entirely disappeared. We are not any longer in exactly the same place that we were, though the increasingly prevalent notion that things are completely different now is laughably simplistic.

DS: But at that moment when this new generation is making these profound demands on the fundamental institutions of the metropolitan state, and there are the troubles in the outer parts of the global periphery pushing refugees to the borders of the metropolitan state, there is also of course the rise of the relevance of the idea of 'culture' in thinking about the principles of the liberal democratic state. I mean 'multiculturalism' itself depends upon the rise of the discursive legitimacy of the idea, however contested, of culture. From now on, the liberal democratic state cannot presume that it stands aside from diversity. It has to recognize something about its own cultural specificity and ask itself whether these Others are people who can themselves participate in the principles of liberal democratic selfhood. So that moment of the 1980s and 1990s is also when culture has come to be a very present category in people's thinking.

SH: Of course, culture has always been at the very centre of the question, because it was never just about diversity and citizenship, but also about forms of life, the construction of subjects and of subject positions. Perhaps some of this is captured by the distinction between the two prevailing terms, 'multi-ethnic' and 'multicultural'. They now tend to be run together but actually point in different directions. The former assumes the continuity of relatively closed, distinct and self-contained communities that bargain their cultural rights with others; the latter is more fluid, discursively more open to 'translation'.

DS: Multi-ethnic is the older term, isn't it?

SH: It is, but they keep running on a sort of parallel track. Multi-ethnic never becomes as popular as multicultural as a way of referring to the general trend, but it is present as a strong element, which has grown stronger with the politicization of religious and cultural differences. It is the image of people remaining more or less separate, but sometimes finding a larger framework within which they can negotiate space without murdering one another in the street. Multiculturalism is about something else. It is about the modes, possibilities, complexities, limit and risks of what Édouard Glissant calls 'entanglement'. And it has a certain conception of the inevitability of cultural change and the erosion of orthodoxy. However, it stops short of assimilation because assimilation will always entail the disappearance of the subordinate into the dominant – whereas multiculturalism retains its unfixed and pluralist fluidity and its innate heteroglossia. And it is fundamentally dialogic. It obeys the modality of a conversation, not a conversion. The transformation it requires is always double-sided: nothing cultural is for ever; can we transform ourselves in their direction as much as we've asked them to transform themselves in ours? I retain the subversive thought that this may be a higher form of 'civilization' than Derrida's hospitality.

DS: What's interesting about this late-twentieth-century multicultural moment (certainly before 9/11) is that in a sense the old racialized and civilizational assumptions are in trouble – at least formally. It's no longer simply possible for the liberal democratic state to decree officially that there are self-evident superiorities and self-evident inferiorities. That set of assumptions has in some profound way been put in question.

I agree with you about the distinction between the 'multicultural' and the 'multi-ethnic'. The multi-ethnic assumes that these are quasi-autonomous ethnic groups and that if they are going to live together they are going to have to hang together within some political structure that enables both their differences to remain intact and their political association to be relatively stable. By contrast, the rise of multiculturalism partly presumes the critique of a civilizational discourse. But one of the things that may have changed since 9/11 is the return of aspects of a civilizational discourse. And this sense in some quarters, as you say, of *threat* – the danger of the Other – to the integrity of the liberal democratic state. That is perhaps what prompts someone like Derrida to make a claim or an appeal (because that is what it is, essentially – an elegant philosophic *appeal*) to that liberal democratic state to be more open to its Others than it is now inclined to be as we face the 'closure', as you put it earlier, of the multicultural opening. Therefore the European state is in crisis and has now to defend its borders against these incursions, so to speak.

SH: Let me say something about the degree to which the civilizational assumptions get undermined. There is a certain level of global interdependence, which just makes it impossible to go on maintaining those old distinctions intact. The system of capitalist globalization stopped working that way, which does not mean that in its new forms it is incapable of creating its own version of a civilizational discourse. In an age of global interdependency, however unequal its terms remain, it is difficult to maintain firm borders and national frontiers. Difficult, but not impossible. Since 9/11, we have witnessed the reconstitution of a civilizational discourse around an ancient enemy in a new disguise: Islam.

Now does this provide the context in which Derrida poses his question? Yes. But it needs to be asked with a greater degree of urgency. I don't feel that this north African-born French philosopher really understands the crisis in liberal republican France, triggered by its Muslim Other living in its midst and knocking at its door. Across Europe, we see borders being more strongly defended, more *sans papiers* refugee camps at the ports, more immigration control agencies, more 'ethnic scanning' at airports. Fortress Europe is alive and well! Observing the speed of closure around new civilizational distinctions is an unnerving experience.

DS: One aspect of globalization that you mentioned is the traffic not only of labour, which we've touched on, but also of *elites* from the periphery. This is eminently a question of hospitality. It is a question of manicured forms of difference that can inhabit with relative ease metropolitan intellectual and artistic institutions and discourses. So I have to wonder whether, for example, the rapid rise over the last fifteen, twenty years of art markets for certain kinds of non-European art (African, Middle Eastern, South Asian, Chinese – not yet Caribbean on a comparable scale) doesn't depend on the circulation of cultivated non-European subjects. And I wonder whether the rise of the new category of the 'contemporary' that is displacing the older idea of the 'modern', even the 'high modern', doesn't also depend on these mobile elites moving around more or less hospitably. For unlike the idea of the 'modern' – in any case, more easily, less reluctantly than the idea of the modern – the idea of the 'contemporary' embodies in it the sense of the *coexistence* and *co-temporality* of difference in artistic production and aesthetic conversation. The contemporary – whatever it is – presupposes the coexistence of diversity, the *co-presentness*, so to say, in preoccupation and sensibility. And this seems to me to depend very much on assumptions about who can move and who can't.

SH: The moment of the 1970s we were talking about posed the question 'Who has and who does not have the right to move?' Significantly, it was also the moment of the emergence of black diaspora arts, in response to the related question 'Who is "in the frame" and who is not?' The second-generation postwar migrants begin to use art, culture, literature and so on to interrogate those dilemmas and non-matching expectations.

DS: Right, it's precisely the moment of the *contemporary* in some sense.

SH: It is an example of 'co-presence of diversities' in your terms – in this case, the vernacular and 'the modern'. You also seemed to be asking the question as to whether people who do *not* belong to the elite might not also participate in this co-presence of diversities. I think something of this hope must have shadowed what was called 'the promise' of world migration at the time, and be responsible for some of its ambivalences. Migration was supposed to be a sign of how poor communities had been exploited and excluded – and excluded from 'the modern'. But wasn't it also a sign of the breakout of their endless colonial provincialization, their potential 'cosmopolitanism' or at least the promise of a cosmopolitanism to come? Was migration not one of the distorted forms, which the old 'internationalist' ideal assumed in these paradoxical times? Borrowing a phrase from the title of *your* book about C. L. R. James and the Haitian Revolution, were we not all, after all, 'conscripts of modernity'?

But you were also talking about this in relation to the circulation of elites. This looks very much like the 'new republicanism' of the transnational, inter-ethnic super-rich, who have a global field of operations and means of accumulation at their disposal, who in a sense belong simultaneously everywhere and nowhere, colonizing art as one of its new provinces, assuming the role of the new global patrons.

Capital's solution to the problem of how to evade the inroads and constraints of the social democratic moment after the war was to 'go global'. And 'going global' meant a new kind of transnationalism among those at the top of the system – new alliances with native elites, new solidarities with the super-rich, assimilation to a new kind of 'cosmopolitan' global consciousness, including access to the precious 'scarcity' and 'conspicuous consumption' value represented by the discourses of high culture and the arts that the rich have always reserved for themselves. In the art market of today, everybody at the top end can be and is a player, including Russian oligarchs who only got their hands on their fortunes thanks to the 'liberation' of the socialist economy the day before yesterday in the bonfire of state assets that followed the fall of the Berlin Wall. However, this comes – as they say – 'at a price': *commodification*. Art must become 'a commodity'; it must enter the circulation circuits of the market, in order to participate in what you are calling 'the contemporary'.

DS: But what this 'go global' moment would presume is that you and I and everybody else can share a *present*-ness; that indeed with our very diversity there is the possibility of sharing a 'now', a present moment, that we can navigate around with each other. And it presumes a curious kind of democratic ethos. It presumes that these diversities inhabit a non-asymmetrical space. They inhabit a flat, egalitarian surface – which of course it does *only* for that very high elite.

SH: Only at one level is it 'democratic'. But it can foster egalitarian illusions. The moment you ask the questions 'Who is closest to that ideal?' and 'What are the modes of participation that must prevail?', the old lines of distinction surface, etched across its face.

DS: So perhaps, then, in closing, if the idea of hospitality is to have any critical purchase it needs a much more rigorous attention to its historical embeddedness in modes and relations of power than has so far been the case.

SH: I profoundly agree with you. Hospitality isn't any longer a very useful, usable concept unless that deconstruction – the recognition of its particularities, its dependency on power and so on – has taken place. Otherwise, it runs the risk of being absorbed into a kind of solipsistic self-delusion.

This conversation took place in London on 12 June 2012.

1   Jacques Derrida and Anne Dufourmantelle, *Of Hospitality*, trans. Rachel Bowlby, Stanford: Stanford University Press, 2000, pp. 11, 35, 37, 113, 115.

Achille Mbembe
The slave: figure of the anti-museum?

I would like to begin with a question that, though seemingly anodyne,
is (in my view at least) crucial for the future of the museum institution.
It is this: 'Should slaves take their place in the museum?'

The manure and the silt

'Slave' is obviously to be construed as a generic term covering various situations
and contexts that have been clearly described by historians and anthropologists.
The Atlantic slave complex, whose core was the plantation system in the
Caribbean, Brazil and the United States, was an obvious link in the formation
of modern capitalism; and it is this complex that inspires the essence of what I
have to say. This Atlantic complex produced neither the same type of society, nor
the same type of slavery, as the Islamic trans-Saharan complex. And if there is
something that distinguishes the regimes of trans-Atlantic slavery from indigenous
forms of slavery in pre-colonial African societies, it is the fact that the latter
were never able to extract from their captives a surplus-value comparable to that
obtained in the New World.

We are therefore primarily concerned with New World slavery, whose
distinctiveness consisted of the fact that it was one of the main cogs in a worldwide
process of accumulation. Through the triple mechanism of capture, oppression
and paralysis, slaves were forcibly bound to a system that prevented them from
making of their lives (and on the basis of their lives) a genuine oeuvre, something
self-standing and endowed with its own substance. In addition, they represented
a radical form of non-autonomy, non-liberty or (if one prefers) subjection within
societies that soon sought to define themselves as free and democratic – that is,
characterized by equality. Depending on the circumstances, slaves were at once
commodities, objects of luxury or utility whose ownership was claimed by others,
and human persons endowed with the gift of speech and capable of using tools.
Deprived of any kinship bond, they were also deprived of any heritage.
While their full humanity was denied by those to whom they belonged, who
extracted unpaid labour from them, it was not completely erased, at least not on
a purely ontological level. By force of circumstance, it was a *floating humanity*,
struggling to escape fixation and repetition and desiring to enter into a dynamic
of autonomous creation.

The peculiarity of this floating humanity, condemned incessantly to re-form
itself, is that it heralded the desire to come. In fact, even when they were legally
defined as personal property, slaves always remained human beings, despite the
practices of cruelty, degradation and dehumanization. Through their labour in the
service of a master, they continued to create a world. Through words and deeds,
they wove relations and a universe of meanings, invented languages, religions,
dances and rituals, and created a 'community'. The destitution and abjection
that had befallen them did not wholly eliminate their capacity for symbolization.
By its very existence, *the community of slaves* constantly stripped the veil of

hypocrisy and lies covering slave societies. Moreover, slaves were capable of rebellion and could on occasion dispose of their own lives through suicide, thereby dispossessing their master of what he regarded as his property and *de facto* abolishing the bond of servitude.

Basically, then, we are dealing with disturbing figures of our humanity, of which slaves form the dark and the scandalous side. Human persons whose name was execrated, whose capacity to continue their line was jammed, whose face was disfigured and labour despoiled, they attest to a mutilated humanity, profoundly stamped by the brand of alienation. But by virtue of the damnation to which their existence was condemned, and the possibility of a radical uprising of which they were nevertheless the bearers (which was never completely destroyed), they also represent a kind of silt of the Earth at the point where a multiplicity of *demi-mondes* produced by the double violence of race and capital converge. Manure of history and subjects beyond subjection, the slaves made a world that reflects this sombre contradiction. Working from the bilges, they were the first stokers of our modernity. And if there is one thing that haunts our modernity from beginning to end, it is precisely the possibility of a unique event – 'the slave revolt' – which would betoken not only the liberation of the enslaved, but also a radical recasting, if not of the system of property and labour, then at least of the mechanisms of its distribution and hence of the foundations of the reproduction of life itself.

Anti-museum

That being the case, my argument is as follows: it is not desirable for such slaves – simultaneously manure and silt of history – to take their place in the museum. Moreover, no museum exists that is capable of hosting them in this dual dimension. To this day, most attempts to stage the history of trans-Atlantic slavery in existing museums have been conspicuous for their vacuity. At best, slaves figure in them as the appendage of a different history: a citation at the foot of a page devoted to someone else, other places, different things. Besides, the moment slaves genuinely took their place in the museum as it exists today, the museum would automatically cease to be a museum. It would signal its own end and it would have to be transformed into something else – a different site, a different stage, with other dispositions and designations, even a different name.

For despite appearances, historically the museum has not invariably been a site for the unconditional reception of the many faces of humanity regarded in its unity. On the contrary, since the modern age it has been a powerful system of segregation. The exhibition of subjugated or humiliated humanities has always obeyed a few elementary rules of injury and violation. And first of all, these humanities have never been entitled to the same treatment, status and dignity as triumphant humanities. They have always been subjected to different rules of classification and different logics of presentation. Added to this logic of separation, or selection, has always been one of allocation. The primary conviction is that since different forms of humanity have produced different objects and different forms of culture, they should be housed and exhibited in distinct sites invested with different, unequal symbolic statuses. The slave's entry into such a museum would doubly sanction the spirit of apartheid underlying this cult of difference, hierarchy and inequality.

Moreover, one function of the museum has also been the production of statues, mummies and fetishes – precisely objects divested of life and restored to the inertia of matter. Statue-making, mummification and fetishization directly correspond to the logic of segregation just evoked. In this case, it is not generally a question of offering peace and repose to the sign long sheltered by the form. The spirit behind the form has been driven out, as in the case of skulls collected during wars of conquest and 'pacification'. To acquire *droit de cité* in the museum as it exists today, slaves, like all the primitive objects that have preceded them there, would have to be drained of their elementary power and energy. The threat this manure-figure and silt-figure might represent, its scandalous potential, would be dispelled, as a precondition of its exhibition. From this point of view, the museum is a space of neutralization and domestication of forces that, prior to their being put in a museum, were living – currents of power. Such remains the essence of its cultural function, particularly in the de-Christianized societies of the West. It is possible that this function (which is also political and cultural) is necessary for the very survival of society, just like the function of forgetting in memory.

But it is precisely necessary to preserve the slave's potential for scandal. Paradoxically, this potential lies in the fact that it is a scandal that people refuse to recognize as such. Including itself in the refusal to recognize it as such, this scandal assigns that figure of humanity its insurrectionary power. To preserve this scandal's power to scandalize, slaves should not take their place in the museum. Consequently, what the history of Atlantic slavery invites us to do is to found a new institution: *the anti-museum*.

Conclusion

Slaves must continue to haunt the museum as it exists today through their absence. Slaves should be everywhere and nowhere, their appearances always occurring in the mode of infraction, never of the institution. That is how we shall preserve the slave's spectral dimension. That is also how we shall prevent facile conclusions being drawn from the abominable event represented by the slave trade.

As to the anti-museum, it is in nowise an institution, but the figure of another place, one of radical hospitality. A place of refuge, the anti-museum also conceives itself as an unconditional place of repose and asylum for all the dregs of humanity and 'damned of the Earth' – those who attest to the sacrificial system constituted by the history of our modernity.

Pelin Tan
The unconditional experience of space

Enemy

Since ancient times, the wall of a walled city has signified the boundary between inside and outside worlds, distinguishing human life (or civilization) that resides within from the wildlife (whether nature or enemy) that lies without. The wall accorded a form of 'citizenship' to the inhabitants inside that was denied to those beyond, the very structure of the wall itself assigning different hierarchies of subjecthood – to law, to power, to capital, etc. – on its two sides. According to Bülent Diken, 'The city is built on the basis of an inside–outside divide, the walls, which are also a symbol of the law, or, the rule. As such, the origin of the city is posited as a distinction between the law and its outside.'[1]

But to consider the wall only as a division or border in this way, or to see it merely as some romantic historical feature, is to misunderstand or to ignore its potentiality as *threshold* – that is to say, not as a barrier, but rather as a space of encounter, negotiation and exchange with the Other, all prerequisites to the formation of the self. As Elizabeth Grozs explains, 'The wall divides us from the world, on one side, and creates another world, a constructed and framed world, on its other side. Though it primarily divides, the wall also provides new connections, new relations, social and interpersonal relations, with those on its other side.'[2]

While this dialectic of inside/outside does not fully express or explain the reality of Istanbul's walls today, it nonetheless provides a useful perspective from which to analyse the construction of subjectivities within the spatial politics of the city. As well as providing layers of space, as a type of threshold or heterotopia, the walls continue to create and preserve the conditions necessary for the 'becoming' of the subject, long after their role as physical limit and divide has been made redundant. The city has continued to expand, of course, and it has long transgressed the bounds of its historic centre. As it has done so, it has left traces of both its expansion and the changing urban conditions and relationships that resulted, which now combine with vestiges of the former sub- and ex-urban realities of others over the wall. In this way, Istanbul's walls are today the site of many different coexisting time–space realms. Perhaps for this reason, they also now provide hospitable situations for several communities and for diverse spatial practices on both sides of the structure and within its labyrinthine spaces. They act at once as temporary shelters; areas for children's play; the burial place of holy people (a surreal narrative from the past, but one that is still meaningful to today's citizens); the location of bird huts and flea markets; and the setting of various daily improvisations, from hanging clothes to urban gardening along the outer wall. All of these practices and more seem to be examples of the unconditional experience of space and the Other that, according to Derrida's notion of 'hospitality', is at the heart of the relationship between host and guest (and potential enemy), as we will see below. Perhaps this manifestation of unconditionality along and inside Istanbul's walls, will allow us to reconsider what we mean by thresholds and to rethink our understanding of how they can exist in the very heart of an urban space.

Threshold

Peter Lang describes areas at the border of or between urban spaces as 'actual territories' that are being continuously transformed. 'Actual territories constitute the built city's negative, the interstitial and the marginal spaces abandoned or in the process of transformation. These are the removed *lieux de la mémoire*, the unconscious becoming of the urban systems, the spaces of confrontation and contamination between the organic and the inorganic, between nature and artifice.'[3] Following Lang's view, the interventions and dwelling practices of Istanbul's walls might represent such a locus and process of urban transformation. The wall is no longer a historical fact, but an artefact that is constantly re-formed by the citizens' everyday application of diverse rituals, practices and uses, sometimes by borrowing from the past, all of which give new meanings to it. What is more, the diverse and connected communities and individuals who live along the wall each create their own spatial relations and ethics specific to their location. In this way, the wall becomes a space of confrontation in urban practice, an 'actual territory'.

The constellation of communities and dwellings in and near Istanbul's walls thus coexists in specific ways to create urban localities. The concept of 'locality' implies an ethics based on a shared spatial experience and communality. But the terms 'local' and 'locality' no longer refer to a homogeneous cultural geography, if they ever did. Instead, urban localities are heterogeneous bodies of diverse communities that are bound together and exist alongside one another. Likewise, 'local' does not simply refer to a geographic place. Especially within an urban sphere, 'local' becomes an act or actions, which are contextualized within the politics of space, economic change, medium and human behaviour. Informal economies, gender, ethnicity and cross-cultural practices all contribute to reshape the local in particular ways. To give a specific example from Istanbul, the municipality's urban transformation of the historical peninsula has extended to the city walls. Yet despite the authorities' attempts to control this territory, inhabitants continue to appropriate the empty spaces for their own purposes, for temporary occupation, weekend activities and the exercise of rituals. Both the conventions of this informal usage (which includes the 'meaning' of the wall in everyday life) and the sanctions of the authorities influence these activities, which then become an outcome and expression of their specific locality.

The 'local', as seen in small-scale examples such as this, is usually positioned in a dualistic structure as the polar opposite of global universalism. Local implications arise from the specific economic, political and cultural conditions of a given society that are related to its unique history, its position in modernization and its place under the effects of globalization. Here, 'local' represents 'particularity'. The local is defined as a communal identity created in response to globalization where a particular local flow of information and capital is 'a defensive historical reaction to globalizing process'.[4] Furthermore, Arjun Appadurai has defined locality as 'primarily relational and contextual rather than scalar or spatial'.[5] And so, in the case of Istanbul, we see various communities and small ethnic groups – the Romany community, say, or the urban gardeners of the city – living and working near the old walls and creating their own sets of ethics and forms of hospitality. Appadurai claims that cities are made up of several layers of such locality, by which he means diverse social or imaginative practices. 'The work of the imagination allows people to inhabit either multiple localities or a kind of single and complex sense of locality, in which many different empirical spaces coexist.'[6] For him, a locality can exist across networks within nation states, or even be transnational in nature, especially within post-colonial social structures. Locality is not exactly defined as a 'community' here, but rather as the experience or the practices of communities in the urban sphere. Similarly, according to Rüdiger Korff, 'a locality must be seen as a response to, and attempt to cope with, the metropolitan environment and the globalization process in particular. Although, of course, spatially bound and referring to specific places, it is not a geographic but first a social category.'[7]

Hospitality

To return to Istanbul, with such a coexistence of diverse localities and multiple overlaid meanings, it seems that the city walls are a hospitable space where any practice or dwelling is possible. The actions of both the authorities and the inhabitants have certainly created a complex form of hospitality. The interventions of TOKİ, the government housing development agency, with its eviction and urban regeneration projects; the municipality's construction of new 'formal' buildings such as swimming pools and ice rinks; and the unofficial, informal and unsanctioned activities of the residents, from flea markets to drug-dealing – all serve to create a sense of threshold, of encounter, of layered localities, of the 'becoming' of subjectivity. Could, then, the city walls be a space of radical experience that is open or welcoming to anything, including even an enemy? The unconditionality of these diverse practices and narratives appears, at the very least, to offer the promise of such a radical experience for whoever wants to dwell in the midst of the walls.

As already stated, the idea of 'radical experience' is based on Derrida's theory of 'hospitality'.[8] With this notion, he set out to theorize a non-canonical concept of absolute friendship. Hospitality for him is the manner in which we relate to ourselves and to others. He asserts the principle of 'unconditional hospitality',[9] in which the condition of meeting, facing and opening yourself to a stranger has no precondition defining the unexpected encounter, which is unconditionally open. Generally, invitation is a prerequisite in hospitality. However, in 'unconditional hospitality', the crucial element is to take the risk of accepting the 'stranger', whoever he or she is, and whether or not he or she is invited. As a result, 'unconditional hospitality' is a radical experiment. It is also, as Derrida makes clear, impossible to achieve.

Derrida's construction of hospitality is also explicitly tied to the idea of 'home', and requires the host to be the 'master' of the house, country or nation, and thereby have the power to be hospitable. The host–guest relationship is thus built on the principles of ownership, property and, by extension, self-identity. Yet all of these concepts are thrown into doubt by our example of Istanbul's city walls, which as we have seen involve a multiplicity of localities in a single space. Both the identity and actions of the various ethnic groups (the Romany community, for instance) and the other residents' informal activities, not to mention the responses of the authorities, create a continuous shift in the host–guest relationship. Who is the guest and who is the host in these conditions is always ambivalent. Here, perhaps more than in most situations, the guest–host relationship is always an antagonistic, fragmented and uncanny one.

Derrida's 'unconditional hospitality' is itself based on a reading of Emmanuel Levinas's philosophy of the face-to-face encounter, from which comes the subject's responsibility to the Other, whose very presence makes demands of the subject before he or she can respond to or ignore the demand.[10] For Levinas, this encounter means that the Other is prior to or superior to the self and is the basis of ethics. Yet it is also based upon an 'impossibility' or, as Simon Critchley has described it, 'a radical and unfulfillable demand',[11] which is akin to the impossible nature of unconditional hospitality. In her article on the work of Krzysztof Wodiczko,[12] Rosalyn Deutsche takes this further by referring to Levinas's assertion that 'my relationship with the Other as neighbour gives meaning to my relations with all the others'. Thus the subject's responsibility is limited not to the Other but extended to Others, making the encounter even more uncanny and traumatic. In this respect, hospitality involves a demanding responsibility.

The city wall of our example is an urban space of confrontation that hosts constellations of fragmented communities and actions, all of which re-creates its meaning as a heterogeneous site. Although it has the form of a border, and once was an actual border, the two sides of the wall and its labyrinthine design now serve as an open structure where several localities coexist at the same time. Its inner spatial design makes it difficult to control the practices inside the wall, which produces uncanny conditions of hospitality. As long as the wall remains a hospitable place hosting diverse inhabitants, informal housing and interventions, and countercultural communities, amid an intense antagonistic relationship with the local authorities and an overwhelming identity of historical heritage, it will continue to create new localities and be a threshold at the heart of the city. In such a situation, the question of who is the 'enemy' will always remain ambivalent. This ambivalence creates a complex urban practice, leading to a radical experience of space.

1   Bülent Diken and Carsten Bagge Lausten, *The Culture of Exception: Sociology Facing The Camp*, London and New York: Routledge, 2005, p. 8.
2   Elizabeth Grozs, *Chaos, Territory, Art: Deleuze and the Framing of the Earth*, New York: Columbia University Press, 2008, p. 14.
3   Peter Lang, 'Stalker on Location', in *Loose Space*, ed. Karen A. Franck and Quentin Stevens, New York: Routledge, 2001, p. 195.
4   Roland Robertson and Jan Aart Scholte (eds.), *Encyclopedia of Globalization*, London and New York: Routledge, 2007, p. 744
5   Arjun Appadurai, 'The production of locality', in *Modernity at Large: Globalization and Cultural Dimension*, Minnesota: University of Minnesota Press, 1996.
6   Ibid.
7   Erhard Berner and Rüdiger Korff, *Globalization and Local Resistance: The Creation of Localities in Manila and Bangkok*, Working Paper no. 205, Southeast Asia Programme. Bielefeld: Bielefeld University, 1994, p. 6. See also Rüdiger Korff, 'City, space and meaning: theoretical perspectives of urbanism', Working Paper no. 140, Southeast Asia Programme, Bielefeld: Bielefield University, 1990, p. 7: 'The city can be described as a kaleidoscope of localities. I would define locality as a socio-spatial clustering of interaction and as interdependency of activities in an area without clear borders. A locality is characterized on one hand by an openness of interaction and social relations, and on the other by an interdependency of activities taking place within the locality.'
8   Jacques Derrida, 'What about hospitality? Politics and friendship', in 'A Discussion with Jacques Derrida', Centre for Modern French Thought, University of Sussex, 1 December 1997.
9   Ibid.
10 As Simon Critchley details: 'The ethical relation begins when I experience being placed in question by the face of the other, an experience that happens both when I respond generously to what Levinas, recalling the Hebrew Bible, calls 'the widow, the orphan, the stranger', but also when I pass them by on the street, silently wishing they were somehow invisible and wincing internally at my callousness.' Simon Critchley, *Infinitely Demanding: Ethics of Commitment, Politics of Resistance*, London: Verso, 2007, p. 56.
11 Ibid, p. 62.
12 Rosalyn Deutsche, 'Sharing strangeness: Krzysztof Wodiczko's Aegis and the question of hospitality', *Grey Room*, no. 6, Winter 2002, pp. 26–43. See also Emmanuel Levinas, *Totality and Infinity: An Essay on Exteriority*, trans. Alphonso Lingis, The Hague, Boston, Mass. and London: Martinus Nijhoff Publishers, 1979; Emmanuel Levinas, *Otherwise than Being*, trans. Alphonso Lingis, Boston, Mass.: Kluwer Academic Publisher, 1991.

Biographies

David Adjaye (b. 1966, Dar es Salaam, Tanzania) is an architect living and working in London, UK. Projects include the Smithsonian Museum of African American Arts and Culture (Washington, DC, USA, 2012) and Museum of Contemporary Art (Denver, Colorado, USA, 2007).

Doug Aitken (b. 1968, California, USA) is an artist living and working in Los Angeles and New York City, USA. Aitken's public-realm projects include *Song 1* (Hirshhorn Museum and Sculpture Garden, Washington DC, USA, 2012), *Black Mirror* (Hydra Island, Greece, 2011) and *Sonic Pavilion* (Brazil, 2009). In 1999, he won the International Prize at the Venice Biennale.

John Akomfrah (b. 1957, Accra, Ghana) is a film-maker, lecturer and writer living and working in London, UK. His films include *The Nine Muses* (2010), *Mnemosyne* (2010–11) and *Seven Songs for Malcolm X* (1993). Akomfrah is one of the founding members of the Black Audio Film Collective.

Chris Alexander (b. 1970, Akron, Ohio, USA) is a poet living and working in New York City, USA. He is the author of *Panda* (Truck Books, 2011) and *McNugget* (Troll Thread, forthcoming).

Hurvin Anderson (b. 1965, Birmingham, UK) is an artist living and working in London, UK. Recent exhibitions include 'Hurvin Anderson: Subtitles' (Michael Werner, New York City, USA, 2011) and 'Art Now: Hurvin Anderson' (Tate Britain, London, UK, 2009). A solo exhibition at Ikon, Birmingham, UK. is forthcoming in 2013.

Janine Antoni (b. 1964, Freeport, Bahamas) is an artist living and working in New York City, USA. Exhibitions include 'Touch' (Museum Kunst der Westküse, Alkersum/Föhr, Germany, 2011), 'At Home in the Body' (University of Virginia Art Museum, Charlottesville, USA, 2010) and 'Up Against' (Luhring Augustine, New York City, USA, 2009).

Keith Arnatt (b. 1930, Oxford, UK; d. 2008, London, UK) was a conceptual artist and photographer, whose photographs have been toured extensively overseas by the British Council. A major retrospective exhibition entitled 'I'm a Real Photographer' was held in 2007 at the Photographers' Gallery (London, UK).

Kader Attia (b. 1970, Paris, France) is an artist living and working in Berlin, Germany. He gained international recognition at the 50th Venice Biennale (Venice, Italy, 2003), where he exhibited 'Flying Rats'. Recent exhibits include 'The Repair of the Occident to Extra-Occidental Cultures', Documenta 13 (Kassel, Germany, 2012).

Yael Bartana (b. 1970, Afula, Israel) is an artist living and working in Israel and The Netherlands. She has had solo exhibitions at the Museum of Modern Art (Warsaw, Poland), the Van Abbemuseum (Eindhoven, The Netherlands) and PS1 (New York City, USA). Bartana participated in the São Paulo Bienal (São Paulo, Brazil, 2010) and Documenta 12 (Kassel, Germany, 2007), and represented Poland in the 54th Venice Biennale (Venice, Italy, 2011).

Jimbo Blachly (b. 1961, Orange, New Jersey, USA) is an artist living and working in New York City, USA. Since 2002, he and the poet Lytle Shaw have been co-editors of the Chadwick Family Papers. Their work has been exhibited at PS1 / Museum of Modern Art (New York City, USA), Tate Modern (London, UK), ICA (Philadelphia, USA) and the Hunt Museum (Limerick, Ireland). They are represented by Winkleman Gallery (New York City, USA).

Sylvie Blocher (b. 1953, Alsace, France) is an artist living and working in Paris, France. Solo exhibitions include 'Les Coupables' (Centre d'Art Contemporain Saint-Restitut, France, 2011), 'What is Missing?' (Museum of Contemporary Art, Sydney, Australia, 2010) and 'Urban Stories / South China' (Nosbaum & Reding Art Contemporain, Luxembourg, 2009).

Riccardo Boglione (b. 1970, Genoa, Italy) is a writer and critic living in Montevideo, Uruguay, where he writes about art for a newspaper and several magazines. He published *Ritmo D.: feeling the blanks* (Gegen, 2009) and *Tapas sin libro* (Gegen, 2011). He is the founder and director of *Crux Desperationis*, the first international journal of conceptual writing.

Christian Bök (b. 1966, Etobicoke, Canada) is an academic and writer based in Calgary, Canada. He is the author of *Crystallography* (Coach House Books, 2003), a pataphysical encyclopedia nominated for the Gerald Lampert Memorial Award, and *Eunoia* (Coach House Books, 2011), a work of experimental literature and winner of the Griffin Prize for Poetic Excellence. He teaches English at the University of Calgary.

Andrea Bowers (b. 1965, Wilmington, Ohio, USA) is an artist living and working in Los Angeles, USA. Solo exhibitions include 'The New Women's Survival Guide' (Andrew Kreps Gallery, New York City, USA, 2011) and 'Ni Una Muerte Mas' (National Museum of Contemporary Art, Athens, Greece, 2011).

Rosi Braidotti (b. 1954, Latisana, Italy) is a philosopher living and working in Utrecht, The Netherlands. She is Distinguished University Professor and founding Director of the Centre for the Humanities at Utrecht University. Her latest books are *Nomadic Subjects* (Columbia University Press, 2011) and *Nomadic Theory: The Portable Rosi Braidotti* (Columbia University Press, 2011).

Stephen Burt (b. 1971, Baltimore, Maryland, USA) is an academic and writer living in Belmont, Massachusetts, USA. He is Professor of English at Harvard University, and his recent books include *The Art of the Sonnet* (with David Mikics; Harvard University Press, 2011) and *Why I Am Not a Toddler And Other Poems by Cooper Bennett Burt (Age One)* (Rain Taxi Books, 2011); a new book of poems, called *Belmont* (after the town where he lives), will appear in 2013.

CAConrad (b. 1966, Topeka, Kansas, USA) is a poet living in Philadelphia, Pennsylvania, USA. He is the author of several poetry books, including *A BEAUTIFUL MARSUPIAL AFTERNOON: New (Soma)tics* (Wave Books, 2012), and *The Book of Frank* (Wave Books, 2010). He is a 2011 Pew Fellow, and a 2012 Ucross Fellow (CAConrad.blogspot.com).

Sophie Calle (b. 1953, Paris, France) is an artist living and working in Paris. Calle's recent solo exhibitions include 'Rachel, Monique' (Palais de Tokyo, Paris, 2010) and 'Talking to Strangers' (Whitechapel Gallery, London, 2009). She has also represented France at the 52nd Venice Biennale (Venice, Italy, 2007).

Libia Castro (b. 1970, Madrid, Spain) and Ólafur Ólafsson (b. 1973, Reykjavik, Iceland) are artists who been working together in Berlin, Germany, and Rotterdam, The Netherlands, since 1997. Solo exhibitions include 'Under Deconstruction' (54th Venice Biennale, Icelandic Pavilion, Venice, Italy, 2011), and 'Tu país no existe' (CAAC Seville, Spain, 2011–12).

Eleanor Clayton is Assistant Curator at Tate Liverpool. She has worked on numerous exhibitions at Tate, most recently 'Alice in Wonderland' and 'Turner Monet Twombly: Later Paintings'. Independent curatorial projects include 'Displacements' (James Taylor Gallery, London, 2010). She has previously worked at Tate Britain and the National Portrait Gallery.

Emily Cormack is curator at Gertrude Contemporary, Melbourne, Australia. She has curated exhibitions throughout the Asia-Pacific region and in Europe, and also writes frequently for *Frieze*, *Art and Australia*, *Art Agenda* and *Kaleidoscope* magazines.

Layla Curtis (b. 1975, Chippenham, UK) is an artist living and working in London, UK. Recent exhibitions include 'A Parliament of Lines' (Edinburgh City Arts Centre, Edinburgh, UK, 2012) and 'Revolver' (Matt's Gallery, London, UK, 2012). Her 1999 Japanese residency culminated in her first solo show, 'Mapping'.

Kieran Daly (b. 1989, Maine, USA; d. 2012, Maine) recently self-published *Empty Sampler, Nullpropriation, Anonymous Abiotic Factor* (2012) and *Plays / For Theatre* (2011).

Enrico David (b. 1966, Ancona, Italy) is an artist living and working in London, UK. He was nominated for the Turner Prize in 2009.

Eugenio Dittborn (b. 1943, Santiago, Chile) is an artist living and working in Santiago. Recent exhibitions include 'Intense Proximity', La Triennale (Palais de Tokyo, Paris, France, 2012), 8th Bienal de Porto Alegre (Porto Alegre, Brazil, 2011) and 'Eugenio Dittborn' (Museo de Artes Visuales (MAVI), Santiago, 2010).

Paul Domela is Programme Director of Liverpool Biennial.

Costas Douzinas is Professor of Law and Director of the Birkbeck Institute for the Humanities, Birkbeck College, University of London, and editor of *Law and Critique*. His books include *Postmodern Jurisprudence* (Routledge, 1993); *The End of Human Rights* (Hart, 2000); *Human Rights and Empire* (Routledge Cavendish, 2007); *Resistance and Philosophy in the Crisis* (Alexandria Publications, 2011); *Law and the Image* (with Lynn Nead; University of Chicago Press, 1999); *Adieu Derrida* (Palgrave Macmillan, 2007) and *The Idea of Communism* (with Slavoj Žižek; Verso, 2010).

Jimmie Durham (b. 1940, Washington, Arkansas, USA) is a sculptor, essayist and poet living and working in Europe. Durham has exhibited solo internationally and has participated in the Venice Biennale (Venice, Italy, 2005, 2003, 2001, and 1999) and Documenta 8 and 9 (Kassel, Germany). He has also had essays and articles published in the *Los Angeles Times*, *Artforum*, *Black Scholar* and *Third Text*.

Craig Dworkin (b. 1969, USA) is a poet, literary theorist and art critic living in Salt Lake City, Utah, USA. He is author of *Strand* (Roof Books, 2005), *Parse* (Atelos, 2008), *The Perverse Library* (information as material, 2010), and *Motes* (Roof Books, 2011). He teaches art and literature at the University of Utah, where he also curates the Eclipse archive <http://english.utah.edu/eclipse>.

Michael Elmgreen (b. 1961, Copenhagen, Denmark) and **Ingar Dragset** (b. 1968, Trondheim, Norway) have been working together in London, UK, and Berlin, Germany, since 1995. Presentations of their work include 'The Fourth Plinth', *Powerless Structures: Fig 101* (Trafalgar Square, London, UK, 2012–13), 'Celebrity: The One and the Many' (ARoS Aarhus Kunstmuseum, Denmark, 2011) and *Happy Days in the Art World* (Performa 11, New York City, USA, 2011).

J. Gordon Faylor (b. 1986, Bethlehem, Pennsylvania, USA) is a writer and editor living and working in Philadelphia, Pennsylvania. He is the editor of *Gauss PDF* and the author of *Docking, Rust Archon* (bas-books, 2012).

Peter Fischli (b. 1952, Zurich, Switzerland) and **David Weiss** (b. 1946, Zurich; d. 2012, Zurich) recently exhibited 'Questions, the Sausage Photographs, and a Quiet Afternoon' (Art Institute of Chicago, 2011) and 'Peter Fischli David Weiss' (21st Century Museum of Contemporary Art, Kanazawa, Japan, 2011).

Robert Fitterman (b. St Louis, Missouri, USA) is the author of twelve books of poetry living in New York City, USA. He teaches writing and poetry at New York University and at the Bard College, Milton Avery School of Graduate Studies. Reviews of his work can be found on his website: http://homepages.nyu.edu/~rmf1.

Lorenzo Fusi is the Liverpool Biennial curator of 'The Unexpected Guest'.

Kristen Gallagher (b. Philadelphia, Pennsylvania, USA) is poet and academic living in New York City, USA, where she teaches Creative Writing at City University of New York City. Forthcoming projects include *Grand Central* and *Things In Marx*.

Dora Garcia (b. 1965, Valladolid) is an artist living and working in Barcelona, Spain. Solo exhibitions include 'KLAU MICH: Radicalism in Society Meets Experiment on TV' (Documenta 13, Kassel, Germany, 2012), 'The Beggar's Things' (Galerie Michel Rein, Paris, France, 2012) and 'L'inadeguato, Lo Inadecuado, The Inadequate' (54th Venice Biennale, Spanish Pavilion, Venice, Italy, 2011).

Steve Giasson (b. 1979, Québec, Canada) is a multi-disciplinary artist (conceptual poetry, installation ...) living and working in Montreal. He intends to transgress genres and undermine notions of authenticity and originality. He has published sixteen books and is currently pursuing a doctorate in fine arts at the Université du Québec à Montréal.

Gilbert Proesch (b. 1943, San Martin de Tor, Italy) and George Passmore (b.1942, Plymouth, UK) have lived and worked together in London, UK, as Gilbert and George since 1968. Recent exhibitions include 'Gilbert and George' (Tate Modern, London, 2007), which travelled to Munich, Turin, Milwaukee, San Francisco and New York City, USA. They represented the United Kingdom at the 51st Venice Biennale (Venice, Italy, 2005), and were awarded the Turner Prize in 1986.

Simryn Gill (b. 1959, Singapore) is an artist living and working in Sydney, Australia. Gill's work was included in Documenta 13 (Kassel, Germany, 2012) and recent exhibitions include 'In Focus: The Tree' (Getty Center, Los Angeles, 2011) and 'Life Stories' (Museum of Contemporary Art, Detroit, 2011).

Kenneth Goldsmith (b. 1961, New York City, USA) is a poet and critic living in New York City. He is the author of ten books of poetry and the founding editor of the online archive UbuWeb.

Dan Graham (b. 1942, Urbana, Illinois, USA) is an artist living and working in New York City, USA. Recent solo exhibitions include 'Pavilions' (Lisson Gallery, London, UK, 2012), 'Dan Graham' (Protocinema, Istanbul, Turkey, 2011) and 'Dan Graham presents New Jersey' (Portikus, Frankfurt am Main, Germany, 2009).

Fritz Haeg (b. 1969, Minnesota, USA) is an artist and architect living and working in Los Angeles, USA. Recent projects include 'Domestic Integrity Field A-1' (Museum of Modern Art, New York City, USA, 2012), 'Wide Open School' (Hayward Gallery, London, UK, 2012), and 'Edible Estate #12: Budapest' (Blood Mountain Foundation, Budapest, Hungary, 2012).

Stuart Hall (b. 1932, Kingston, Jamaica) came to England to study at Oxford (1951–7). A founder of *New Left Review*, then director of the Centre for Cultural Studies (1964–1979), he has acted as chair of the Institute for International Visual Arts and the Association of Black Photography and contributed to the foundation of the Rivington Place centre for diversity in the visual arts, all in London, UK.

Mona Hatoum (b. 1952, Beirut, Lebanon) is an artist living and working in London, UK, and Berlin, Germany. Recent solo exhibitions include 'Projection' (Joan Miró Foundation, Barcelona, Spain, 2012), 'You are Still Here' (Arter, Istanbul, Turkey, 2012) and 'Bunker' (White Cube, London, 2011).

Jeanne van Heeswijk (b. 1965, Schijndel, The Netherlands) is an artist living and working in Rotterdam, The Netherlands. Projects include 'Freehouse: Radicalising The Local' (Rotterdam South, 2009 – present) and '2Up 2Down/Homebaked' (Anfield, Liverpool, UK, 2009 – present).

Oded Hirsch (b. 1976, Kibbutz Afikim, Israel) is an artist living and working in New York City, USA. Exhibitions include 'Nothing New' (Thierry Goldberg Gallery, New York City, 2012), 'The Workers' (MASS MoCA, Massachusets, USA, 2011) and 'Family Files' (Jewish Museum, Munich, Germany, 2010).

Thomas Hirschhorn (b. 1957, Bern, Switzerland) is an artist living and working in Paris, France. His work is shown internationally, including in the Swiss Pavilion at the 54th Venice Biennale (Venice, Italy, 2011), the Carnegie International (Pittsburgh, USA, 2008), and the São Paulo Bienal, (São Paulo, Brazil, 2006).

Hsieh Ying-Chun (b. 1954, Taichung County, Taiwan) is an architect living and working in Sun Moon Lake, Taiwan. Recent projects with his studio Atelier-3 include a new rural village development in Henan (Guangzhou, China, 2012 – present), an Aboriginal community reconstruction following Typhoon Morakot (Taiwan, 2009 – present) and Tibetan herders settlement housing (Namuhu, Tibet, China, 2010).

Lanny Jordan Jackson (b. Lubbock, Texas, 1986) is an artist, editor, designer, publisher and archivist living

in New York City. Lanny's art practice combines text-generation, performance and audio/video. He is the editor-designer of bas-books and curator of the second volume of *Collective Task*, an experimental collective project involving poets and artists.

Nadia Kaabi-Linke (b. 1978, Tunis, Tunisia) is an artist living and working in Tunis, Tunisia and Berlin, Germany. Exhibitions include 'Chkoun Ahna: On the Track of History' (National Museum of Carthage, Carthage, Tunisia, 2012), 'Lines of Control' (Herbert F. Johnson Museum, Ithaca, USA, 2012), and 'Black is the New White' (Lawrie Shabibi Gallery, Dubai, UAE, 2012).

Markus Kåhre (b. 1969, Helsinki, Finland) is an artist living and working in Espoo, Finland. His work has been presented at Tampere Art Museum (Tampere, Finland, 2011), Suomesta Galleria (Berlin, Germany, 2011) and Scultor (Helsinki, Finland, 2011).

Josef Kaplan (b. 1985, Santa Monica, California, USA) is a poet and critic living in New York City, USA. He is the author of *Democracy is Not for the People* (Truck Books, 2012).

Bill Kennedy is the artistic director of the Scream Literary Festival in Toronto, a poetry editor for Coach House Books, and an organizer of the Lexiconjury Reading Series. With Darren Wershler, he is the author of *Update* (Snare Books 2010) and *apostrophe* (ECW Press, 2006). He lives in Toronto.

William Kentridge (b. 1955, Johannesburg, South Africa) is an artist and film-maker. Recently his work has been seen at the Metropolitan Opera and Museum of Modern Art (both New York City, USA), Musée du Louvre and Jeu de Paume (both Paris, France), the Albertina Museum and La Scala (both Vienna, Austria), and Documenta 13 (Kassel, Germany).

Omar Kholeif is a writer and a curator at FACT, Foundation for Art and Creative Technology Liverpool, a visiting curator at Cornerhouse, Manchester, and a curator at the Arab British Centre, London. He is founding director of the UK's Arab Film Festival, co-curator of Abandon Normal Devices, and a contributing curator to Liverpool Biennial. He's also a senior editor at Ibraaz Publishing and Portal 9 (Beirut).

Anja Kirschner (b. 1977, Munich, Germany) and David Panos (b. 1971, Athens, Greece) are artists living and working together in London, UK. Solo exhibitions include 'Living truthfully under imaginary circumstances' (Transmission Gallery, Glasgow, Scotland, 2012), and 'The Empty Plan' (Kunsthalle Oslo, Oslo, Norway, 2011).

Jakob Kolding (b. 1971, Albertslund, Denmark) is an artist living and working in Berlin, Germany. Solo exhibitions include 'Blocks' (Team Gallery, New York City, USA, 2011), 'Stakes is High' (Stedelijk Museum Bureau Amsterdam, Amsterdam, The Netherlands, 2010) and 'Radical World' (Studio Dabbeni, Lugano, Switzerland, 2009).

Jiří Kovanda (b. 1953, Prague) is an artist living and working in Prague, Czech Republic. Solo exhibitions include 'Jiri Kovanda' (Museo Nacional Centro de Arte Reina Sofía, Madrid, Spain, 2012), 'White Blanket' (Secession, Vienna, Austria, 2010), and '1, 2, 3,' (Andrew Kreps Gallery, New York City, USA, 2009).

Suzanne Lacy (b. 1945, Wasco, California, USA) is an artist and writer living and working in Los Angeles, USA. Recent exhibitions include 'Wide Open School'

(Hayward Gallery, London, UK, 2012), and
'Under the Big Black Sun: California Art 1974–1981'
(Museum of Contemporary Art, Los Angeles,
USA, 2011). Books include *Leaving Art: Writings
on Performance, Politics and Publics, 1974–2007*
(Duke University Press, 2010).

Runo Lagomarsino (b. 1977, Lund, Sweden) is an artist
living and working in Malmö, Sweden, and São Paulo,
Brazil. Exhibitions include 'Unfinished Journeys'
(National Museum of Norway, Oslo, 2012), 'Untitled',
12th Istanbul Biennial (Istanbul, Turkey, 2011) and
'Speech Matters', 54th Venice Biennale, Danish
Pavilion, Venice, Italy, 2011.

Dr Sook-Kyung Lee is Exhibitions and Displays Curator
at Tate Liverpool. Born in South Korea, Lee has worked
as curator, lecturer and art writer both in South Korea
and the UK, and has curated a number of exhibitions,
including 'Nam June Paik' (2010) and 'Liu Jianhua:
Regular / Fragile' (2007).

Tan Lin (b. 1957, Seattle, Washington, USA) is a writer
and critic living and working in New York City, USA.
He has authored over ten books, including *Heath
Course Pak* (Counterpath Press, 2011), *Insomnia and
the Aunt* (Kenning Editions, 2011) and *7 Controlled
Vocabularies and Obituary 2004: The Joy of Cooking*
(Wesleyan, 2010). He is the recipient of a 2012
Foundation for Contemporary Arts Award for poetry
and a Getty Distinguished Scholar Grant to complete
a book on Andy Warhol's writings.

Trisha Low (b. 1988, New York City, USA) is a writer
living and working in New York City. She is the author
of *Confessions [of a variety]* (Gauss PDF, 2010).
Other works have appeared in *Against Expression:
An Anthology of Conceptual Writing*, *P-QUEUE* and
Elective Affinities.

Jorge Macchi (b. 1963, Buenos Aires, Argentina)
is an artist living and working in Buenos Aires.
Solo exhibitions include 'Music Stand Still' (SMAK,
Ghent, Belgium, 2011), 'Crónicas eventuales'
(Ruth Benzacar Gallery, Buenos Aires, 2010), and
'10:51' (Kunstlerhaus Bremen, Germany, 2009).

Achille Mbembe (b. 1957, Otélé, Cameroon) is
a philosopher and political scientist based in
Johannesburg, South Africa. He is Professor of
Social Theory at Stellenbosch University, South Africa,
where he convenes the Locations and Locutions
lecture series. At the University of the Witwatersrand,
he co-convenes the Johannesburg Workshop in
Theory and Criticism. He has written extensively
on African history and politics including (in English)
On Private Indirect Government (CODESRIA, 2000)
and *On the Postcolony* (University of California
Press, 2001).

Stephen McLaughlin (b. New Jersey, USA) is
a writer and web broadcaster currently living
in Philadelphia. He directs PennSound Radio,
a 24-hour online poetry stream, and creates
podcasts for Jacket2.org. His monthly reading
series is titled Principal Hand Presents
(PrincipalHand.net).

Dane Mitchell (b. 1976, Auckland, New Zealand) is
an artist living and working in Auckland, New Zealand,
and Berlin, Germany. Exhibitions include 'Radiant
Matter II' (Dunedin Public Art Gallery, Dunedin,
New Zealand, 2011), and 'Afterlife' (Nederlands
Uitvaart Museum Tot Zover, Amsterdam, The
Netherlands, 2011).

Sabelo Mlangeni (b. 1980, Driefontein, South Africa)
is an artist living and working in Johannesburg,
South Africa. Exhibitions include 'Black Men in
Dress and Iimbali' (Stevenson Gallery, Johannesburg,
South Africa, 2012), 'Figures and Fictions:
Contemporary South African Photography'
(V&A, London, UK, 2011) and 'I Am Not Afraid:
The Market Photo Workshop' (Johannesburg Art
Gallery, Johannesburg, 2010).

Debbie Morgan (b. 1963, Liverpool, UK) is a writer
living and working in Liverpool. In the past she
has worked as a chambermaid, a bingo caller, a
dressmaker, and a primary-school teacher. Her
first novel, *Disappearing Home*, was published by
Tindal Street Press in March 2012 and has received
widespread critical acclaim.

Simon Morris (b. 1968, Chichester, UK) is a conceptual
writer living and working in York, UK. Morris has
been called 'philosophically irresponsible', a 'literary
pervert' and an 'inspired lunatic'. In 2002, he founded
the publishing imprint 'information as material',
which has subsequently become the world's largest
publisher of uncreative literature.

Tracie Morris (b. New York City, USA) is a poet,
performer and scholar and works extensively
as a sound artist, writer, bandleader and actor.
She is Professor of Humanities and Media Studies
at Pratt Institute.

Mark Morrisroe (b. 1959, Malden, Massachusetts;
d. 1989, Jersey City, New Jersey) was an artist who
lived and worked in Boston and New York City, USA.
Recent exhibitions include Mark Morrisroe (Museum
Villa Stuck, Munich, Germany, 2012; Fotomuseum
Winterthur, Winterthur, Switzerland, 2010–11),
'From This Moment On' (Artists Space, New York City,
USA, 2011) and 'Punk: No One is Innocent' (Kunsthalle
Wien, Vienna, Austria, 2008).

Patrick Murphy's work is interdisciplinary, employing
a diverse range of media, techniques and skills.
He is concerned with creating a dialogue with our
surroundings and each other. Altering the original
context of objects and themes so they appear
simultaneously familiar and unfamiliar, encouraging
a sense of questioning from the viewer.

Eileen Myles (b. 1949, Cambridge, Massachusetts,
USA) moved to New York City (where she still lives) in
1974 to be a poet. Latest books are *Snowflake/different
streets* (Wave Books, 2012), *Inferno (a poet's novel)*
(OR Books, 2010) and *The Importance of Being Iceland:
Travel Essays in Art* (Semiotext(e), 2009), for which she
received a Creative Capital/Warhol Art Writing Grant.
She is a 2012 Guggenheim Fellow.

Ahmet Öğüt (b. 1981, Diyarbakir, Turkey) is an artist
living and working in Amsterdam, The Netherlands.
Exhibitions include 'Or Whistle Spontaneously'
(Delfina Foundation, London, UK, 2012), 'Modern
Essays 1: Across the Slope' (SALT, Istanbul,
Turkey, 2011) and 'Black Diamond – Het Oog 3' (Van
Abbemuseum, Eindhoven, The Netherlands, 2010).

Trevor Paglen (b. 1974, Maryland, USA) is an artist
and writer living and working in New York City,
USA. Exhibitions include 'After the Gold Rush'
(Metropolitan Museum of Art, New York City, USA,
2011–12) and 'Trevor Paglen' (Secession, Vienna,
Austria, 2010–11). Books include *Blank Spots on the
Map: The Dark Geography of the Pentagon's Secret
World* (Dutton, 2009).

Pak Sheung Chuen (b. 1977, Fujian, China) is a conceptual and performance artist living and working in Hong Kong. He is also well known as a regular arts columnist in the local newspaper *Mingpao*. He represented Hong Kong at the 53rd Venice Biennale (Venice, Italy, 2009). He was awarded the 2005 Overseas Exchange Prize (Chinese Performance Art) from Macao Museum of Art.

Christodoulos Panayiotou (b. 1978, Limassol, Cyprus) is an artist living and working in Berlin, Germany. Solo exhibitions include 'One Thousand and One Days' (Museum of Contemporary Art, St Louis, USA, 2012), Documenta 13 (Kassel, Germany, 2012) and 'Christodolous Panayiotou '(Museum of Contemporary Art, Leipzig, Germany, 2011).

Martin Parr (b. 1952, Epsom, UK) is an artist living and working in Bristol, UK. He earned an international reputation for his oblique approach to social-documentary photography, and in 1994 he became a member of Magnum. Parr's work has been displayed worldwide, as well as contributing to major exhibitions such as 'Street and Studio' (Tate Modern, London, UK, 2008).

Vanessa Place (b. 1968, Stratford, South Dakota, USA) is a poet, critic, criminal defence lawyer living in Los Angeles, USA. She is co-director of Les Figues Press and was the first poet to perform as part of the Whitney Biennial (New York, USA).

Nina Power is a writer and academic living and working in London, UK. Her books include *One Dimensional Woman* (Zero Books, 2009) and *On Beckett* (co-edited with Alain Badiou, Clinamen Press, 2002). She is Senior Lecturer in Philosophy at Roehampton University, UK.

Jacques Rancière (b. 1940, Algiers, Algeria) is a philosopher and writer living and working in France. Translated works include *The Emancipation of the Spectator* (Verso, 2009), *Hatred of Democracy* (Verso, 2007) and *The Names of History: On the Poetics of Knowledge* (University of Minnesota Press, 1994). Rancière is Professor Emeritus at the Université de Paris and Professor of Philosophy at the European Graduate School.

Pedro Reyes (b. 1972, Mexico City, Mexico) is an artist living and working in Mexico City. Recent solo exhibitions include 'Rompecabezas' (LABOR Gallery, Mexico City, 2012), 'Babymarx' (Walker Art Gallery, Minneapolis, USA), and 'Sanatorium' (Guggenheim Museum, New York City, USA).

Kim Rosenfield (b. 1966, Los Angeles, USA) is a poet and psychoanalytically oriented psychotherapist living and working in NYC. She is the author of five books of poetry, the latest of which, *Lividity*, was published by Les Figues Press in 2012. *USO (I'll Be Seeing You)* will be published by Ugly Duckling Presse in 2013.

Pamela Rosenkranz (b. 1979, Sils-Maria, Switzerland) is an artist living and working in Amsterdam, The Netherlands. Recent solo exhibitions include 'Because They Try to Bore Holes' (Miguel Abreu, New York City, USA, 2012), 'No Core' (Centre d'Art Contemporain, Geneva, Switzerland, 2010) and 'On Sun' (Istituto Svizzero di Roma, Venice, Italy, 2009).

María Salgado (b. 1984, Madrid, Spain) is a low-tech poet living and working in Madrid. She curates perfomative readings, experimental sound bands, and Contrabando (an exchange of Panamerican and Spanish texts). She is the author of *ferias* (Universidad Popular José Hierro, 2007), *31 poemas* (Puerta del Mar, 2010) and *ready* (arrebato, 2012). She writes at globorapido.net and laliteraturadelpobre.wordpress.com.

David Scott is a Jamaican scholar living in New York City, where he is a professor in the Department of Anthropology, Columbia University. His new book, *Omens of Adversity: Tragedy, Time, Memory, Justice*, will be published in 2013. He is the editor of the journal *Small Axe*.

Vijay Seshadri (b. 1954, Bangalore, India) is a poet and academic living and working in New York City. He came to America at the age of five and has lived in many parts of the country, and has been employed in many ways. He is the author of four books of poetry: *Wild Kingdom* (Graywolf Press, 1996) and *The Long Meadow* (Graywolf Press, 2004), *The Disappearances* (HarperCollins India, 2007), and *3 Sections* (forthcoming). He currently teaches at Sarah Lawrence College, Bronxville, New York.

Don Share (b. 1957, Ohio, USA) is a poet, translator, podcaster and editor living in Chicago, USA. His most recent books are *Wishbone* (Black Sparrow Books, 2012), *Bunting's Persia* (Flood Editions, 2012), and *100 Poems, 100 Years of Poetry Magazine* (University of Chicago Press, 2012). He is also senior editor of *Poetry* magazine in Chicago.

George Shaw (b. 1966, Coventry, UK) is an artist living and working in Devon, UK. Recent exhibitions include 'I Woz Ere at The Herbert' (Coventry, UK, 2011), 'The Sly and Unseen Day' (Baltic Centre for Contemporary Art, Gateshead; South London Gallery, London, 2011) and 'Looking for Baz, Shaz, Gaz and Daz' (Void, Derry, UK, 2010). Shaw was nominated for the Turner Prize in 2011.

Lytle Shaw (b. 1967, Ithaca, New York) is a poet and critic living in New York City. His books include *The Moiré Effect* (Book Horse/Cabinet Books, 2012), *The Clifford Chadwick Clifford Collection* (An Endless Supply, 2011) and *Frank O'Hara: The Poetics of Coterie* (University of Iowa Press, 2006). He is Associate Professor of English at New York University.

Ara Shirinyan (b. 1977, Soviet Armenia) is a poet, writer, translator and teacher living in Los Angeles, USA. He is the author of numerous works of poetry, among them *Syria is in the World* (Palm Press, 2007), *Your Country Is Great* (Futurepoem, 2008), and *Handsome Fish Offices* (Insert Blanc Press, 2008).

Stephanie Smith is Deputy Director and Chief Curator at the Smart Museum of Art. She is an affiliate member of the University of Chicago's Department of Visual Arts, a founding member of its Open Practice Committee, and a contributing editor at *Afterall*. Smith's work focuses on socially engaged public practice and questions of sustainability, notably in the exhibitions and publications *Beyond Green: Toward a Sustainable Art* (2005), *Heartland* (2009), and *Feast: Radical Hospitality in Contemporary Art* (2012).

Mikhael Subotzky (b. 1981, Cape Town, South Africa) is an artist living and working in Johannesburg, South Africa. Recent exhibitions include 'Out of Focus' (Saatchi Gallery, London, UK, 2012), 'State of the Art Photography' (NRW-Forum, Düsseldorf, Germany, 2012), and 'Figures and Fictions: Contemporary South African Photography' (V&A, London, UK, 2011).

Sun Xun (b. 1980, Fuxin, China) is an artist living in Beijing, China. He studied printmaking at the China Academy of Fine Arts before founding his own animation studio in 2006. His practice brings together drawing, text and moving image to create large-scale installations that explore a variety of historical and political contexts.

Superflex is an artists' group based in Copenhagen, Denmark, founded in 1993 by Jakob Fenger (b. 1968, Copenhagen), Rasmus Nielsen (b. 1969, Copenhagen) and Bjørnstjerne Christiansen (b. 1969, Copenhagen). Recent exhibitions include 'Prouvé in Africa / Bent, Pressed, Compressed, Welded and then Copied' (Musée d'Art Moderne, St-Etienne, France, 2012), 'Superkilen' (public intervention, Copenhagen, 2012) and 'Power Toilets/JPMorgan Chase' (commissioned by Creative Time, New York City, USA, 2011).

Sally Tallant is Director of Liverpool Biennial.

Pelin Tan is Assistant Professor at the New Media Department, KHAS University, Istanbul and a Fellow of the Japan Foundation researching artist-run spaces in Japan. Between 2001 and 2011, she worked in Art History ITU, where she completed a doctorate on socially engaged art practices in urban space.

Sinta Tantra (b. 1979, New York City, USA) is an artist living and working in London, UK. Her public-realm works include *A Beautiful Sunset Mistaken for a Dawn* (Canary Wharf, London, 2012), *A Good time and a Half!* (Southbank Centre, London, 2008) and *Thoughts on the Education of Daughters* (Camden Town Hall, London, 2008).

Althea Thauberger (b. 1970, Saskatoon, Canada) is an artist living and working in Vancouver, Canada. Recent exhibitions include 'Althea Thauberger' (Musée d'Art Contemporain de Montréal, Canada, 2012), 'Ecce Homo' (Vancouver City Centre Station, Canada, 2012) and 'Terms of Belonging' (Institut for Samtidskunst, Copenhagen, Denmark, 2011).

Nick Thurston (b. 1982, UK) is an academic living and working in Yorkshire, UK, and co-editor of the publishing imprint 'information as material'. He is the author of two books, numerous journal articles and artists' pages, plus two chapbooks. His third book, *Of The Sub-Contract*, is forthcoming.

Mark Titchner (b. 1973, Luton, UK) is an artist living and working in London, UK. Recent solo shows include 'Be True To Your Oblivion' (New Art Gallery, Walsall, UK, 2011) and 'Run Black River, Run' (Baltic Centre for Contemporary Art, Gateshead, UK, 2008). Titchner was nominated for the Turner Prize in 2006.

José Angel Vincench (b. 1973, Holguín, Cuba) is an artist living and working in Havana, Cuba. Recent exhibitions include the 11th Havana Biennial (Havana, 2012), 'Light and Darkness' (Havana Gallery, Zürich, Switzerland, 2011) and 'Cuban Visions' (Metropolitan Pavilion Gallery, New York City, USA, 2011).

Mark Wallinger (b. 1959, Essex, UK) is an artist living and working in London, UK. Wallinger was awarded the Turner Prize in 2007, and has exhibited worldwide, recently in 'Metamorphosis: Titian 2012' at the National Gallery (London, UK, 2012), Baltic Centre for Contemporary Art (Gateshead, UK, 2012), and Museum De Pont (Tilburg, The Netherlands, 2011).

Patrick Waterhouse (b. 1981, Bath, UK) is an artist living and working between Italy, England and South Africa. Recent exhibitions include 'State of the Art Photography' (NRW-Forum, Düsseldorf, Germany, 2012), 'High Rise: Idea and Reality (Museum für Gestaltung, Zürich, Switzerland, 2011–12) and 'Appropriated Landscapes' (Walther Collection, Neu-Ulm, Germany, 2011).

Darren Wershler (b. 1966, Winnipeg, Canada) is a writer and scholar living in Montreal. He is the Concordia University Research Chair in Media and Contemporary Literature, and the author or co-author of twelve books, most recently, *Guy Maddin's My Winnipeg* (University of Toronto Press, 2010) and *Update* (with Bill Kennedy; Snare Books 2010).

Ming Wong (b. 1971, Singapore) is an artist living and working in Berlin, Germany. Recent exhibitions include 'A Trip to the Moon: Before and after Cinema' (Bonniers Konsthall, Stockholm, Sweden, 2012), 'Persona Performa' (Performa 11 at the Museum of Moving Image, New York City, USA, 2011) and 'Invisible of Visibleness' (MoCA Taipei, Taiwan, 2011).

Jemima Wyman (b. 1977, Sydney, Australia) is an artist living and working in Los Angeles, USA, and Brisbane, Australia. Recent exhibitions include 'Render: New Construction in Video Art' (UCR / California Museum of Photography, Riverside, USA) and 'Inner Voices' (21st Century Museum of Contemporary Art, Kanazawa, Japan, 2011).

Kohei Yoshiyuki (b. 1946, Hiroshima, Japan) is an artist living and working in Japan. Recent exhibitions include 'Camera Work' (Adam Art Gallery, Wellington, New Zealand, 2012) and 'Night Vision: Photography After Dark' (Metropolitan Museum of Art, New York City, USA, 2011).

Yukinori Yanagi (b. 1959, Fukuoka, Japan) is an artist living and working in Hiroshima, Japan. He recently exhibited in 'Study for American Art' (Miyake Fine Art, Tokyo, Japan, 2012) and the 8th Mercosul Biennial (Porto Alegre, Brazil, 2011).

Akram Zaatari (b. 1966, Saida, Lebanon) is an artist living and working in Beirut, Lebanon. Recent exhibitions include 'Photography: New Documentary Forms' (Tate Modern, London, UK, 2012), 'Composition for Two Wings' (Contemporary Art Centre, Vilnius, Lithuania, 2012), and 'Seeing is Believing' (KunstWerke, Berlin, Germany, 2011).

Steven Zultanski (b. 1981, Princeton, New Jersey, USA) is a doctoral student in English at SUNY Buffalo, living in New York City. He is the author of *Pad* (Make Now Press, 2010), *Cop Kisser* (BookThug, 2010) and *Agony* (BookThug, 2012). He curates the Segue Reading Series at the Segue Foundation, New York City.

Project supporters

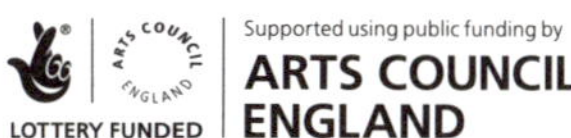 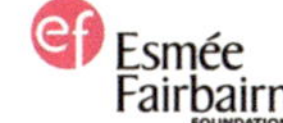 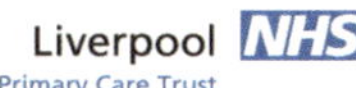 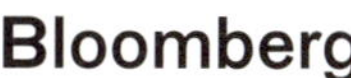

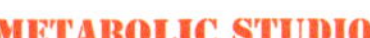 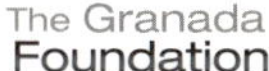 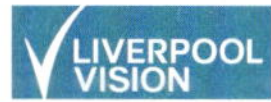 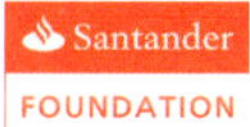 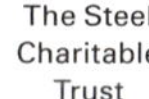 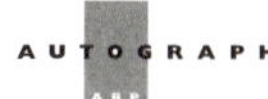

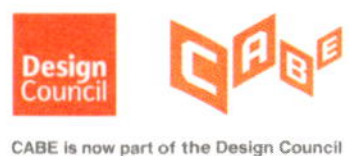  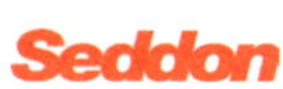 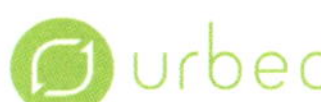 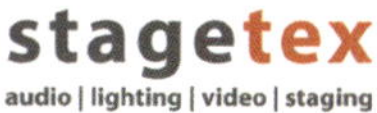

Sky Arts Ignition: Doug Aitken – *The Source* with additional support from Tate Liverpool Members

International agencies and galleries

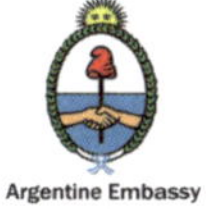 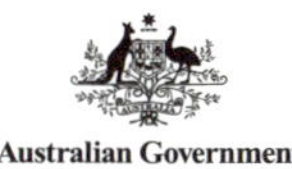 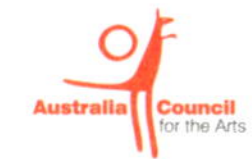

This project has been assisted by the Australian Government through the Australia Council, its arts funding and advisory body.

 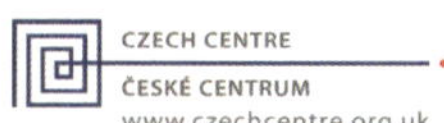 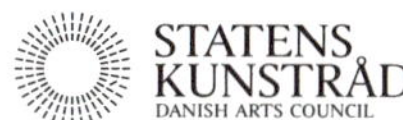 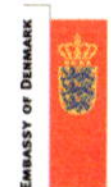

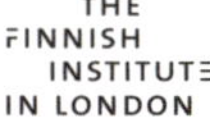 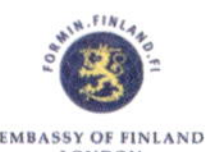 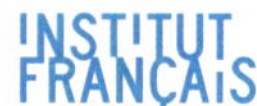 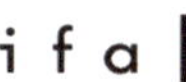

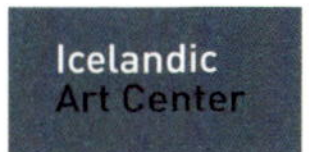 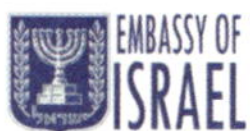  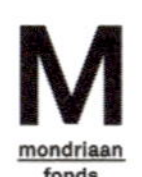 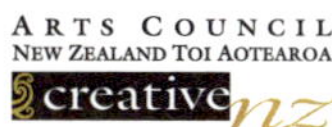

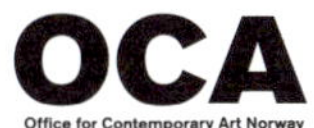 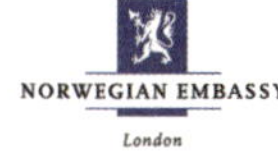 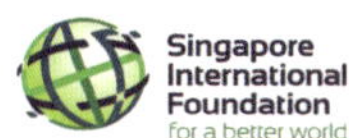 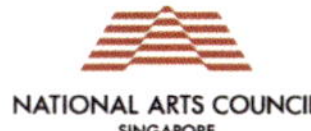 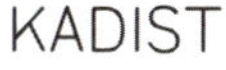

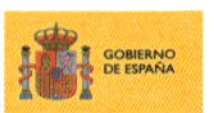 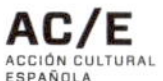 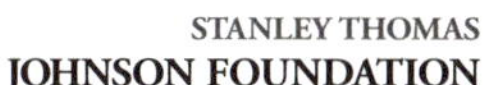 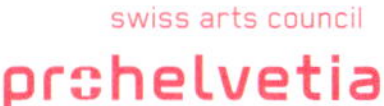 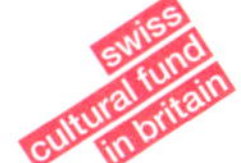 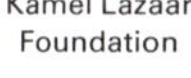

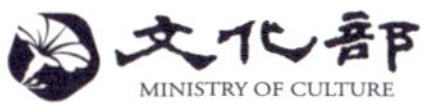 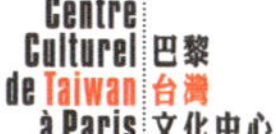

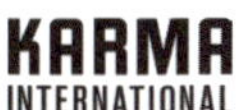

Acknowledgments

7th Liverpool Biennial
15 September – 25 November 2012

Sally Tallant, Artistic Director

'The Unexpected Guest' curated by

Liverpool Biennial
Lorenzo Fusi, Rosie Cooper,
Lucy Johnston, Laurie Peake

The Bluecoat
Bryan Biggs, Sara-Jayne Parsons

FACT
Omar Kholeif, Mike Stubbs

Open Eye Gallery
Karen Newman

METAL Liverpool
Jenny Porter

Walker Art Gallery
Ann Bukantas

Victoria Gallery and Museum
Moira Lindsay

The Royal Standard

Sky Arts Ignition: Doug Aitken – The Source
and Tate Liverpool, 'Thresholds'
Sook-Kyung Lee, Eleanor Clayton,
Jose Diaz

Liverpool Biennial trustees

Dawn Ades OBE, FBA; Lesley Chalmers; Jim Gill OBE; Paul Hyland; Peter Mearns; Prof. Gerald Pillay FRSA DL; Paula Ridley CBE DL; John Shield; Jane Wentworth; Tony Wilson

Liverpool Biennial staff

Beatrice Boatto *Marketing and communications assistant*; Vanessa Boni *Assistant curator*; Lisa Bradshaw *Development officer*; Maria Brewster *Project producer*; Rosie Cooper *Project curator*; Zainab Djavanroodi *Operations administrator*; Paul Domela *Programme director*; Lorenzo Fusi *Curator*; Lucy Johnston *Assistant curator*; Cecilia Kinnear *Visitor services leader*; Sally Lupton *Development manager*; Allison Mottram *Finance officer*; Sally Parker *Development and finance assistant*; Laurie Peake *Programme director (Public art)*; Antony Pickthall *Head of marketing and communications*; Hannah Pierce *Programme assistant*; Kealey Puckering *Creative apprentice*; Paul Smith *Executive director*; Sally Tallant *Director*; Francesca Williams *Partnership coordinator*; Sally Wong *IT support officer*

Interns

Katie Henry; Simon Job; Amy Jones; Rosanna Mollica; Alex Patterson

Thanks to

Donna Berry; Alexandra Bradley; Tim Brunsden; Charlie Burke; Sarah Cable; Katie Craven; Lee Currie; Jonathan Falkingham; Thomas Godwin; Monika Golinska; Harriet Gray; Tony Greenall; Teresa Gruber; Simon Job; Mark Jones; Mathew Kel; Laura Köönikkä; Alessandro Leggio; Timo Linke; Frances Loeffler; Jo McClellan; Charlotte Mears; Sharon Merone; Kira Meyer; Lily Mitchell; Gabi Ngcobo; Sharon Oldale; Stephen Osuhor; Alex Patterson; Marta Rincón Areitio; Shaun Ross; Jess Rowe; Mark Sealy; Ian Simmons; Alan Smith; Claire Thomas; Hayley Trowbridge; Andrew Willoughby; Ami Yesufu